바람의 나라

KINGDOM OF THE WINDS

Vol. 2

Kimjin

NETCOMICS

바람의 나라
KINGDOM OF THE WINDS **Vol. 2**

Story and Art by Kimjin

English translation rights arranged by
Ecomix Media Company
Seoul, Korea
info@ecomixmedia.com

- Produced by Ecomix Media Company
- Translator Soyoung Jung
- Cover Designer purj
- Graphic Designer Hyoeun Na
- Editor Philip Daay
- Production Manager Sunghwan Park
- President & Publisher Heewoon Chung

P.O. Box 4004, Glendale, CA 91222-0004
info@netcomics.com
www.NETCOMICS.com

ISBN: 978-1-60009-252-7

First printing: April 2008
10 9 8 7 6 5 4 3 2 1
Printed in Korea

바람의 나라

KINGDOM OF THE WINDS

Vol. 2

Kimjin

바람의 나라
KINGDOM OF THE WINDS

Characters

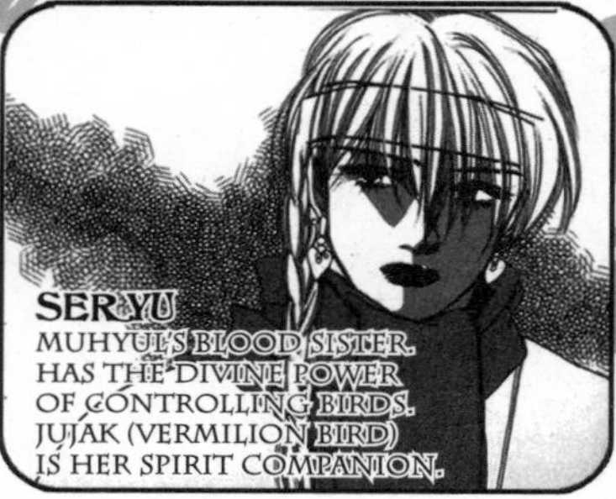

SERYU
MUHYUL'S BLOOD SISTER.
HAS THE DIVINE POWER
OF CONTROLLING BIRDS.
JUJAK (VERMILION BIRD)
IS HER SPIRIT COMPANION.

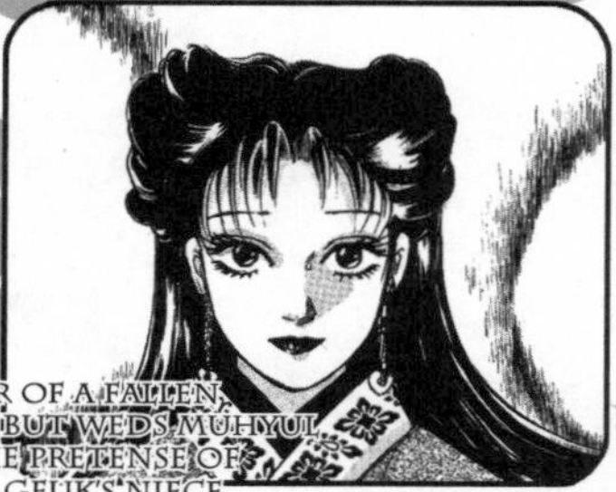

EJI
DAUGHTER OF A FALLEN
RETAINER, BUT WEDS MUHYUL
UNDER THE PRETENSE OF
BEING BAE GEUK'S NIECE.
IS THE MOTHER OF HAEWOO,
KING MOBON.

GAHEE
DAUGHTER OF THE CREATOR.
HER LOVE FOR GOEYU MADE
HER ENTER THE HUMAN
WORLD. HER ORIGINAL FORM
WAS AN AMARANTHINE FLOWER.

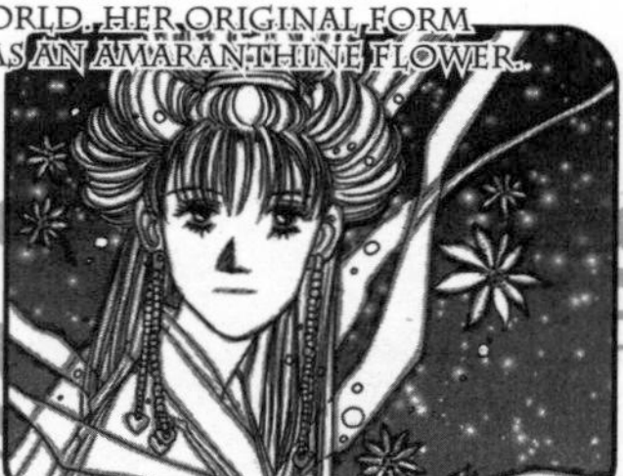

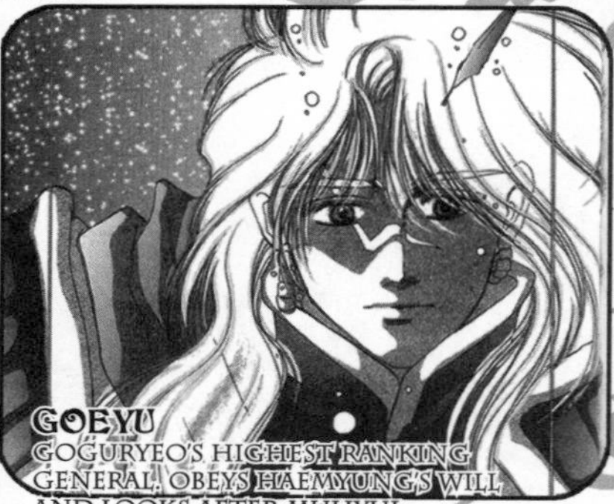

GOEYU
GOGURYEO'S HIGHEST RANKING
GENERAL. OBEYS HAEMYUNG'S WILL
AND LOOKS AFTER MUHYUL.
BAEKHO (WHITE TIGER)
IS HIS SPIRIT COMPANION.

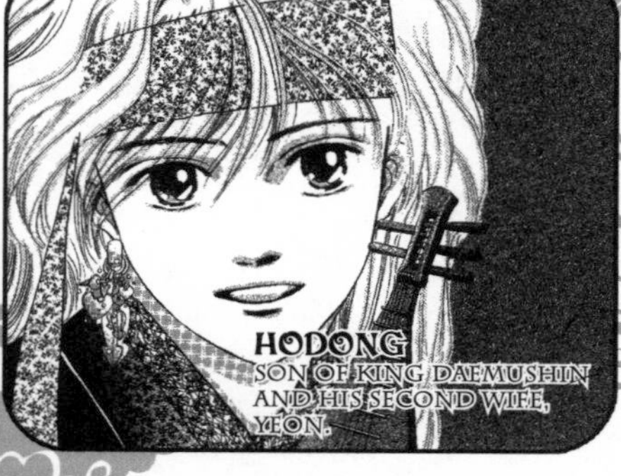

HODONG
SON OF KING DAEMUSHIN
AND HIS SECOND WIFE,
YEON.

CHICK
(PHOENIX)
COMES FROM THE SUN. IT HAS
A STRONG AVERSION TO MUHYUL'S
BLUE DRAGON. HODONG'S SPIRIT
COMPANION.

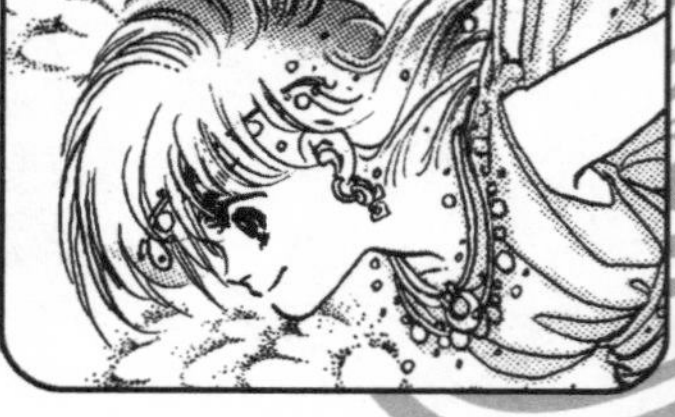

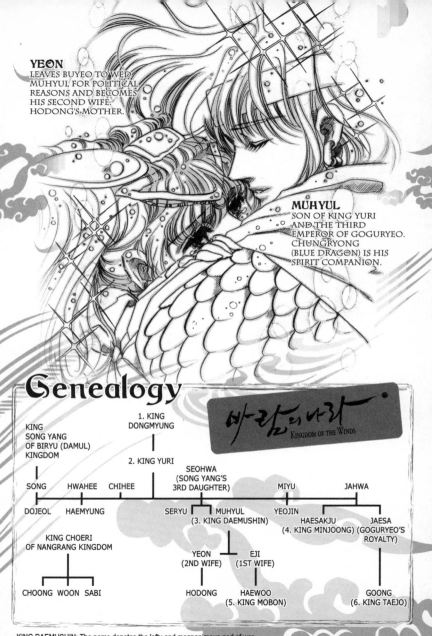

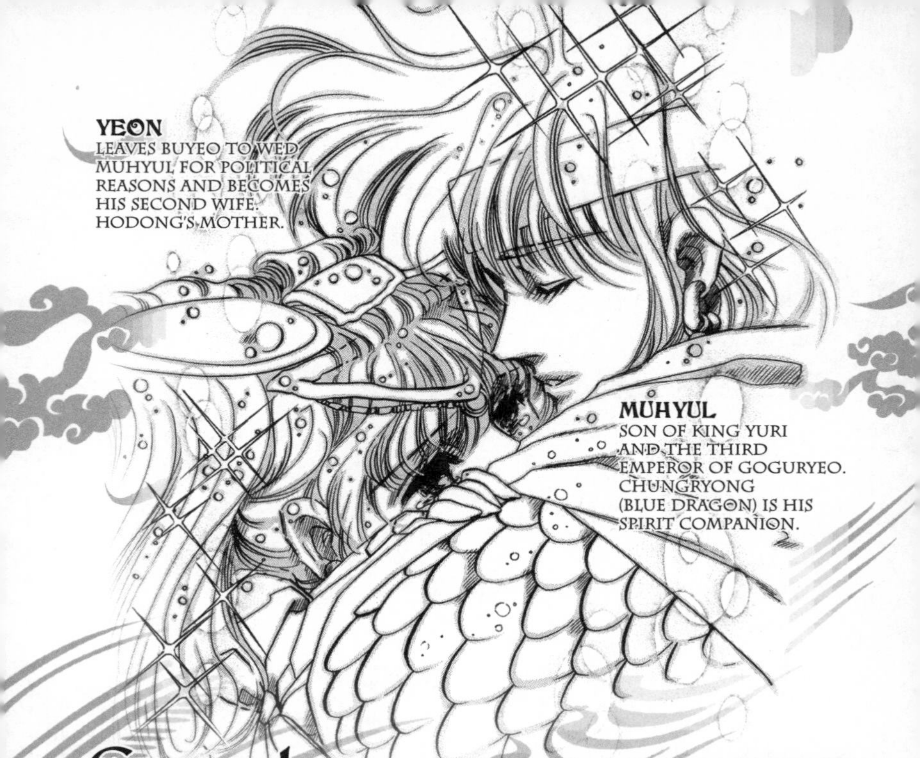
YEON
LEAVES BUYEO TO WED MUHYUL FOR POLITICAL REASONS AND BECOMES HIS SECOND WIFE. HODONG'S MOTHER.
MUHYUL
SON OF KING YURI AND THE THIRD EMPEROR OF GOGURYEO. CHUNGRYONG (BLUE DRAGON) IS HIS SPIRIT COMPANION.

Genealogy

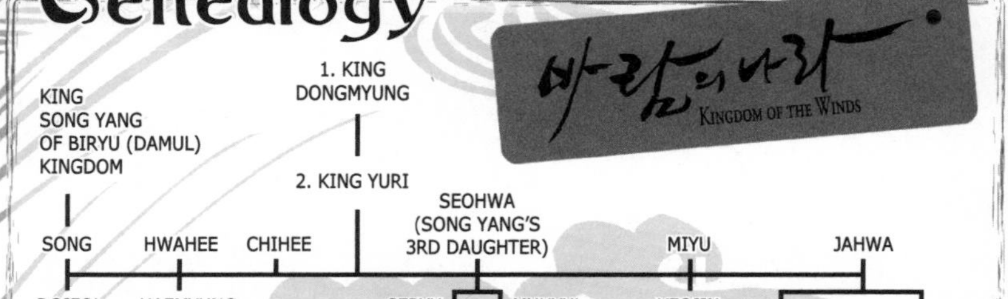
바람의 나라
KINGDOM OF THE WINDS
1. KING DONGMYUNG
2. KING YURI
KING SONG YANG OF BIRYU (DAMUL) KINGDOM
SONG
HWAHEE
CHIHEE
SEOHWA (SONG YANG'S 3RD DAUGHTER)
MIYU
JAHWA
DOJEOL
HAEMYUNG
SERYU
MUHYUL (3. KING DAEMUSHIN)
YEOJIN
HAESAKJU (4. KING MINJOONG)
JAESA (GOGURYEO'S ROYALTY)
KING CHOERI OF NANGRANG KINGDOM
YEON (2ND WIFE)
EJI (1ST WIFE)
CHOONG
WOON
SABI
HODONG
HAEWOO (5. KING MOBON)
GOONG (6. KING TAEJO)

KING DAEMUSHIN: The name denotes the lofty and magnanimous god of war.

Contents

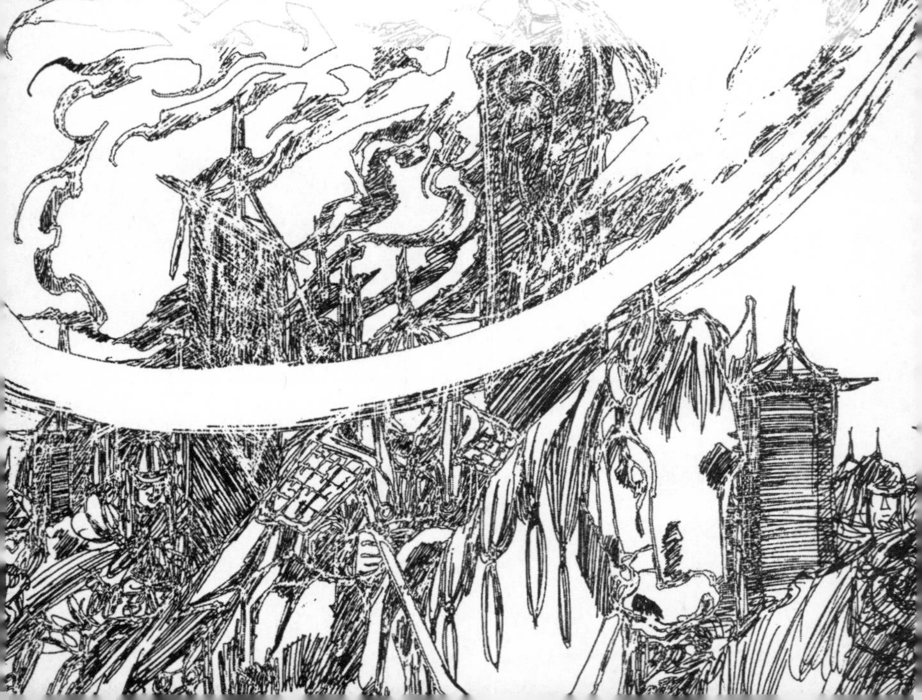

PART 1 Chapter 11
(continued from Volume 1)

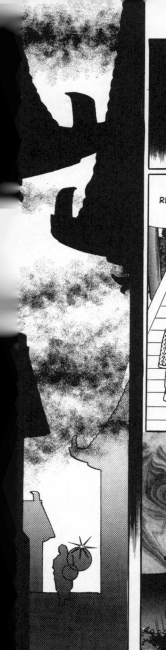

THE SERVANT RETURNS.

REPORT.

THE CROWN PRINCESS WAS GREATLY DISPLEASED BY THE COMMOTION WE CAUSED.

DID YOU HEAR THAT, YOUR MAJESTY?

......

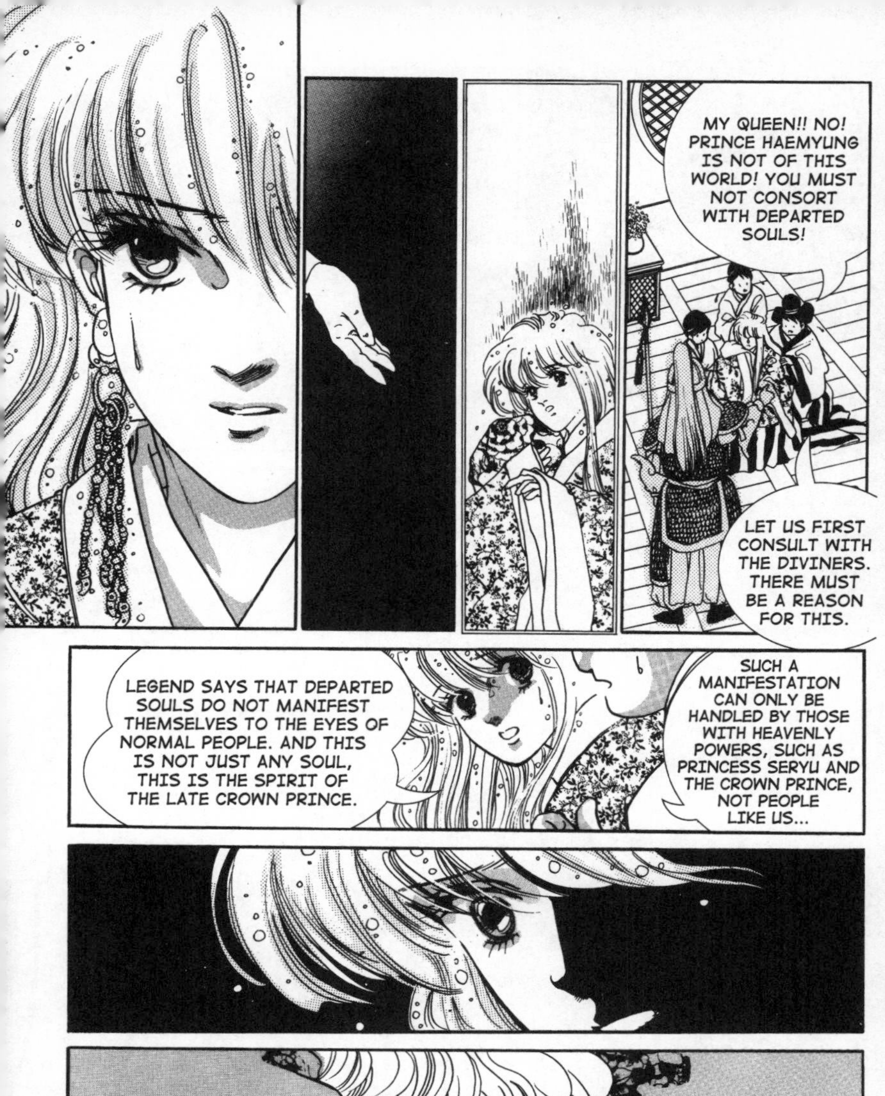
MY QUEEN!! NO! PRINCE HAEMYUNG IS NOT OF THIS WORLD! YOU MUST NOT CONSORT WITH DEPARTED SOULS!
LET US FIRST CONSULT WITH THE DIVINERS. THERE MUST BE A REASON FOR THIS.
LEGEND SAYS THAT DEPARTED SOULS DO NOT MANIFEST THEMSELVES TO THE EYES OF NORMAL PEOPLE. AND THIS IS NOT JUST ANY SOUL, THIS IS THE SPIRIT OF THE LATE CROWN PRINCE.
SUCH A MANIFESTATION CAN ONLY BE HANDLED BY THOSE WITH HEAVENLY POWERS, SUCH AS PRINCESS SERYU AND THE CROWN PRINCE, NOT PEOPLE LIKE US...

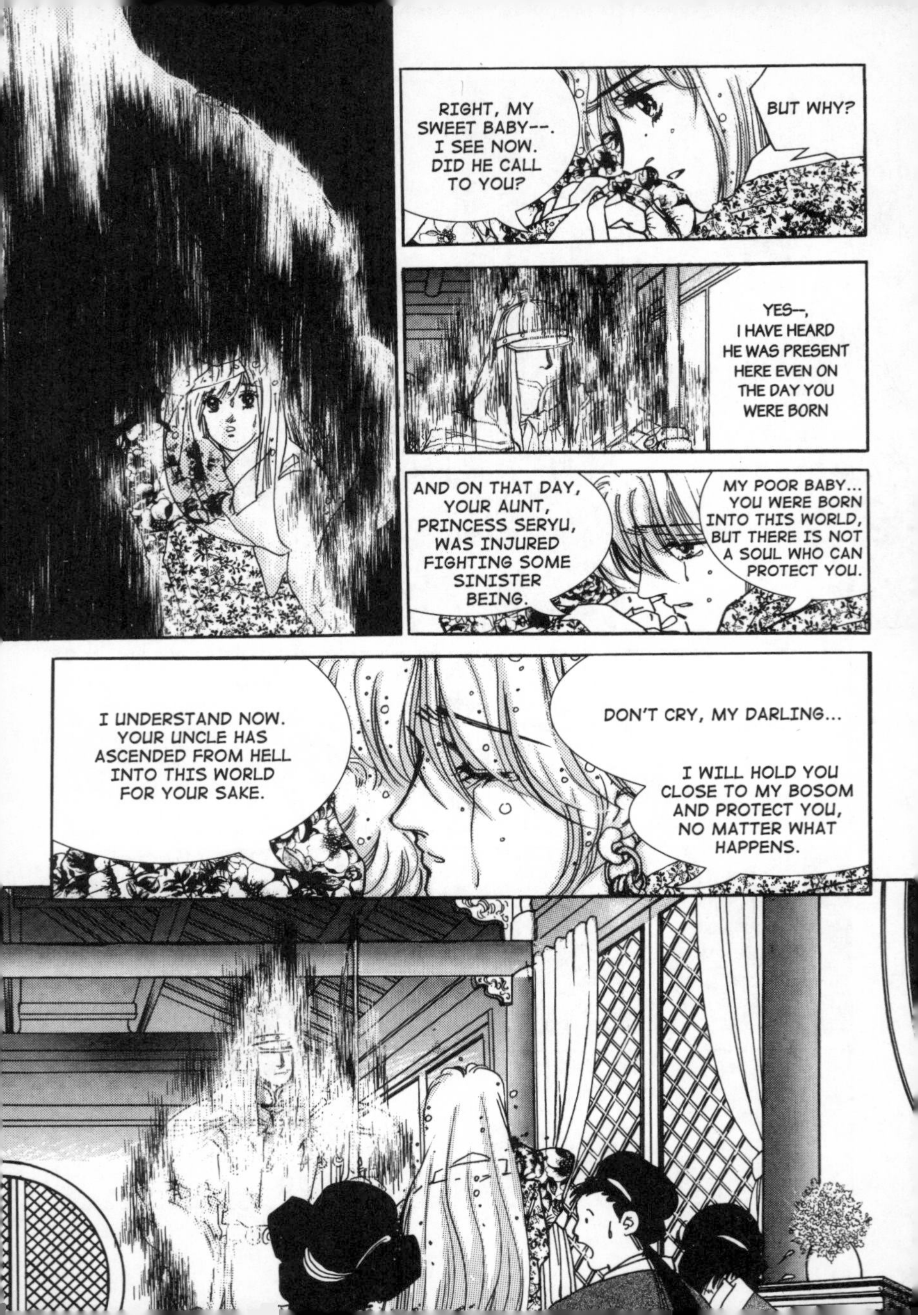
RIGHT, MY SWEET BABY--. I SEE NOW. DID HE CALL TO YOU?
BUT WHY?
YES--, I HAVE HEARD HE WAS PRESENT HERE EVEN ON THE DAY YOU WERE BORN
AND ON THAT DAY, YOUR AUNT, PRINCESS SERYU, WAS INJURED FIGHTING SOME SINISTER BEING.
MY POOR BABY... YOU WERE BORN INTO THIS WORLD, BUT THERE IS NOT A SOUL WHO CAN PROTECT YOU.
I UNDERSTAND NOW. YOUR UNCLE HAS ASCENDED FROM HELL INTO THIS WORLD FOR YOUR SAKE.
DON'T CRY, MY DARLING...
I WILL HOLD YOU CLOSE TO MY BOSOM AND PROTECT YOU, NO MATTER WHAT HAPPENS.

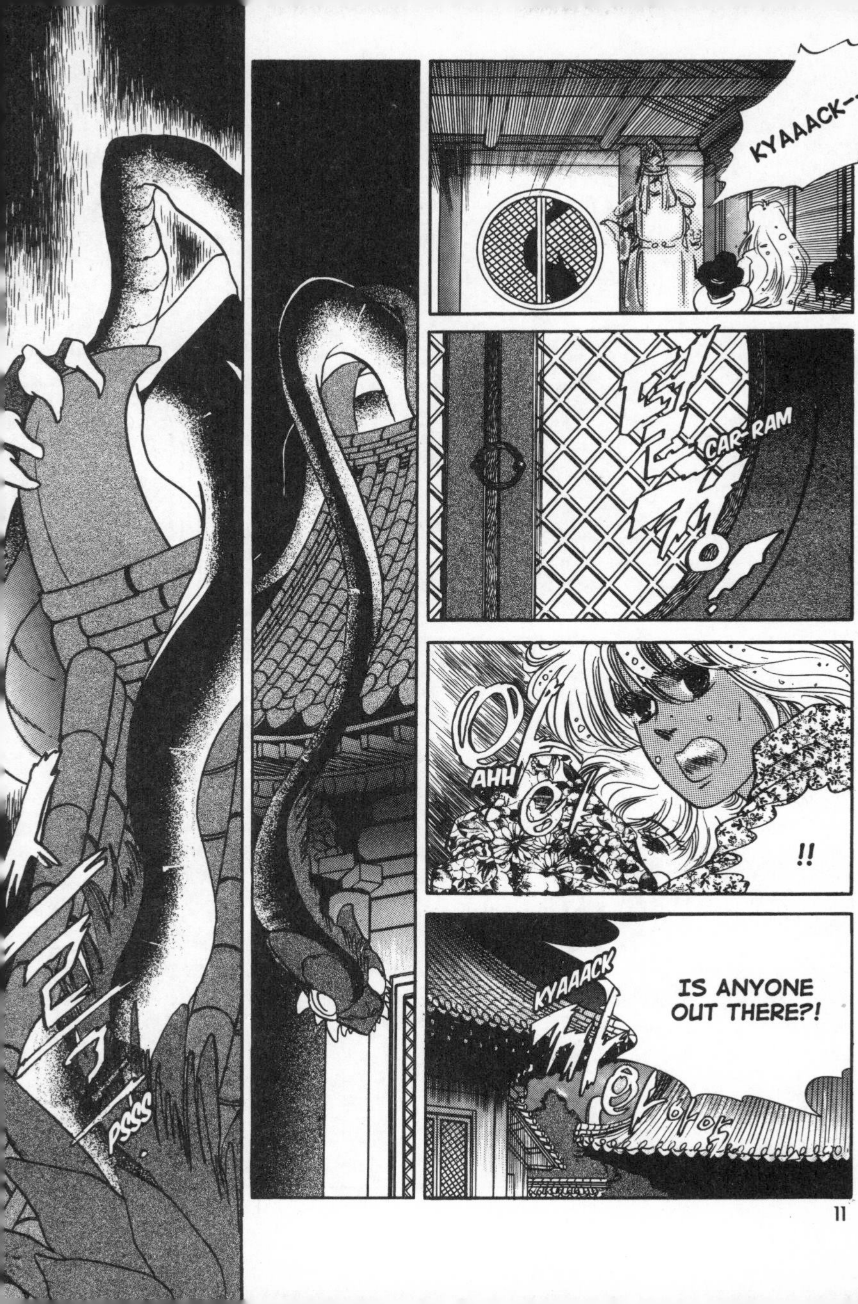
PSSS
KYAAACK---!
CAR-RAM
AHH
!!
KYAAACK
IS ANYONE OUT THERE?!

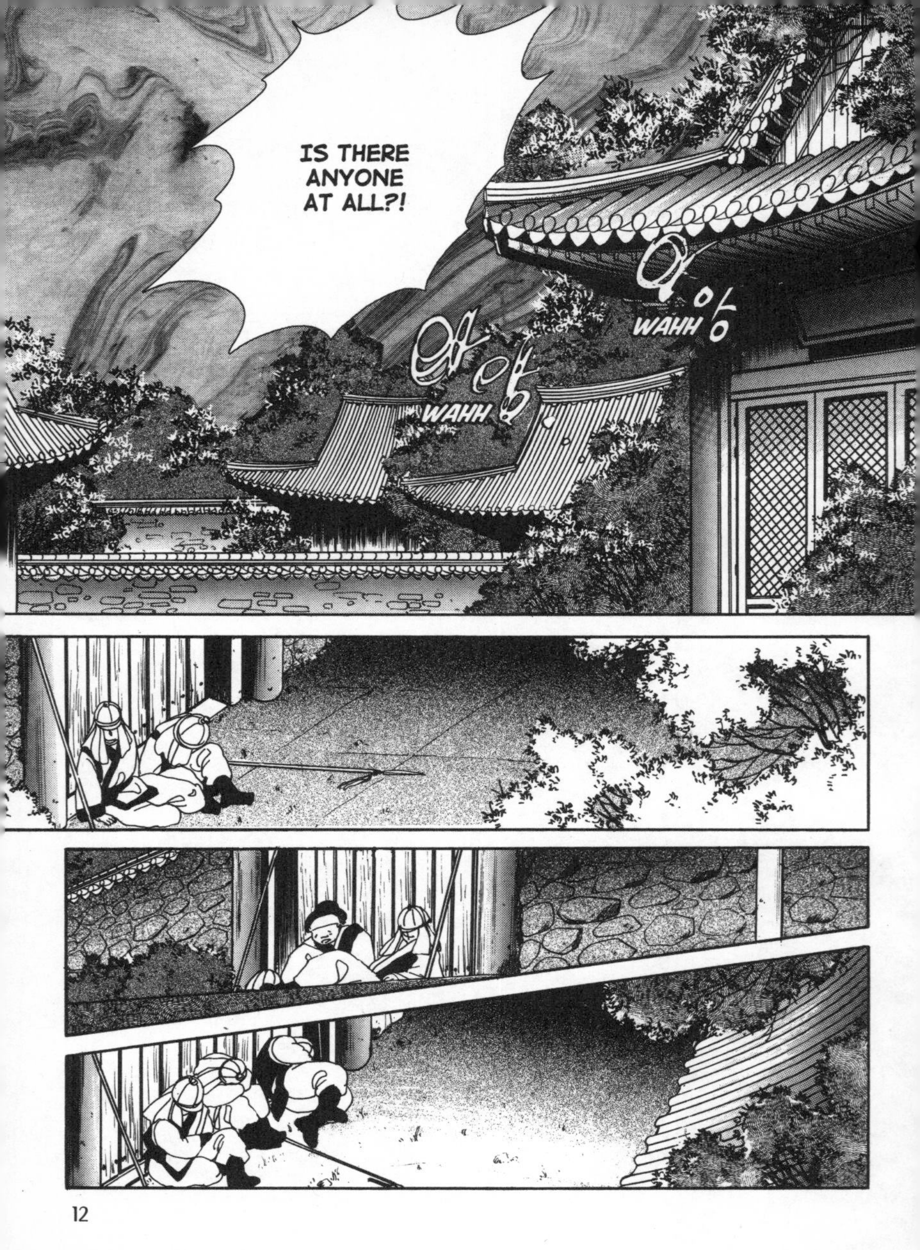
IS THERE ANYONE AT ALL?!
WAHH
WAHH

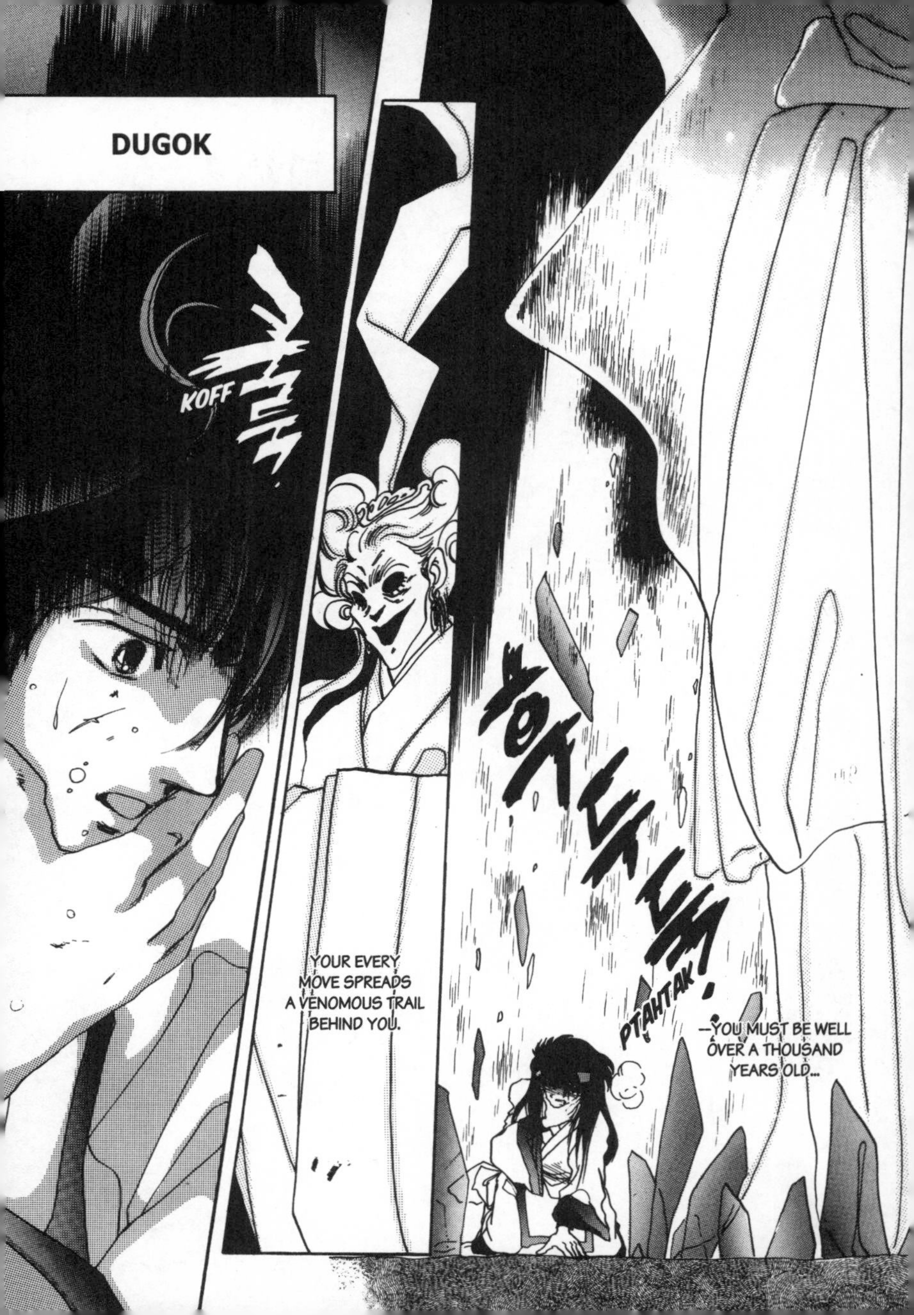
DUGOK
KOFF
YOUR EVERY MOVE SPREADS A VENOMOUS TRAIL BEHIND YOU.
PTAHTAK!
—YOU MUST BE WELL OVER A THOUSAND YEARS OLD...

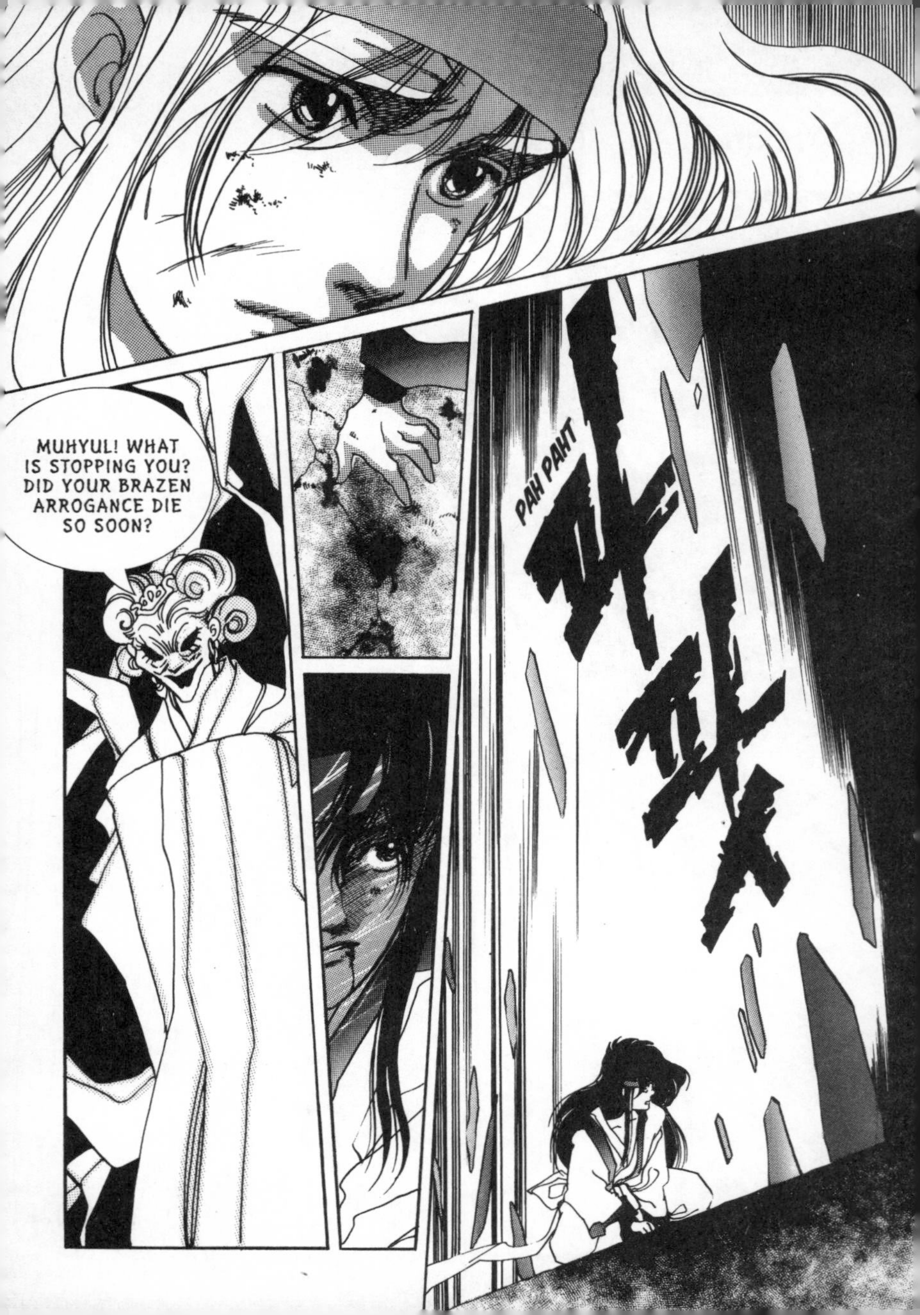
MUHYUL! WHAT IS STOPPING YOU? DID YOUR BRAZEN ARROGANCE DIE SO SOON?
PAH PAHT

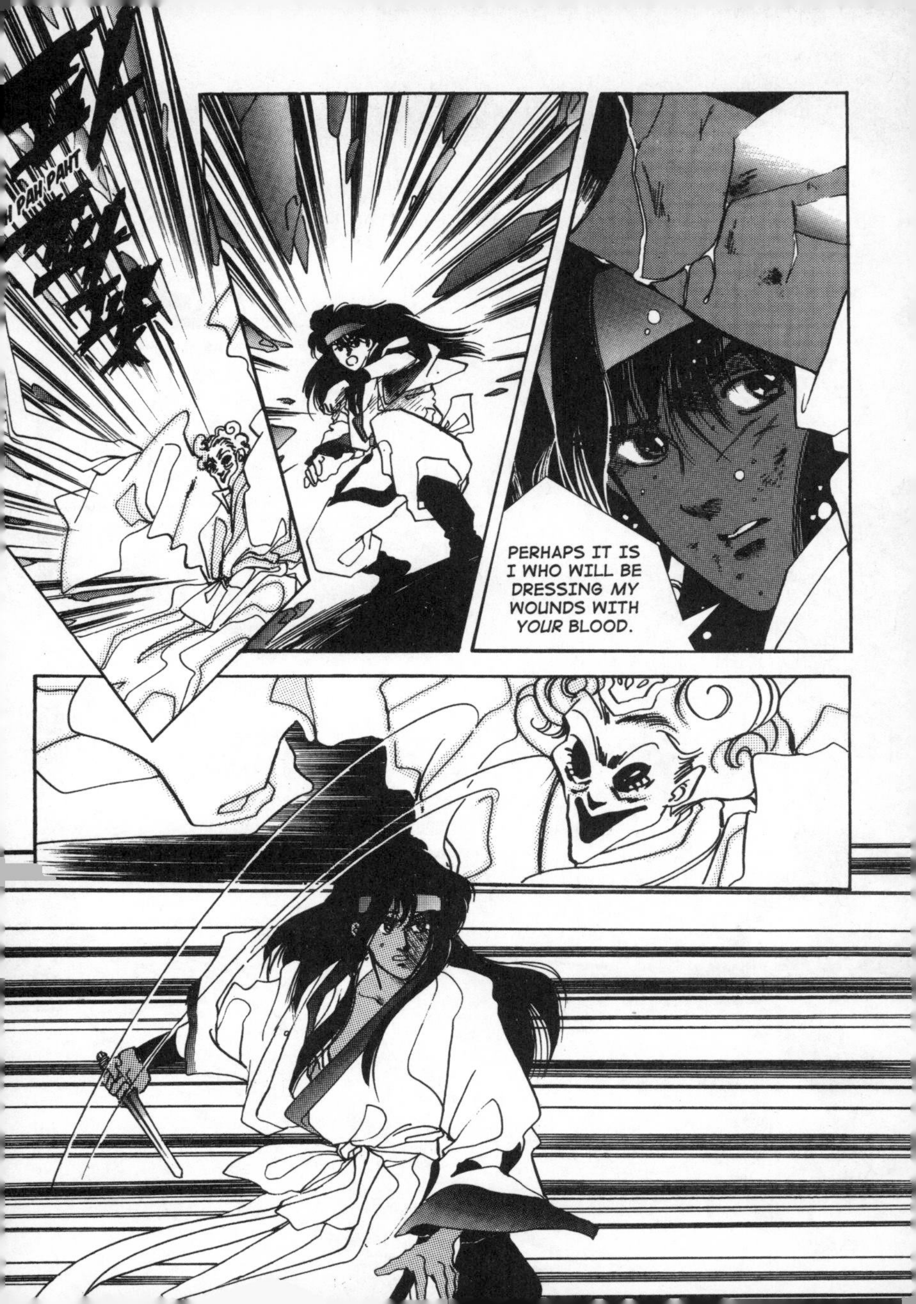
PAH PAH PAHT
PERHAPS IT IS I WHO WILL BE DRESSING MY WOUNDS WITH YOUR BLOOD.

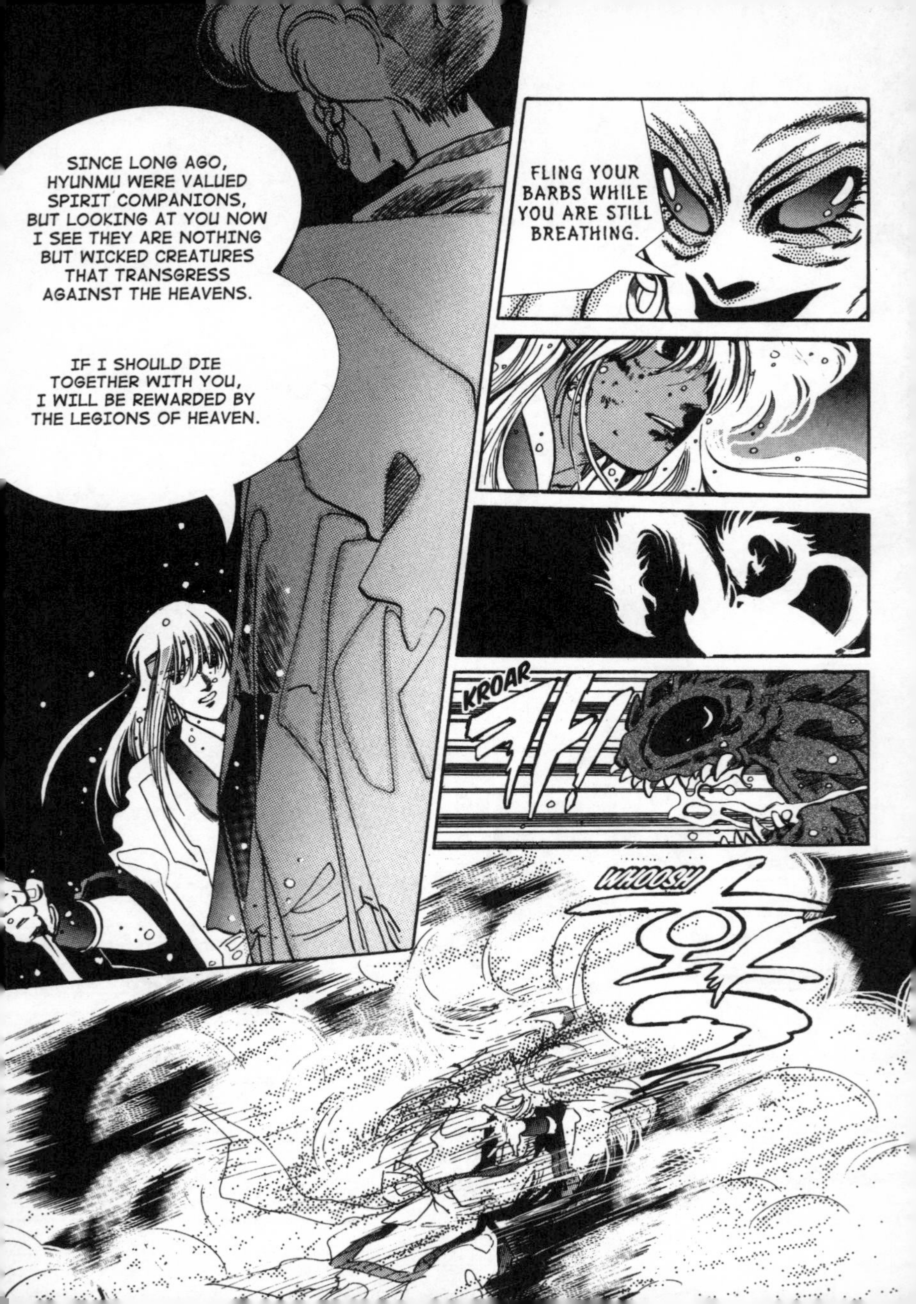
SINCE LONG AGO, HYUNMU WERE VALUED SPIRIT COMPANIONS, BUT LOOKING AT YOU NOW I SEE THEY ARE NOTHING BUT WICKED CREATURES THAT TRANSGRESS AGAINST THE HEAVENS.
IF I SHOULD DIE TOGETHER WITH YOU, I WILL BE REWARDED BY THE LEGIONS OF HEAVEN.
FLING YOUR BARBS WHILE YOU ARE STILL BREATHING.
KROAR
WHOOSH

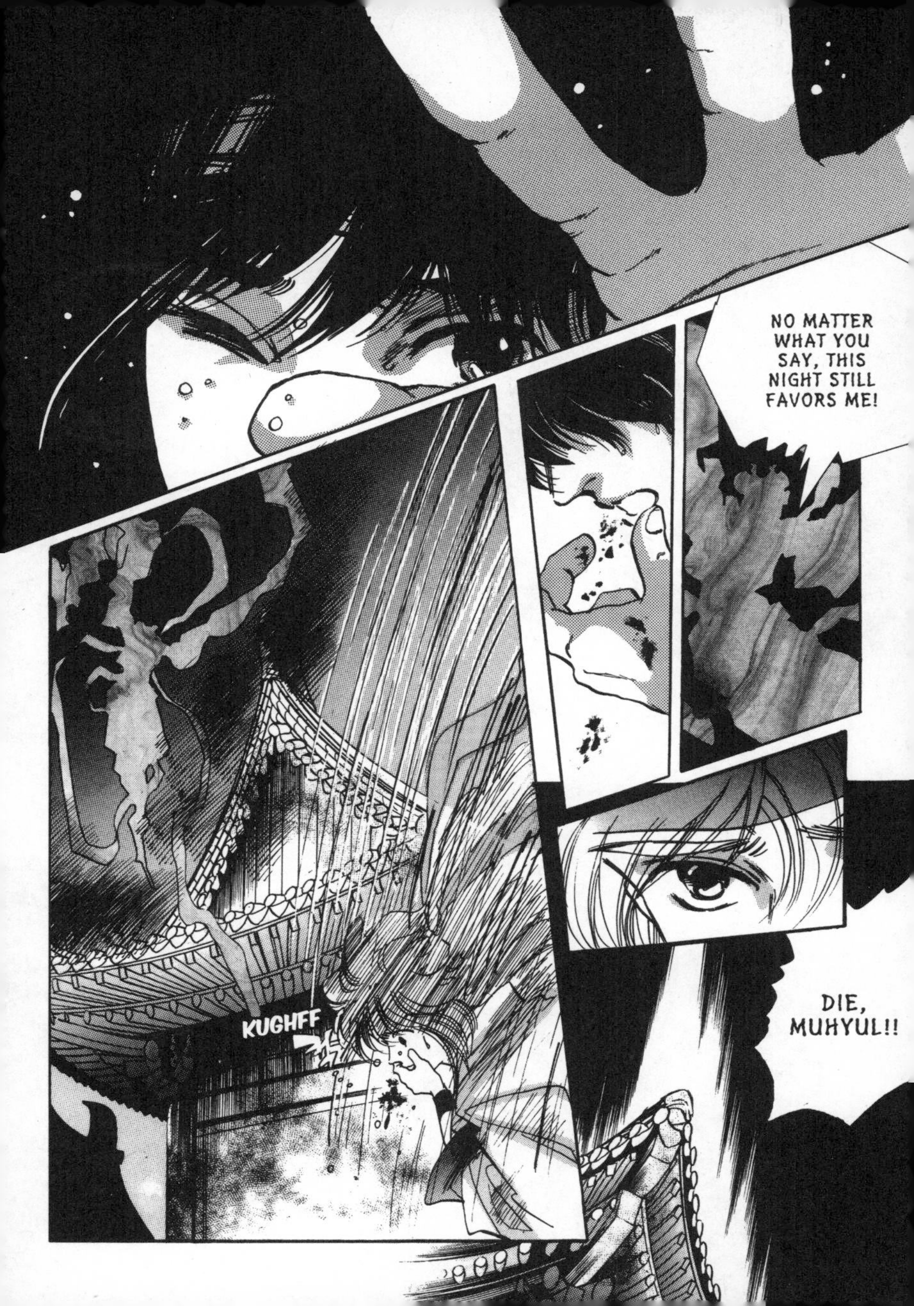
NO MATTER WHAT YOU SAY, THIS NIGHT STILL FAVORS ME!
KUGHFF
DIE, MUHYUL!!

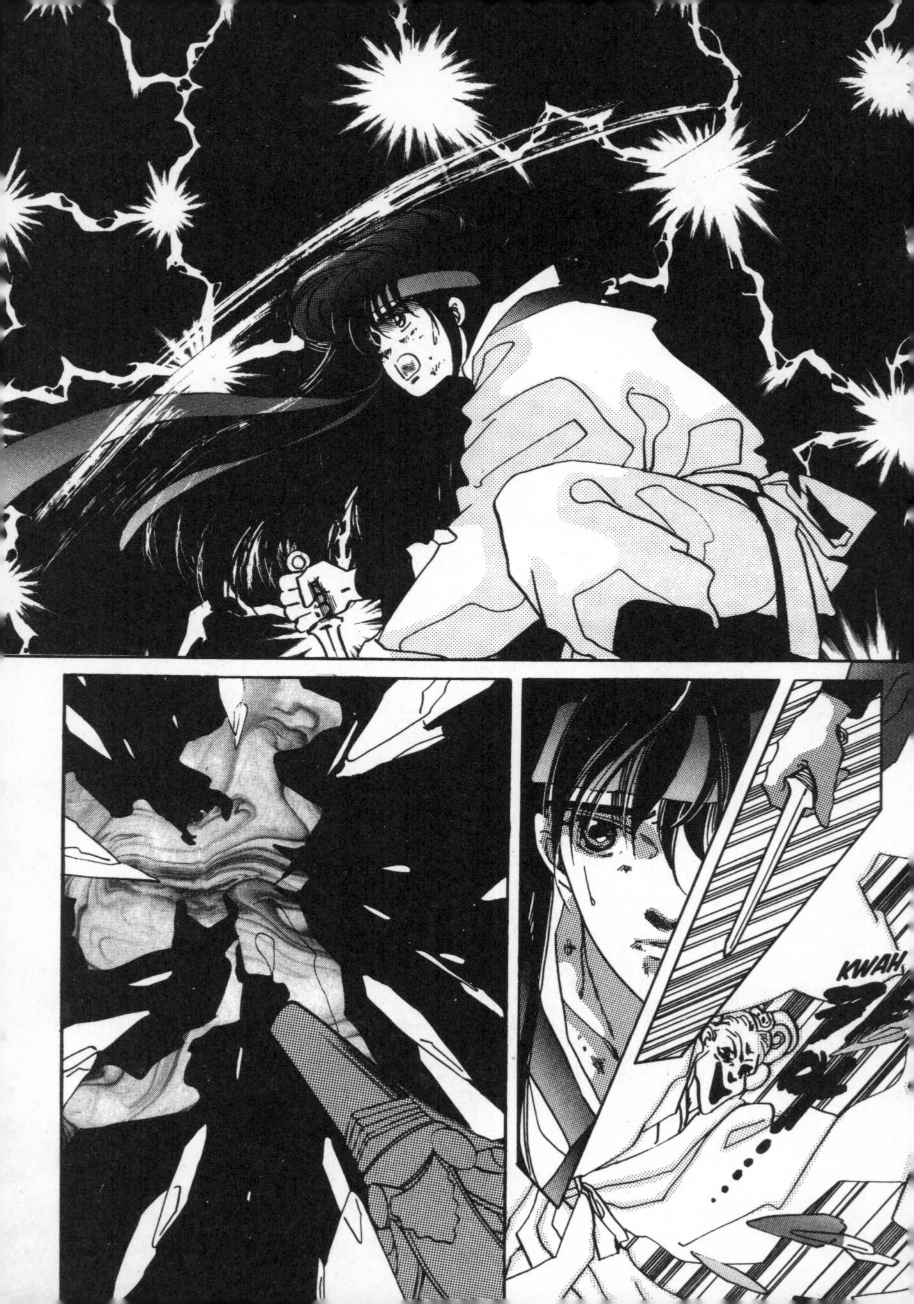
KWAH

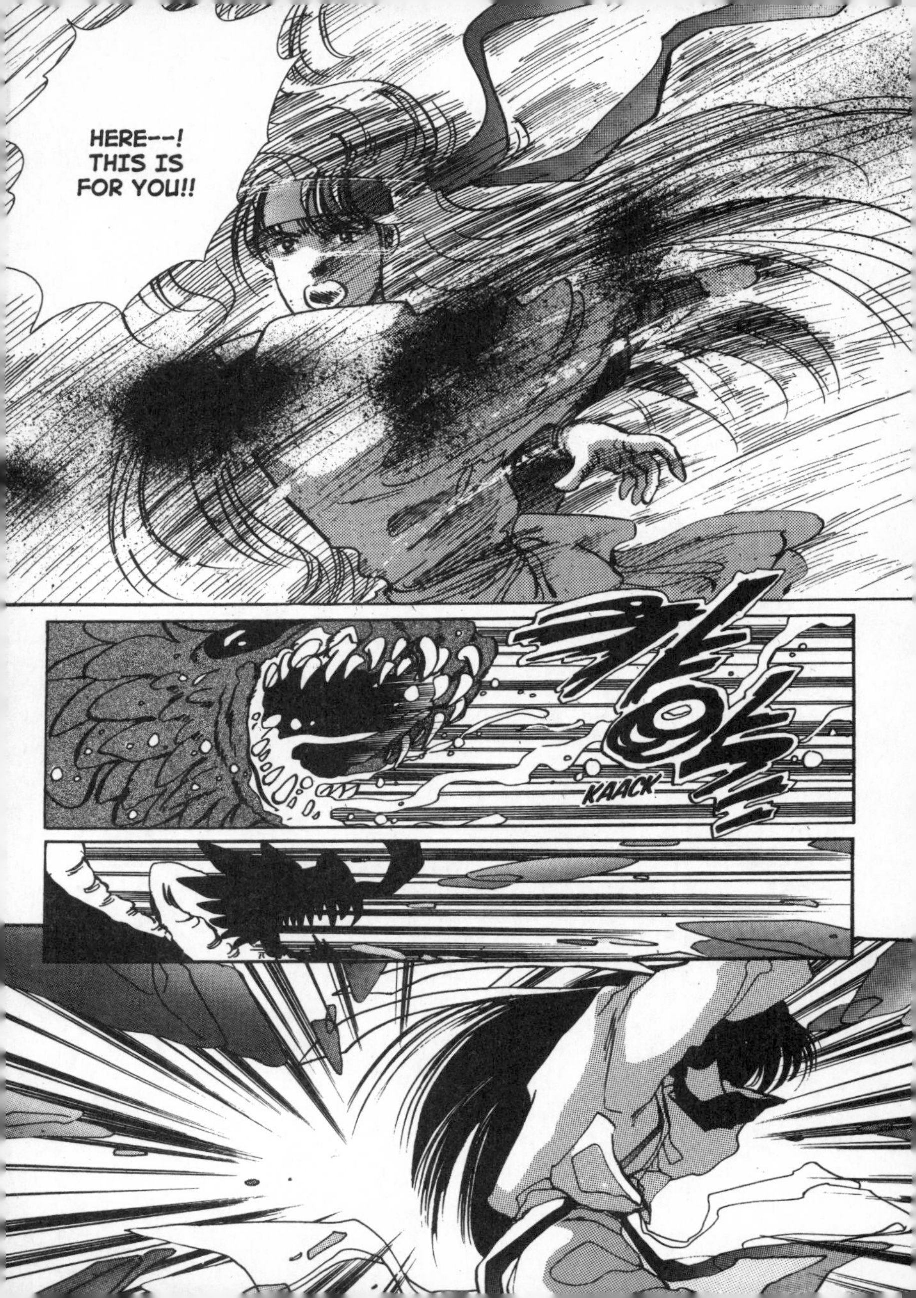
HERE--! THIS IS FOR YOU!!
KAACK

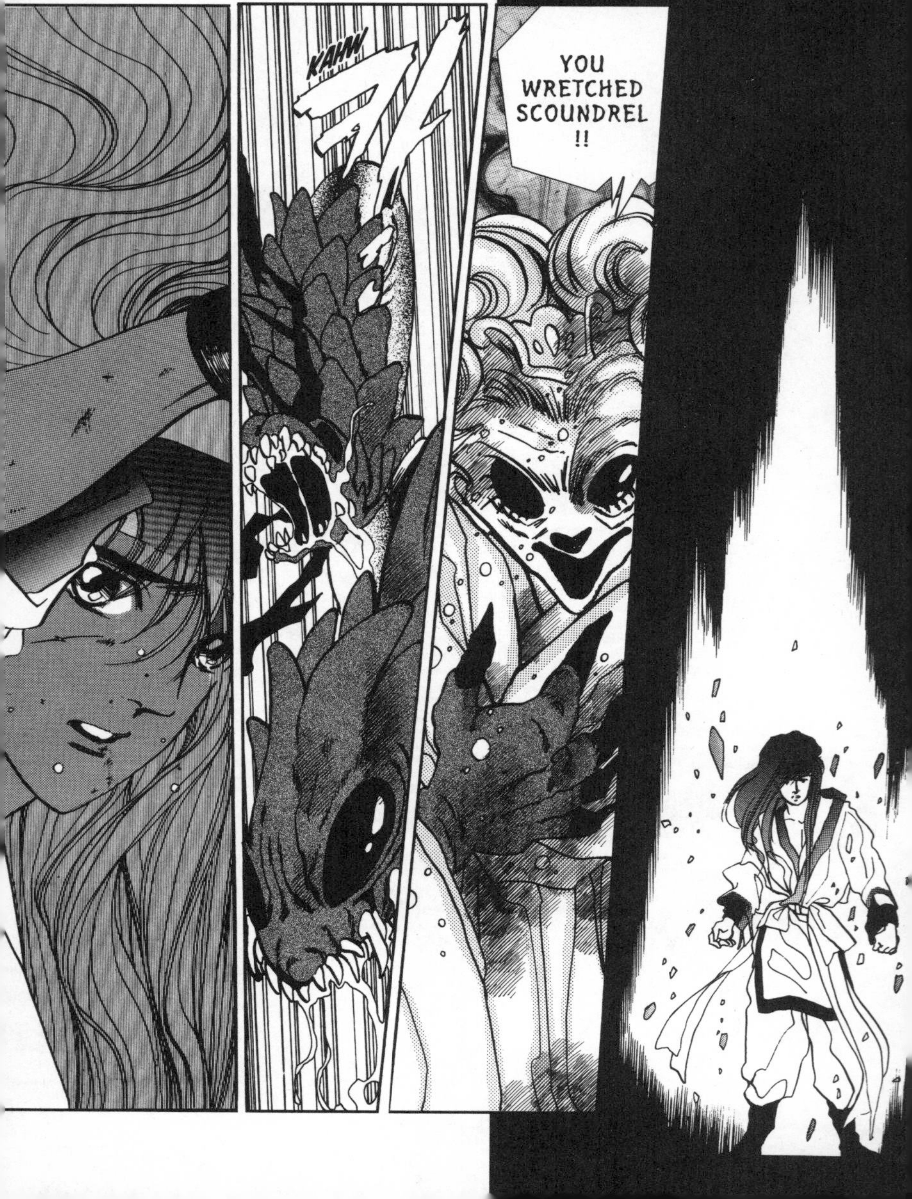
KAHW
YOU WRETCHED SCOUNDREL !!

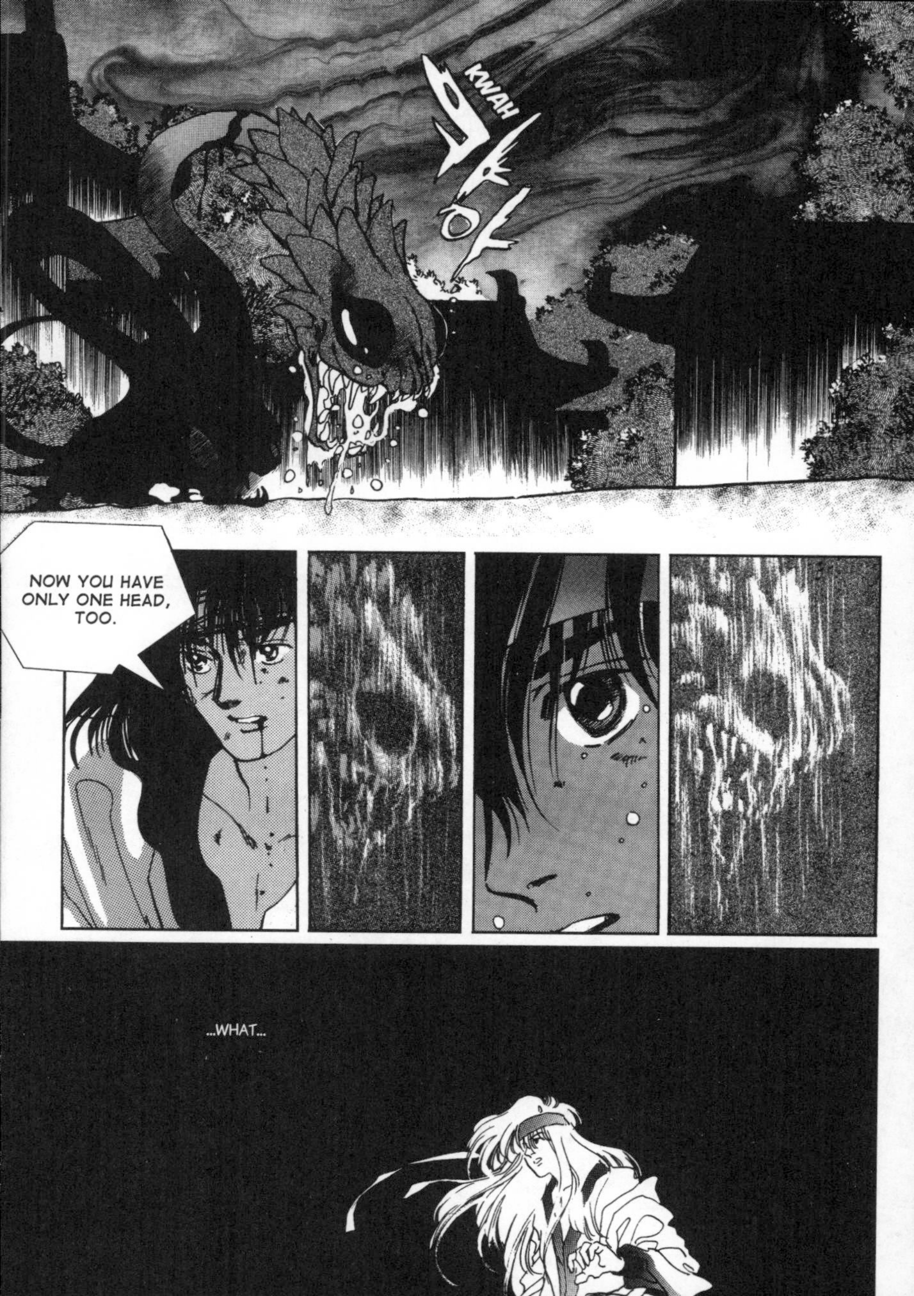
KWAH
NOW YOU HAVE ONLY ONE HEAD, TOO.
...WHAT...

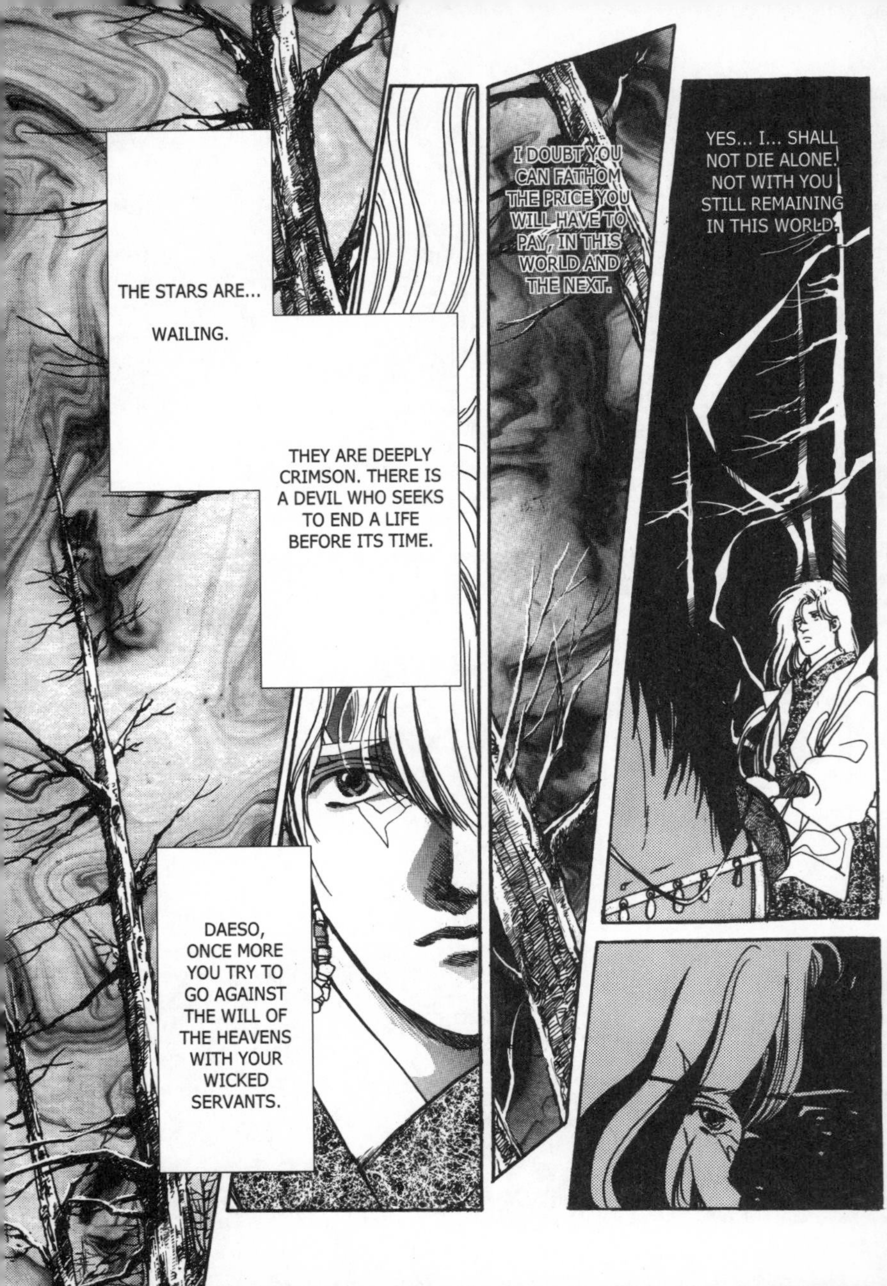
THE STARS ARE...
WAILING.
THEY ARE DEEPLY CRIMSON. THERE IS A DEVIL WHO SEEKS TO END A LIFE BEFORE ITS TIME.
DAESO, ONCE MORE YOU TRY TO GO AGAINST THE WILL OF THE HEAVENS WITH YOUR WICKED SERVANTS.
I DOUBT YOU CAN FATHOM THE PRICE YOU WILL HAVE TO PAY, IN THIS WORLD AND THE NEXT.
YES... I... SHALL NOT DIE ALONE. NOT WITH YOU STILL REMAINING IN THIS WORLD.

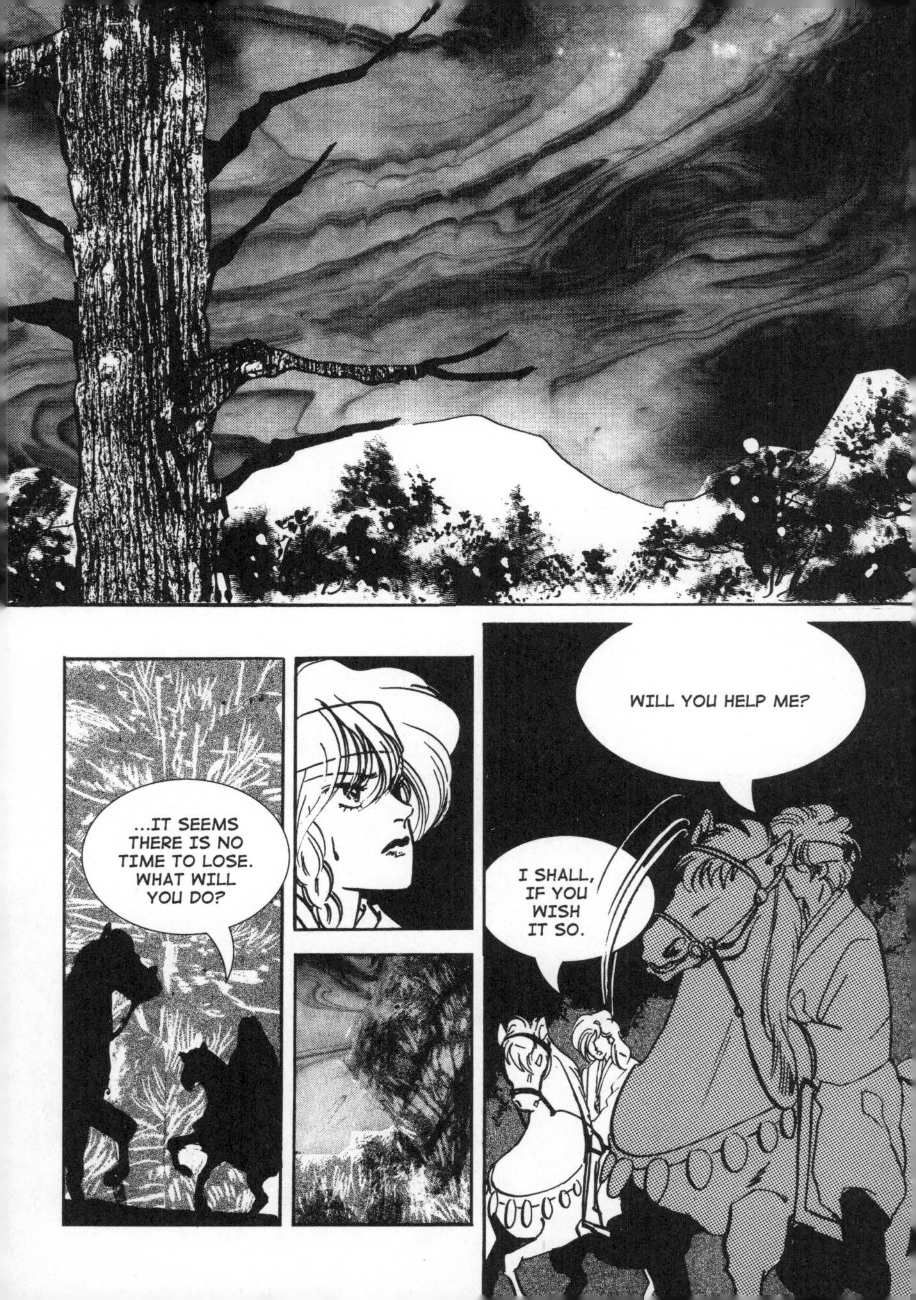
...IT SEEMS THERE IS NO TIME TO LOSE. WHAT WILL YOU DO?
WILL YOU HELP ME?
I SHALL, IF YOU WISH IT SO.

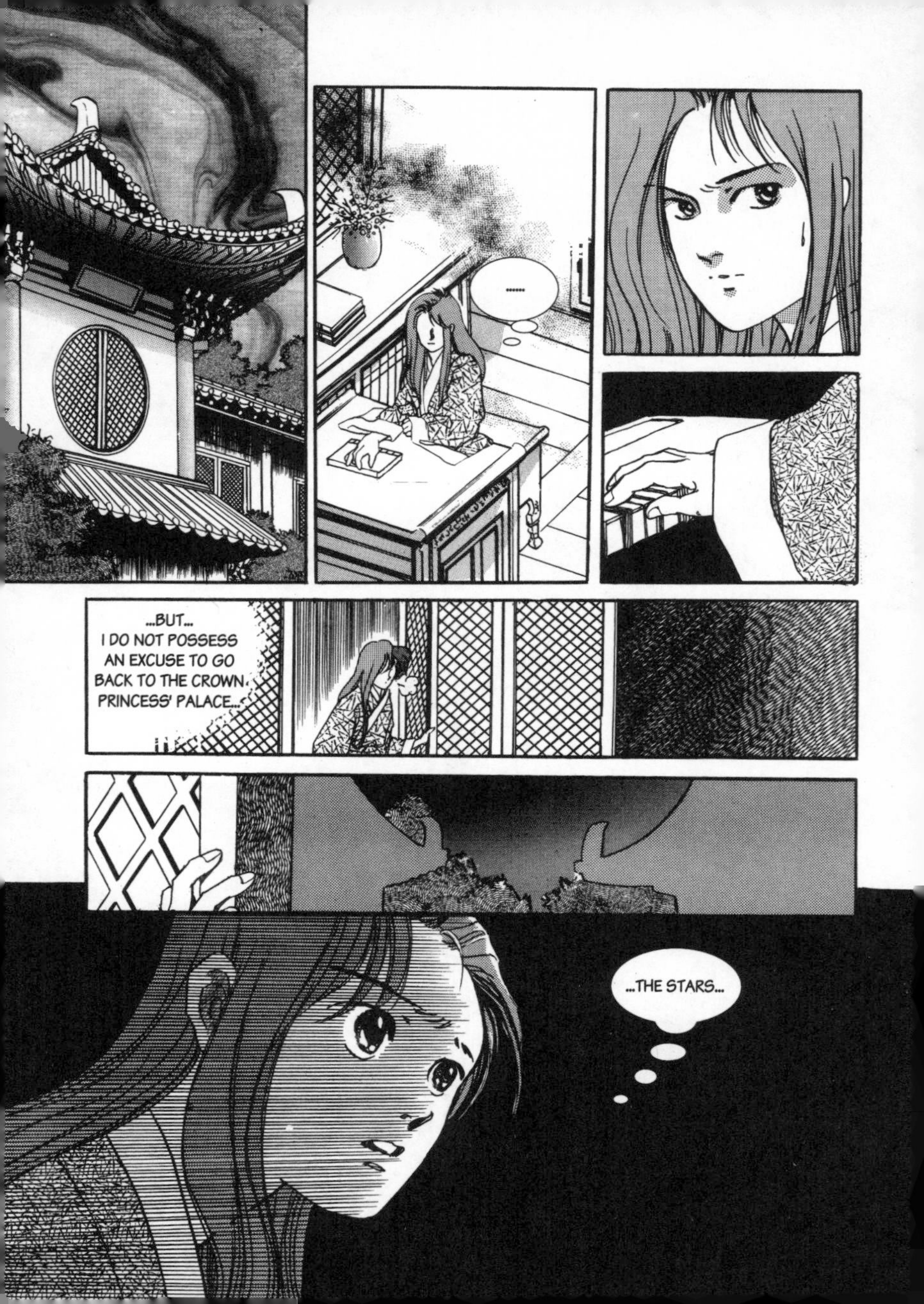
......
...BUT... I DO NOT POSSESS AN EXCUSE TO GO BACK TO THE CROWN PRINCESS' PALACE...
...THE STARS...

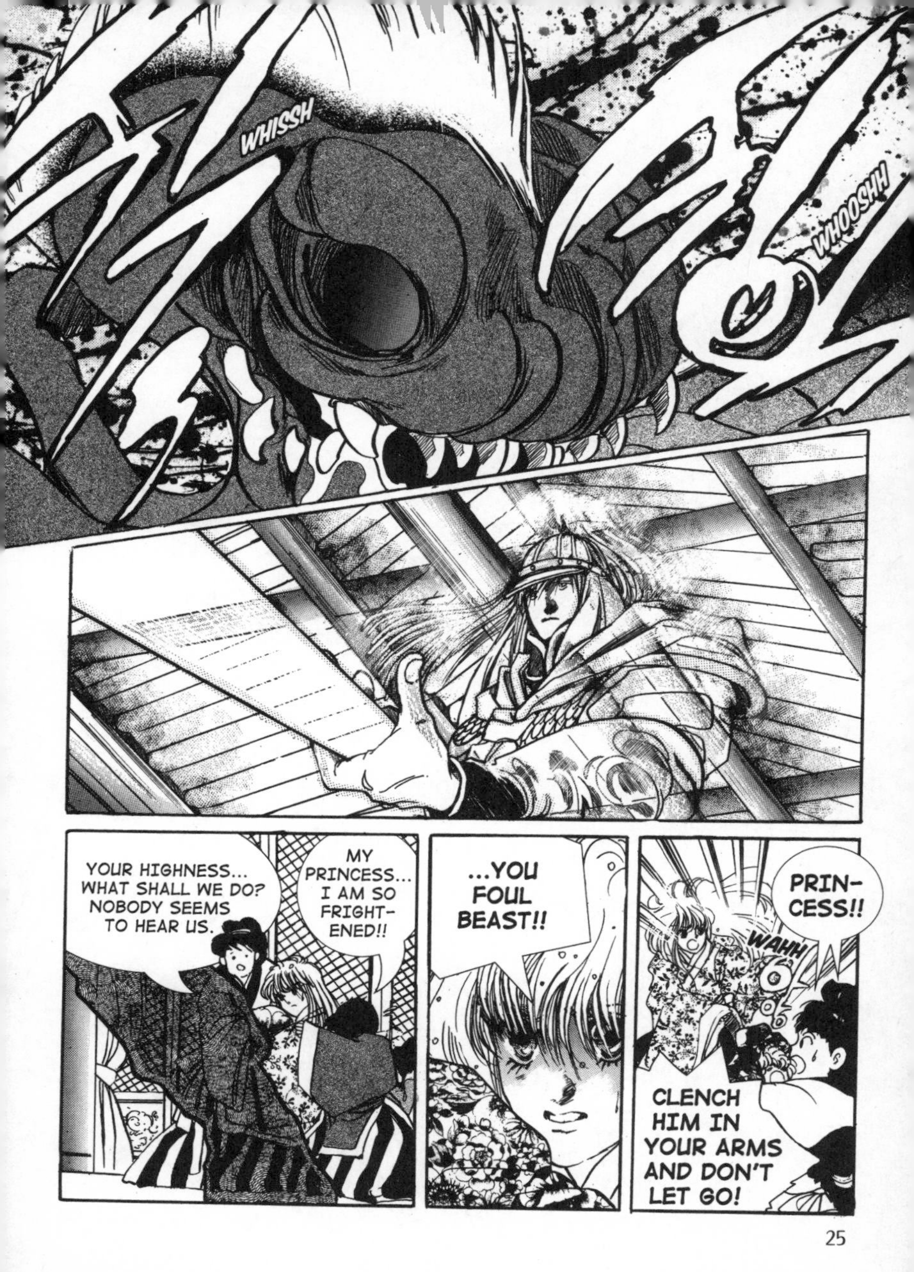
WHISSH
WHOOSHH
YOUR HIGHNESS... WHAT SHALL WE DO? NOBODY SEEMS TO HEAR US.
MY PRINCESS... I AM SO FRIGHT-ENED!!
...YOU FOUL BEAST!!
PRIN-CESS!!
WAHH
CLENCH HIM IN YOUR ARMS AND DON'T LET GO!

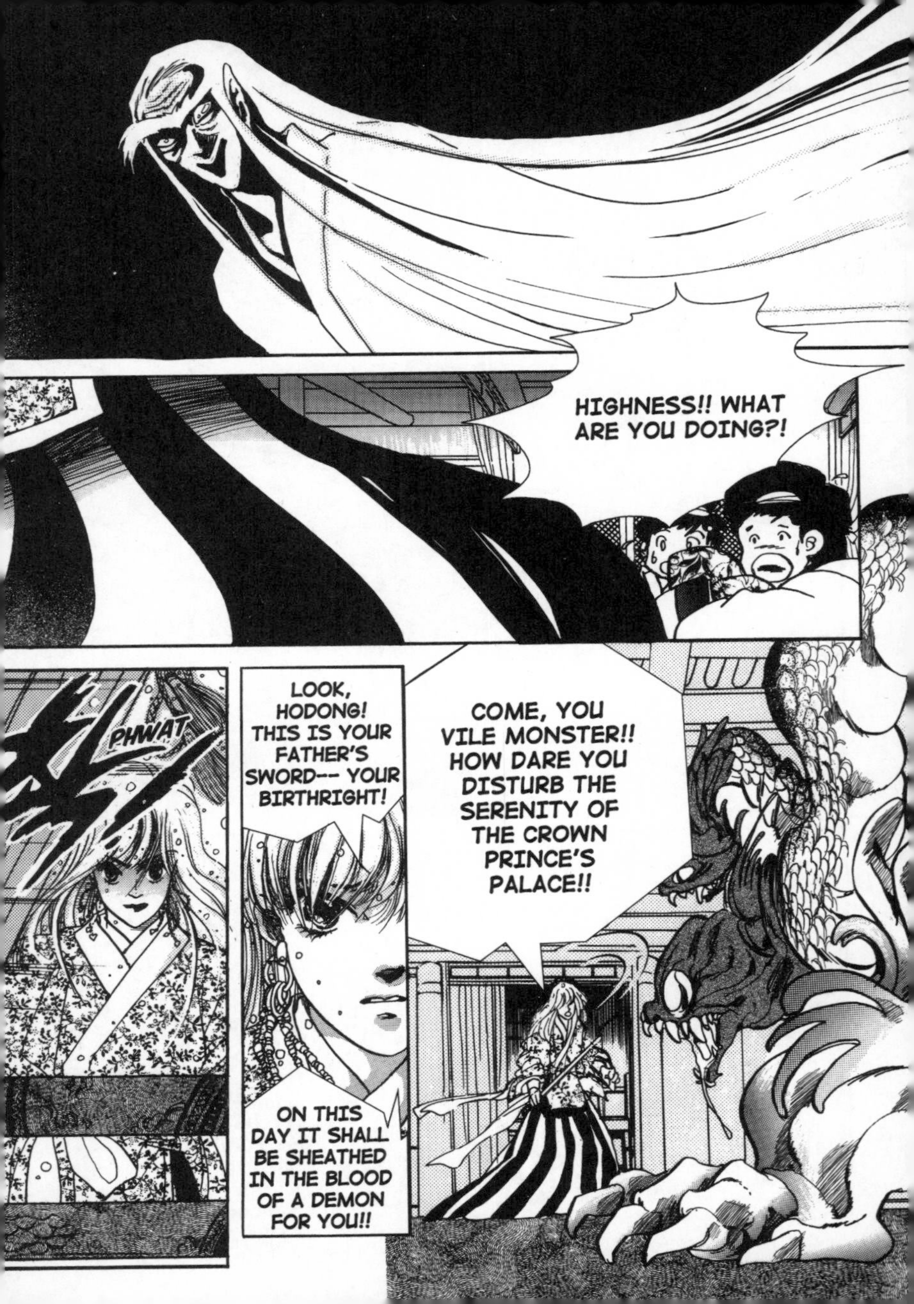
HIGHNESS!! WHAT ARE YOU DOING?!
PHWAT
LOOK, HODONG! THIS IS YOUR FATHER'S SWORD-- YOUR BIRTHRIGHT!
ON THIS DAY IT SHALL BE SHEATHED IN THE BLOOD OF A DEMON FOR YOU!!
COME, YOU VILE MONSTER!! HOW DARE YOU DISTURB THE SERENITY OF THE CROWN PRINCE'S PALACE!!

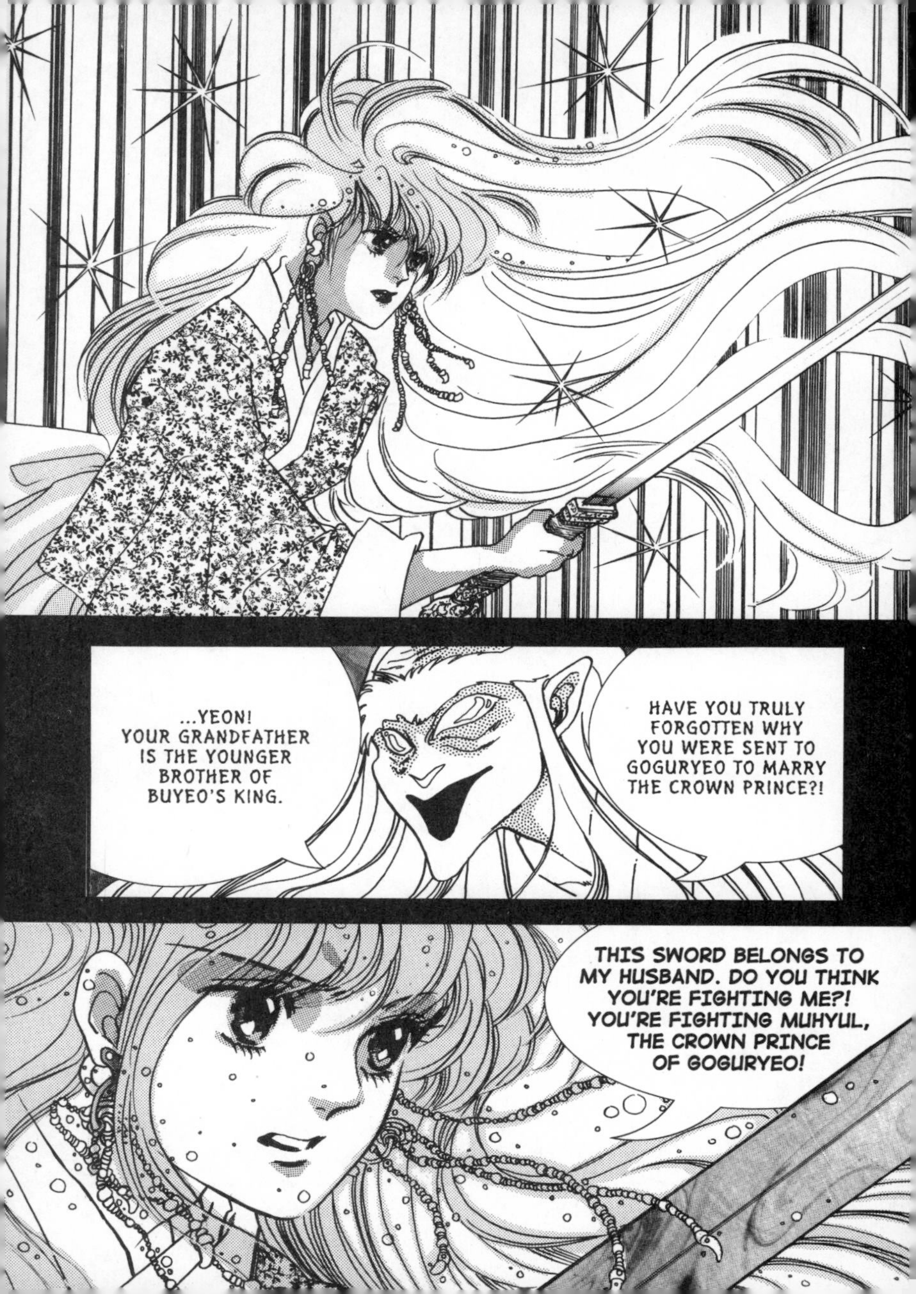
...YEON! YOUR GRANDFATHER IS THE YOUNGER BROTHER OF BUYEO'S KING.
HAVE YOU TRULY FORGOTTEN WHY YOU WERE SENT TO GOGURYEO TO MARRY THE CROWN PRINCE?!
THIS SWORD BELONGS TO MY HUSBAND. DO YOU THINK YOU'RE FIGHTING ME?! YOU'RE FIGHTING MUHYUL, THE CROWN PRINCE OF GOGURYEO!

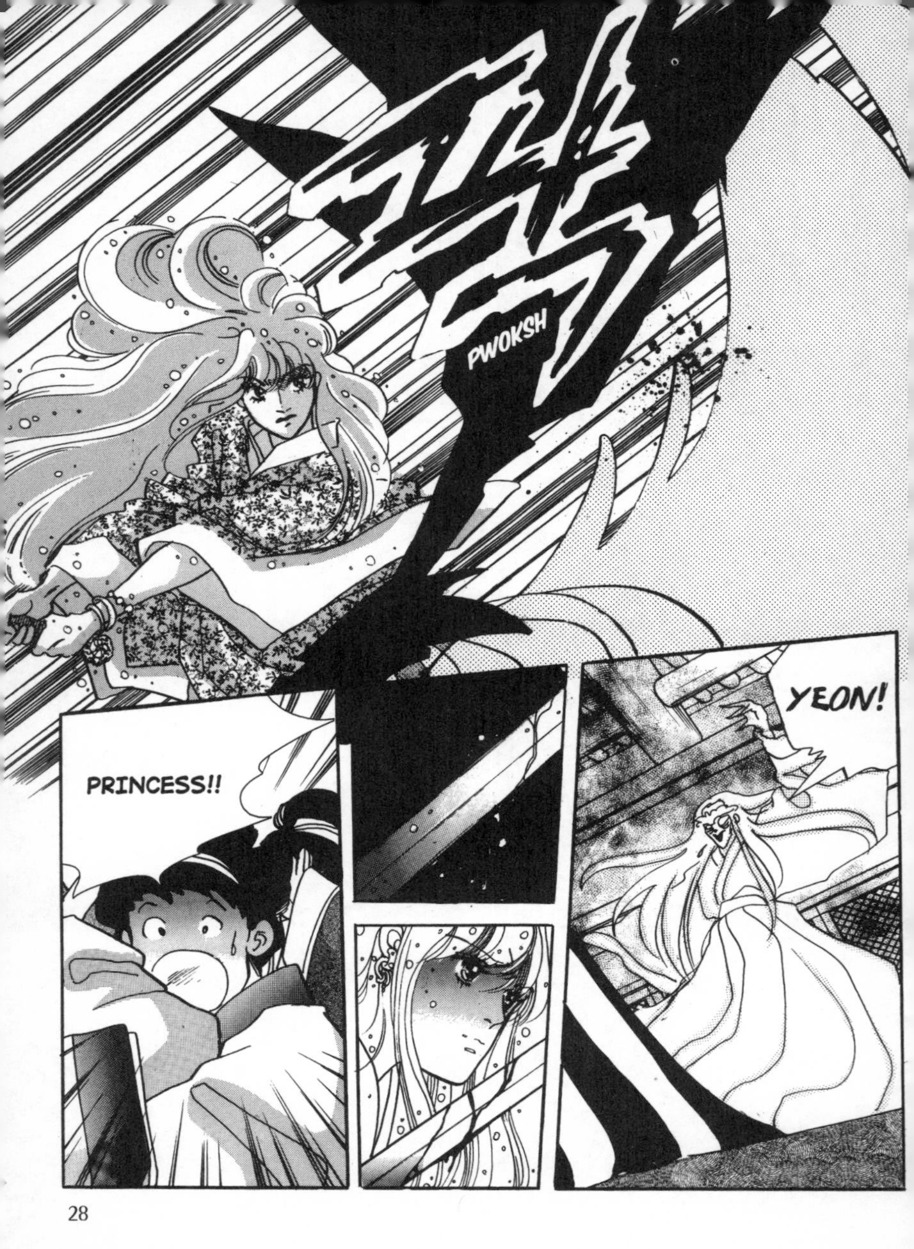
PWOKSH
PRINCESS!!
YEON!

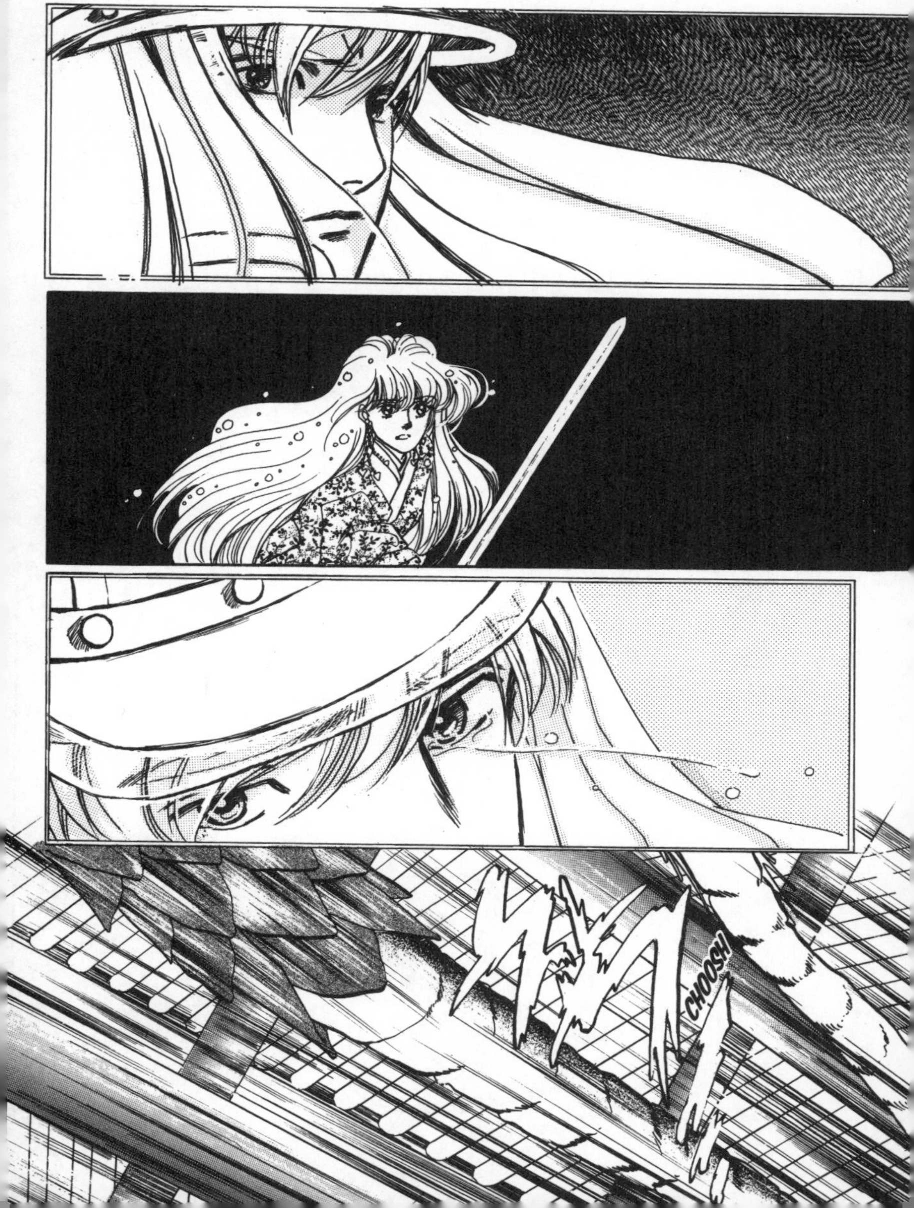
CHOOSH

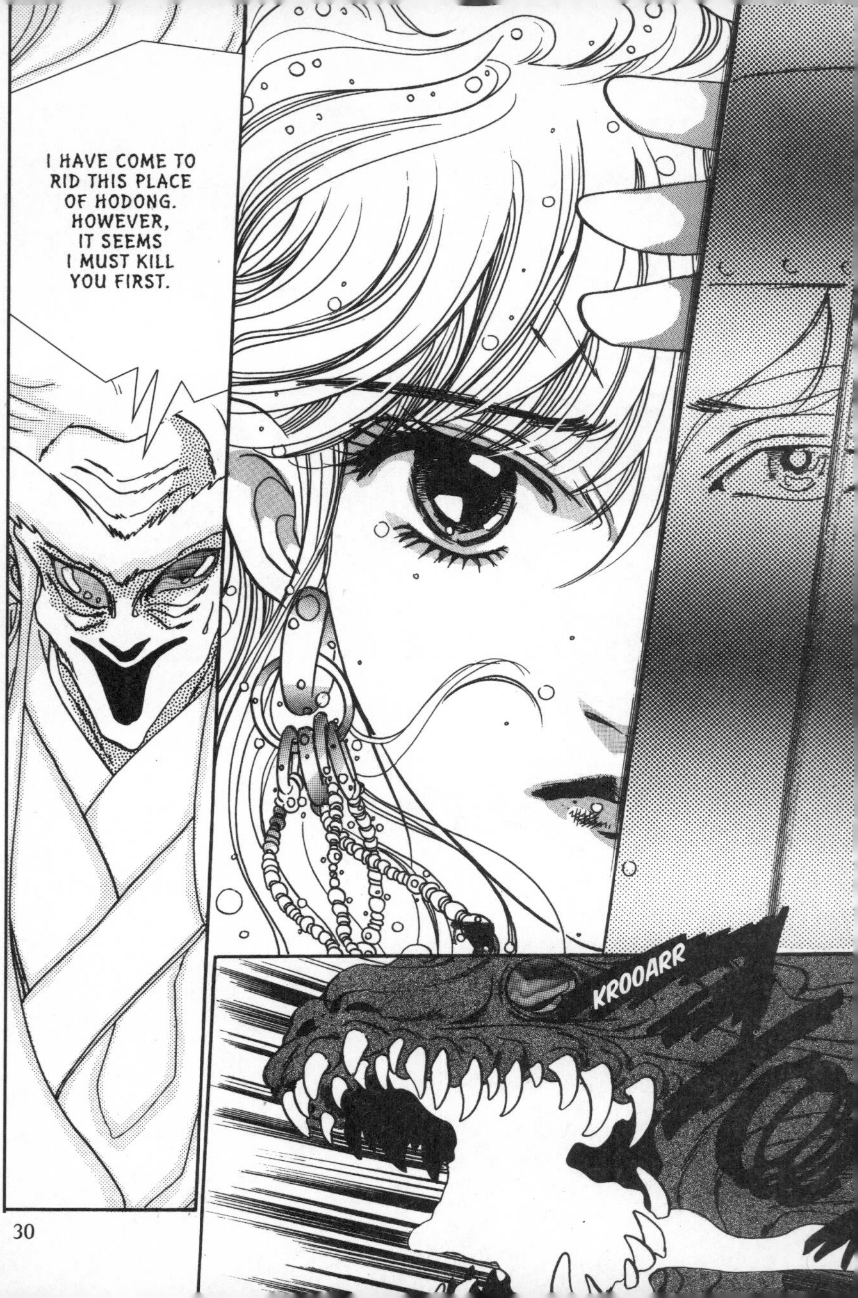
I HAVE COME TO RID THIS PLACE OF HODONG. HOWEVER, IT SEEMS I MUST KILL YOU FIRST.
KROOARR

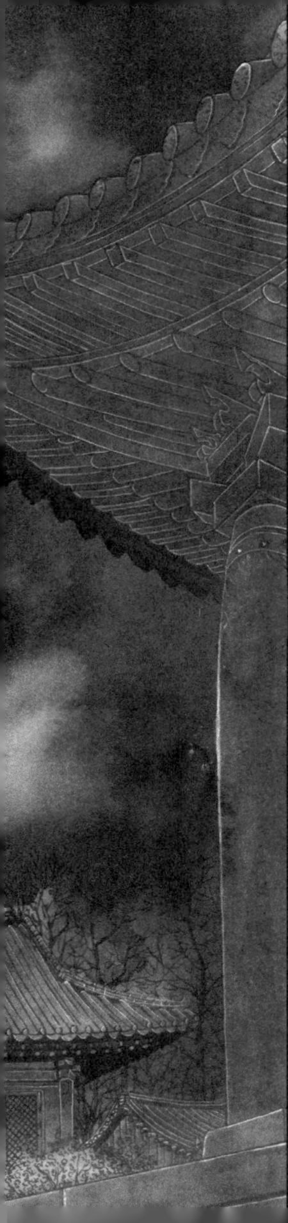

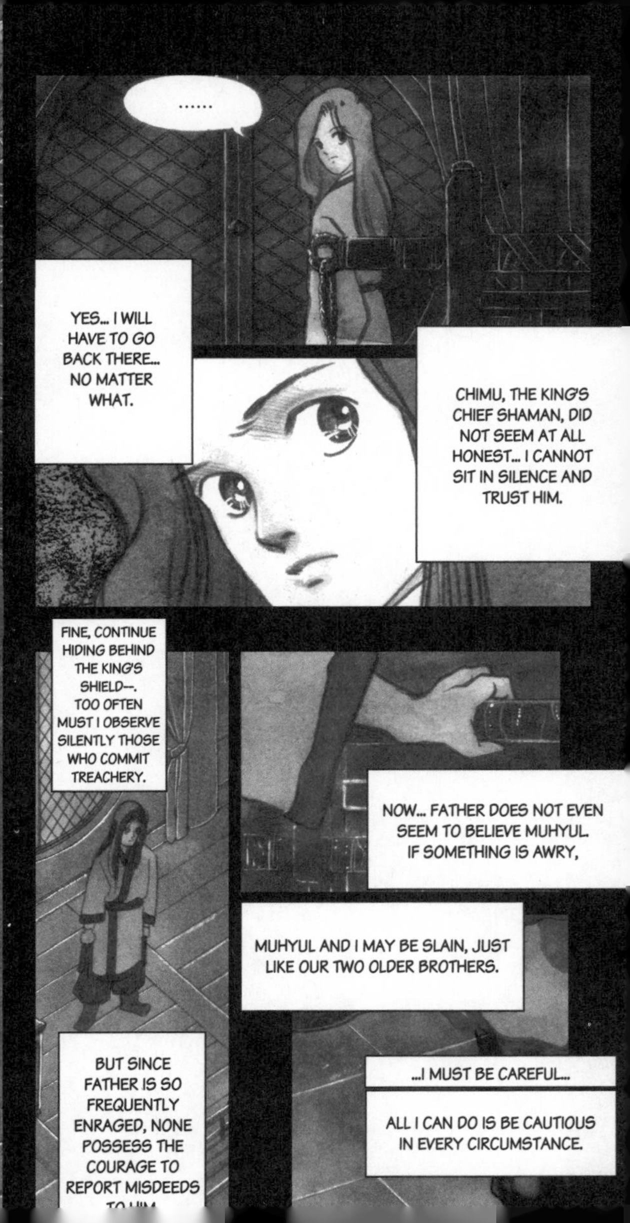

......
YES... I WILL HAVE TO GO BACK THERE... NO MATTER WHAT.
CHIMU, THE KING'S CHIEF SHAMAN, DID NOT SEEM AT ALL HONEST... I CANNOT SIT IN SILENCE AND TRUST HIM.
FINE, CONTINUE HIDING BEHIND THE KING'S SHIELD--. TOO OFTEN MUST I OBSERVE SILENTLY THOSE WHO COMMIT TREACHERY.
BUT SINCE FATHER IS SO FREQUENTLY ENRAGED, NONE POSSESS THE COURAGE TO REPORT MISDEEDS
NOW... FATHER DOES NOT EVEN SEEM TO BELIEVE MUHYUL. IF SOMETHING IS AWRY,
MUHYUL AND I MAY BE SLAIN, JUST LIKE OUR TWO OLDER BROTHERS.
...I MUST BE CAREFUL...
ALL I CAN DO IS BE CAUTIOUS IN EVERY CIRCUMSTANCE.

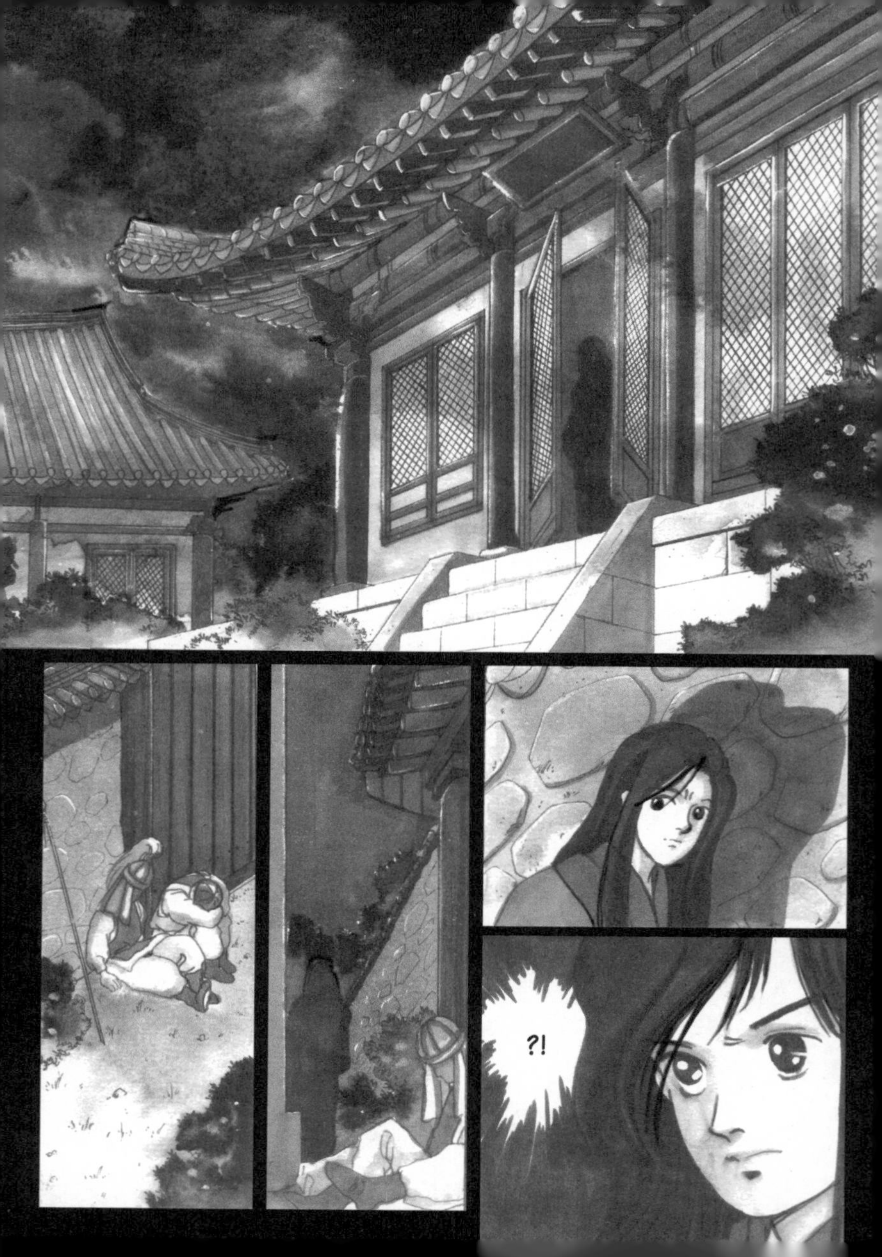
?!

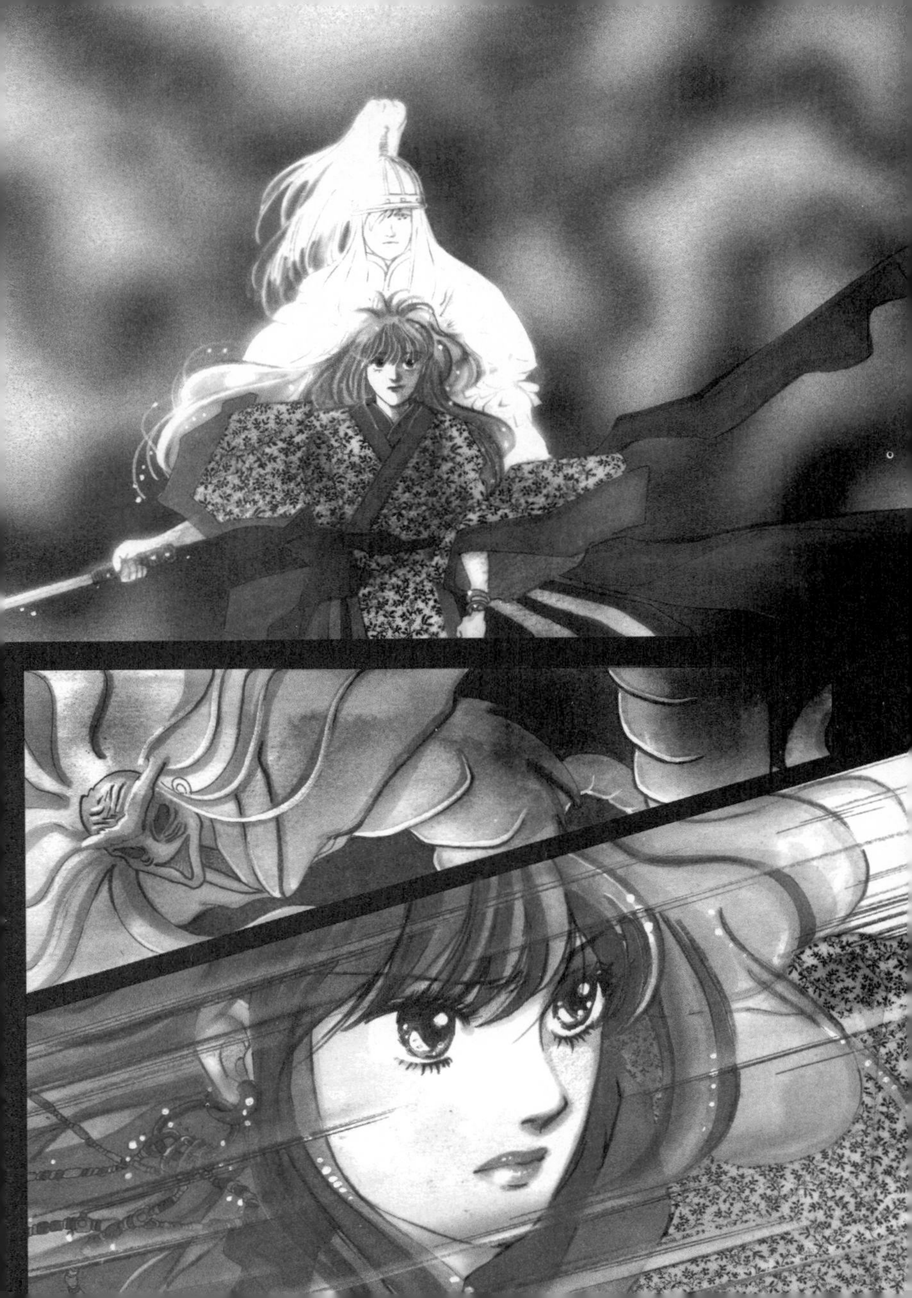

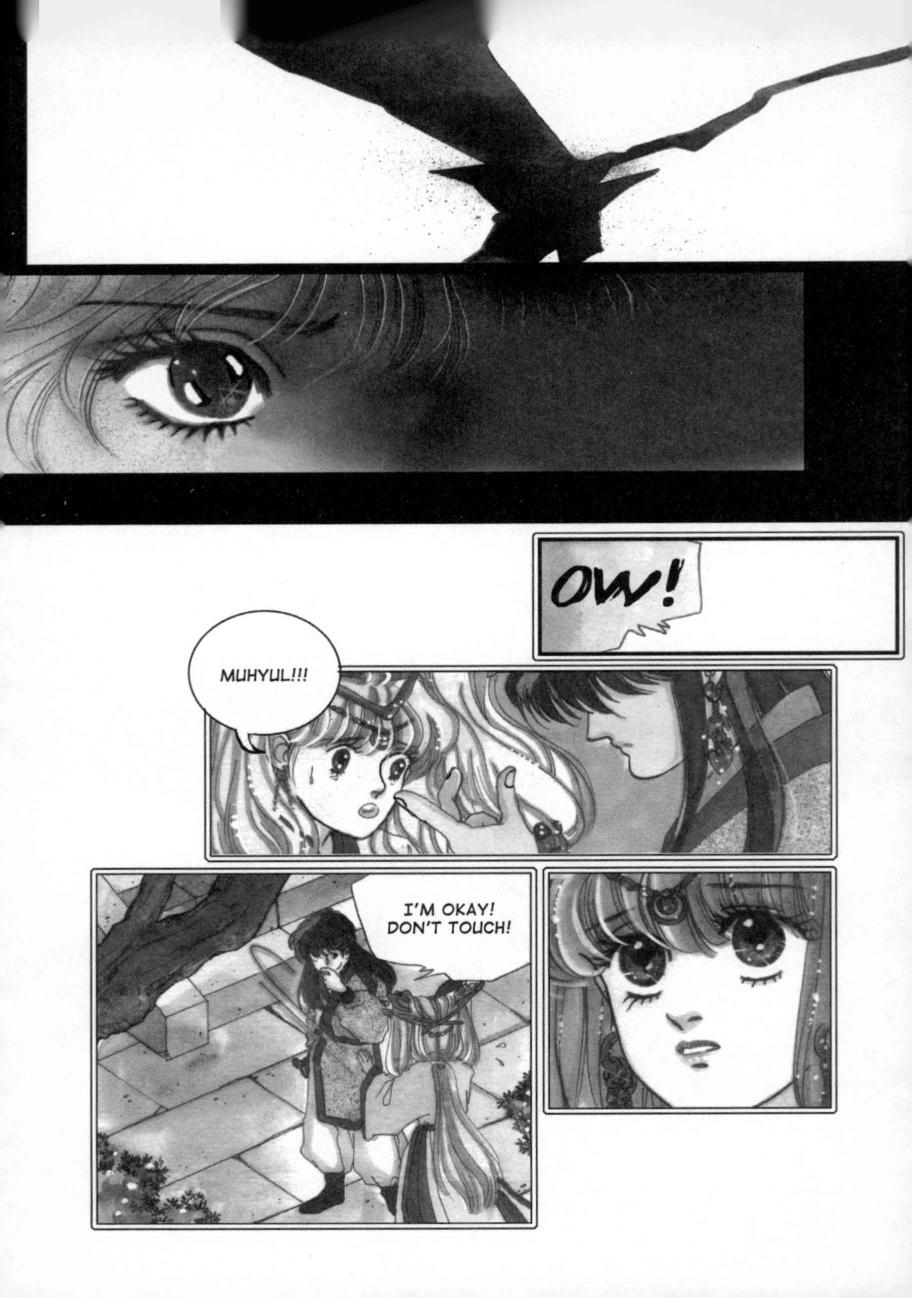
OW!
MUHYUL!!!
I'M OKAY! DON'T TOUCH!

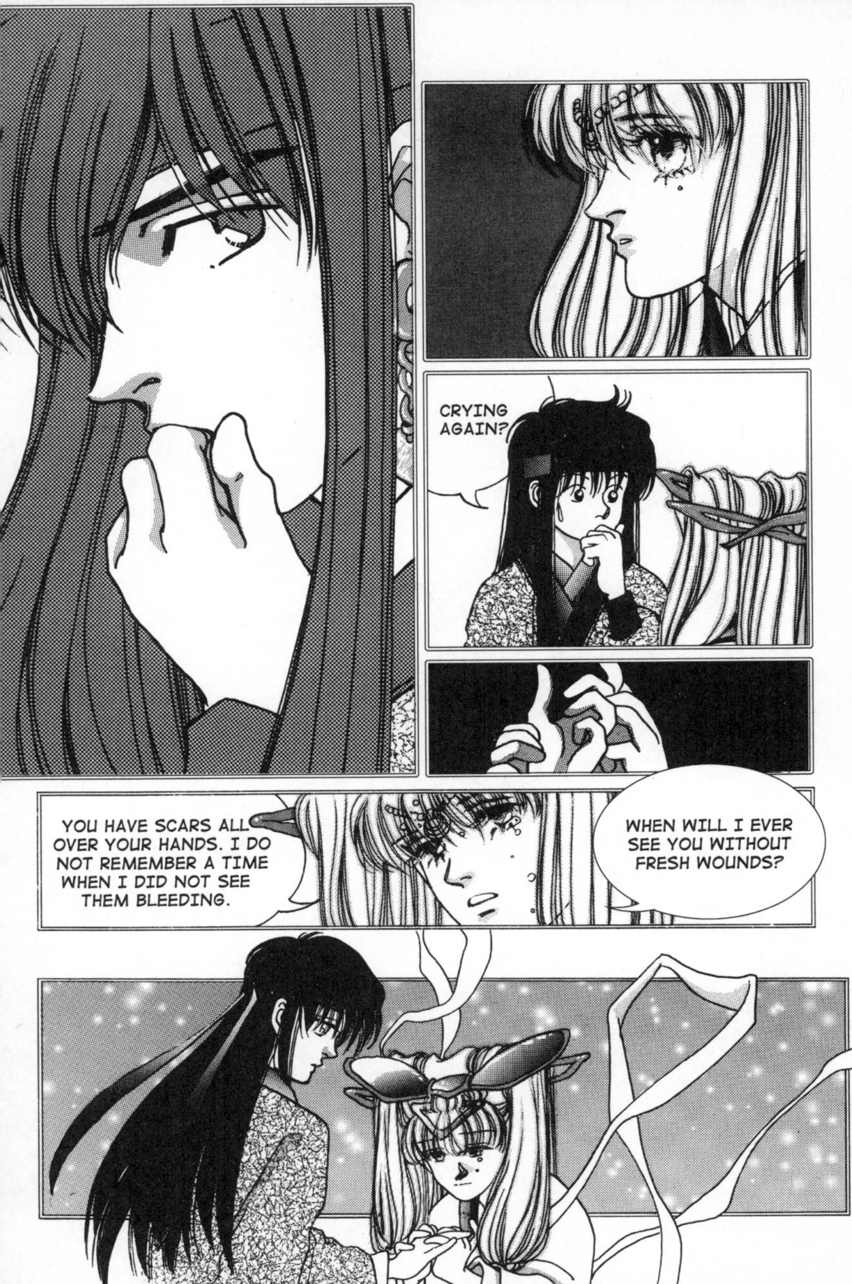
CRYING AGAIN?
YOU HAVE SCARS ALL OVER YOUR HANDS. I DO NOT REMEMBER A TIME WHEN I DID NOT SEE THEM BLEEDING.
WHEN WILL I EVER SEE YOU WITHOUT FRESH WOUNDS?

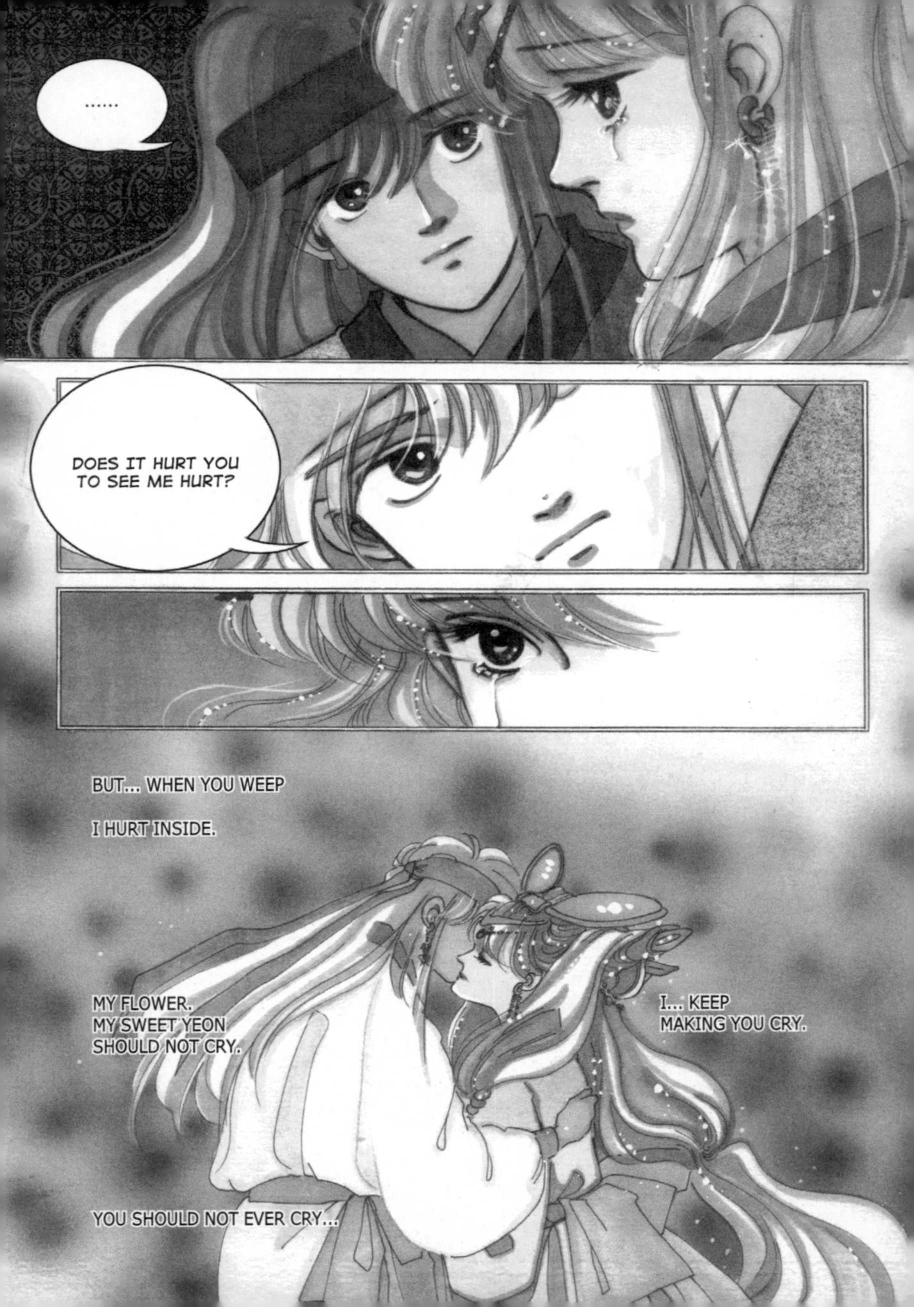
......
DOES IT HURT YOU TO SEE ME HURT?
BUT... WHEN YOU WEEP
I HURT INSIDE.
MY FLOWER. MY SWEET YEON SHOULD NOT CRY.
I... KEEP MAKING YOU CRY.
YOU SHOULD NOT EVER CRY...

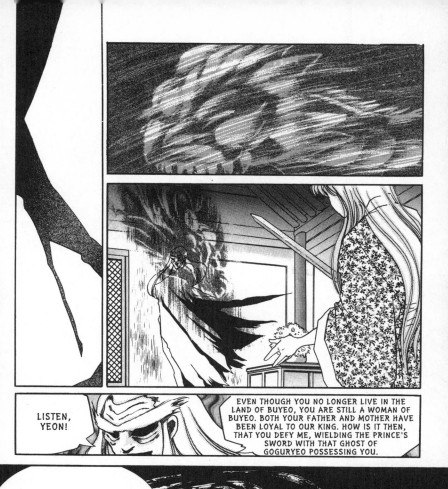

LISTEN, YEON!

EVEN THOUGH YOU NO LONGER LIVE IN THE LAND OF BUYEO, YOU ARE STILL A WOMAN OF BUYEO. BOTH YOUR FATHER AND MOTHER HAVE BEEN LOYAL TO OUR KING. HOW IS IT THEN, THAT YOU DEFY ME, WIELDING THE PRINCE'S SWORD WITH THAT GHOST OF GOGURYEO POSSESSING YOU.

WHAT WOULD YOUR PARENTS SAY OF YOU NOW?

HOW IS THIS ANYTHING BUT A BETRAYAL? THINK OF THE GREATER GOOD. HOW CAN YOU CLING TO YOUR OWN PERSONAL SENTIMENTS AND STAND WITH OUR ENEMY AGAINST THE SERVANTS OF YOUR HOMELAND?

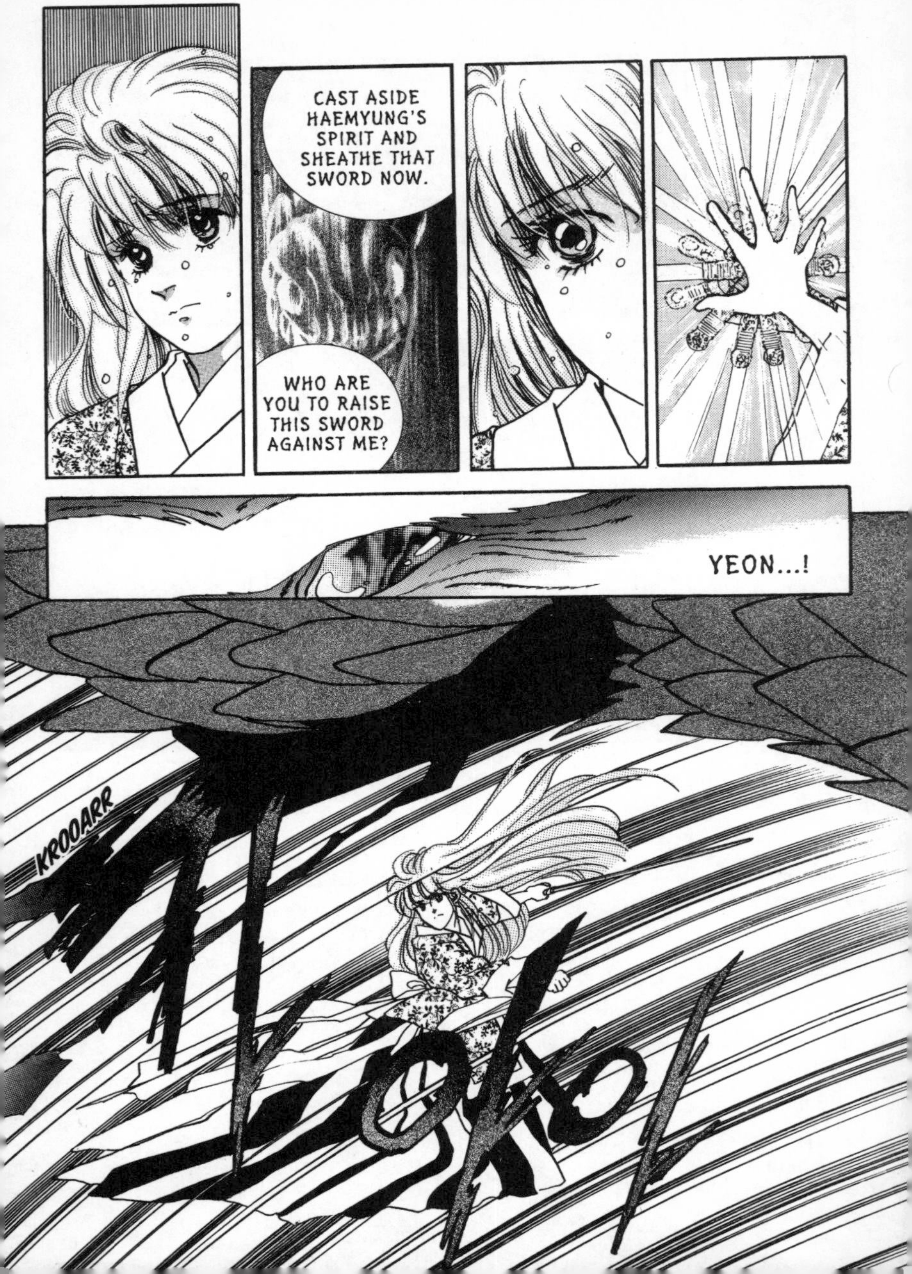
CAST ASIDE HAEMYUNG'S SPIRIT AND SHEATHE THAT SWORD NOW.
WHO ARE YOU TO RAISE THIS SWORD AGAINST ME?
YEON...!
KROOARR

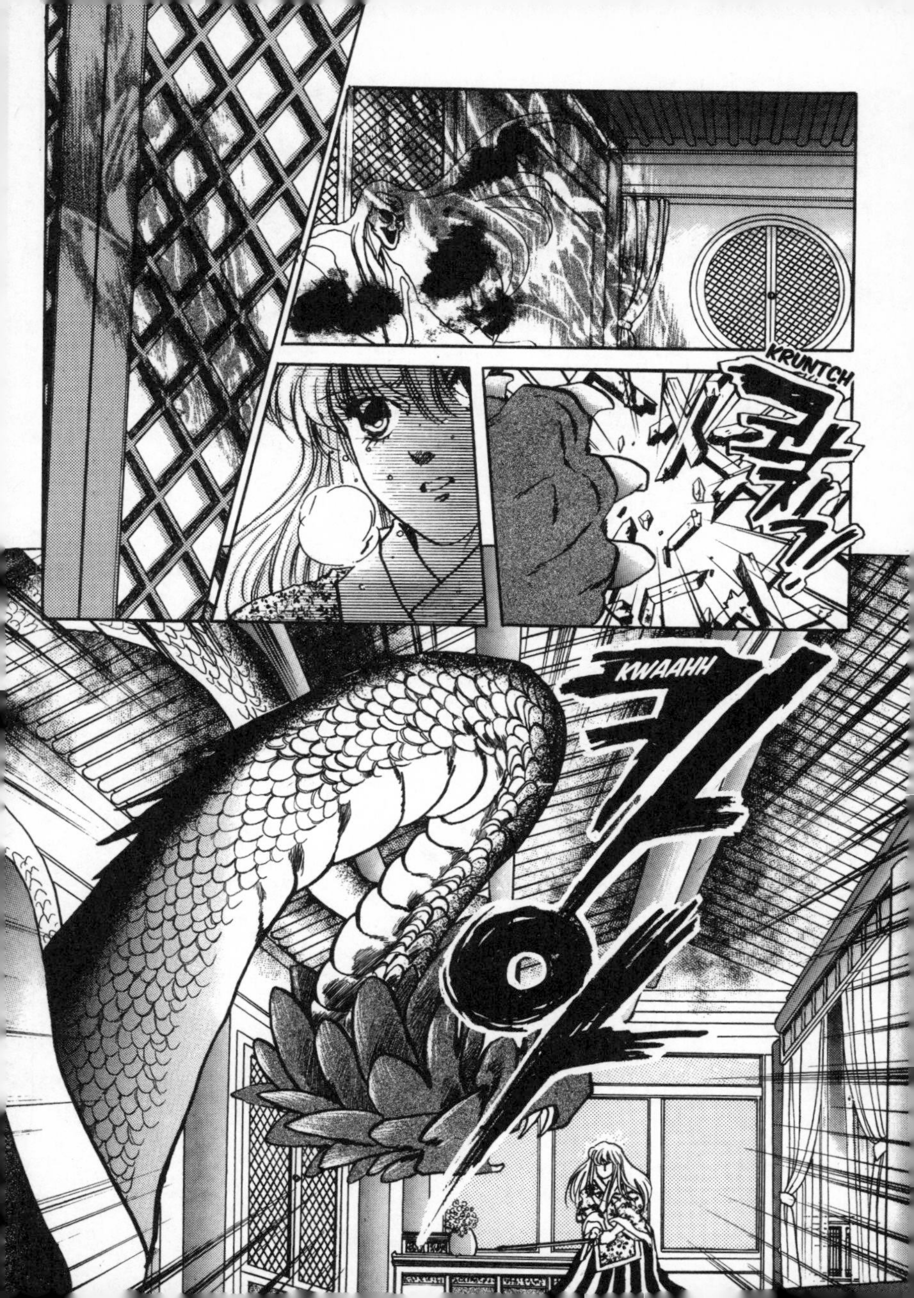
KRUNTCH
KWAAHH

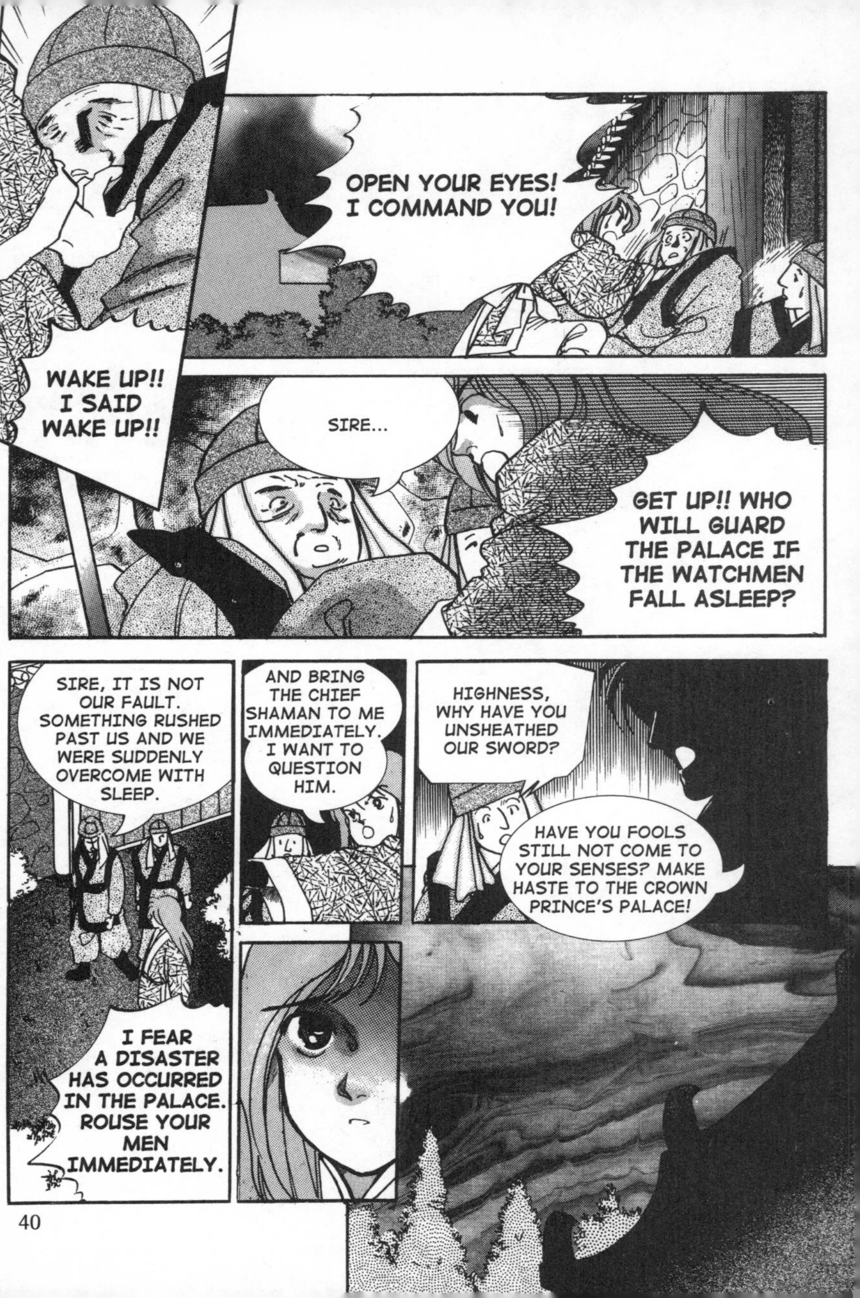
WAKE UP!! I SAID WAKE UP!!
OPEN YOUR EYES! I COMMAND YOU!
SIRE...
GET UP!! WHO WILL GUARD THE PALACE IF THE WATCHMEN FALL ASLEEP?
SIRE, IT IS NOT OUR FAULT. SOMETHING RUSHED PAST US AND WE WERE SUDDENLY OVERCOME WITH SLEEP.
I FEAR A DISASTER HAS OCCURRED IN THE PALACE. ROUSE YOUR MEN IMMEDIATELY.
AND BRING THE CHIEF SHAMAN TO ME IMMEDIATELY. I WANT TO QUESTION HIM.
HIGHNESS, WHY HAVE YOU UNSHEATHED OUR SWORD?
HAVE YOU FOOLS STILL NOT COME TO YOUR SENSES? MAKE HASTE TO THE CROWN PRINCE'S PALACE!

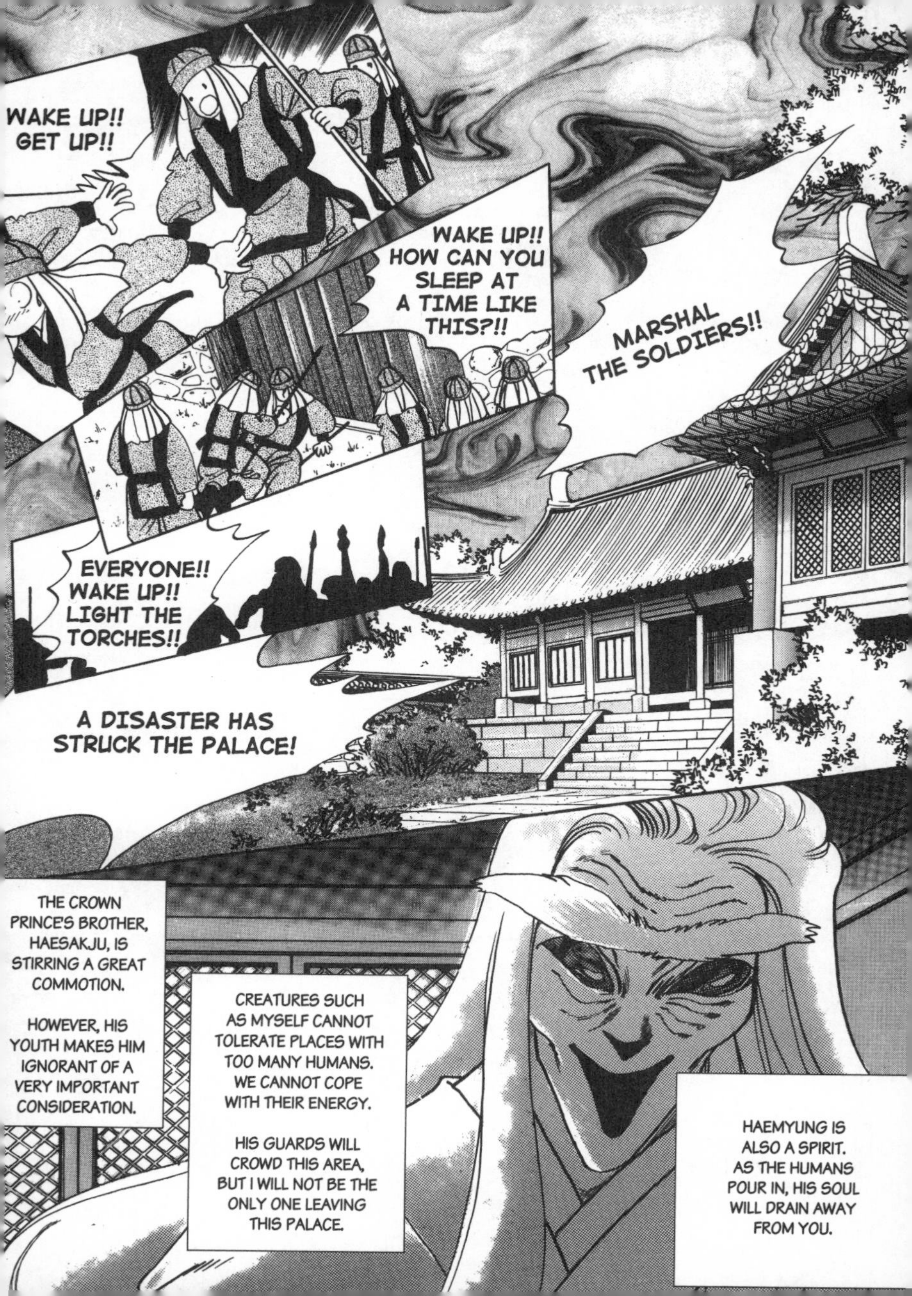
WAKE UP!! GET UP!!
WAKE UP!! HOW CAN YOU SLEEP AT A TIME LIKE THIS?!!
MARSHAL THE SOLDIERS!!
EVERYONE!! WAKE UP!! LIGHT THE TORCHES!!
A DISASTER HAS STRUCK THE PALACE!
THE CROWN PRINCE'S BROTHER, HAESAKJU, IS STIRRING A GREAT COMMOTION.
HOWEVER, HIS YOUTH MAKES HIM IGNORANT OF A VERY IMPORTANT CONSIDERATION.
CREATURES SUCH AS MYSELF CANNOT TOLERATE PLACES WITH TOO MANY HUMANS. WE CANNOT COPE WITH THEIR ENERGY.
HIS GUARDS WILL CROWD THIS AREA, BUT I WILL NOT BE THE ONLY ONE LEAVING THIS PALACE.
HAEMYUNG IS ALSO A SPIRIT. AS THE HUMANS POUR IN, HIS SOUL WILL DRAIN AWAY FROM YOU.

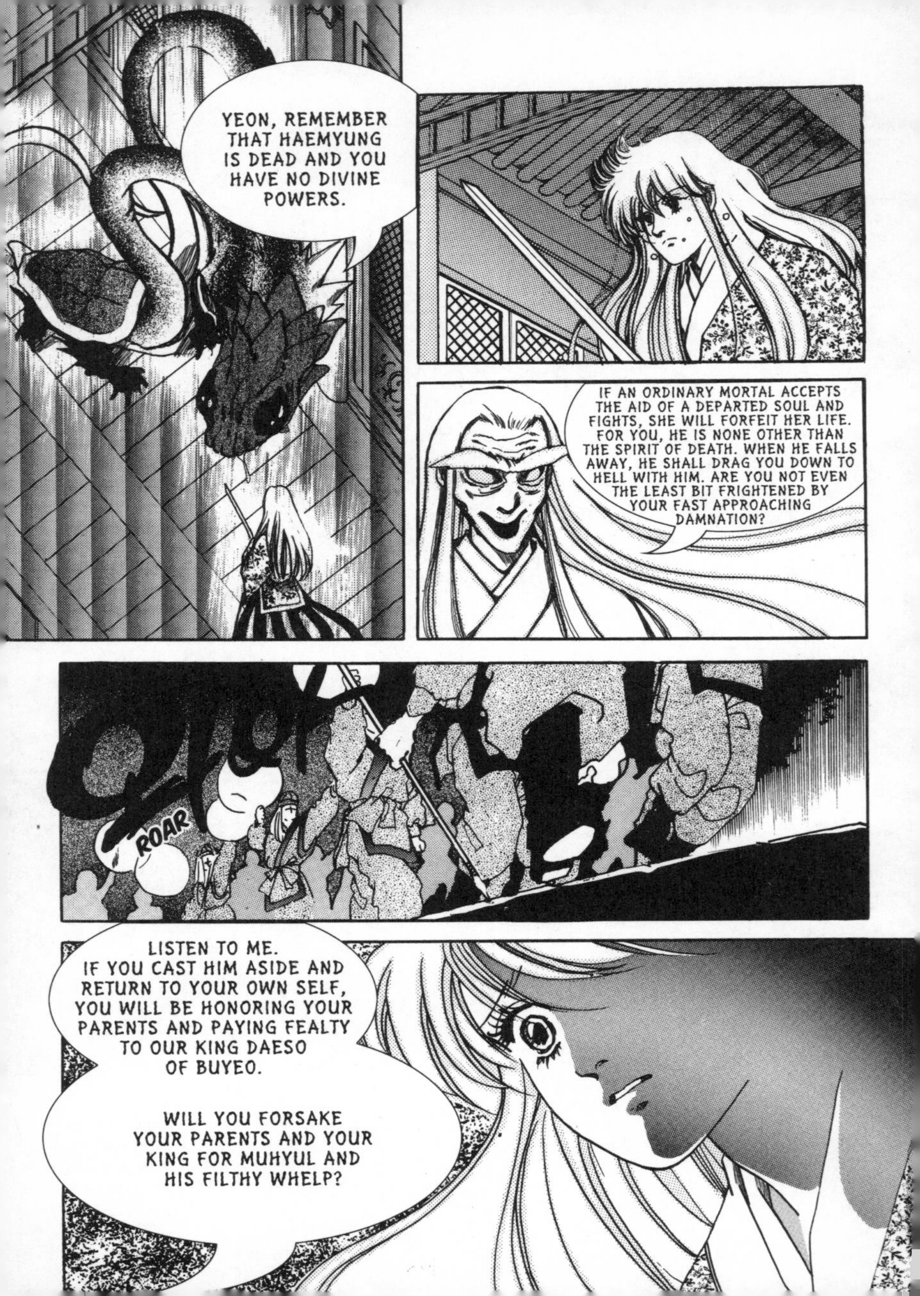
YEON, REMEMBER THAT HAEMYUNG IS DEAD AND YOU HAVE NO DIVINE POWERS.
IF AN ORDINARY MORTAL ACCEPTS THE AID OF A DEPARTED SOUL AND FIGHTS, SHE WILL FORFEIT HER LIFE. FOR YOU, HE IS NONE OTHER THAN THE SPIRIT OF DEATH. WHEN HE FALLS AWAY, HE SHALL DRAG YOU DOWN TO HELL WITH HIM. ARE YOU NOT EVEN THE LEAST BIT FRIGHTENED BY YOUR FAST APPROACHING DAMNATION?
ROAR
LISTEN TO ME. IF YOU CAST HIM ASIDE AND RETURN TO YOUR OWN SELF, YOU WILL BE HONORING YOUR PARENTS AND PAYING FEALTY TO OUR KING DAESO OF BUYEO.
WILL YOU FORSAKE YOUR PARENTS AND YOUR KING FOR MUHYUL AND HIS FILTHY WHELP?

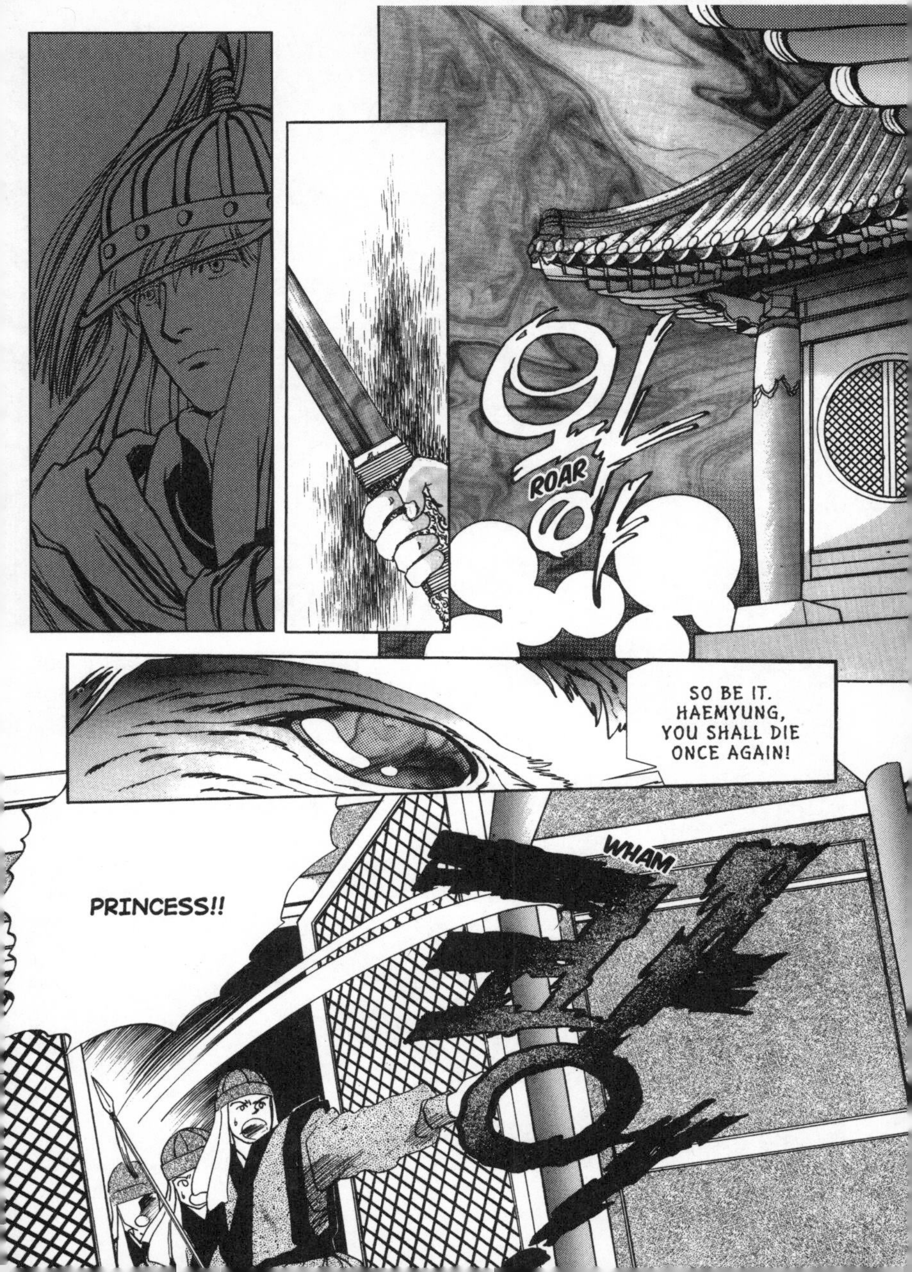
ROAR
SO BE IT. HAEMYUNG, YOU SHALL DIE ONCE AGAIN!
PRINCESS!!
WHAM

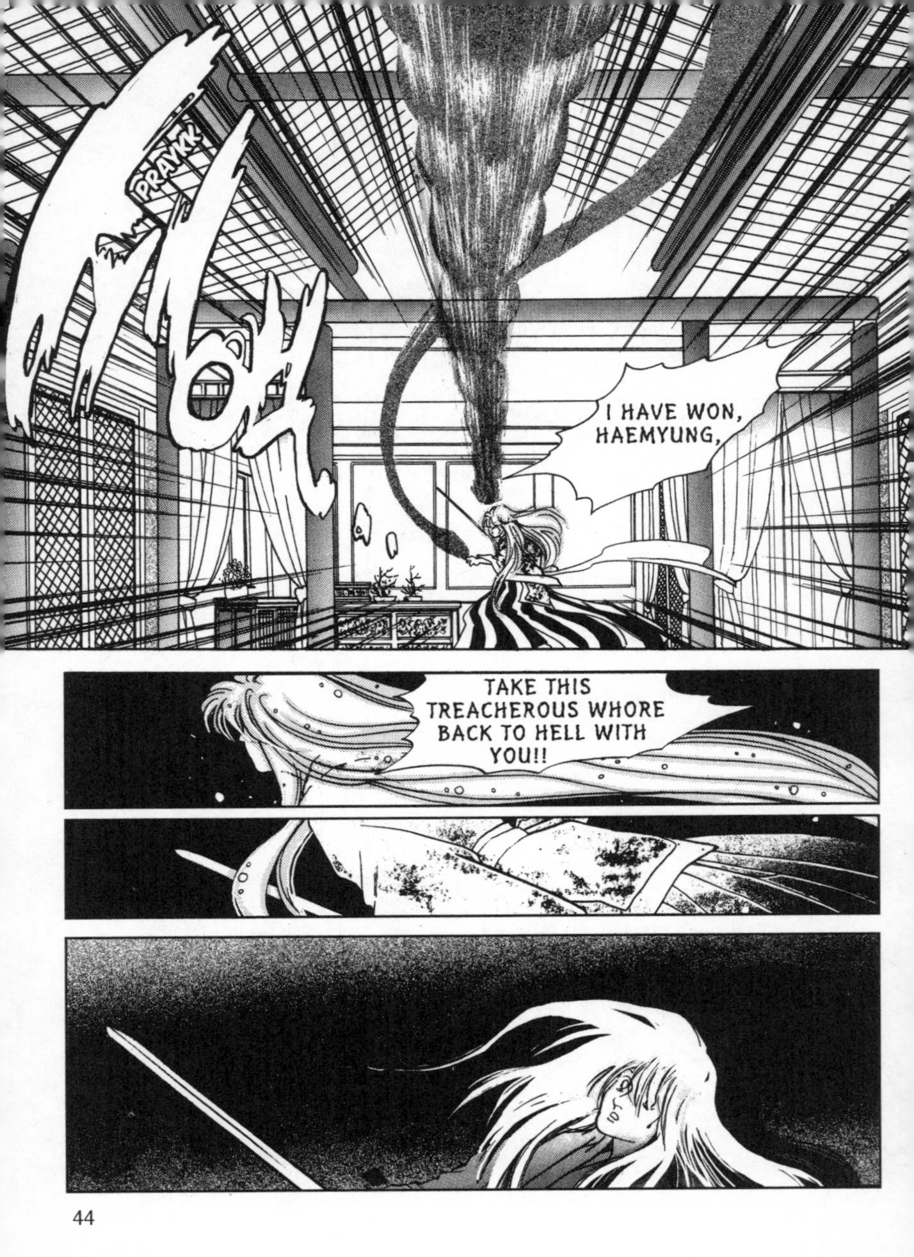
PRAYKK
I HAVE WON, HAEMYUNG,
TAKE THIS TREACHEROUS WHORE BACK TO HELL WITH YOU!!

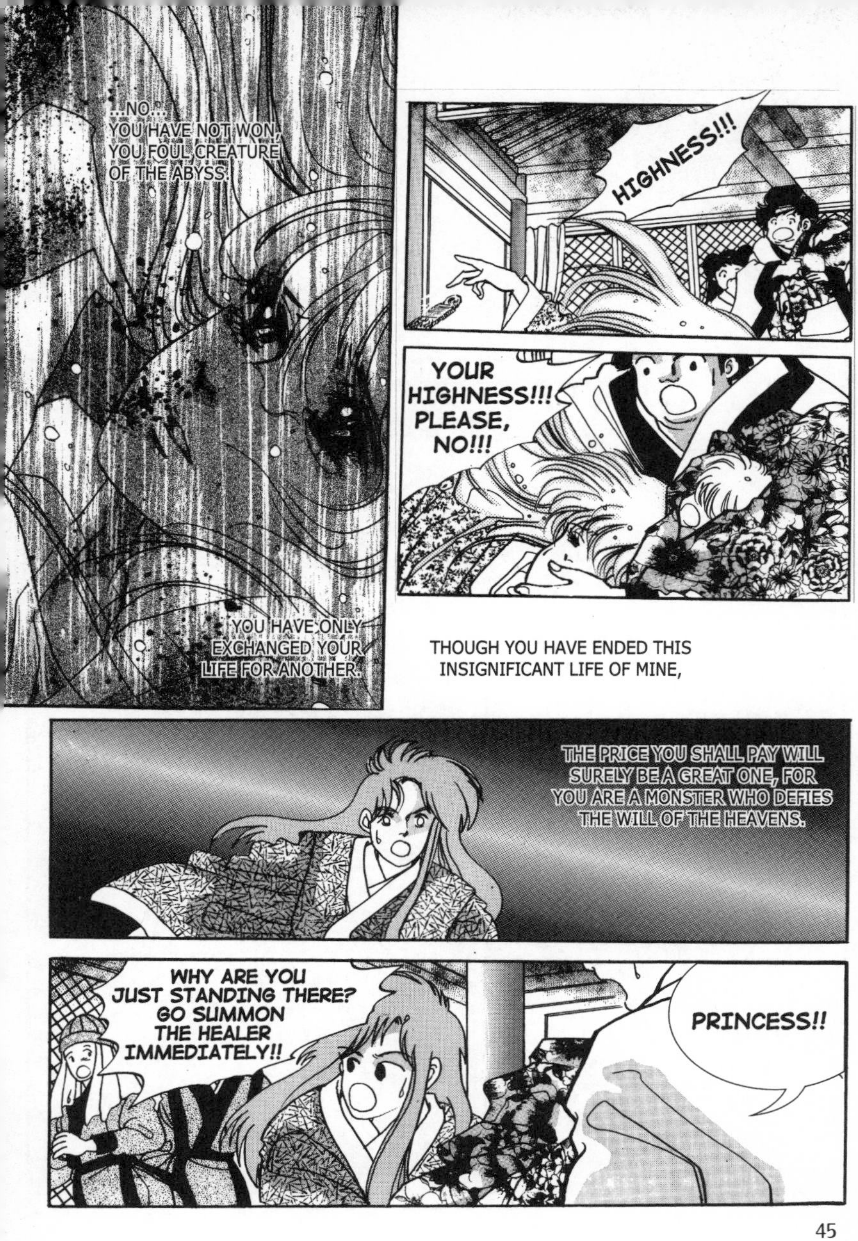
...NO...
YOU HAVE NOT WON,
YOU FOUL CREATURE
OF THE ABYSS.
YOU HAVE ONLY
EXCHANGED YOUR
LIFE FOR ANOTHER.
HIGHNESS!!!
YOUR
HIGHNESS!!!
PLEASE,
NO!!!
THOUGH YOU HAVE ENDED THIS
INSIGNIFICANT LIFE OF MINE,
THE PRICE YOU SHALL PAY WILL
SURELY BE A GREAT ONE, FOR
YOU ARE A MONSTER WHO DEFIES
THE WILL OF THE HEAVENS.
WHY ARE YOU
JUST STANDING THERE?
GO SUMMON
THE HEALER
IMMEDIATELY!!
PRINCESS!!

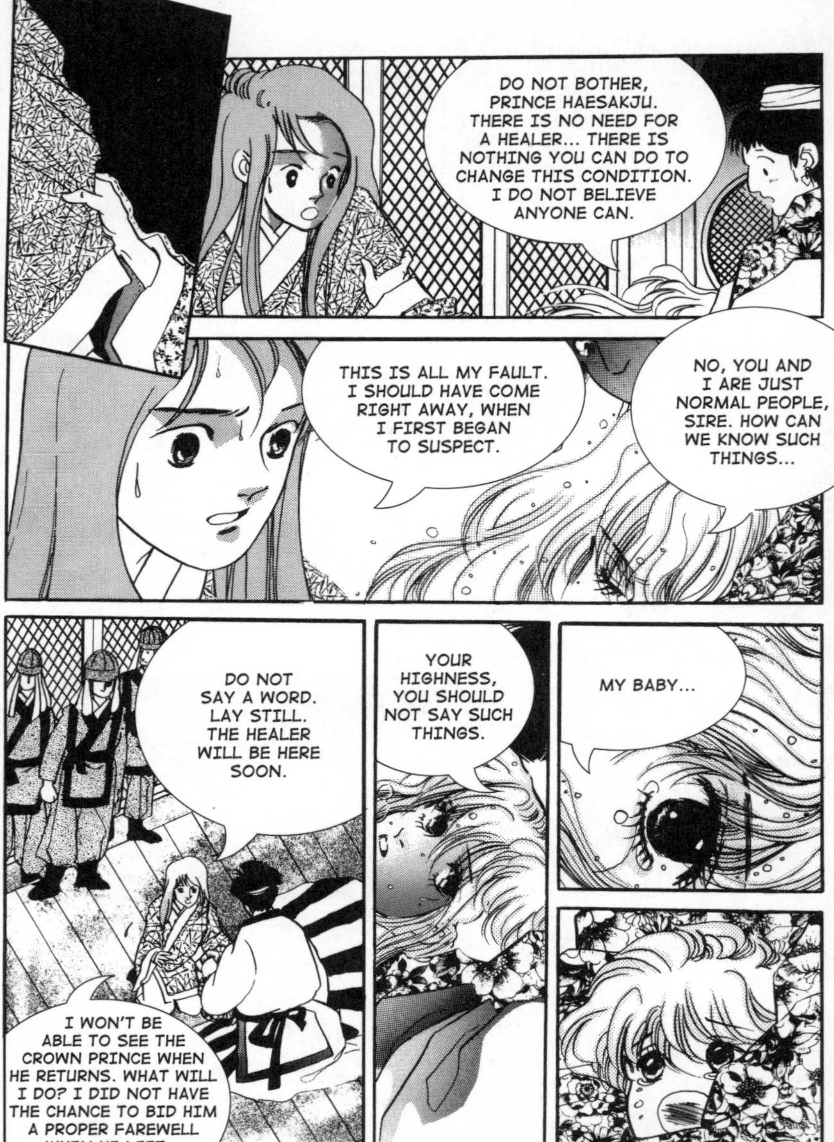
DO NOT BOTHER, PRINCE HAESAKJU. THERE IS NO NEED FOR A HEALER... THERE IS NOTHING YOU CAN DO TO CHANGE THIS CONDITION. I DO NOT BELIEVE ANYONE CAN.
THIS IS ALL MY FAULT. I SHOULD HAVE COME RIGHT AWAY, WHEN I FIRST BEGAN TO SUSPECT.
NO, YOU AND I ARE JUST NORMAL PEOPLE, SIRE. HOW CAN WE KNOW SUCH THINGS...
DO NOT SAY A WORD. LAY STILL. THE HEALER WILL BE HERE SOON.
I WON'T BE ABLE TO SEE THE CROWN PRINCE WHEN HE RETURNS. WHAT WILL I DO? I DID NOT HAVE THE CHANCE TO BID HIM A PROPER FAREWELL WHEN HE LEFT...
YOUR HIGHNESS, YOU SHOULD NOT SAY SUCH THINGS.
MY BABY...

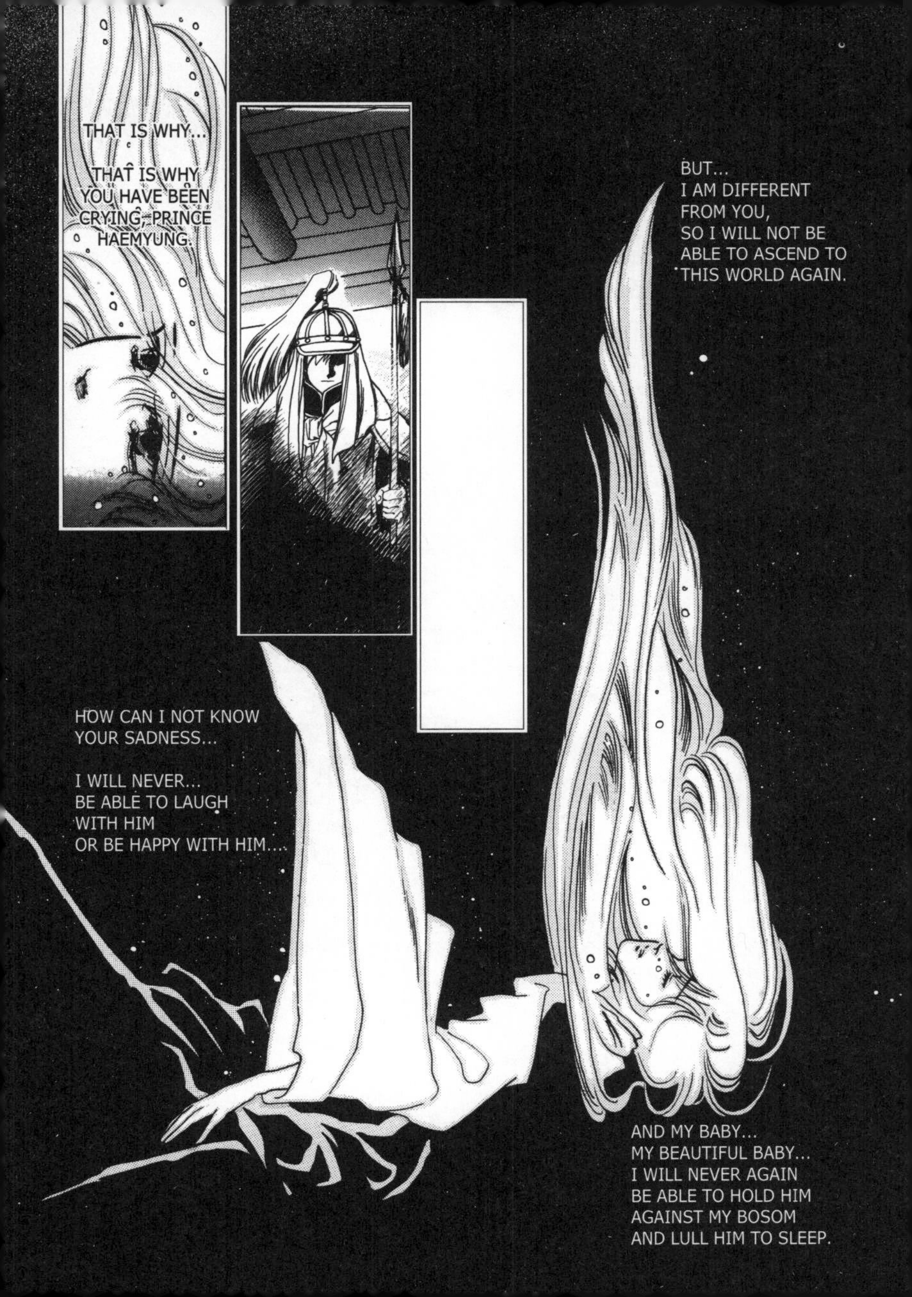
THAT IS WHY...
THAT IS WHY YOU HAVE BEEN CRYING, PRINCE HAEMYUNG.
BUT...
I AM DIFFERENT FROM YOU,
SO I WILL NOT BE ABLE TO ASCEND TO THIS WORLD AGAIN.
HOW CAN I NOT KNOW YOUR SADNESS...
I WILL NEVER...
BE ABLE TO LAUGH WITH HIM
OR BE HAPPY WITH HIM....
AND MY BABY...
MY BEAUTIFUL BABY...
I WILL NEVER AGAIN
BE ABLE TO HOLD HIM
AGAINST MY BOSOM
AND LULL HIM TO SLEEP.

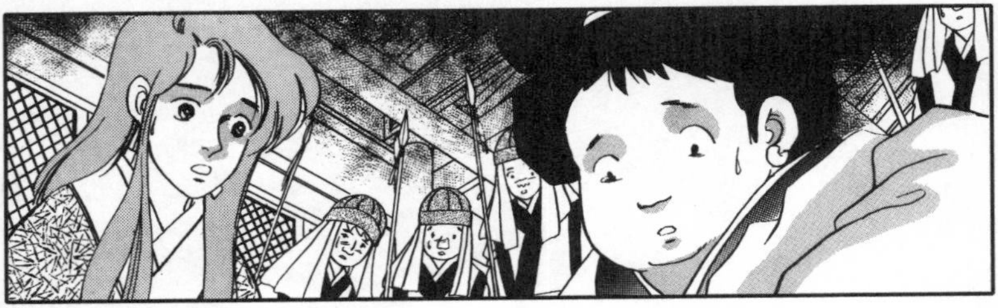

AS I DIE NOW...
AS I DIE AND WAIT

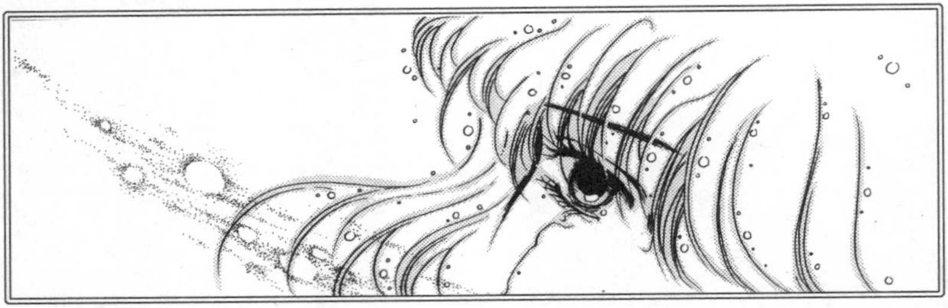

WILL HE COME AND LIE NEXT TO ME...

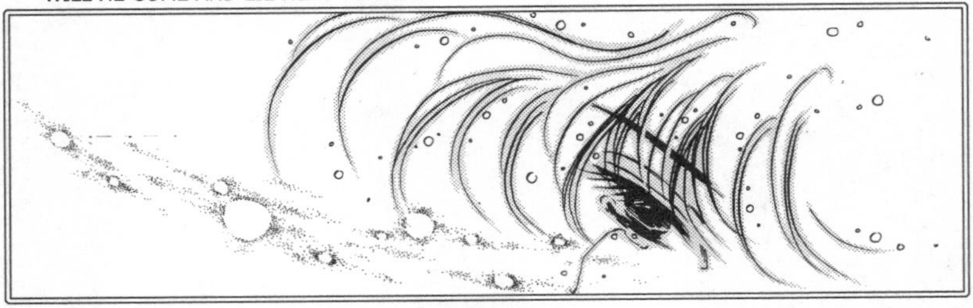

WILL HE FOREVERMORE CONSOLE ME WITH HIS SONGS
WHEN THE NIGHTS ARE BATHED IN MOONLIGHT, AS HE ALWAYS HAS...

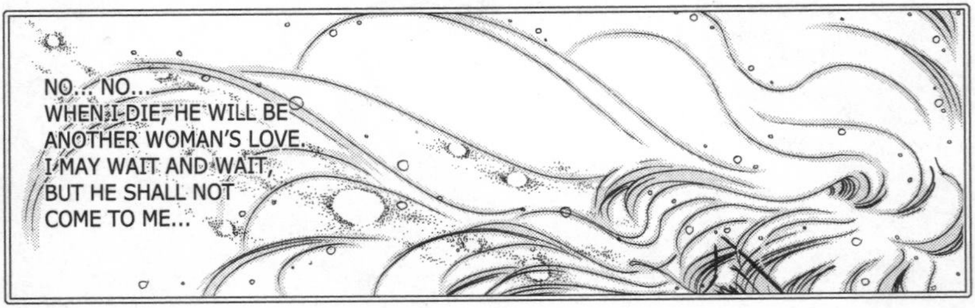
NO... NO...
WHEN I DIE, HE WILL BE
ANOTHER WOMAN'S LOVE.
I MAY WAIT AND WAIT,
BUT HE SHALL NOT
COME TO ME...

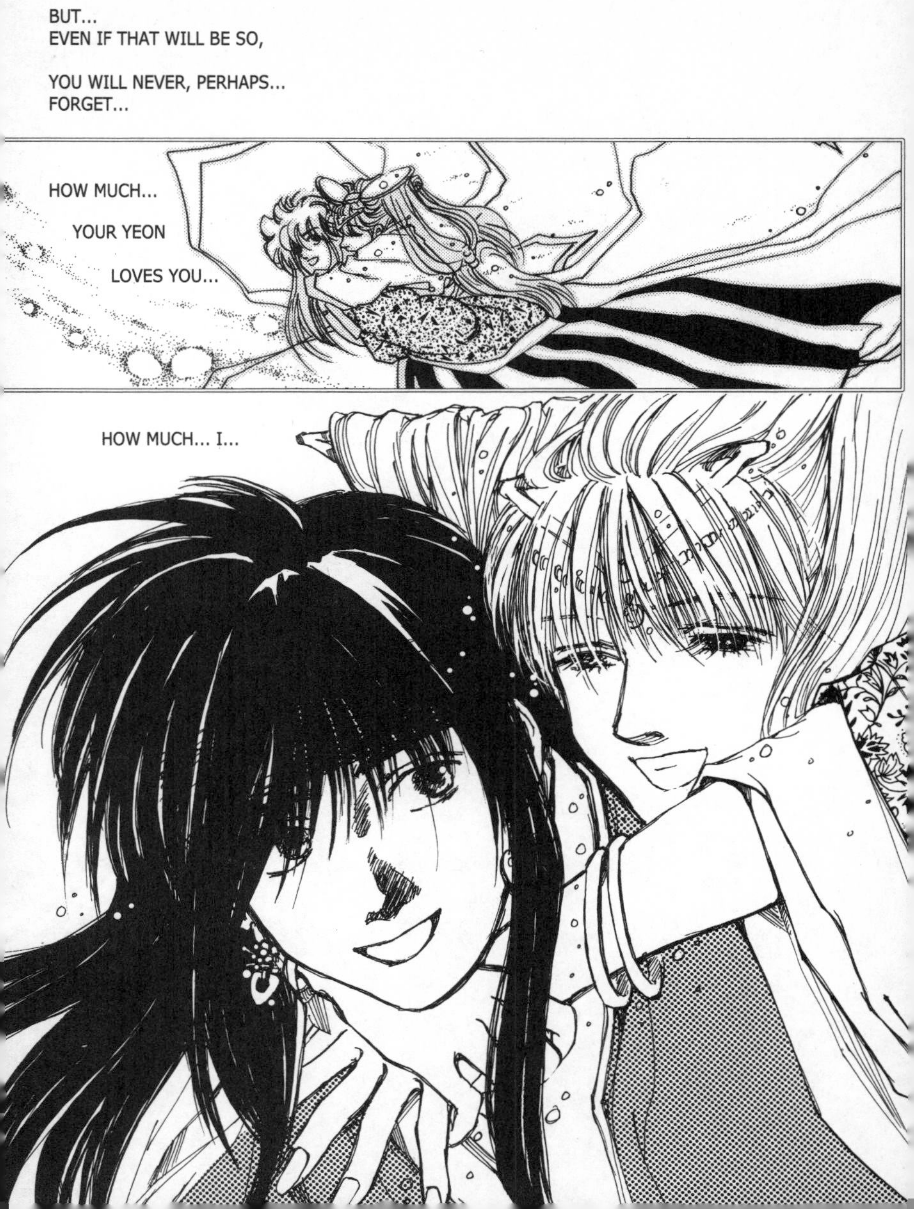
BUT...
EVEN IF THAT WILL BE SO,
YOU WILL NEVER, PERHAPS...
FORGET...
HOW MUCH...
YOUR YEON
LOVES YOU...
HOW MUCH... I...

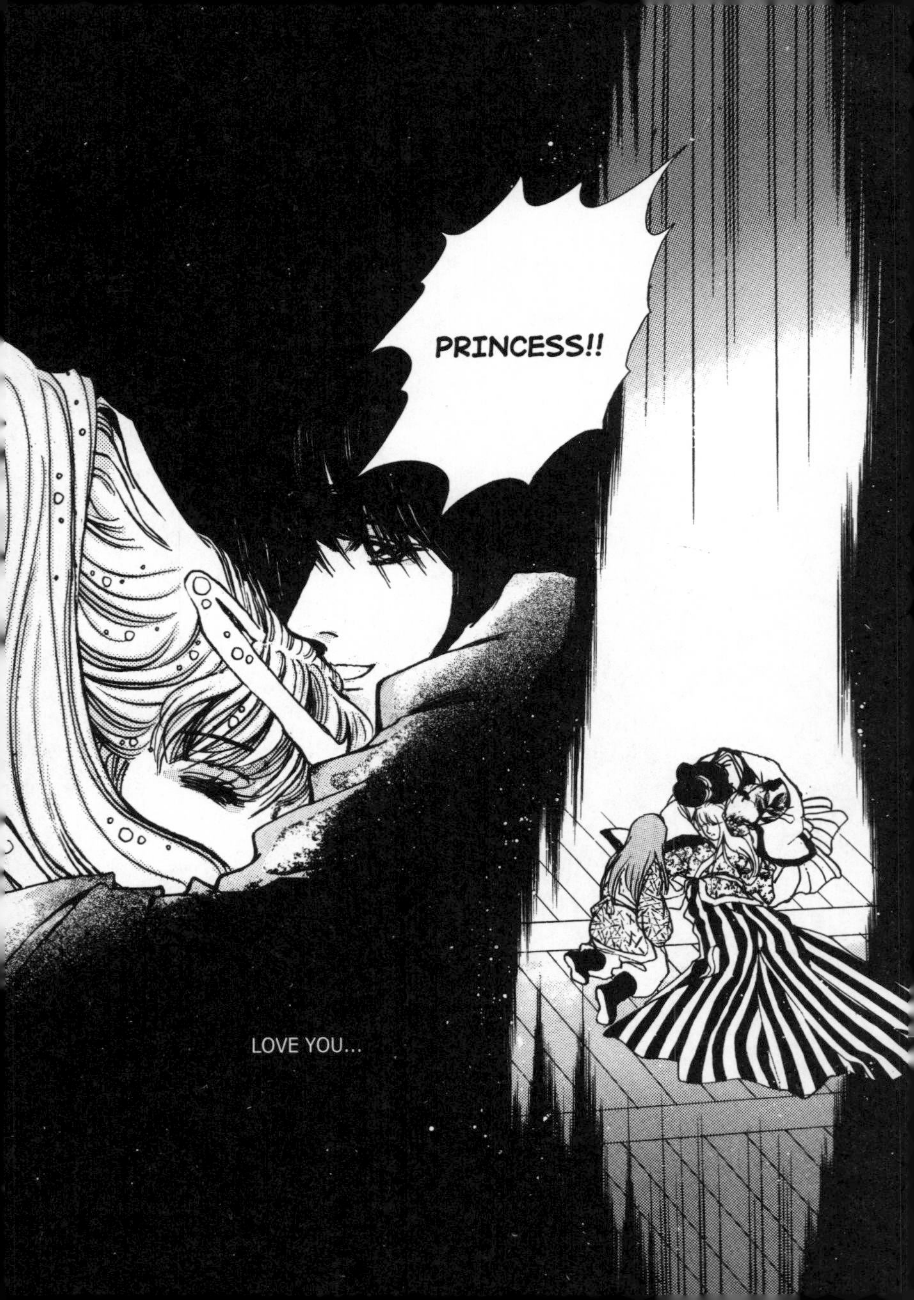
PRINCESS!!
LOVE YOU...

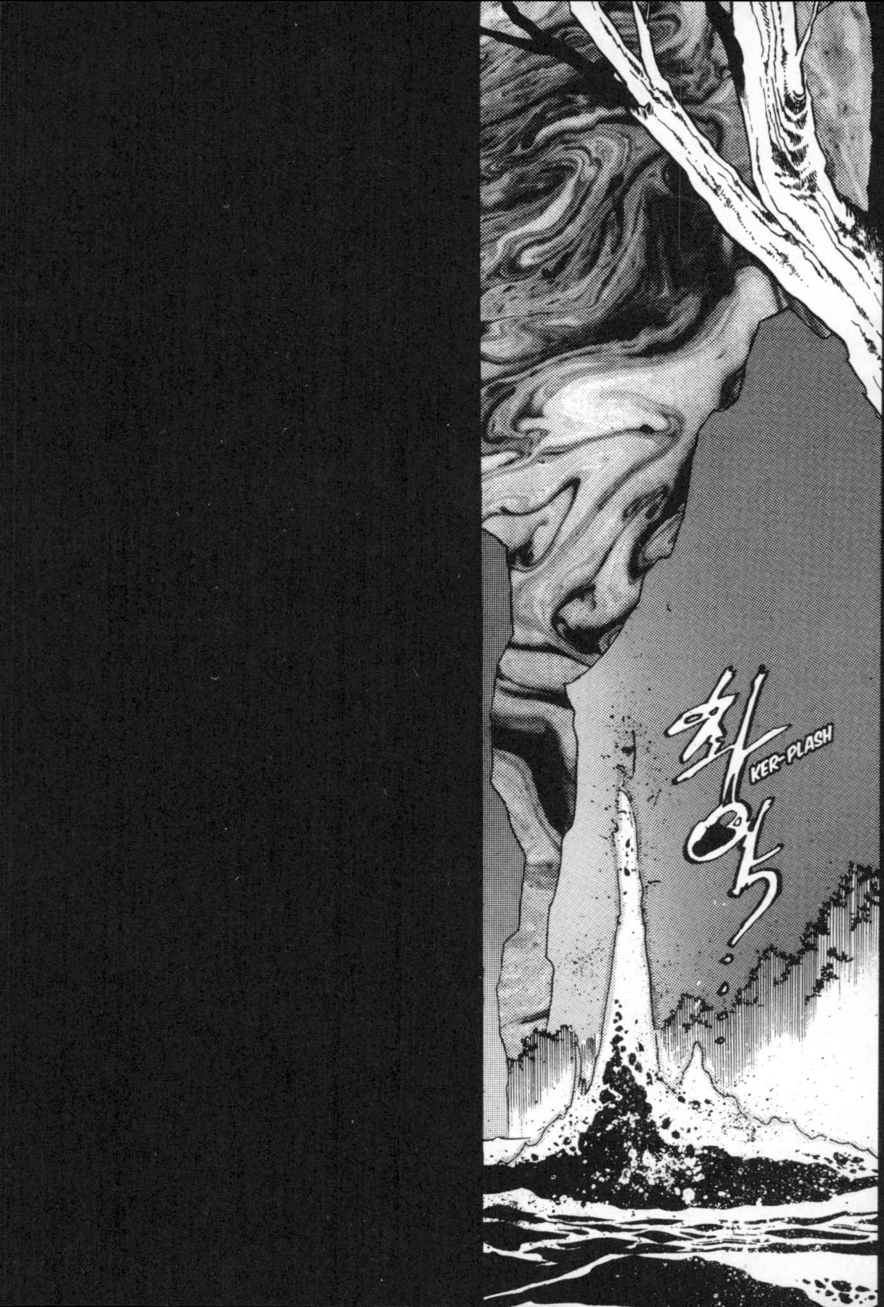
촤앙
KER-PLASH

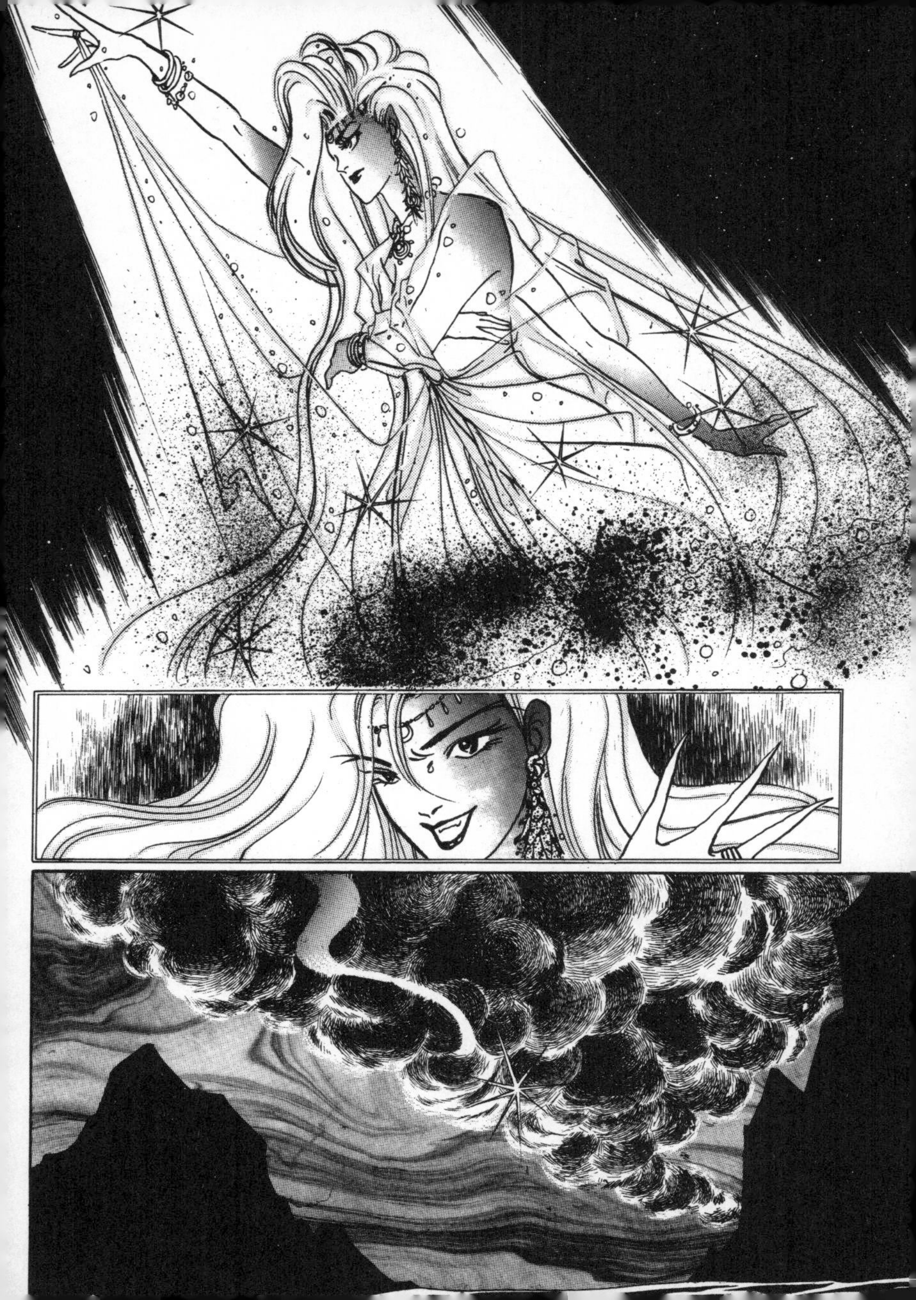

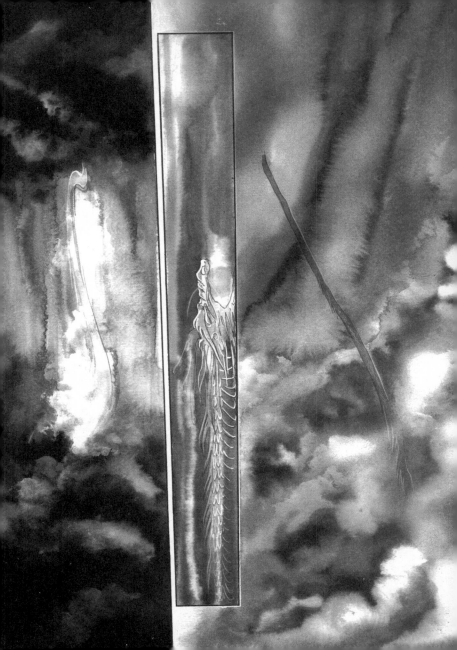

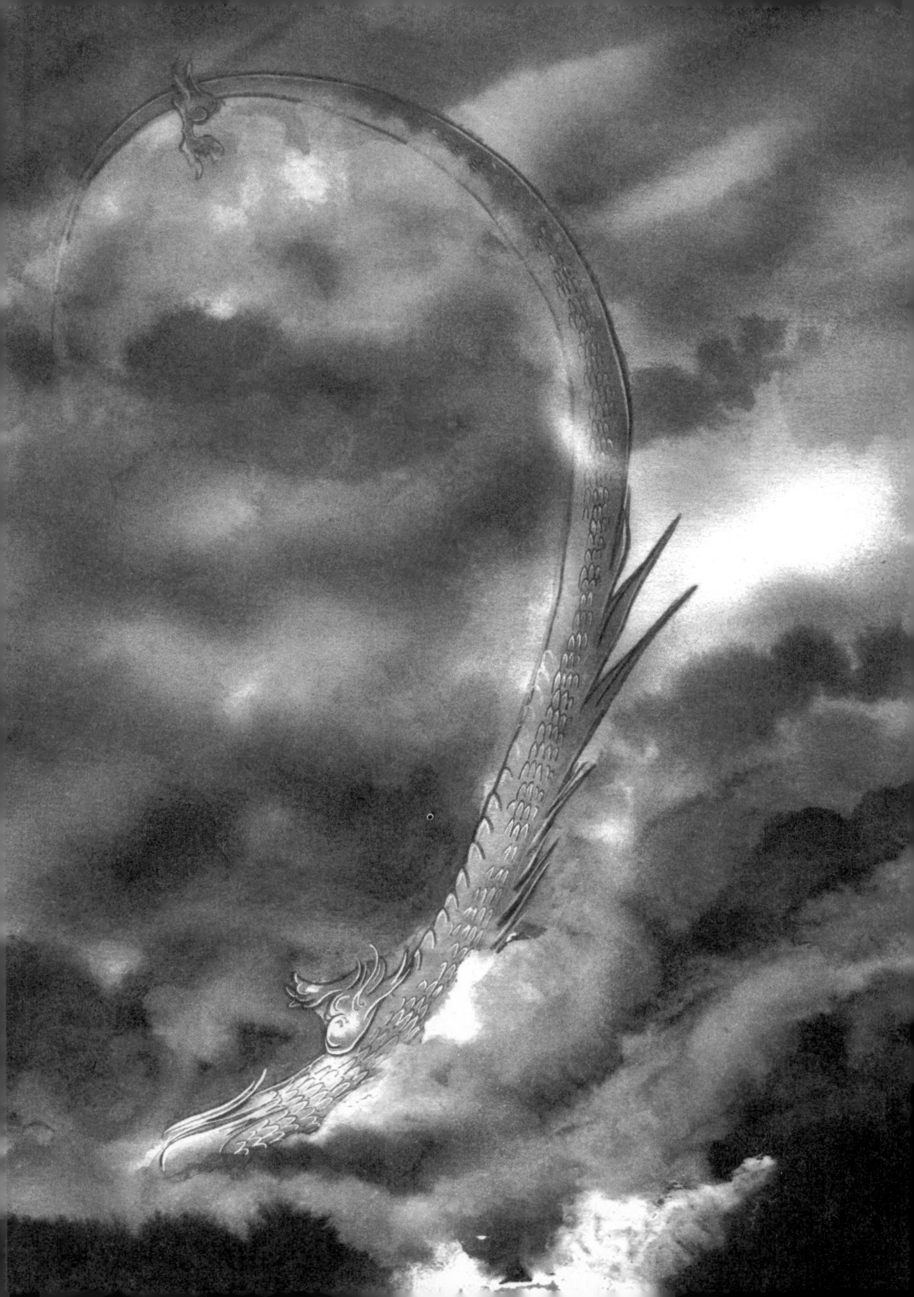

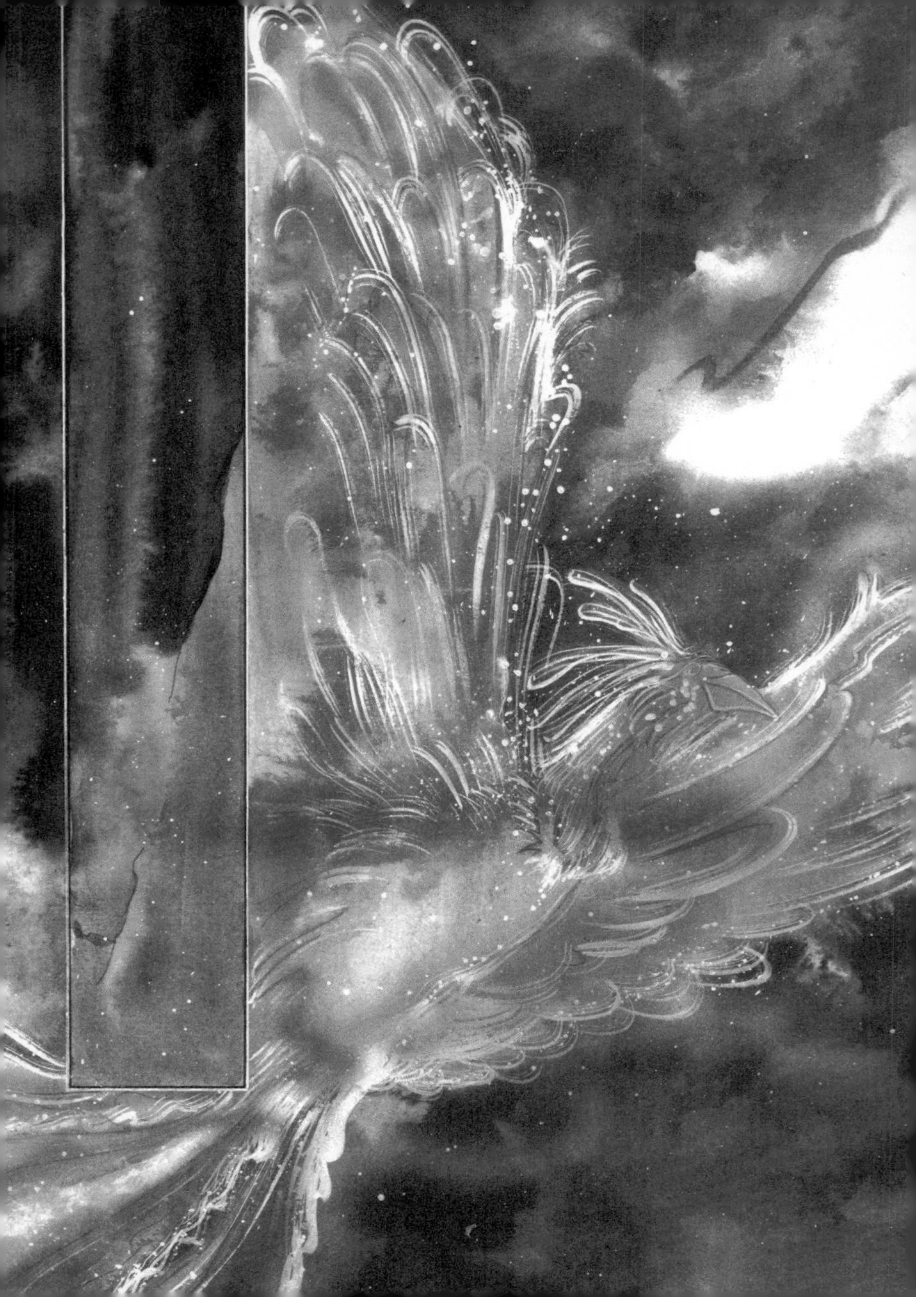

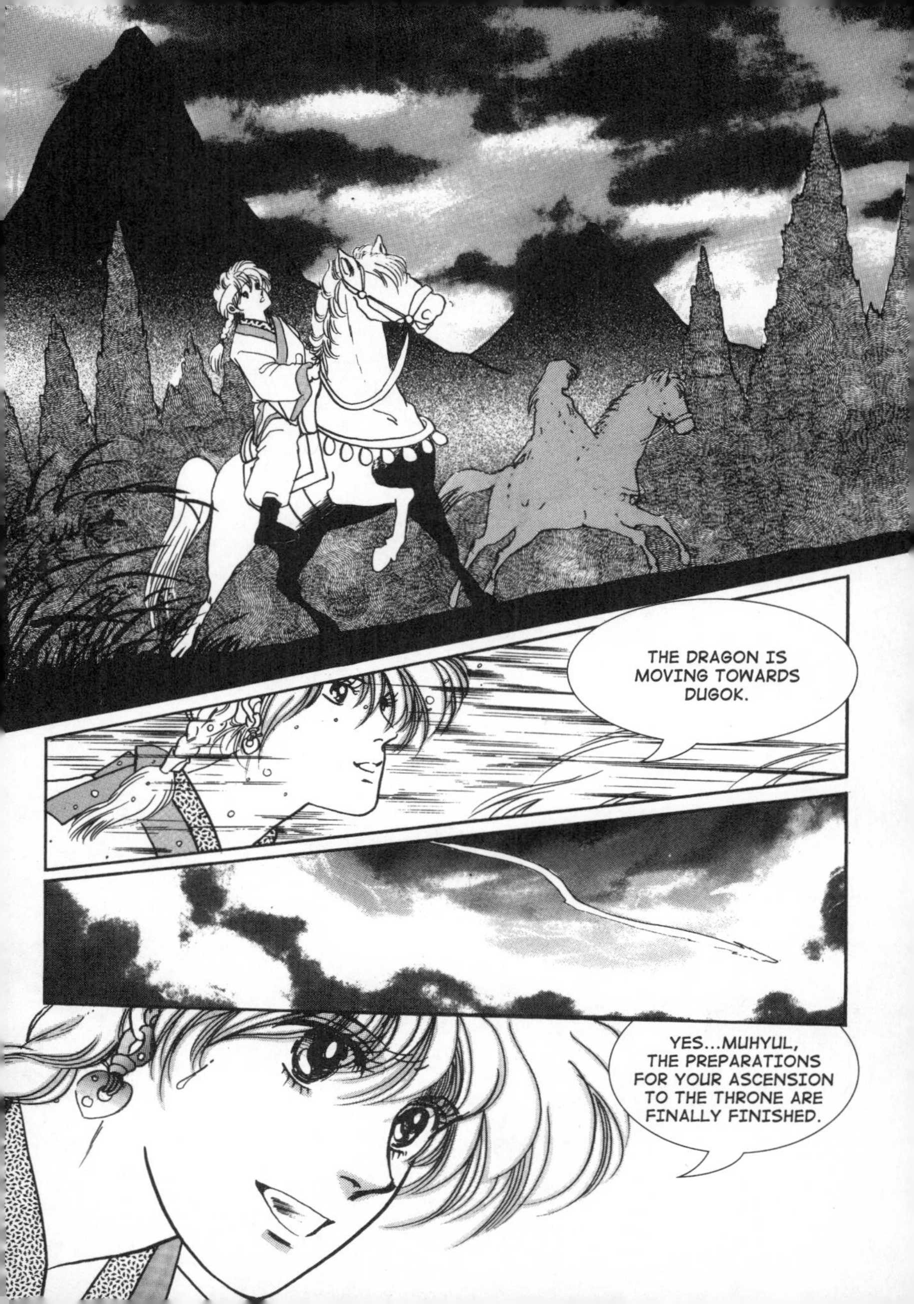
THE DRAGON IS MOVING TOWARDS DUGOK.
YES...MUHYUL, THE PREPARATIONS FOR YOUR ASCENSION TO THE THRONE ARE FINALLY FINISHED.

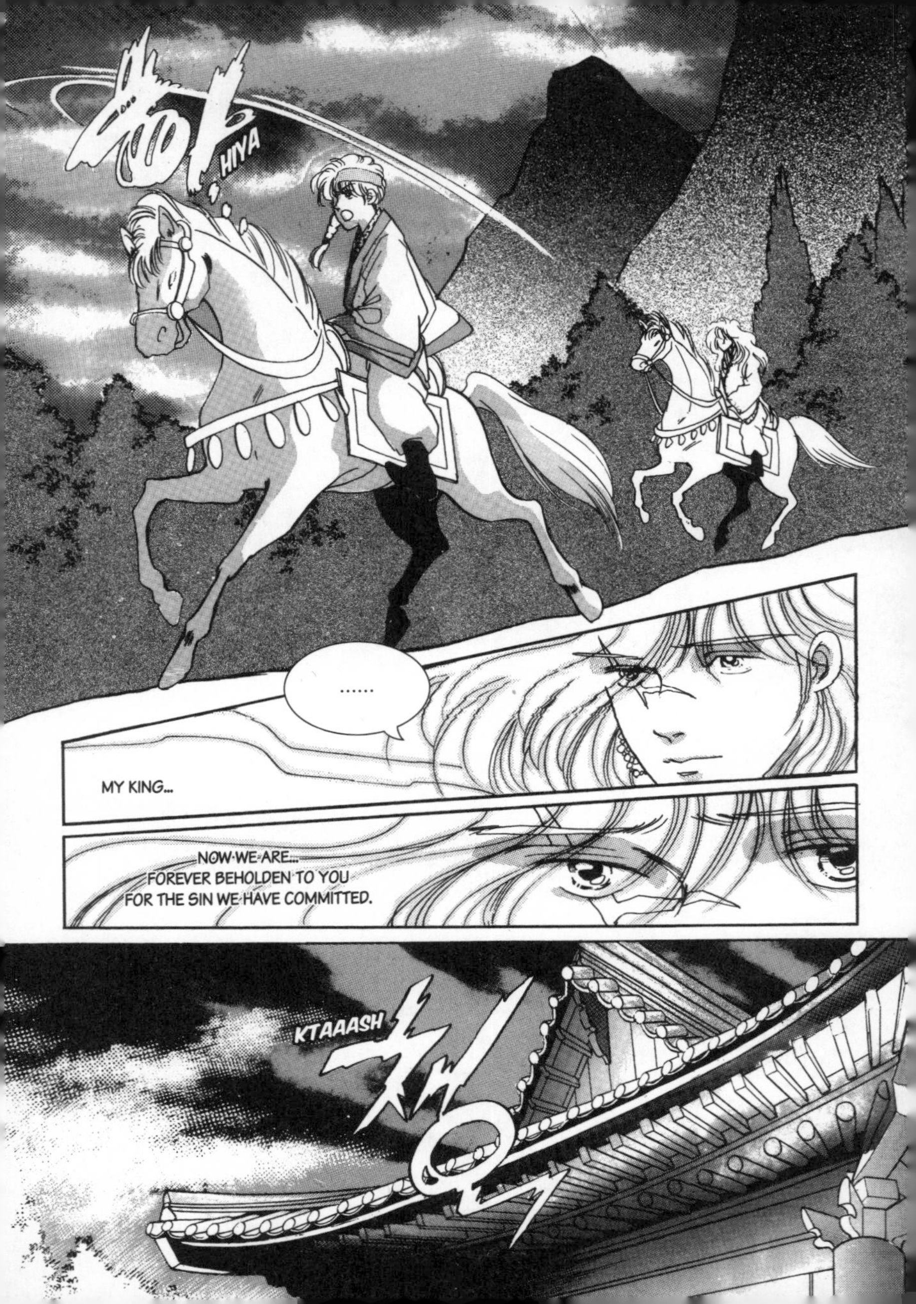
HIYA
......
MY KING...
NOW WE ARE...
FOREVER BEHOLDEN TO YOU
FOR THE SIN WE HAVE COMMITTED.
KTAAASH

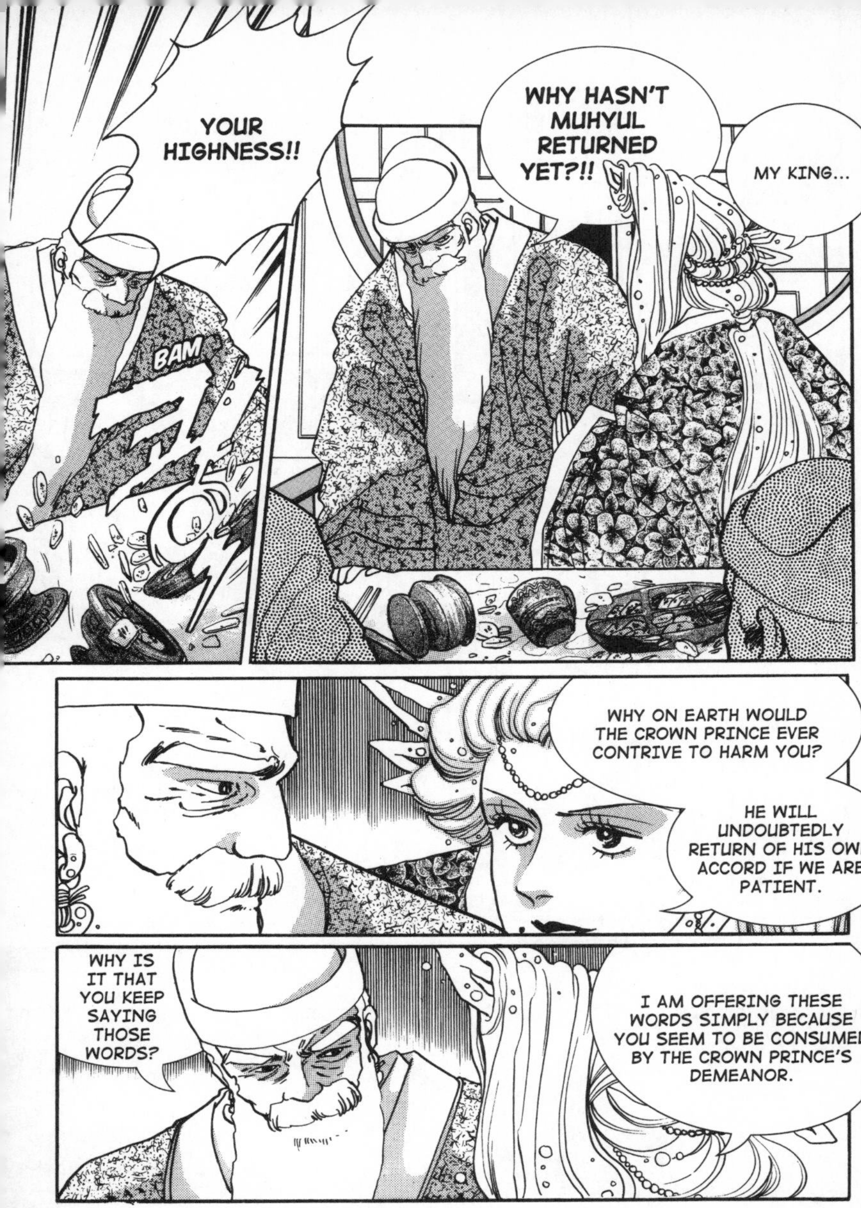
YOUR HIGHNESS!!
BAM
WHY HASN'T MUHYUL RETURNED YET?!!
MY KING...
WHY ON EARTH WOULD THE CROWN PRINCE EVER CONTRIVE TO HARM YOU?
HE WILL UNDOUBTEDLY RETURN OF HIS OWN ACCORD IF WE ARE PATIENT.
WHY IS IT THAT YOU KEEP SAYING THOSE WORDS?
I AM OFFERING THESE WORDS SIMPLY BECAUSE YOU SEEM TO BE CONSUMED BY THE CROWN PRINCE'S DEMEANOR.

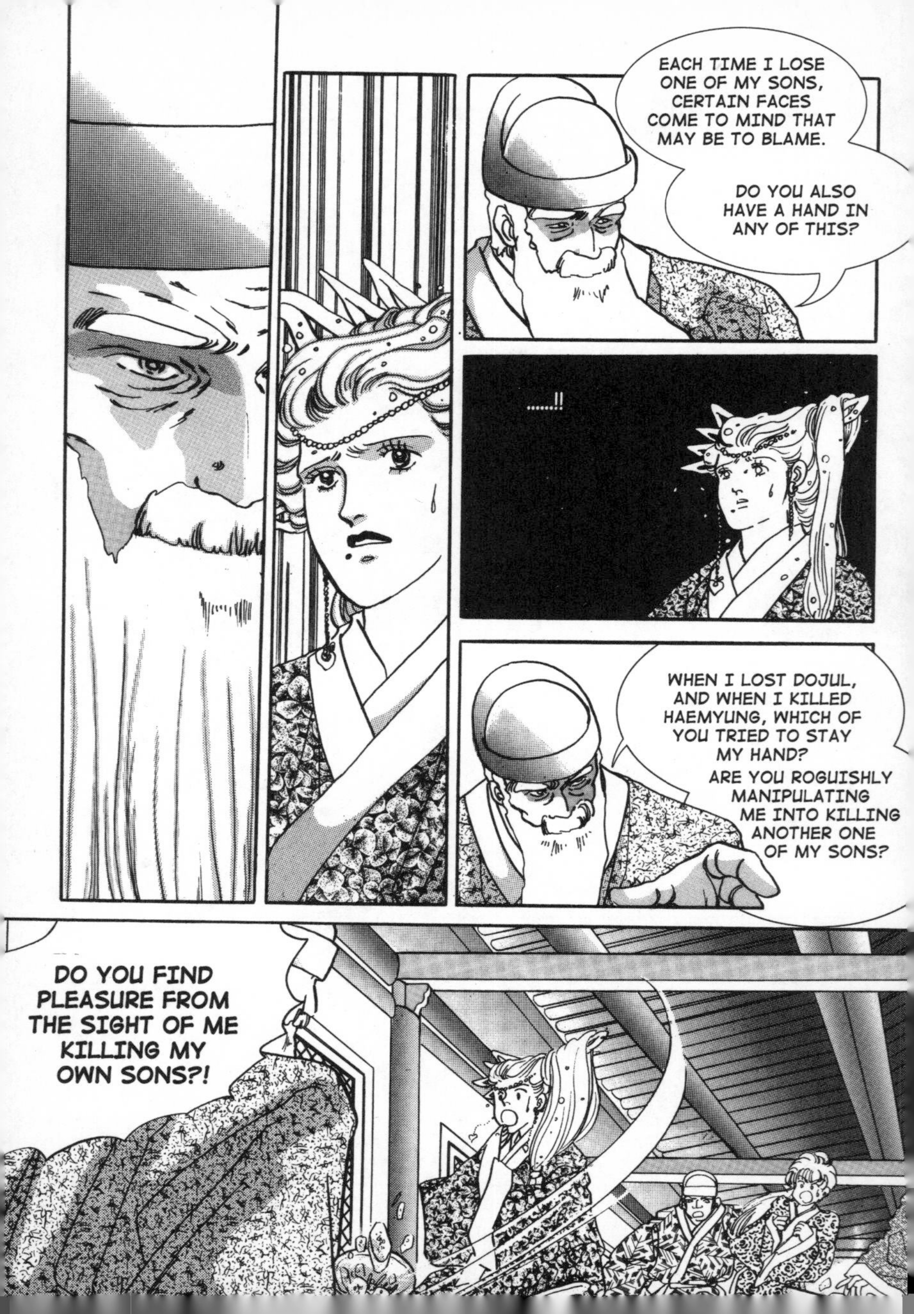
EACH TIME I LOSE ONE OF MY SONS, CERTAIN FACES COME TO MIND THAT MAY BE TO BLAME.
DO YOU ALSO HAVE A HAND IN ANY OF THIS?
......!!
WHEN I LOST DOJUL, AND WHEN I KILLED HAEMYUNG, WHICH OF YOU TRIED TO STAY MY HAND?
ARE YOU ROGUISHLY MANIPULATING ME INTO KILLING ANOTHER ONE OF MY SONS?
DO YOU FIND PLEASURE FROM THE SIGHT OF ME KILLING MY OWN SONS?!

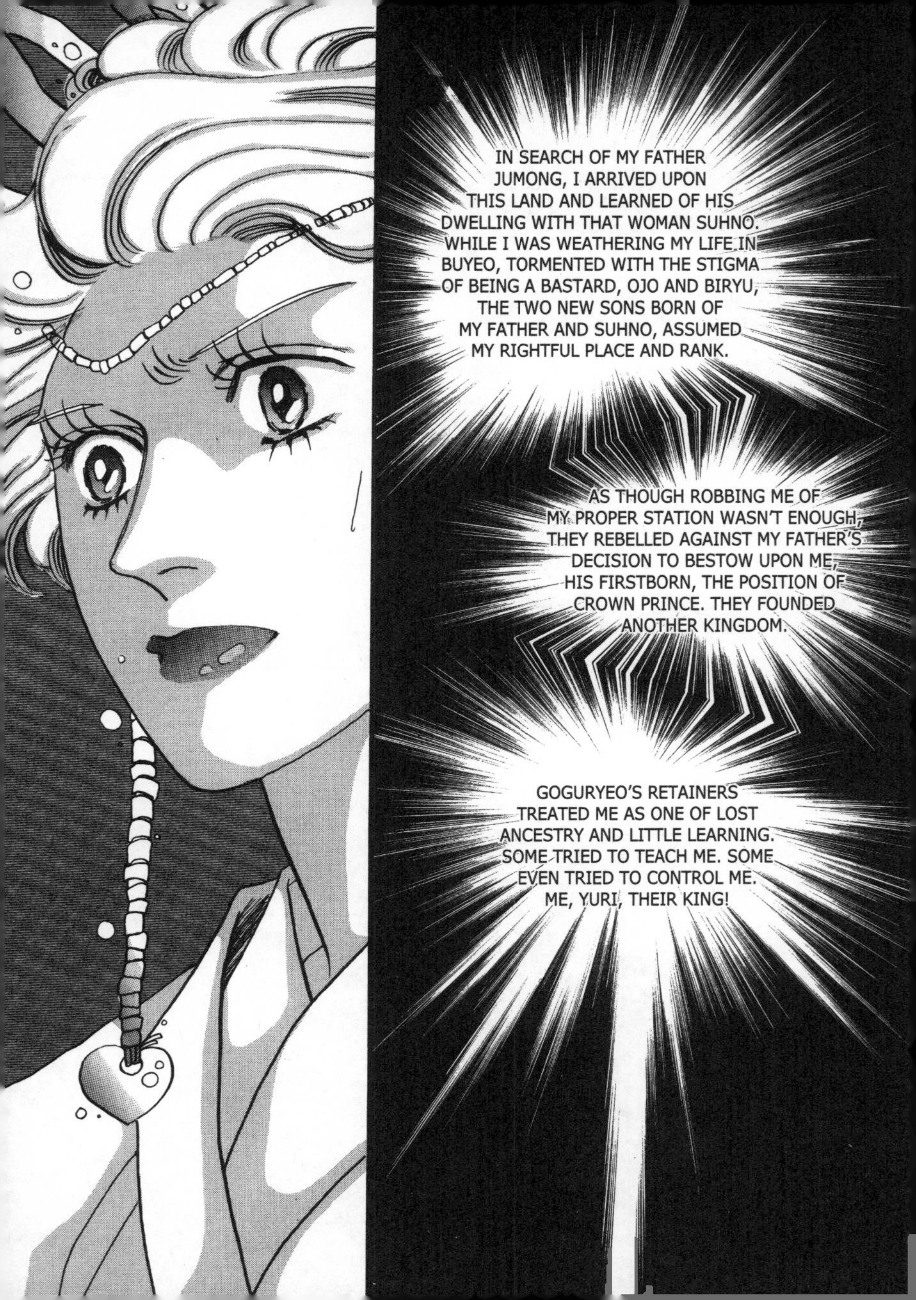
IN SEARCH OF MY FATHER JUMONG, I ARRIVED UPON THIS LAND AND LEARNED OF HIS DWELLING WITH THAT WOMAN SUHNO. WHILE I WAS WEATHERING MY LIFE IN BUYEO, TORMENTED WITH THE STIGMA OF BEING A BASTARD, OJO AND BIRYU, THE TWO NEW SONS BORN OF MY FATHER AND SUHNO, ASSUMED MY RIGHTFUL PLACE AND RANK.
AS THOUGH ROBBING ME OF MY PROPER STATION WASN'T ENOUGH, THEY REBELLED AGAINST MY FATHER'S DECISION TO BESTOW UPON ME, HIS FIRSTBORN, THE POSITION OF CROWN PRINCE. THEY FOUNDED ANOTHER KINGDOM.
GOGURYEO'S RETAINERS TREATED ME AS ONE OF LOST ANCESTRY AND LITTLE LEARNING. SOME TRIED TO TEACH ME. SOME EVEN TRIED TO CONTROL ME. ME, YURI, THEIR KING!

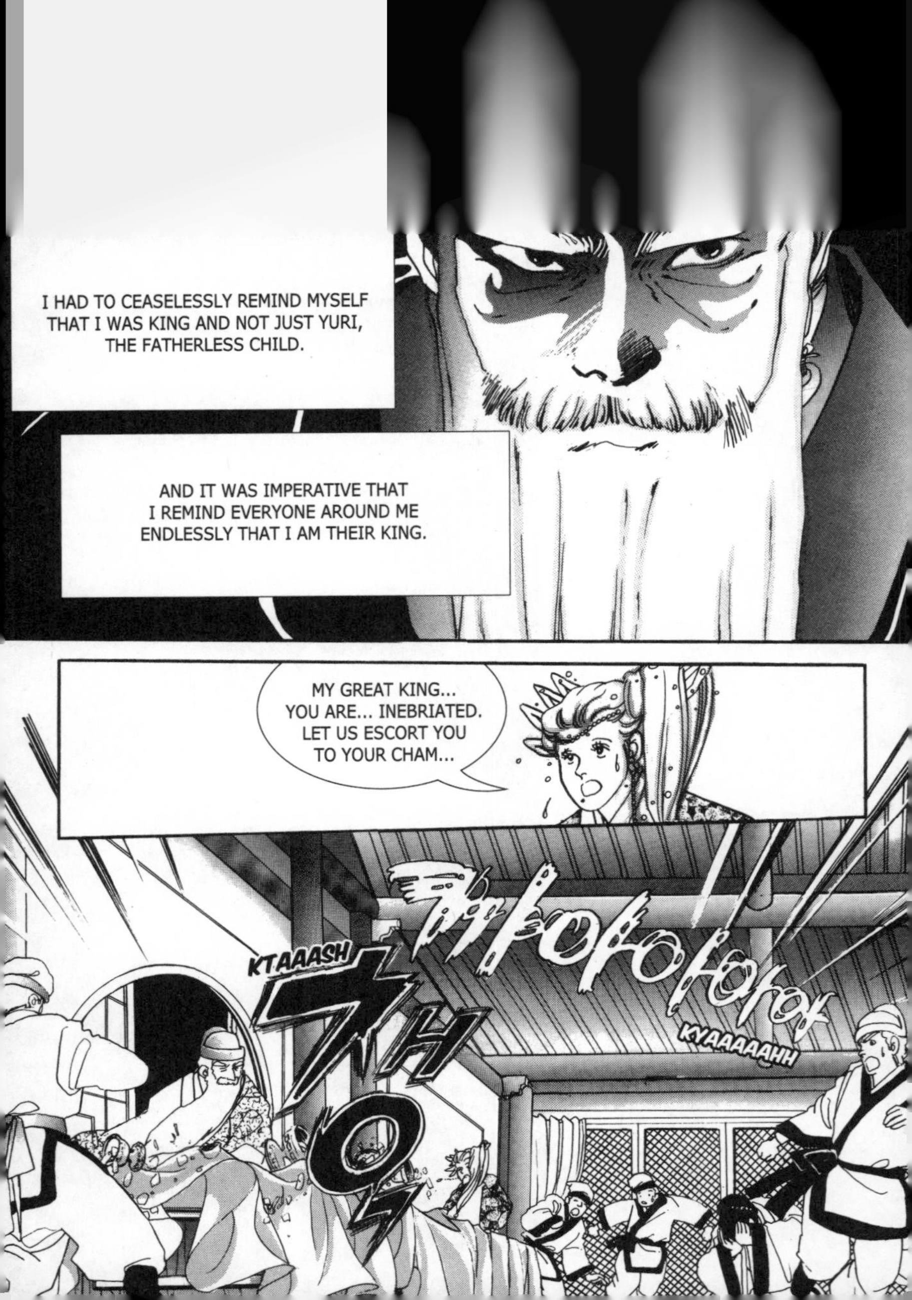
I HAD TO CEASELESSLY REMIND MYSELF THAT I WAS KING AND NOT JUST YURI, THE FATHERLESS CHILD.
AND IT WAS IMPERATIVE THAT I REMIND EVERYONE AROUND ME ENDLESSLY THAT I AM THEIR KING.
MY GREAT KING... YOU ARE... INEBRIATED. LET US ESCORT YOU TO YOUR CHAM...
KTAAASH
KYAAAAAHH

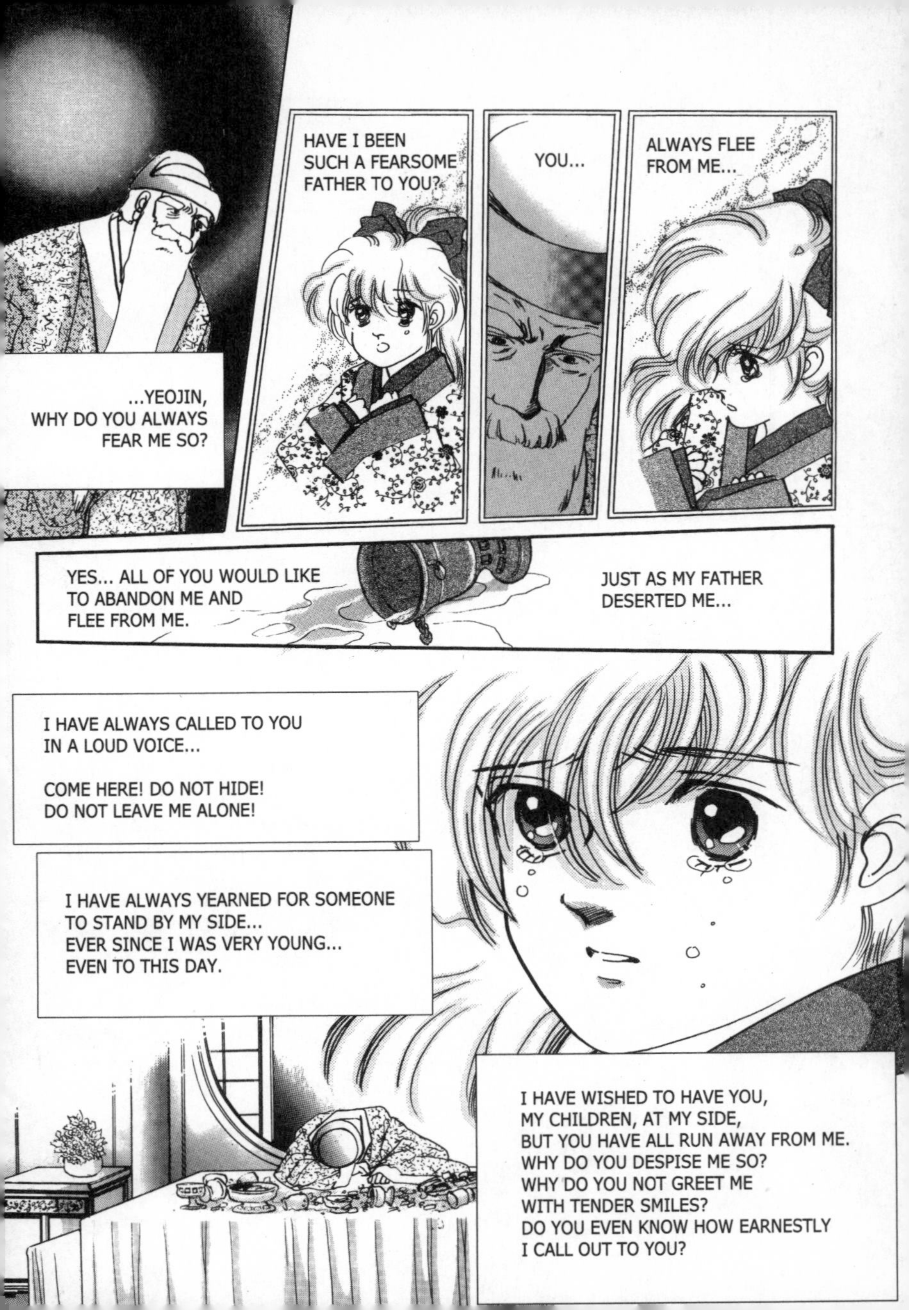
...YEOJIN, WHY DO YOU ALWAYS FEAR ME SO?
HAVE I BEEN SUCH A FEARSOME FATHER TO YOU?
YOU...
ALWAYS FLEE FROM ME...
YES... ALL OF YOU WOULD LIKE TO ABANDON ME AND FLEE FROM ME.
JUST AS MY FATHER DESERTED ME...
I HAVE ALWAYS CALLED TO YOU IN A LOUD VOICE...
COME HERE! DO NOT HIDE! DO NOT LEAVE ME ALONE!
I HAVE ALWAYS YEARNED FOR SOMEONE TO STAND BY MY SIDE... EVER SINCE I WAS VERY YOUNG... EVEN TO THIS DAY.
I HAVE WISHED TO HAVE YOU, MY CHILDREN, AT MY SIDE, BUT YOU HAVE ALL RUN AWAY FROM ME. WHY DO YOU DESPISE ME SO? WHY DO YOU NOT GREET ME WITH TENDER SMILES? DO YOU EVEN KNOW HOW EARNESTLY I CALL OUT TO YOU?

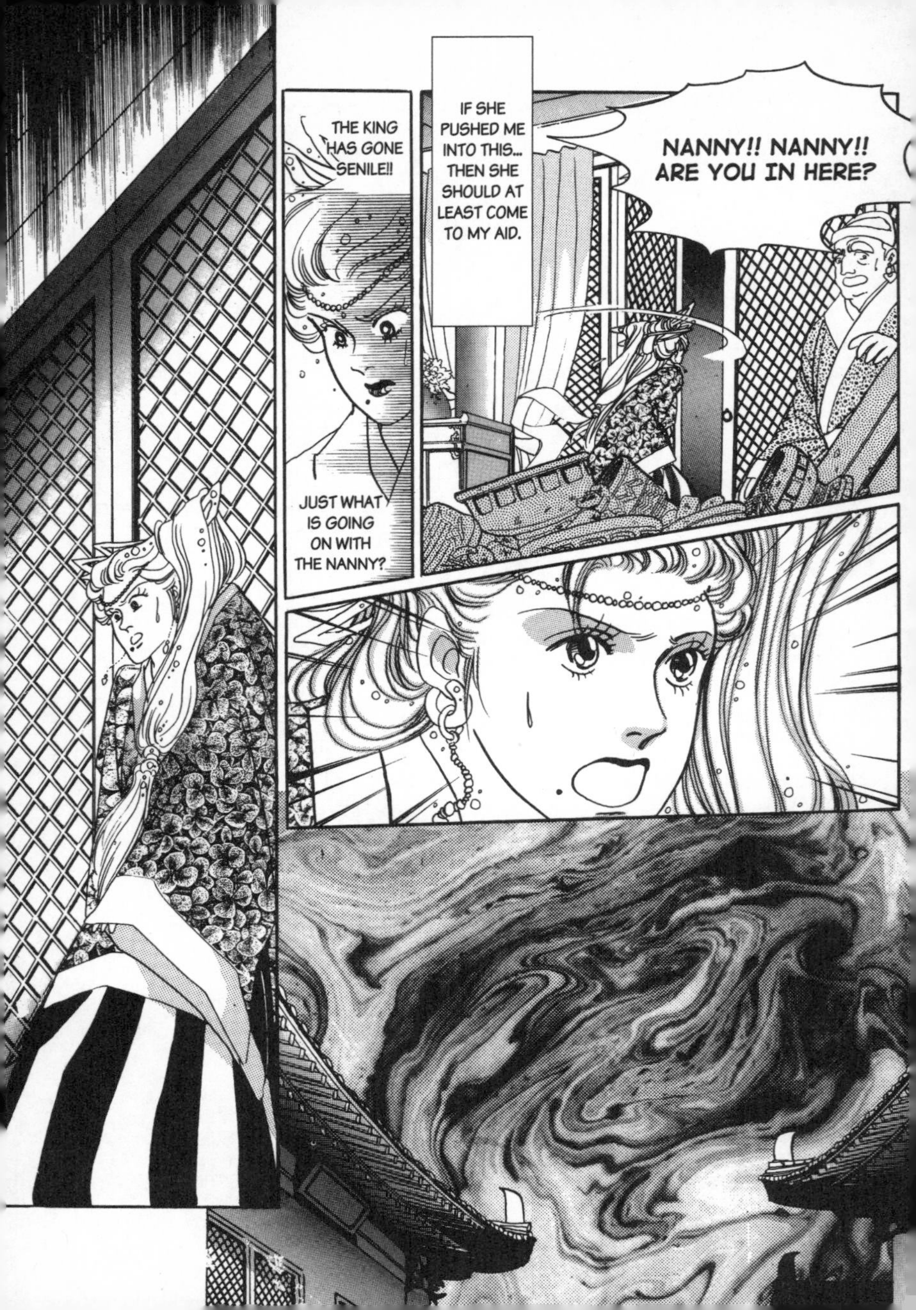
THE KING HAS GONE SENILE!!
JUST WHAT IS GOING ON WITH THE NANNY?
IF SHE PUSHED ME INTO THIS... THEN SHE SHOULD AT LEAST COME TO MY AID.
NANNY!! NANNY!! ARE YOU IN HERE?

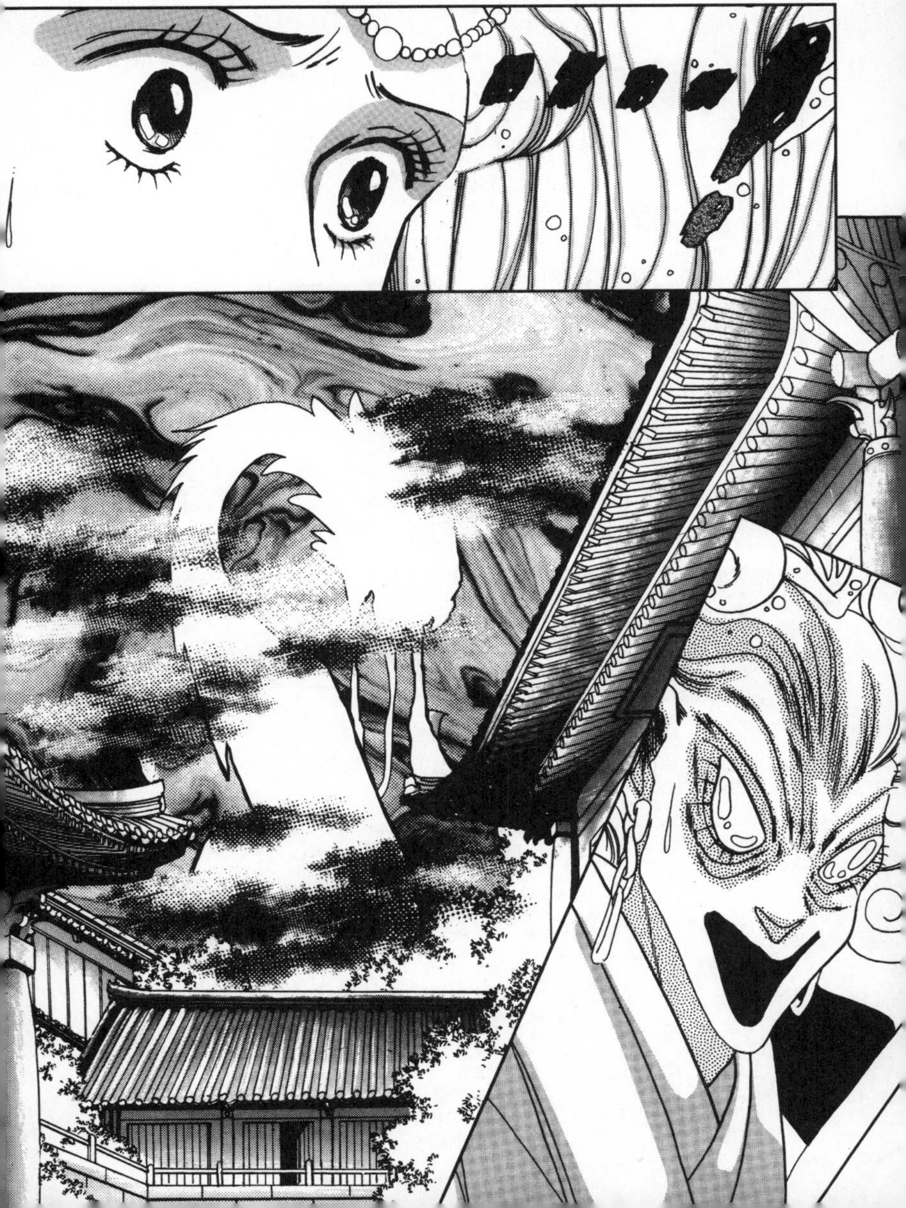
....!

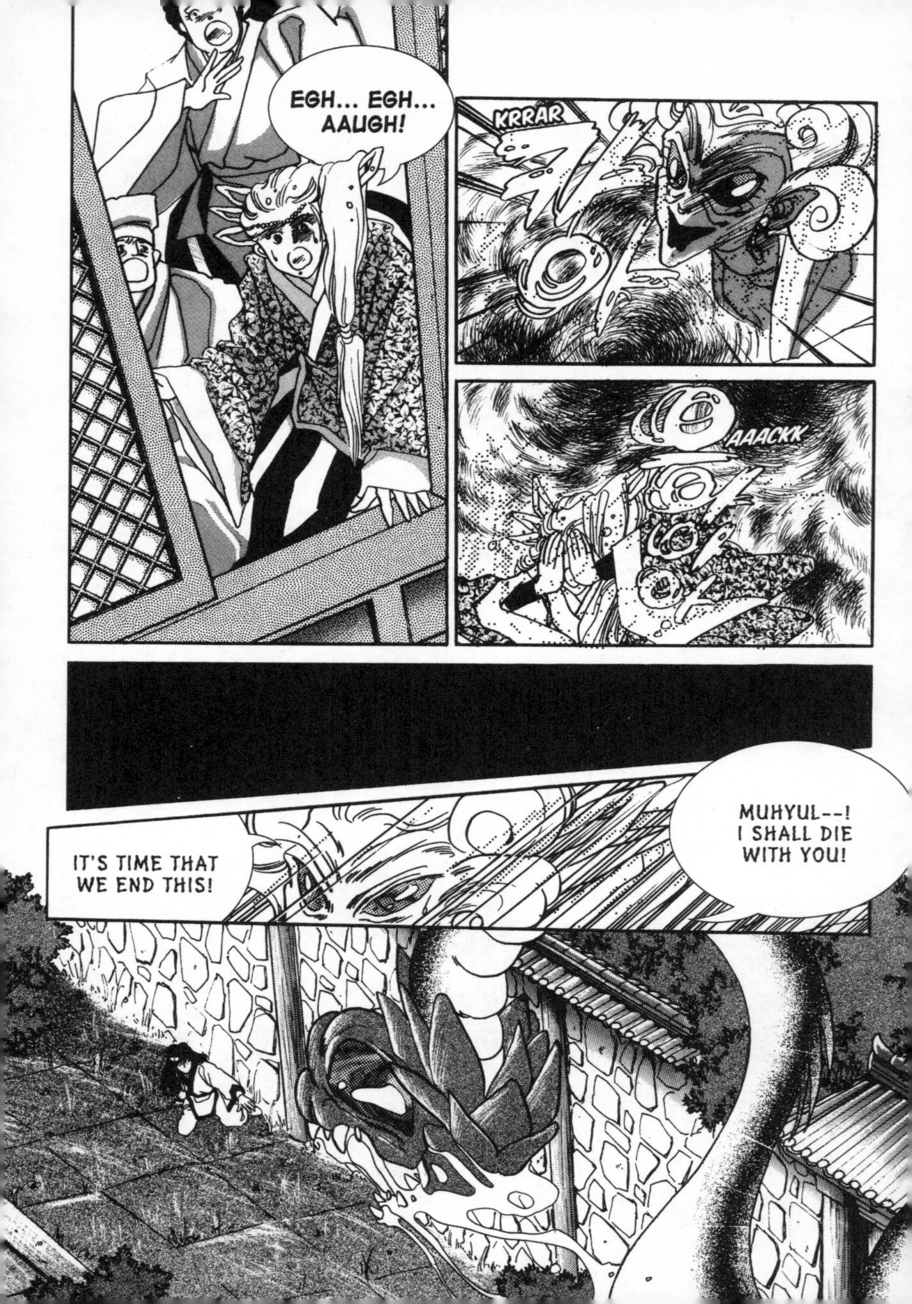
EGH... EGH... AAUGH!
KRRAR
AAACKK
IT'S TIME THAT WE END THIS!
MUHYUL--! I SHALL DIE WITH YOU!

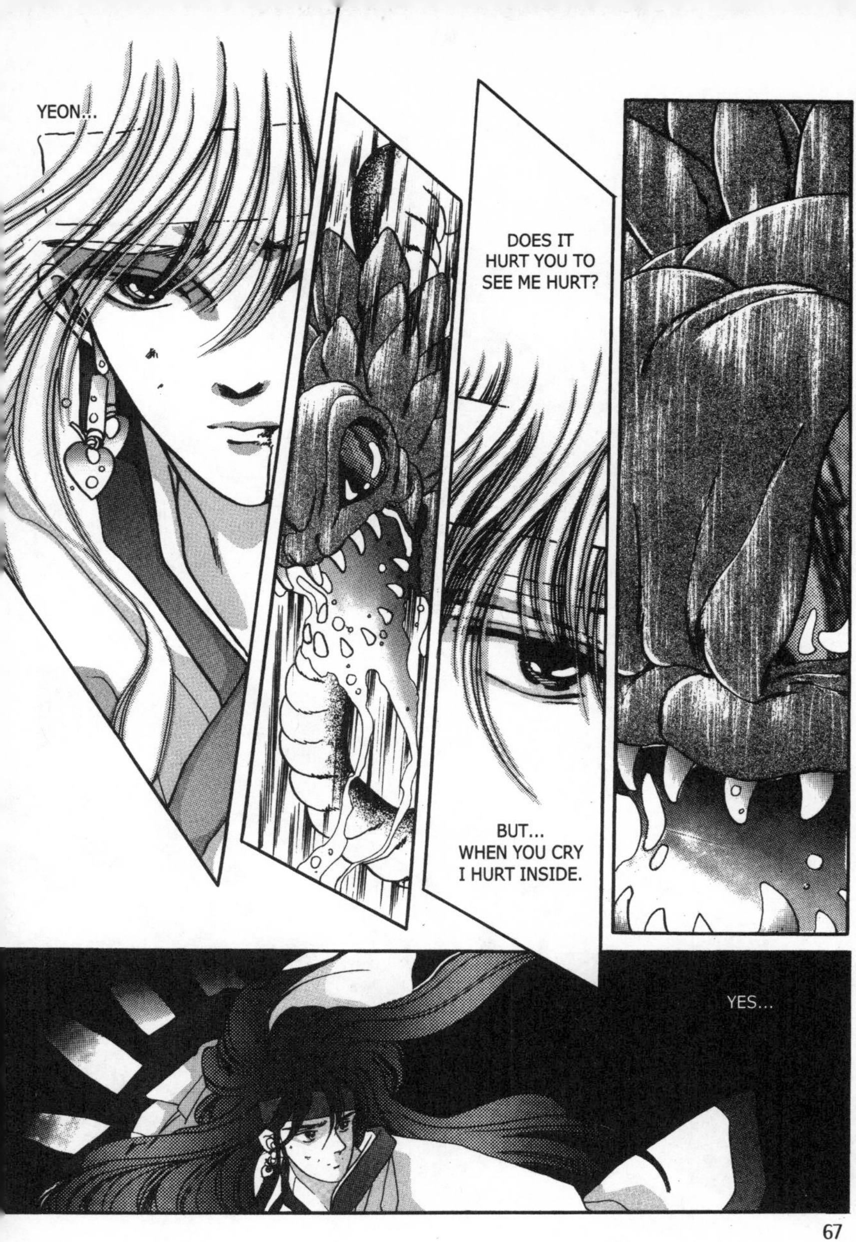
YEON...
DOES IT HURT YOU TO SEE ME HURT?
BUT... WHEN YOU CRY I HURT INSIDE.
YES...

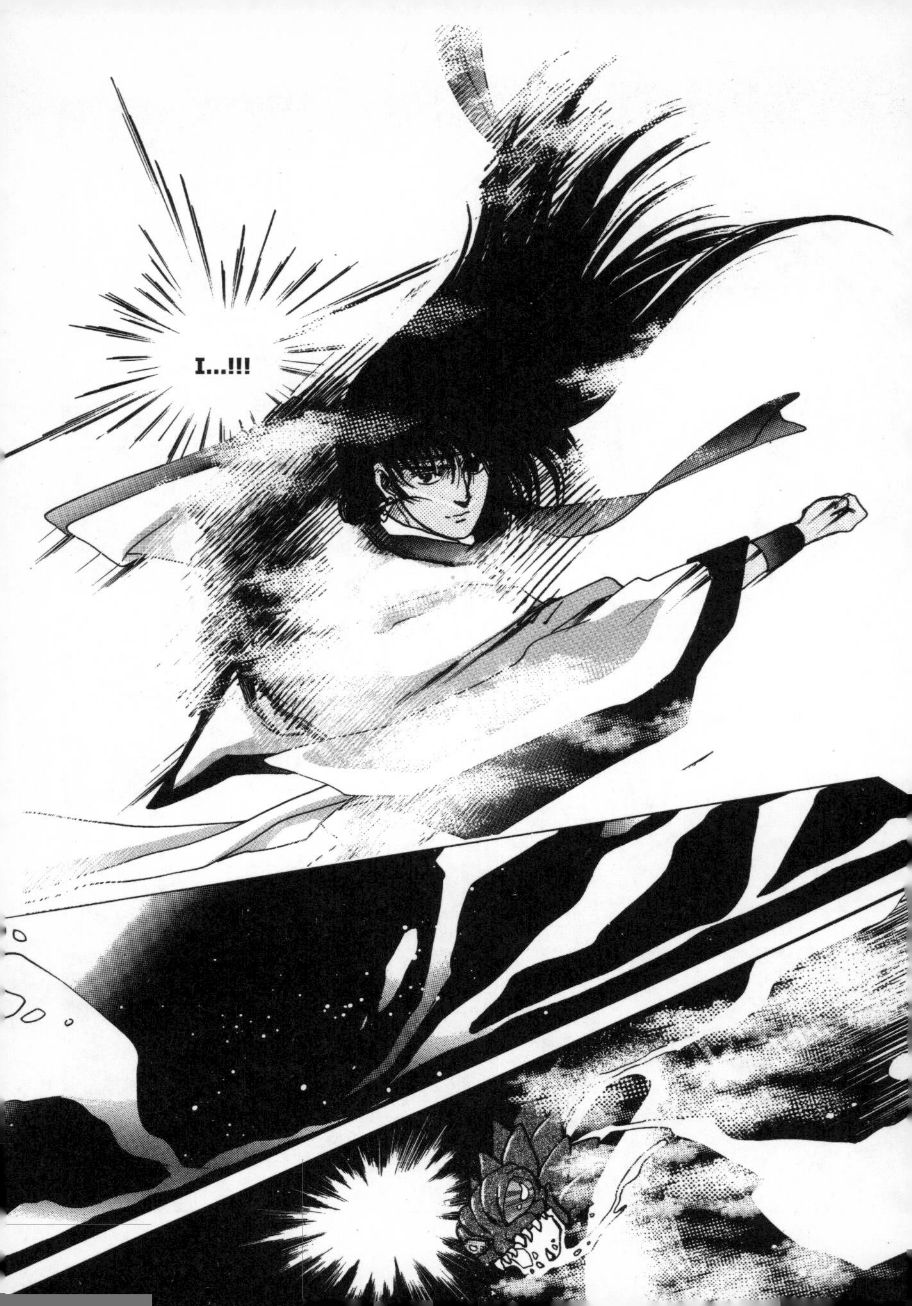
I...!!!

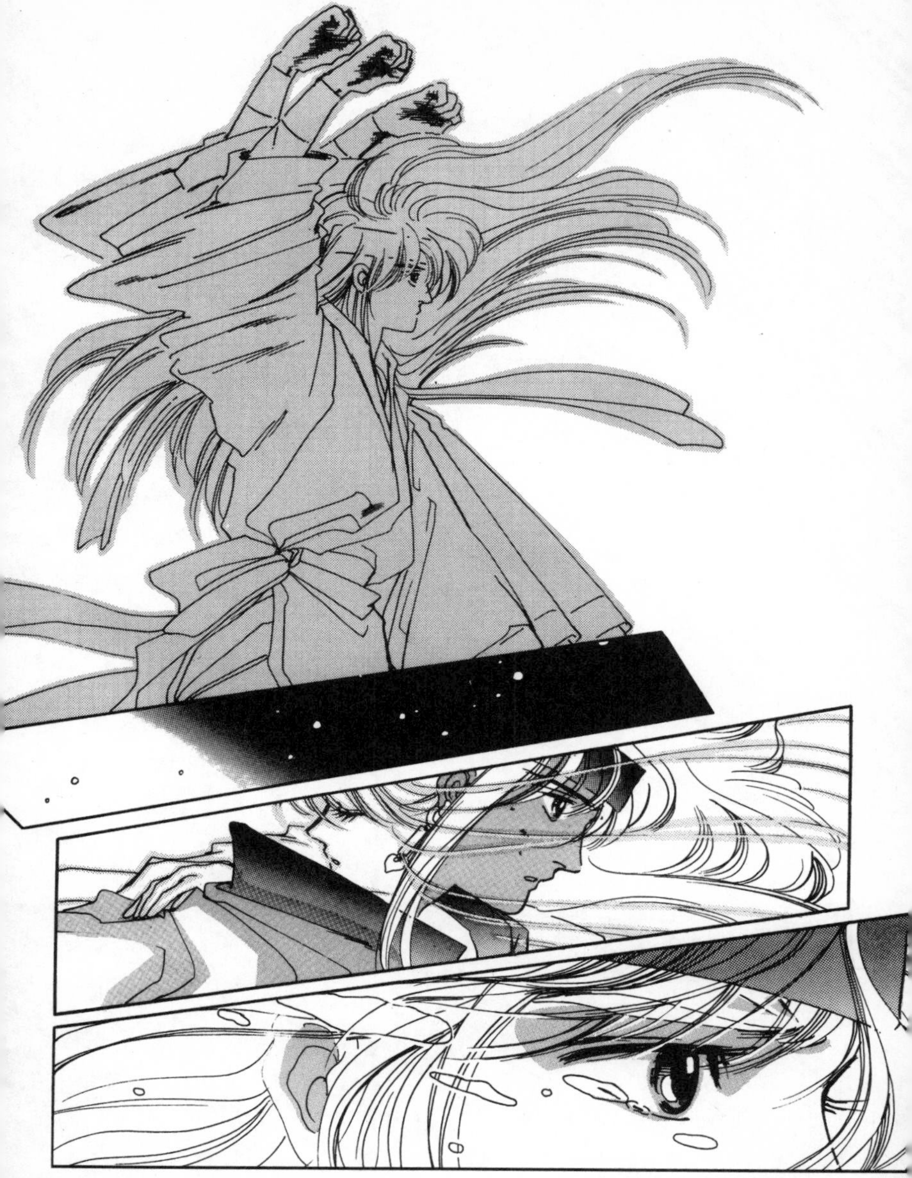

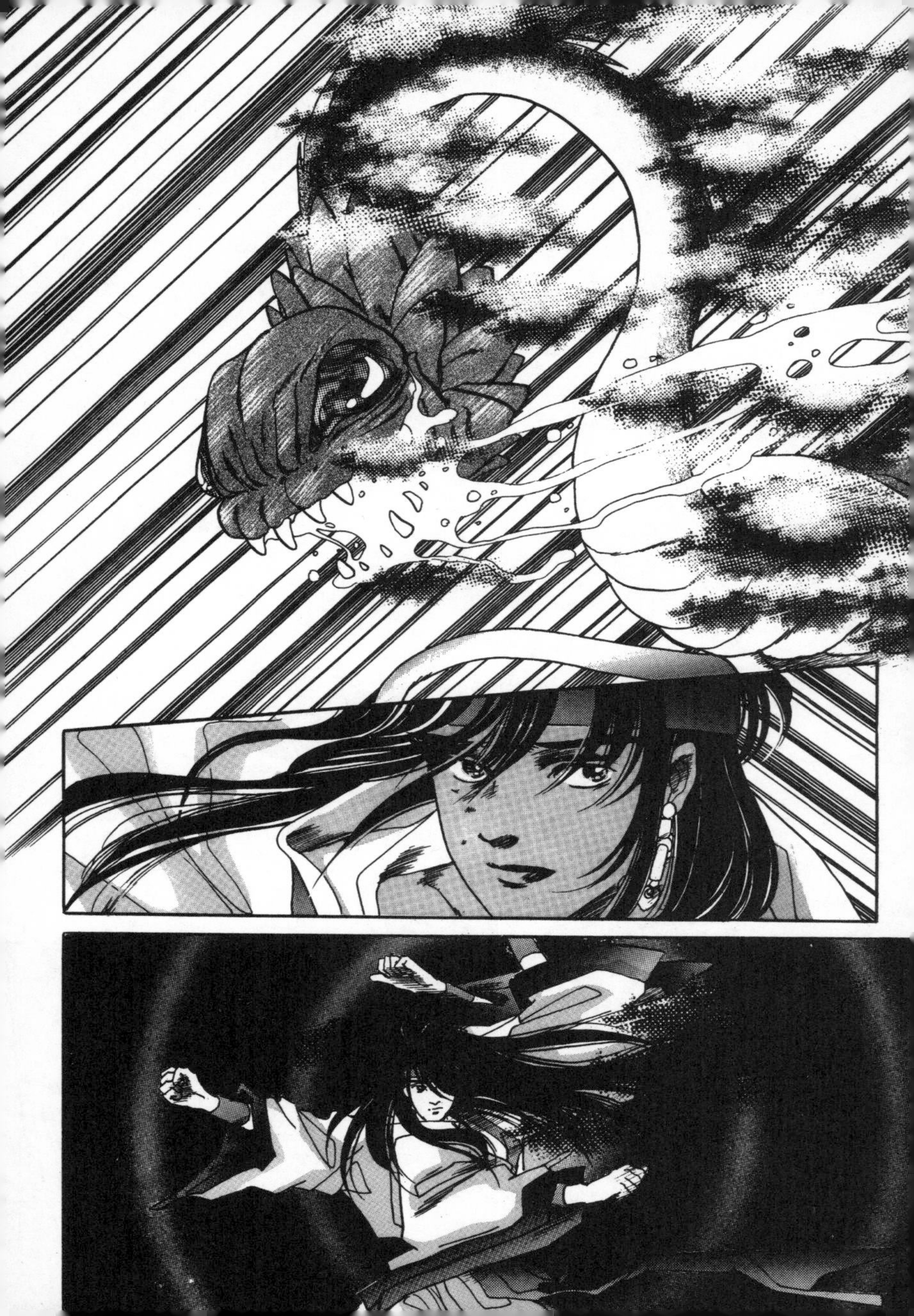

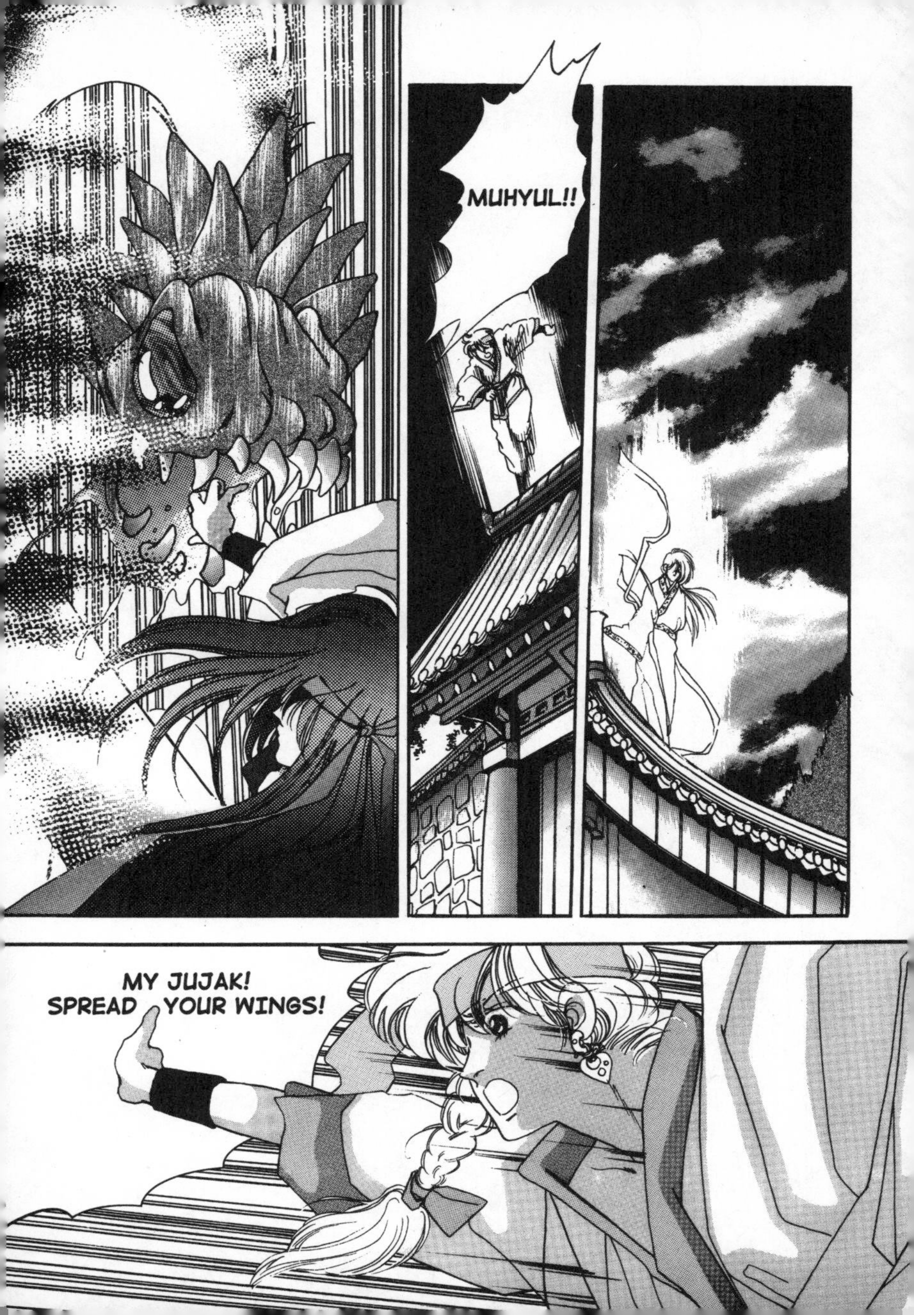
MUHYUL!!
MY JUJAK! SPREAD YOUR WINGS!

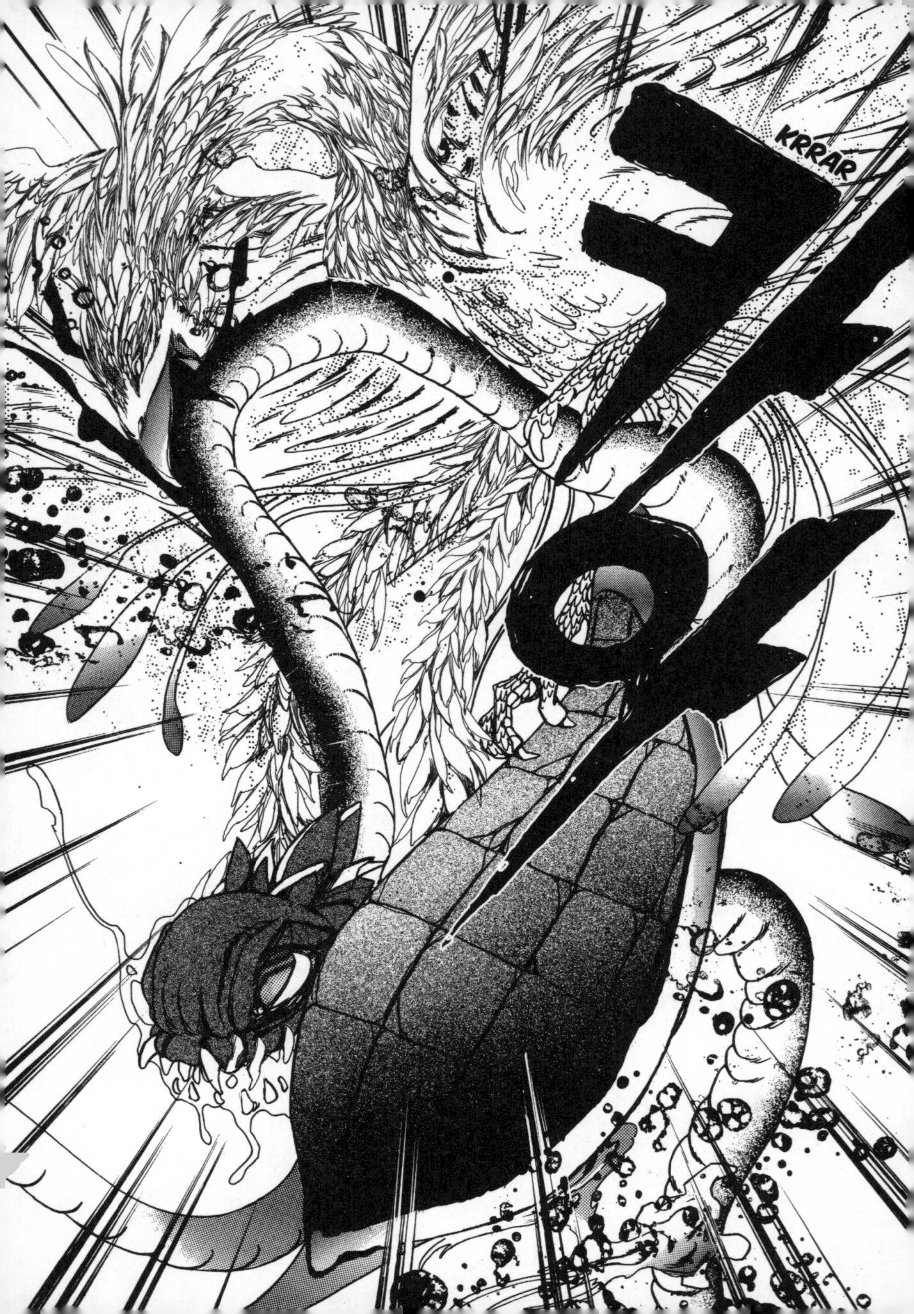
KRRAR

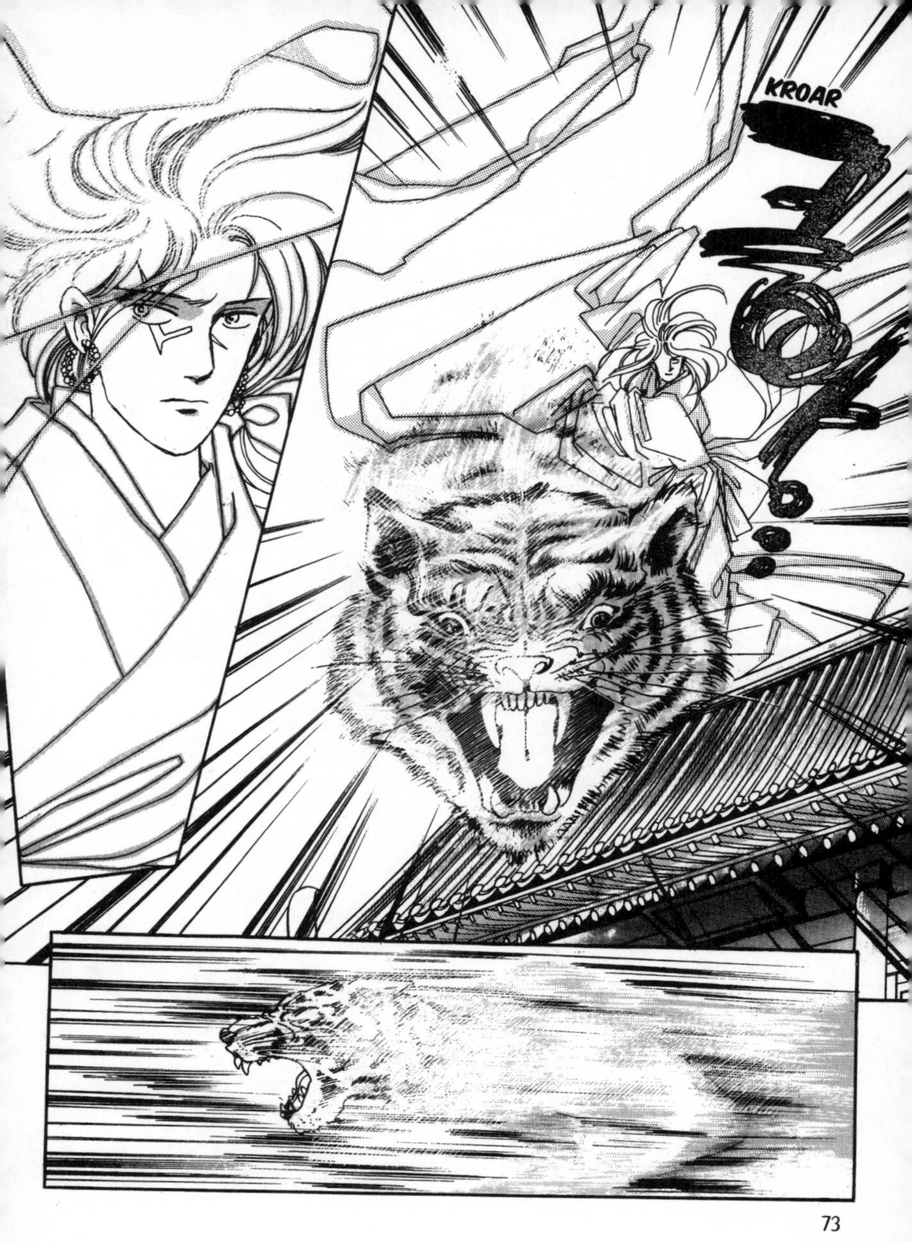
KROAR

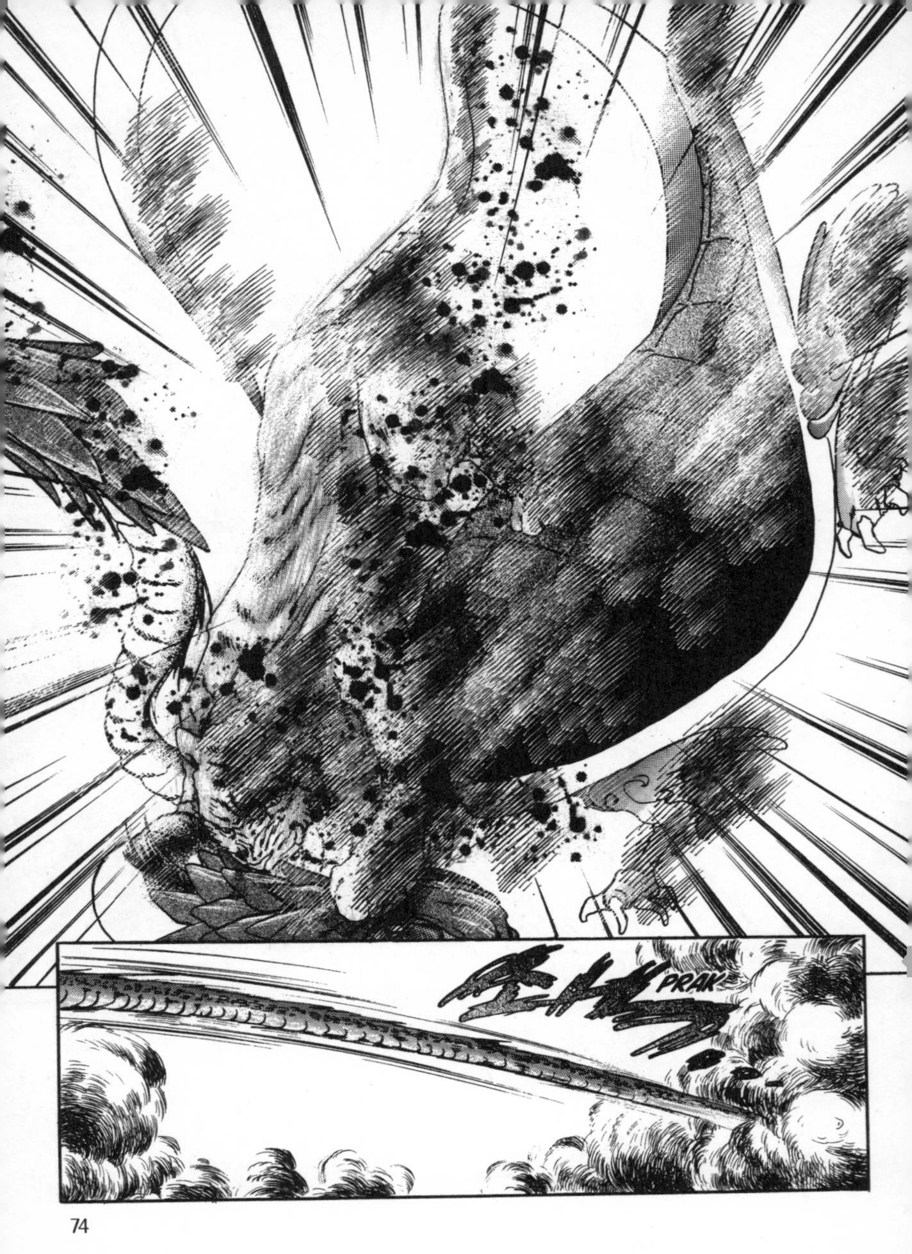
PRAK

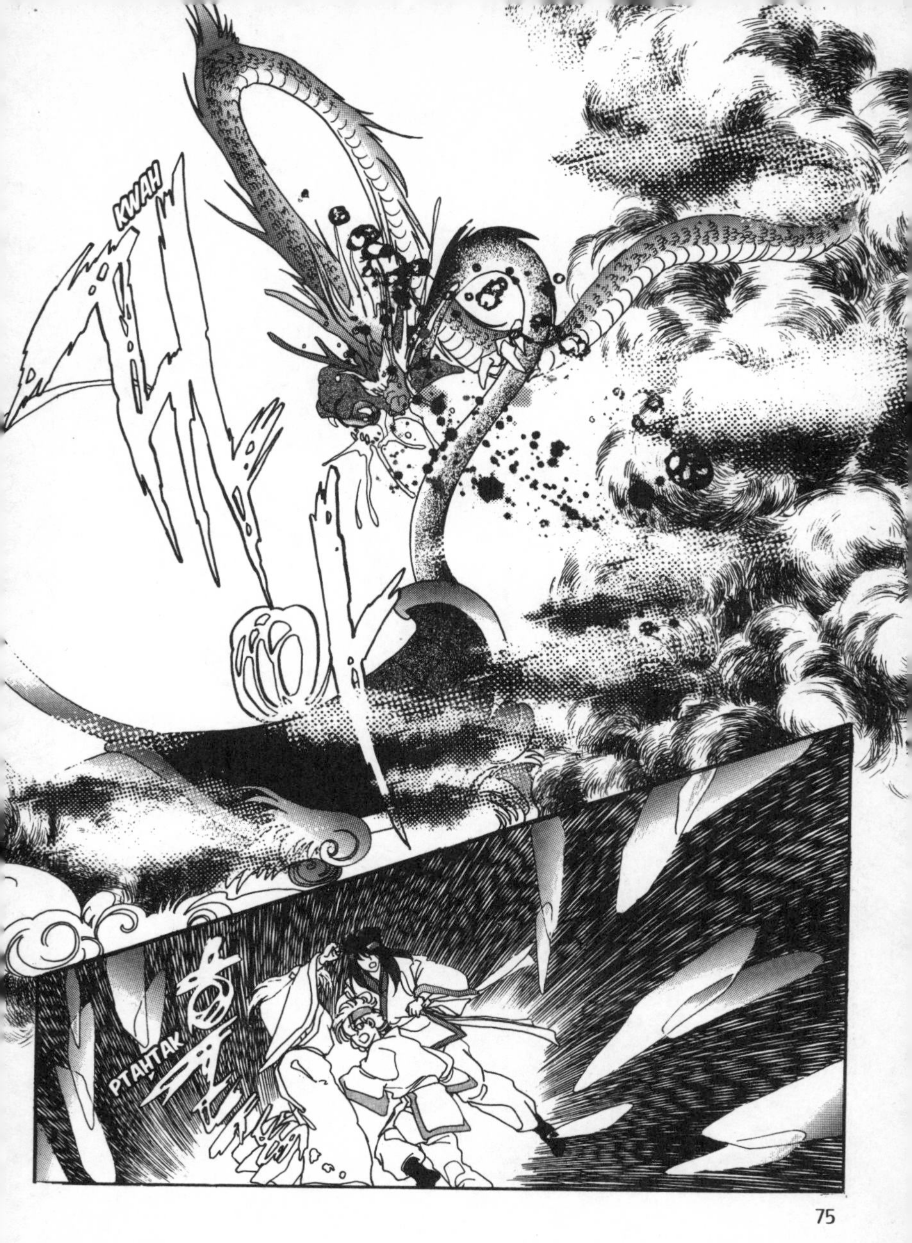
KWAH
PTAHTAK

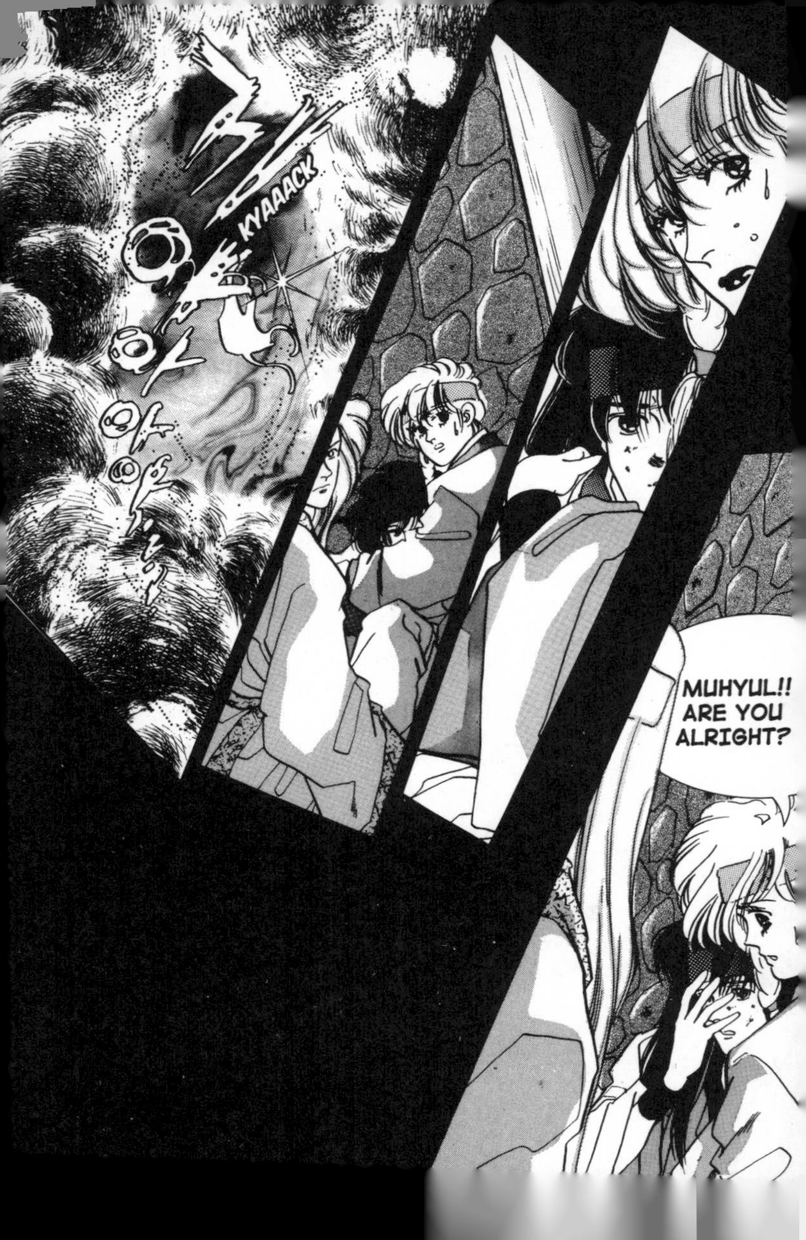
KYAAACK
MUHYUL!! ARE YOU ALRIGHT?

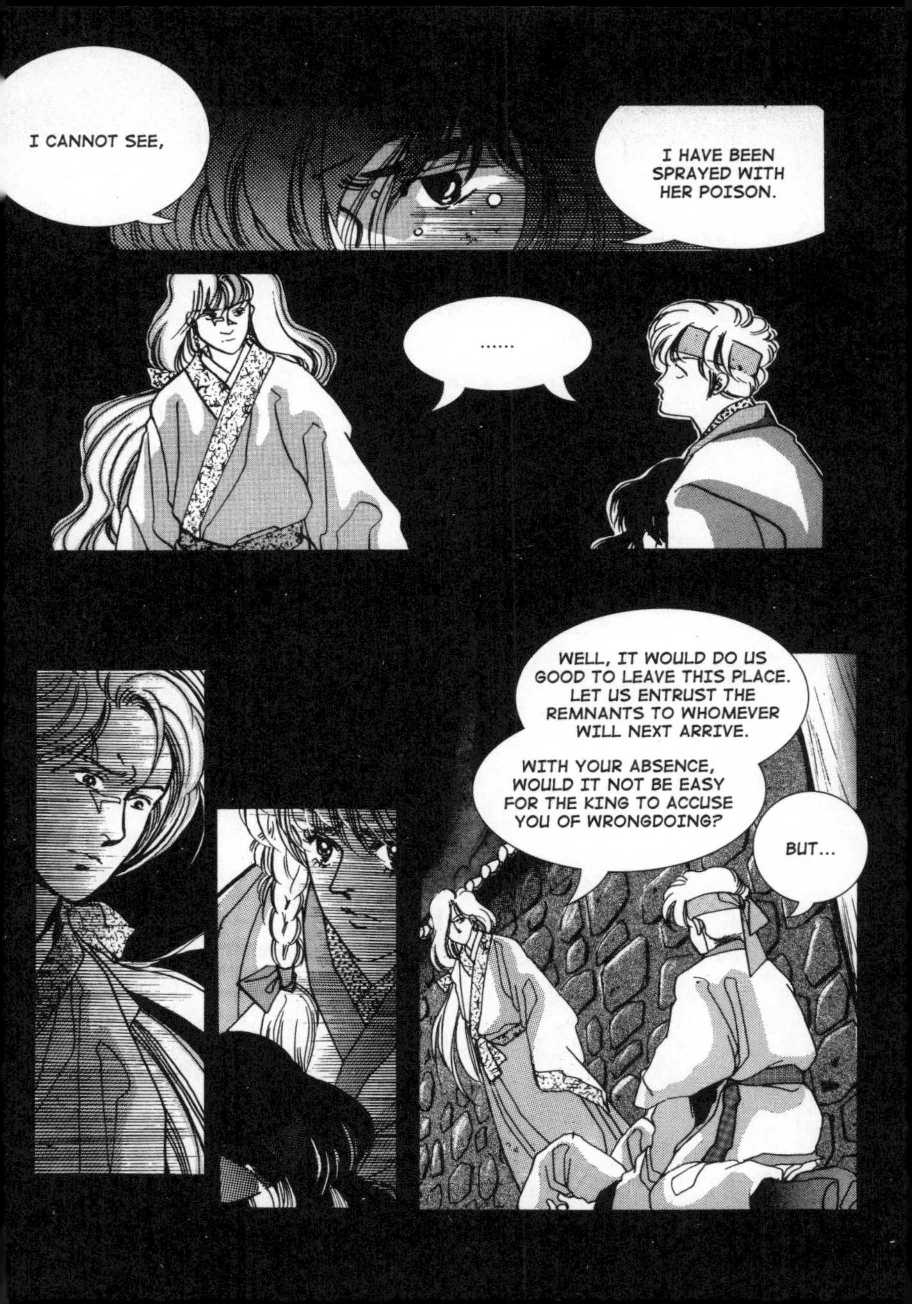
I CANNOT SEE,
I HAVE BEEN SPRAYED WITH HER POISON.
......
WELL, IT WOULD DO US GOOD TO LEAVE THIS PLACE. LET US ENTRUST THE REMNANTS TO WHOMEVER WILL NEXT ARRIVE.
WITH YOUR ABSENCE, WOULD IT NOT BE EASY FOR THE KING TO ACCUSE YOU OF WRONGDOING?
BUT...

I SUPPOSE IT WOULD BE A GOOD IDEA FOR ME TO GO MY OWN SEPARATE WAY. I AM NOT IN ANY POSITION TO REVEAL MY PRESENCE.
I TRULY STILL HAVE NO CLUE WHAT YOU REALLY ARE.
...MUHYUL... TAKE CARE OF YOURSELF.
I THINK IT WOULD BE BEST IF I LEFT WITH HIM. I WILL CONTACT YOU SOON.
WA...WAIT... IT WILL BE ALRIGHT IF I LEAVE YEON IN YOUR CARE, YES?
VISIT HER ONCE... BEFORE YOU SET OUT ON YOUR JOURNEY. THE BABY, AS WELL...

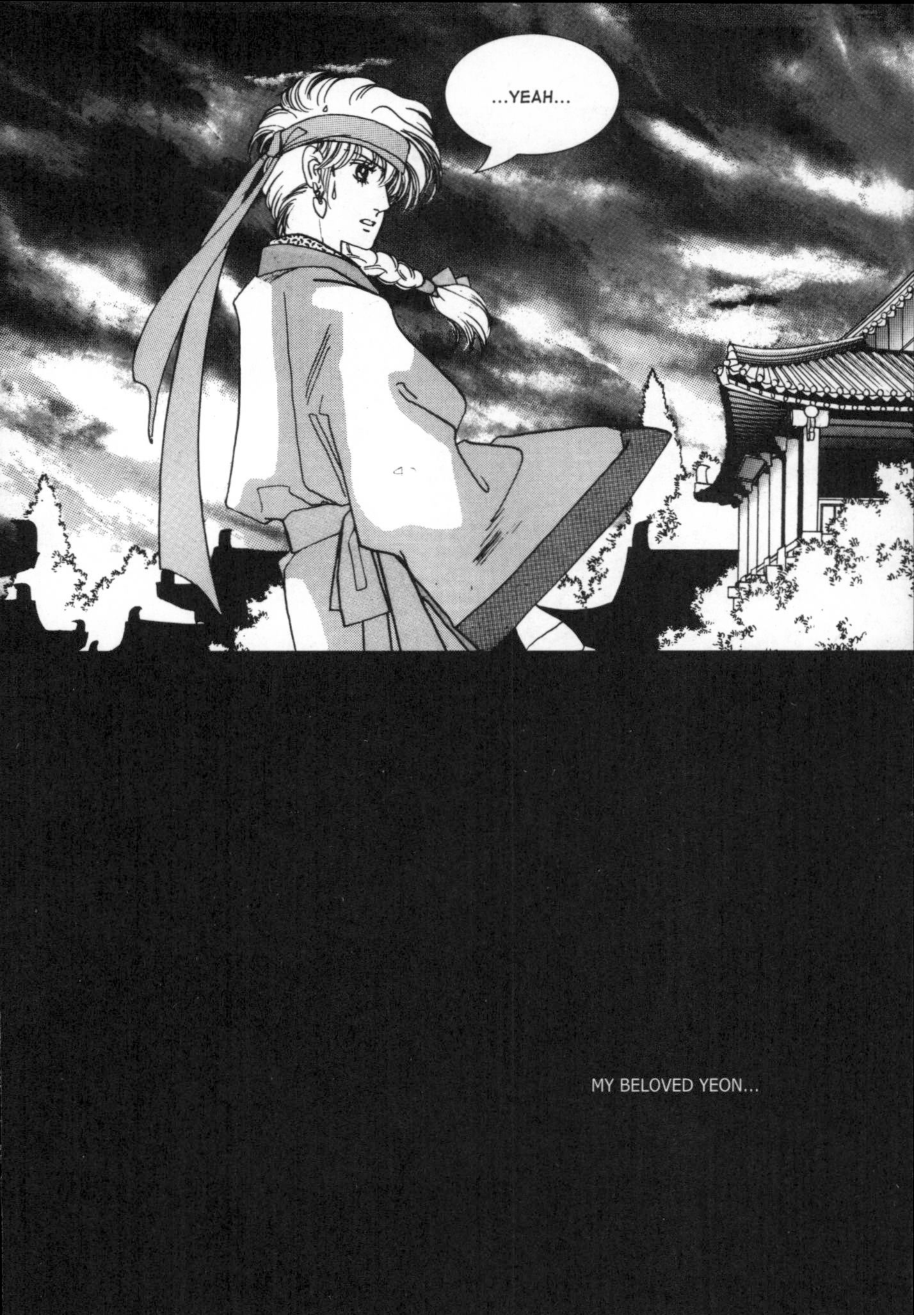
...YEAH...
MY BELOVED YEON...

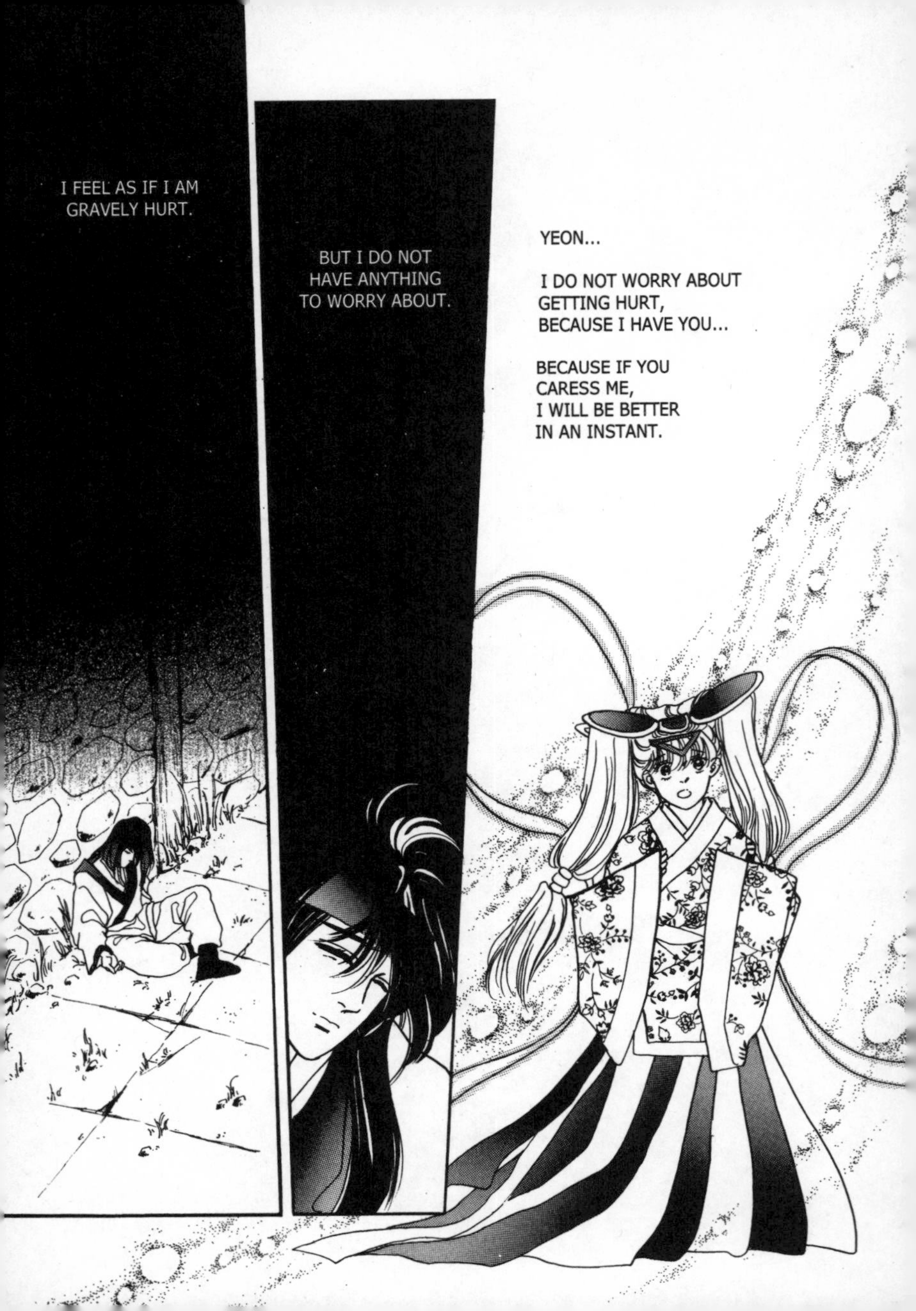
I FEEL AS IF I AM GRAVELY HURT.
BUT I DO NOT HAVE ANYTHING TO WORRY ABOUT.
YEON...
I DO NOT WORRY ABOUT GETTING HURT, BECAUSE I HAVE YOU...
BECAUSE IF YOU CARESS ME, I WILL BE BETTER IN AN INSTANT.

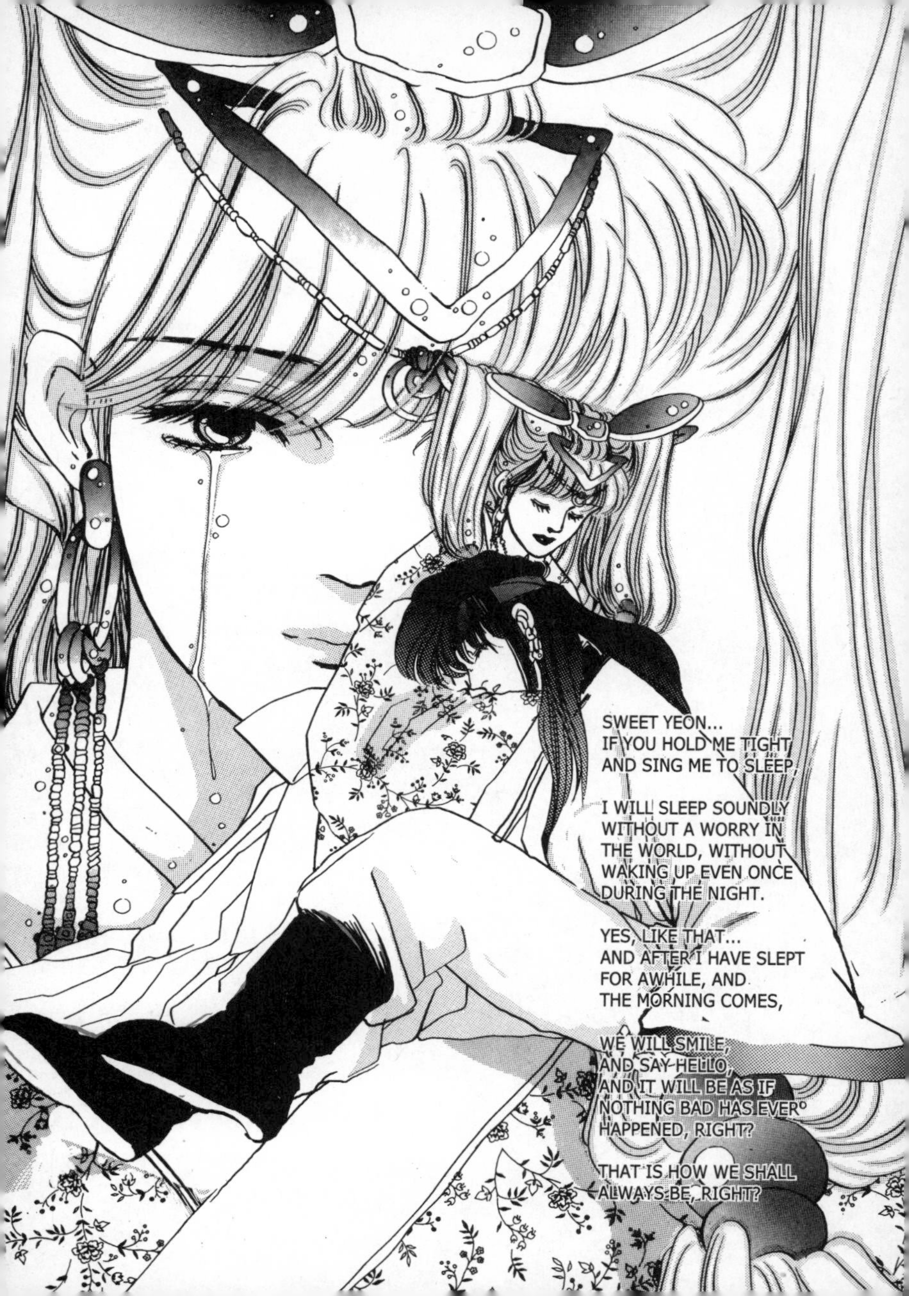
SWEET YEON...
IF YOU HOLD ME TIGHT AND SING ME TO SLEEP,
I WILL SLEEP SOUNDLY WITHOUT A WORRY IN THE WORLD, WITHOUT WAKING UP EVEN ONCE DURING THE NIGHT.
YES, LIKE THAT...
AND AFTER I HAVE SLEPT FOR AWHILE, AND THE MORNING COMES,
WE WILL SMILE, AND SAY HELLO, AND IT WILL BE AS IF NOTHING BAD HAS EVER HAPPENED, RIGHT?
THAT IS HOW WE SHALL ALWAYS BE, RIGHT?

IN 18 A. D. (THE 37TH YEAR OF KING YURI'S REIGN), KING YURI CHOOSES TO MAKE HIS ABODE IN DUGOK, WITHIN THE TOWN'S SECONDARY PALACE, AND EVENTUALLY DIES THERE. HIS BURIAL CEREMONY WAS HELD IN THE EAST GARDEN WHERE HE WAS GRANTED THE POSTHUMOUS EPITHET "KING YURIMYUNG".

- EXCERPT FROM SAMGUK SAGI, BOOK 1 OF GOGURYEO, CHAPTER: KING YURI.

KING DAEMUSHIN ASCENDS THE THRONE. MOTHER SEOHWA IS THE DAUGHTER OF KING SONG YANG OF DAMUL. HE WAS CROWNED DURING KING YURI'S 33RD YEAR OF REIGN. MUHYUL WAS 11.

- EXCERPT FROM SAMGUK SAGI, BOOK 2 OF GOGURYEO, CHAPTER: KING DAEMUSHIN.

The end of PART I

SAMGUK SAGI (Chronicles of the Three Kingdoms): a historical record of the Three Kingdoms of Korea: Goguryeo, Baekje, and Shilla

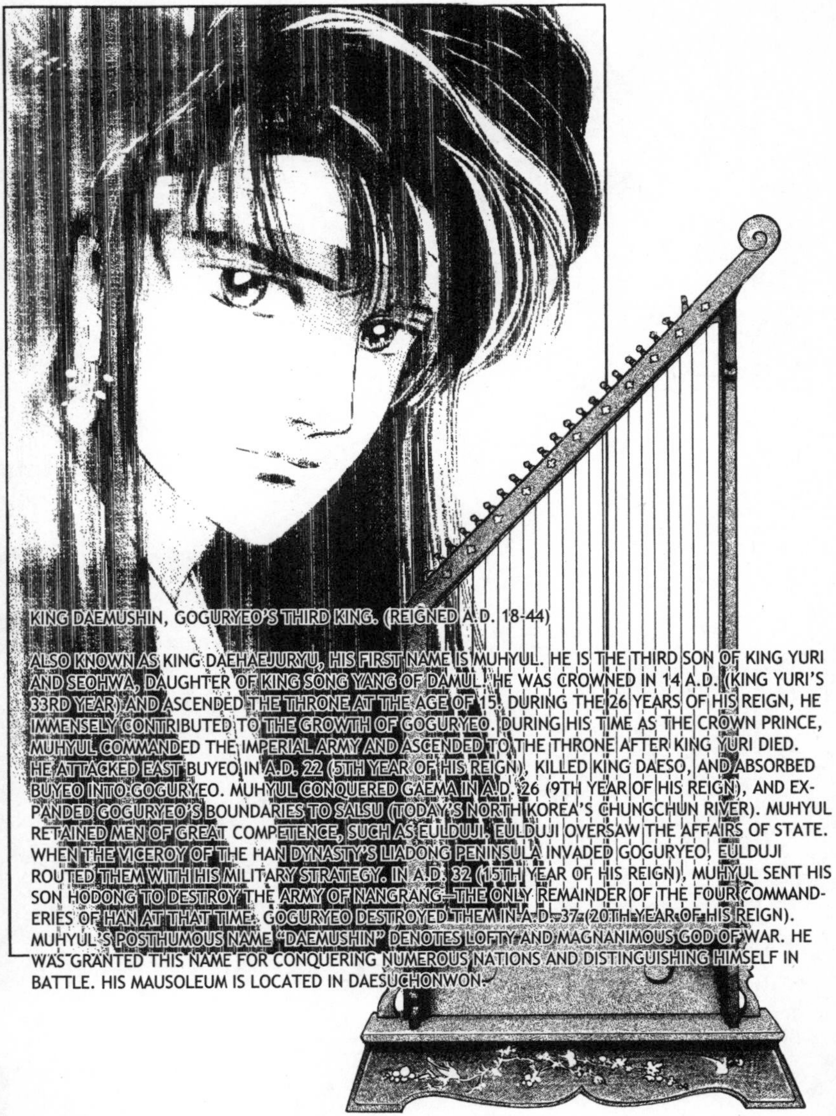

KING DAEMUSHIN, GOGURYEO'S THIRD KING. (REIGNED A.D. 18-44)

ALSO KNOWN AS KING DAEHAEJURYU, HIS FIRST NAME IS MUHYUL. HE IS THE THIRD SON OF KING YURI AND SEOHWA, DAUGHTER OF KING SONG YANG OF DAMUL. HE WAS CROWNED IN 14 A.D. (KING YURI'S 33RD YEAR) AND ASCENDED THE THRONE AT THE AGE OF 15. DURING THE 26 YEARS OF HIS REIGN, HE IMMENSELY CONTRIBUTED TO THE GROWTH OF GOGURYEO. DURING HIS TIME AS THE CROWN PRINCE, MUHYUL COMMANDED THE IMPERIAL ARMY AND ASCENDED TO THE THRONE AFTER KING YURI DIED. HE ATTACKED EAST BUYEO IN A.D. 22 (5TH YEAR OF HIS REIGN), KILLED KING DAESO, AND ABSORBED BUYEO INTO GOGURYEO. MUHYUL CONQUERED GAEMA IN A.D. 26 (9TH YEAR OF HIS REIGN), AND EXPANDED GOGURYEO'S BOUNDARIES TO SALSU (TODAY'S NORTH KOREA'S CHUNGCHUN RIVER). MUHYUL RETAINED MEN OF GREAT COMPETENCE, SUCH AS EULDUJI. EULDUJI OVERSAW THE AFFAIRS OF STATE. WHEN THE VICEROY OF THE HAN DYNASTY'S LIADONG PENINSULA INVADED GOGURYEO, EULDUJI ROUTED THEM WITH HIS MILITARY STRATEGY. IN A.D. 32 (15TH YEAR OF HIS REIGN), MUHYUL SENT HIS SON HODONG TO DESTROY THE ARMY OF NANGRANG—THE ONLY REMAINDER OF THE FOUR COMMANDERIES OF HAN AT THAT TIME. GOGURYEO DESTROYED THEM IN A.D. 37 (20TH YEAR OF HIS REIGN). MUHYUL'S POSTHUMOUS NAME "DAEMUSHIN" DENOTES LOFTY AND MAGNANIMOUS GOD OF WAR. HE WAS GRANTED THIS NAME FOR CONQUERING NUMEROUS NATIONS AND DISTINGUISHING HIMSELF IN BATTLE. HIS MAUSOLEUM IS LOCATED IN DAESUCHONWON.

SHOULD IT NOT BE CONTRARY TO YOUR WILL, ALLOW ME TO REMAIN BY MY BROTHER'S SIDE. LET ME BE THE ONE WHO SHALL WITNESS HIS LAST BREATH.
I BESEECH YOU, MY HEAVENLY FATHER, DO NOT TO LET HIM SPEND IN VAIN THE TIME THAT YOU HAVE GRANTED HIM BY YOUR ROYAL SANCTION...

EVEN AFTER HE COMPLETES HIS QUEST, HIS TIES TO THE HEAVENS HAVE ALREADY BEEN SEVERED. WHY DO YOU TORMENT YOURSELF IN SUCH A FUTILE MANNER?
DURING THAT FRIGHTFUL TRIAL I EXPERIENCED, YOU HEARD MY MOTHER'S PRAYERS AND DELIVERED ME FROM THE CALAMITY BELOW TO THIS PLACE.
PLEASE REMEMBER THE GRACIOUS HEART YOU SHOWED TO ME ON THAT DAY. ALLOW ME TO DIE TOGETHER WITH HIM...
ALTHOUGH I HAVE RETURNED TO THE HEAVENS IN MY CELESTIAL GARB AND HAVE FOREVER PARTED WITH HIM, I CANNOT HELP BUT KEEP HIM IN MY HEART. AND SO, I HAVE CONTINUED TO SHED MY TEARS LIKE A FOOL.
EVERY CREATURE IN THE WORLD HAS ITS OWN COUNTERPART. AS SUCH, I SUPPOSE MY BROTHER ALSO HAS HIS OTHER HALF. HE MAY FIND HER ON EARTH.
FATE HAS DEALT US A CRUEL LOT. I ALREADY UNDERSTAND THAT HE DOES NOT BELONG TO ME. HOWEVER, IF YOU WOULD PERMIT IT, LET ME STAY AT HIS SIDE, PROTECTING HIM WHILE HE STILL LIVES.
BUT EVEN BEFORE HE BECAME MY BROTHER, HE IS MY LOVER FROM LONG AGO. I WISH TO RETURN TO HIM.
AND WHEN HE DIES, LET ME LIVE TOGETHER WITH HIM IN THAT OTHER WORLD WHERE HUMANS ARE SAID TO GO WHEN THEY DIE.

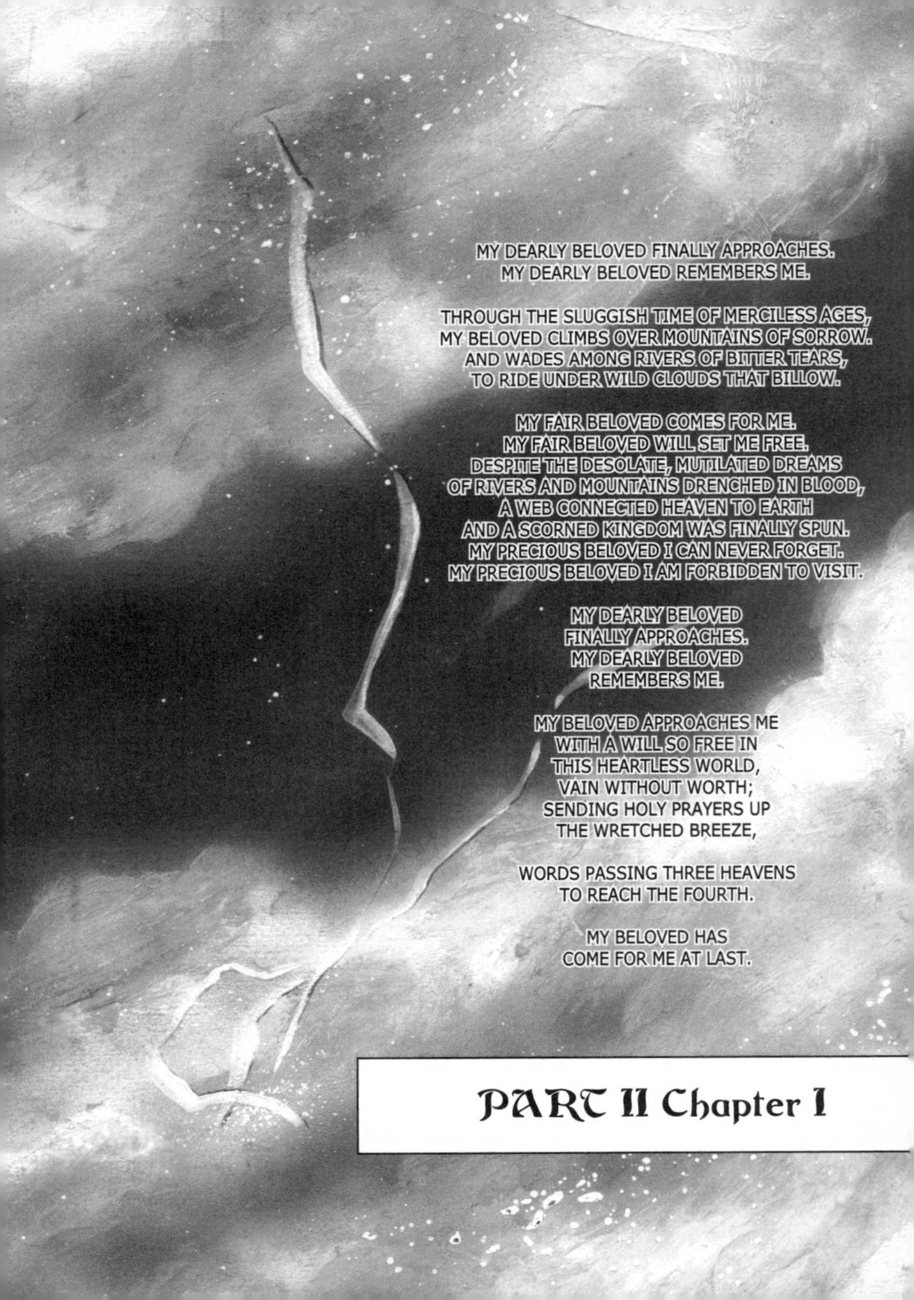
MY DEARLY BELOVED FINALLY APPROACHES.
MY DEARLY BELOVED REMEMBERS ME.
THROUGH THE SLUGGISH TIME OF MERCILESS AGES,
MY BELOVED CLIMBS OVER MOUNTAINS OF SORROW.
AND WADES AMONG RIVERS OF BITTER TEARS,
TO RIDE UNDER WILD CLOUDS THAT BILLOW.
MY FAIR BELOVED COMES FOR ME.
MY FAIR BELOVED WILL SET ME FREE.
DESPITE THE DESOLATE, MUTILATED DREAMS
OF RIVERS AND MOUNTAINS DRENCHED IN BLOOD,
A WEB CONNECTED HEAVEN TO EARTH
AND A SCORNED KINGDOM WAS FINALLY SPUN.
MY PRECIOUS BELOVED I CAN NEVER FORGET.
MY PRECIOUS BELOVED I AM FORBIDDEN TO VISIT.
MY DEARLY BELOVED
FINALLY APPROACHES.
MY DEARLY BELOVED
REMEMBERS ME.
MY BELOVED APPROACHES ME
WITH A WILL SO FREE IN
THIS HEARTLESS WORLD,
VAIN WITHOUT WORTH;
SENDING HOLY PRAYERS UP
THE WRETCHED BREEZE,
WORDS PASSING THREE HEAVENS
TO REACH THE FOURTH.
MY BELOVED HAS
COME FOR ME AT LAST.
PART II Chapter I

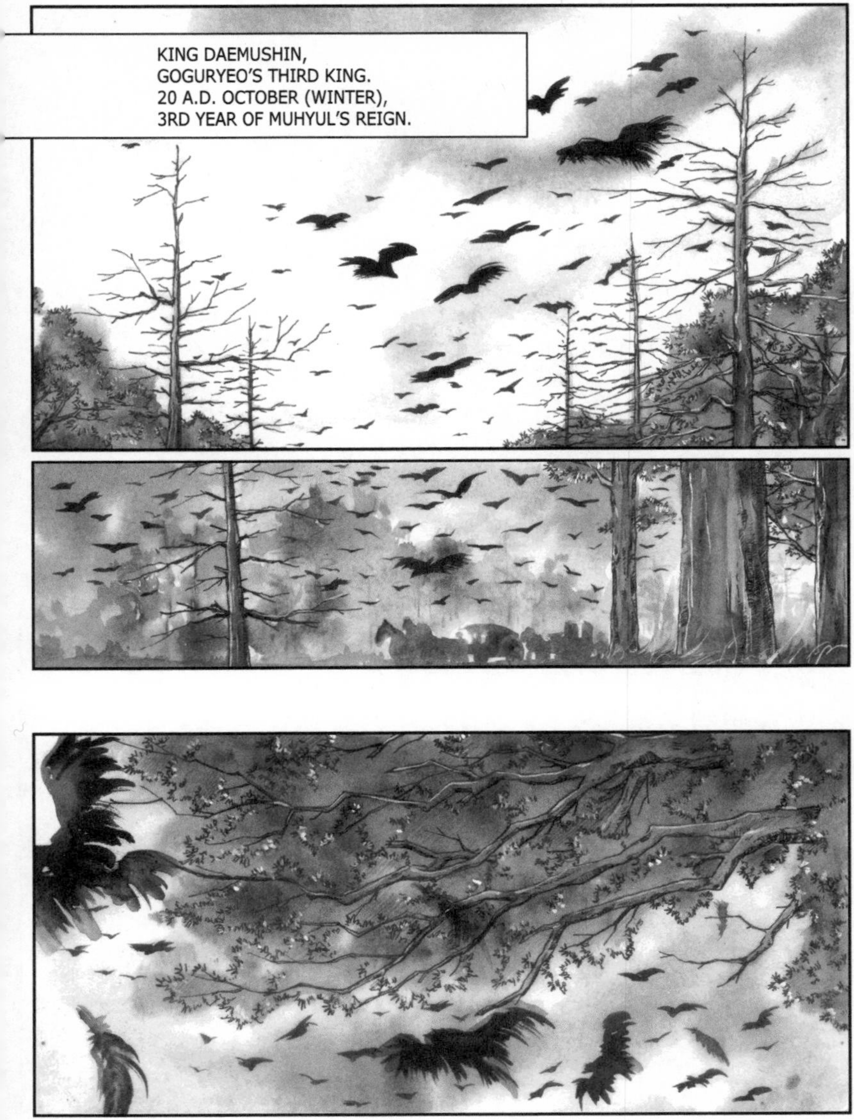
KING DAEMUSHIN,
GOGURYEO'S THIRD KING.
20 A.D. OCTOBER (WINTER),
3RD YEAR OF MUHYUL'S REIGN.

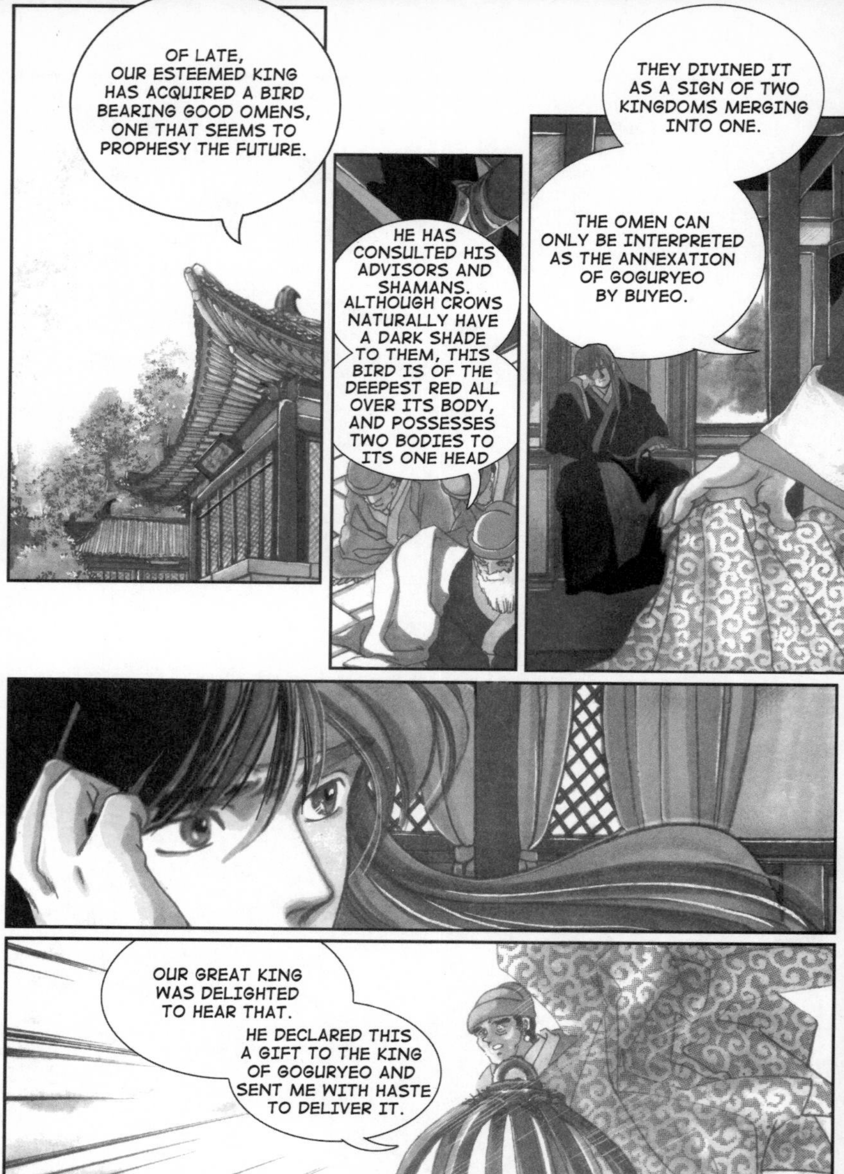
OF LATE, OUR ESTEEMED KING HAS ACQUIRED A BIRD BEARING GOOD OMENS, ONE THAT SEEMS TO PROPHESY THE FUTURE.
HE HAS CONSULTED HIS ADVISORS AND SHAMANS. ALTHOUGH CROWS NATURALLY HAVE A DARK SHADE TO THEM, THIS BIRD IS OF THE DEEPEST RED ALL OVER ITS BODY, AND POSSESSES TWO BODIES TO ITS ONE HEAD
THEY DIVINED IT AS A SIGN OF TWO KINGDOMS MERGING INTO ONE.
THE OMEN CAN ONLY BE INTERPRETED AS THE ANNEXATION OF GOGURYEO BY BUYEO.
OUR GREAT KING WAS DELIGHTED TO HEAR THAT.
HE DECLARED THIS A GIFT TO THE KING OF GOGURYEO AND SENT ME WITH HASTE TO DELIVER IT.

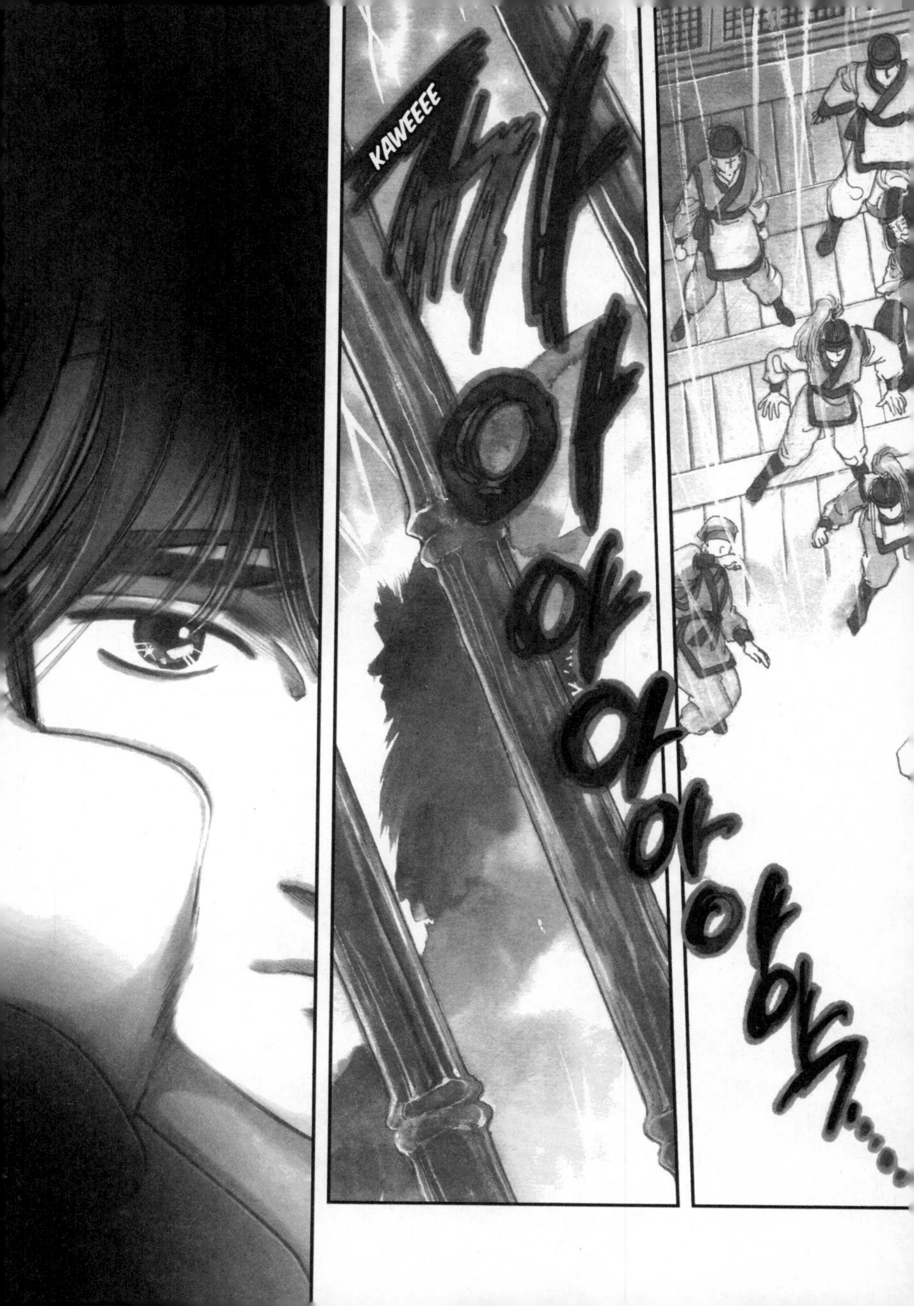
KAWEEEE

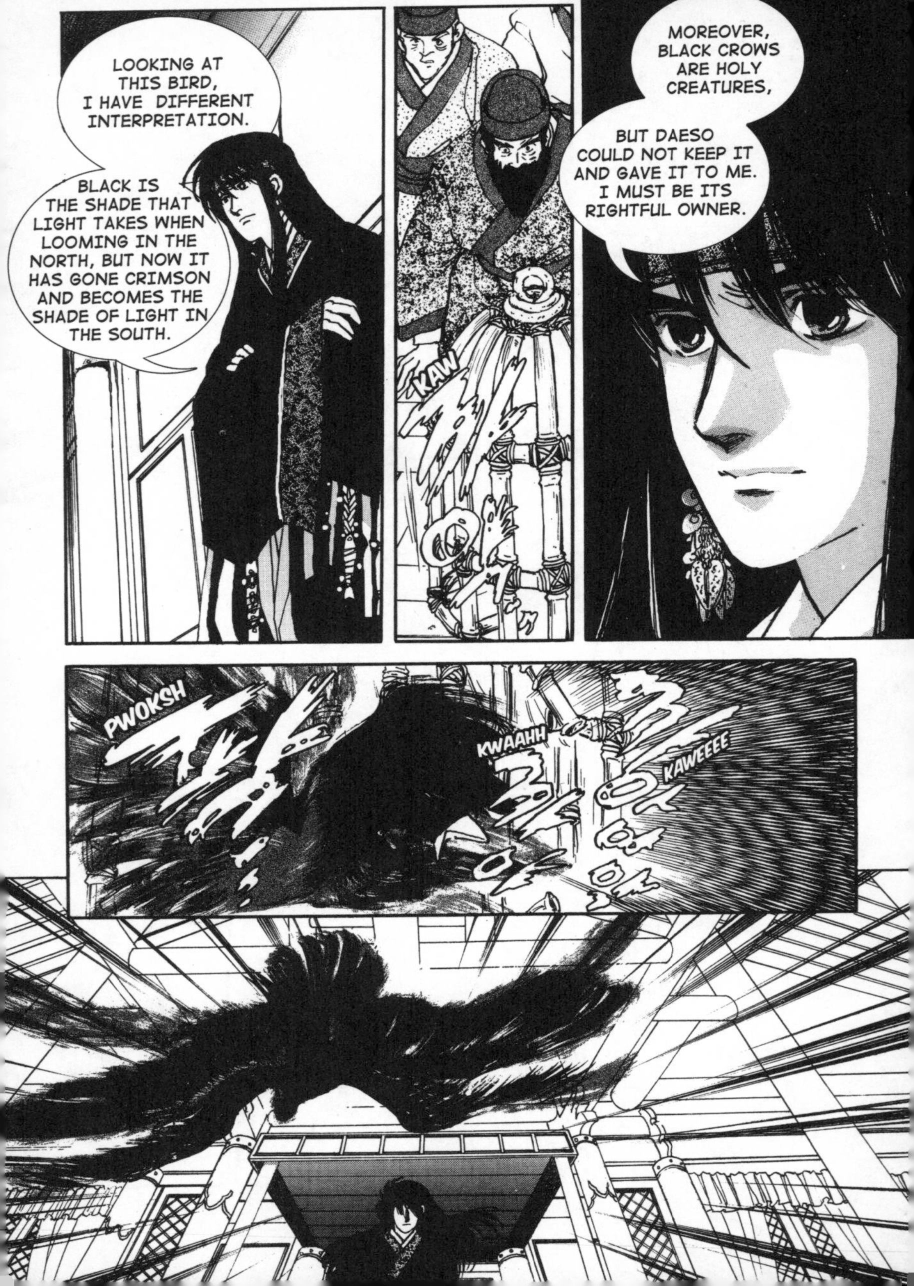
LOOKING AT THIS BIRD, I HAVE DIFFERENT INTERPRETATION.
BLACK IS THE SHADE THAT LIGHT TAKES WHEN LOOMING IN THE NORTH, BUT NOW IT HAS GONE CRIMSON AND BECOMES THE SHADE OF LIGHT IN THE SOUTH.
KAW
MOREOVER, BLACK CROWS ARE HOLY CREATURES,
BUT DAESO COULD NOT KEEP IT AND GAVE IT TO ME. I MUST BE ITS RIGHTFUL OWNER.
PWOKSH
KWAAHH
KAWEEEE

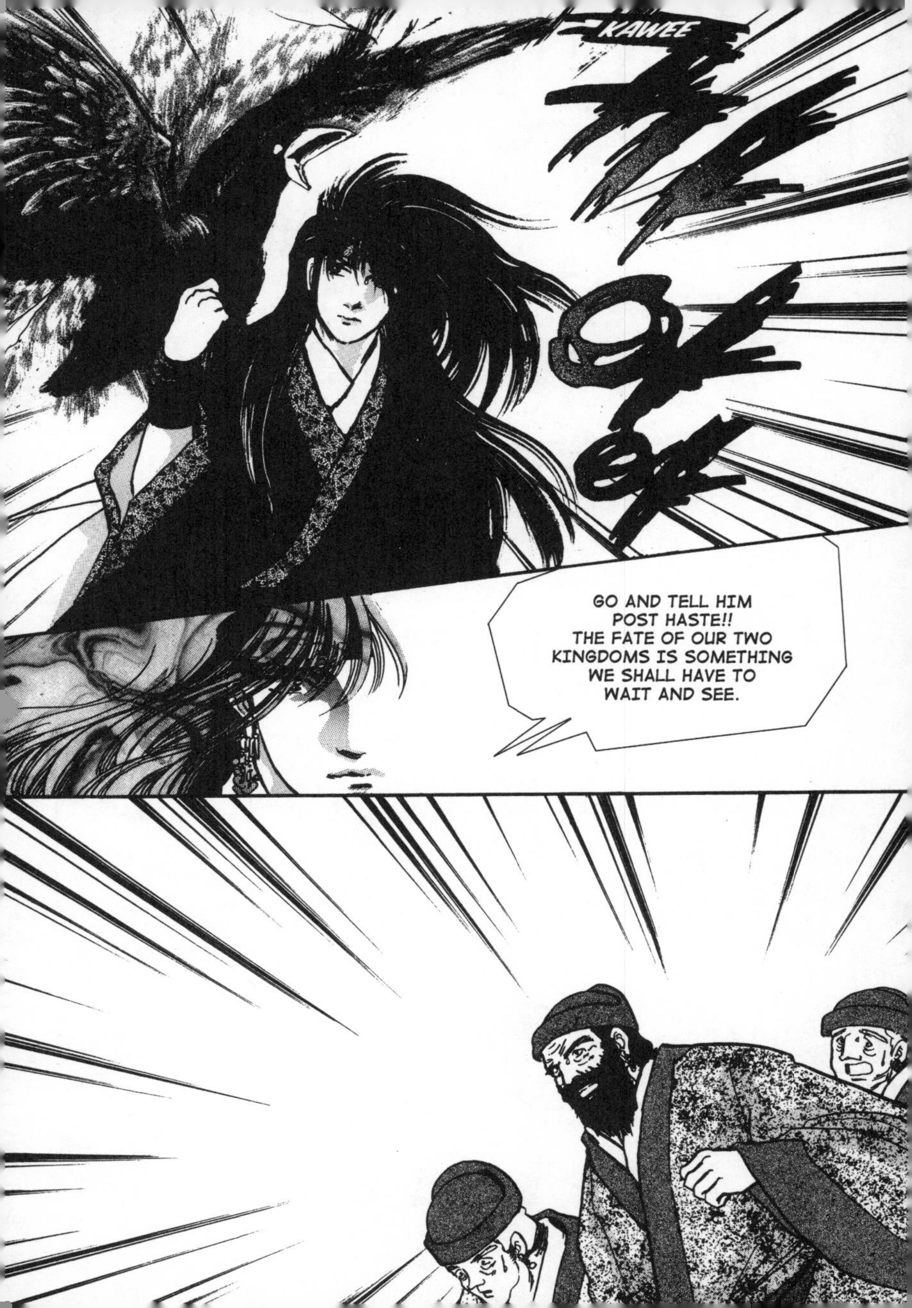
KAWEE
GO AND TELL HIM POST HASTE!! THE FATE OF OUR TWO KINGDOMS IS SOMETHING WE SHALL HAVE TO WAIT AND SEE.

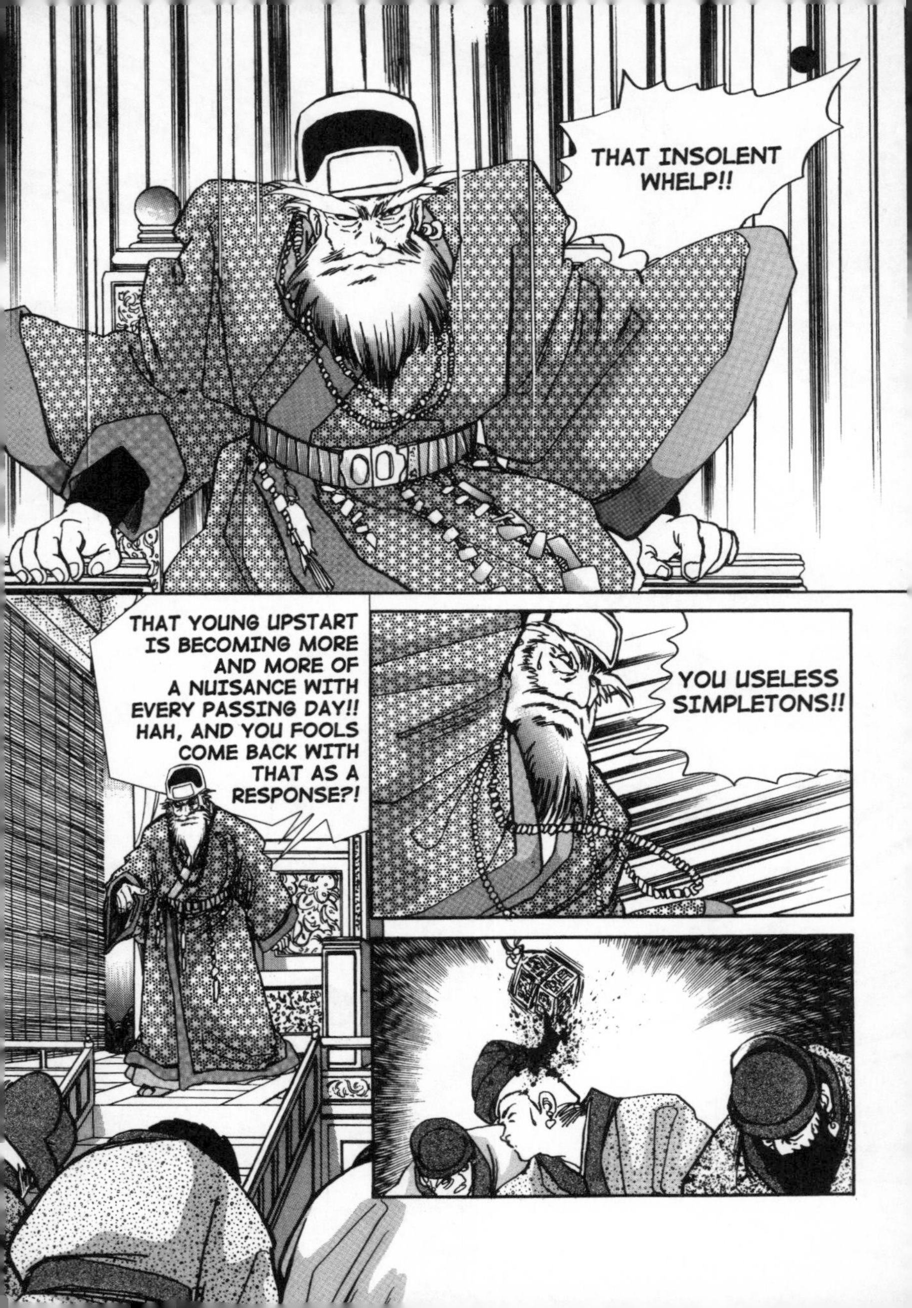
THAT INSOLENT WHELP!!
THAT YOUNG UPSTART IS BECOMING MORE AND MORE OF A NUISANCE WITH EVERY PASSING DAY!! HAH, AND YOU FOOLS COME BACK WITH THAT AS A RESPONSE?!
YOU USELESS SIMPLETONS!!

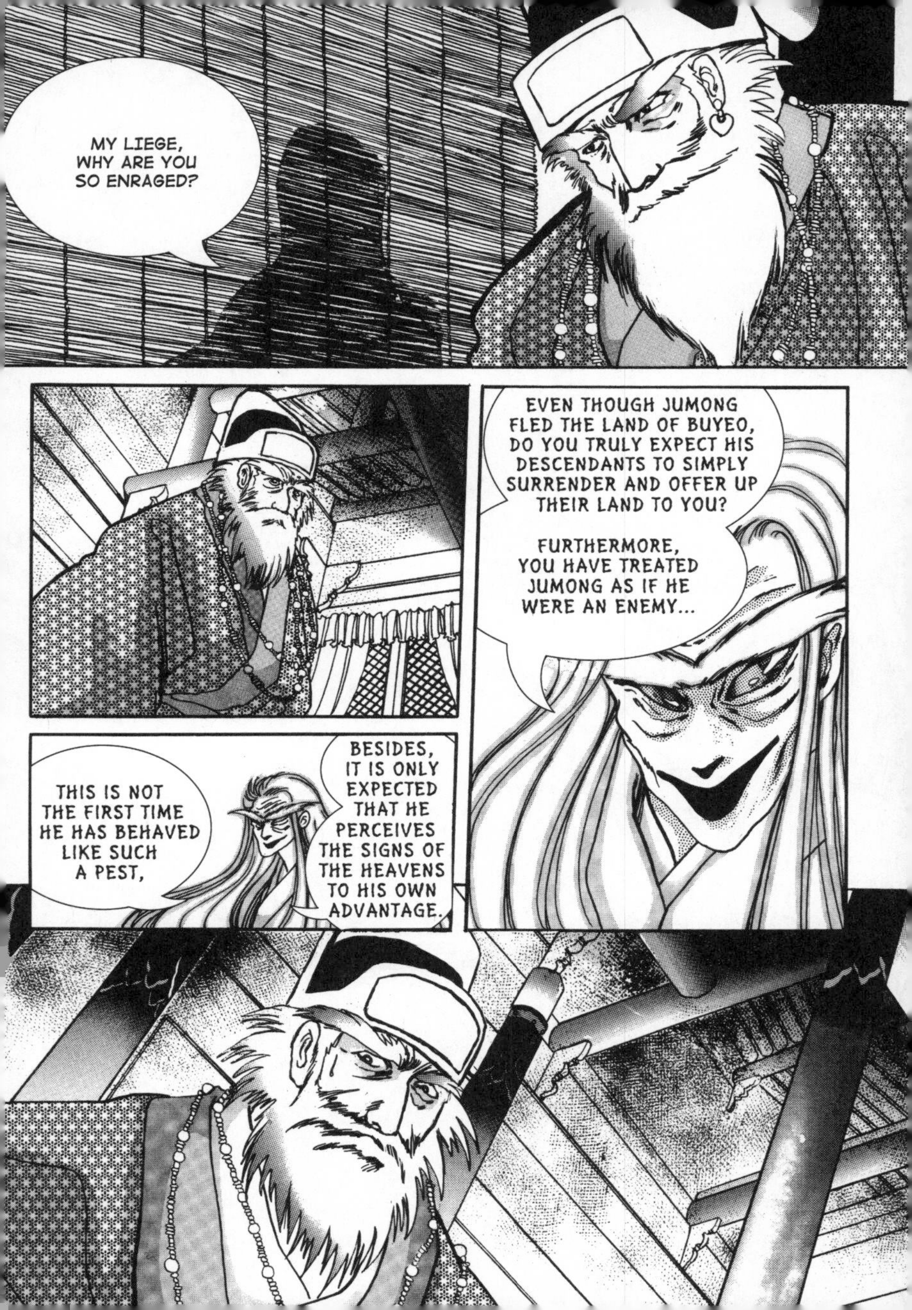
MY LIEGE, WHY ARE YOU SO ENRAGED?
EVEN THOUGH JUMONG FLED THE LAND OF BUYEO, DO YOU TRULY EXPECT HIS DESCENDANTS TO SIMPLY SURRENDER AND OFFER UP THEIR LAND TO YOU?
FURTHERMORE, YOU HAVE TREATED JUMONG AS IF HE WERE AN ENEMY...
THIS IS NOT THE FIRST TIME HE HAS BEHAVED LIKE SUCH A PEST,
BESIDES, IT IS ONLY EXPECTED THAT HE PERCEIVES THE SIGNS OF THE HEAVENS TO HIS OWN ADVANTAGE.

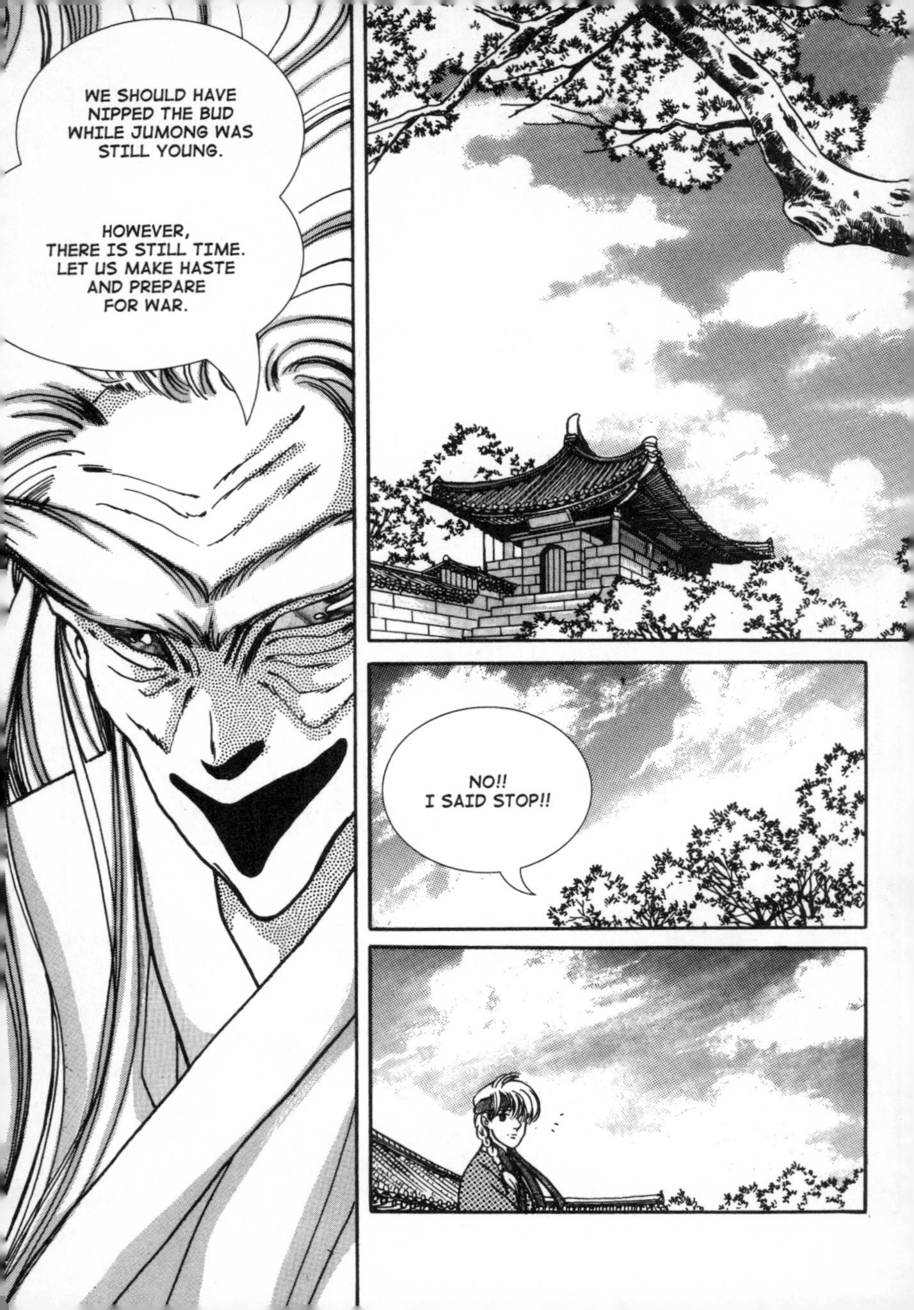
WE SHOULD HAVE NIPPED THE BUD WHILE JUMONG WAS STILL YOUNG.
HOWEVER, THERE IS STILL TIME. LET US MAKE HASTE AND PREPARE FOR WAR.
NO!! I SAID STOP!!

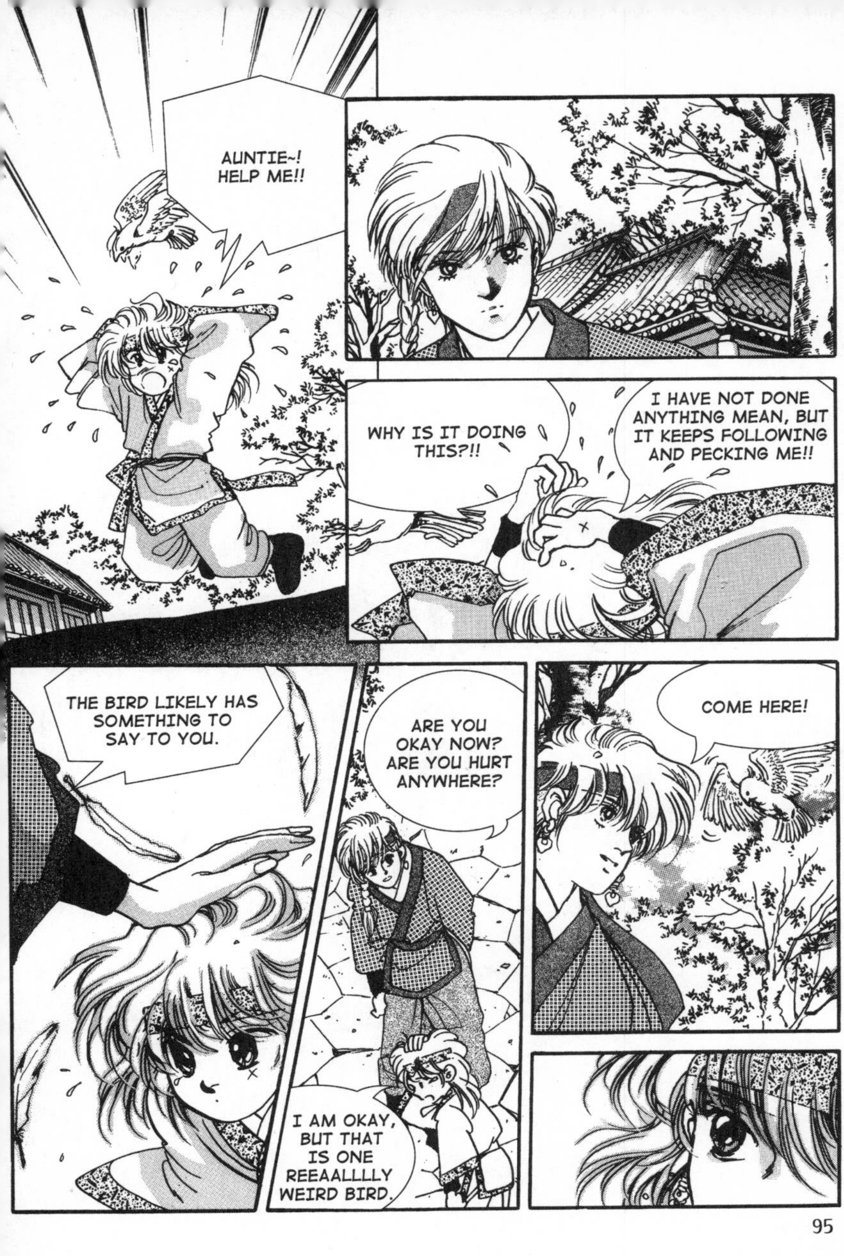
AUNTIE~! HELP ME!!
WHY IS IT DOING THIS?!!
I HAVE NOT DONE ANYTHING MEAN, BUT IT KEEPS FOLLOWING AND PECKING ME!!
THE BIRD LIKELY HAS SOMETHING TO SAY TO YOU.
ARE YOU OKAY NOW? ARE YOU HURT ANYWHERE?
I AM OKAY, BUT THAT IS ONE REEAALLLLY WEIRD BIRD.
COME HERE!

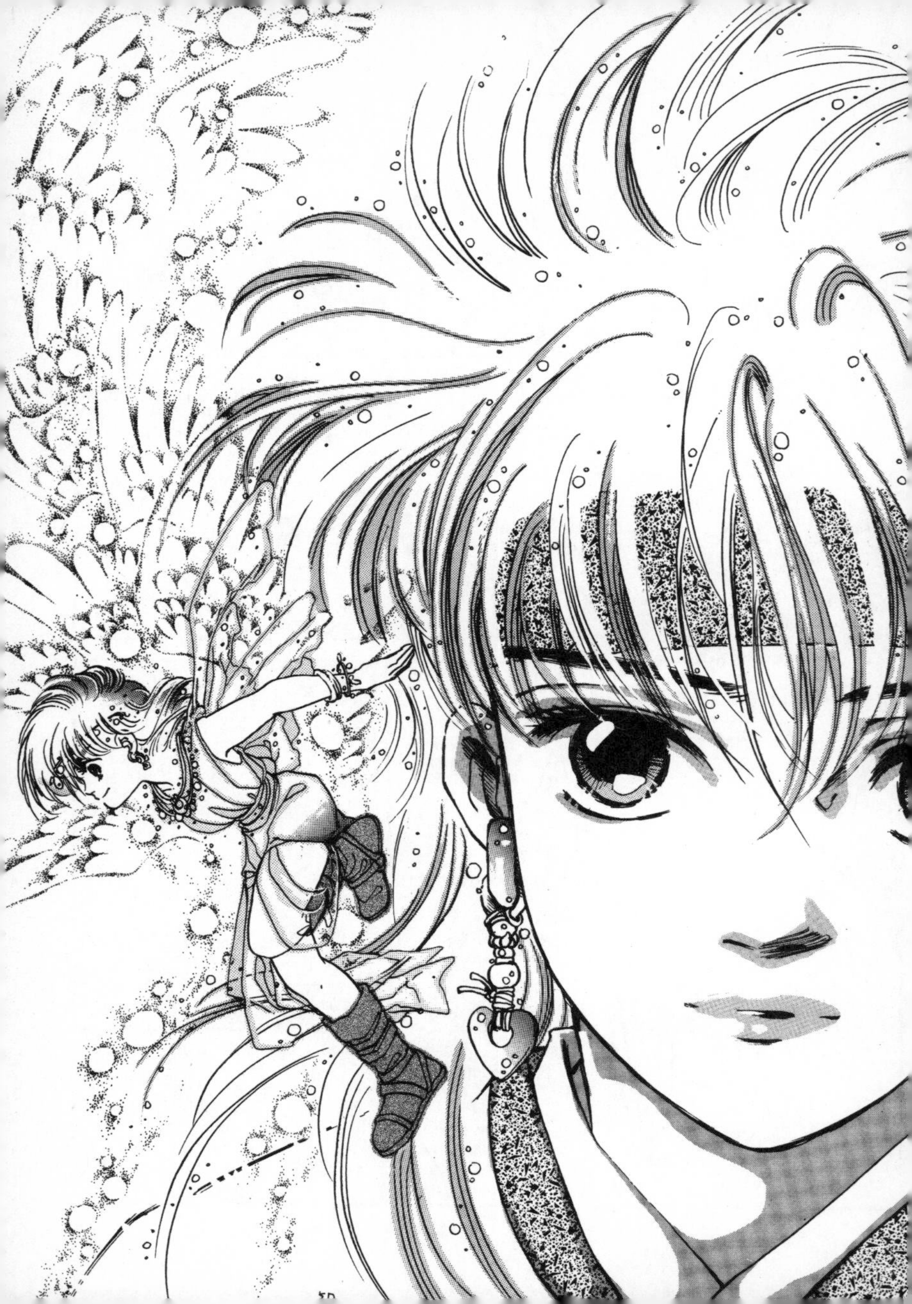

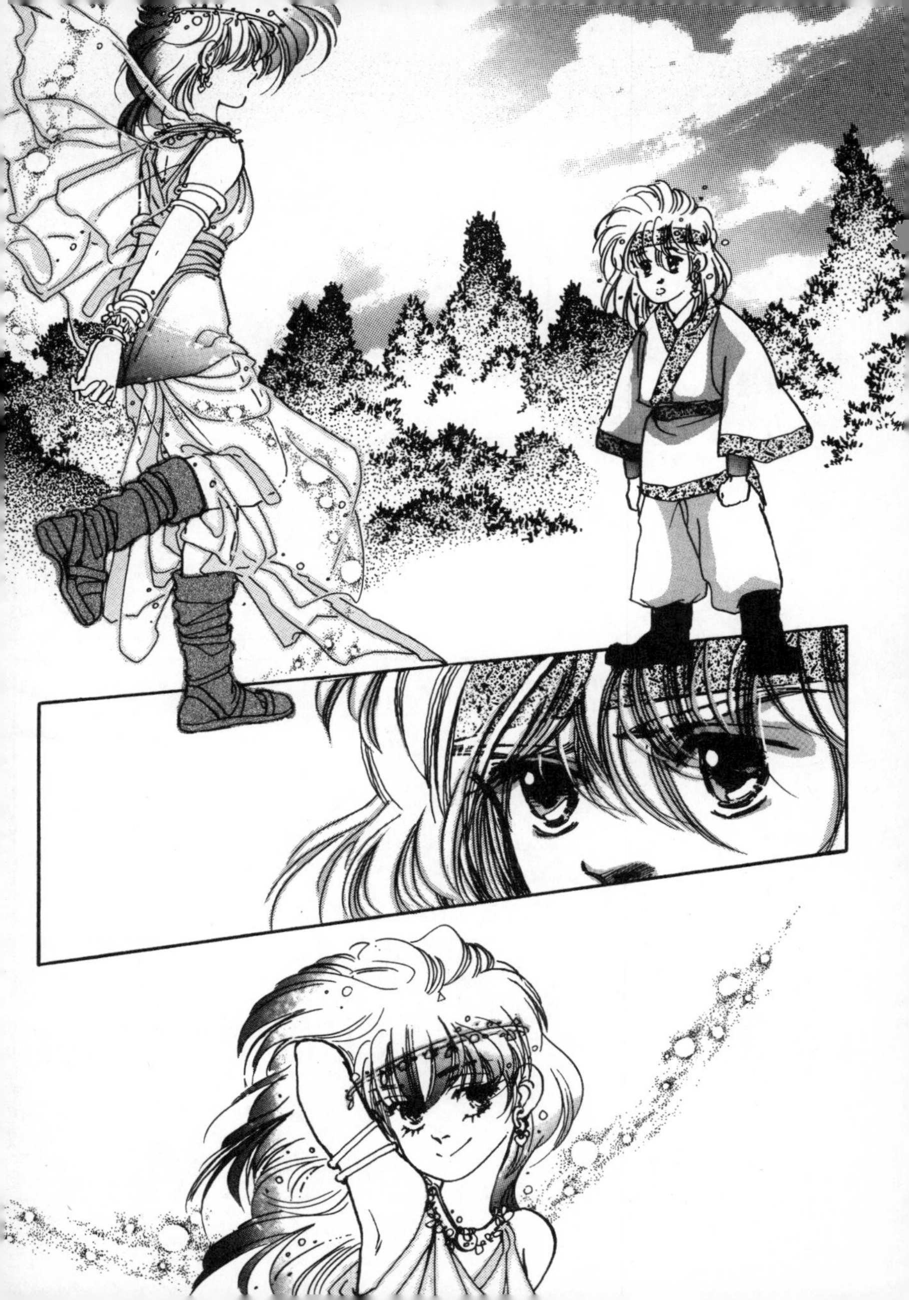

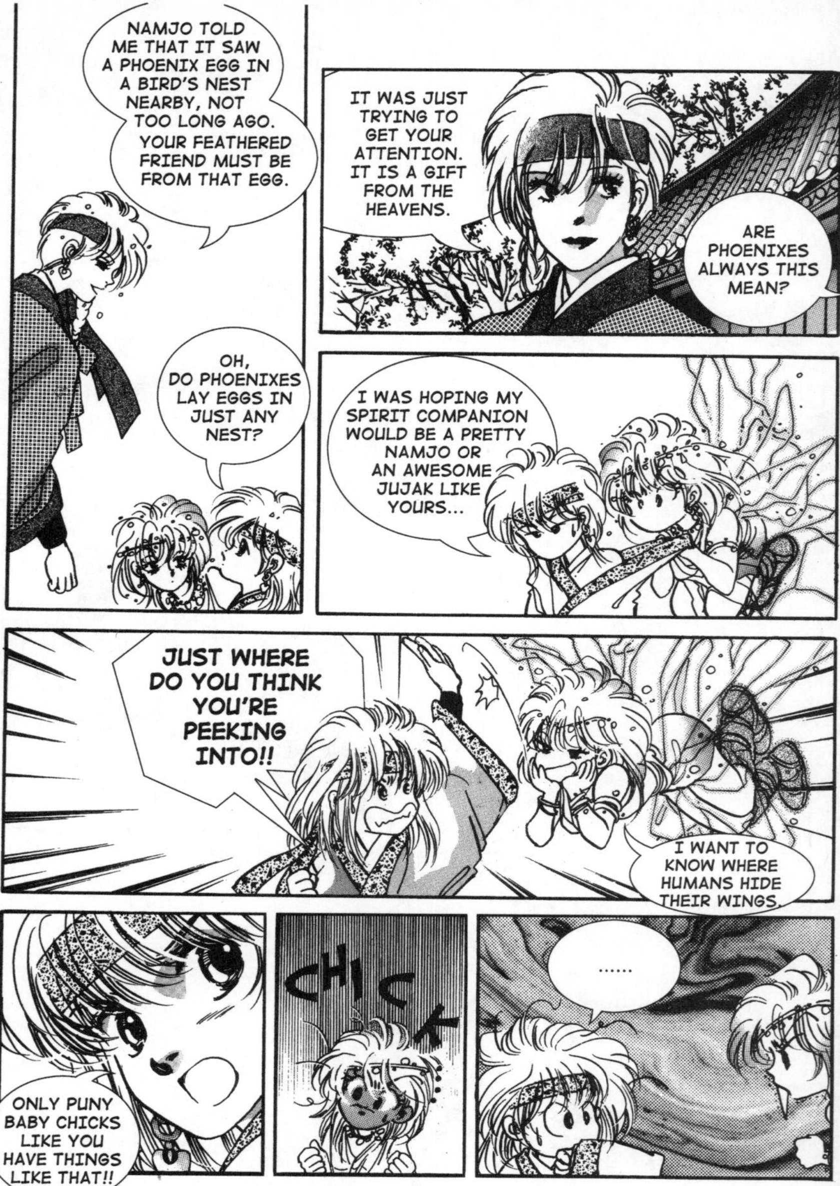
NAMJO TOLD ME THAT IT SAW A PHOENIX EGG IN A BIRD'S NEST NEARBY, NOT TOO LONG AGO. YOUR FEATHERED FRIEND MUST BE FROM THAT EGG.
IT WAS JUST TRYING TO GET YOUR ATTENTION. IT IS A GIFT FROM THE HEAVENS.
ARE PHOENIXES ALWAYS THIS MEAN?
OH, DO PHOENIXES LAY EGGS IN JUST ANY NEST?
I WAS HOPING MY SPIRIT COMPANION WOULD BE A PRETTY NAMJO OR AN AWESOME JUJAK LIKE YOURS...
JUST WHERE DO YOU THINK YOU'RE PEEKING INTO!!
I WANT TO KNOW WHERE HUMANS HIDE THEIR WINGS.
ONLY PUNY BABY CHICKS LIKE YOU HAVE THINGS LIKE THAT!!
CHICK
......

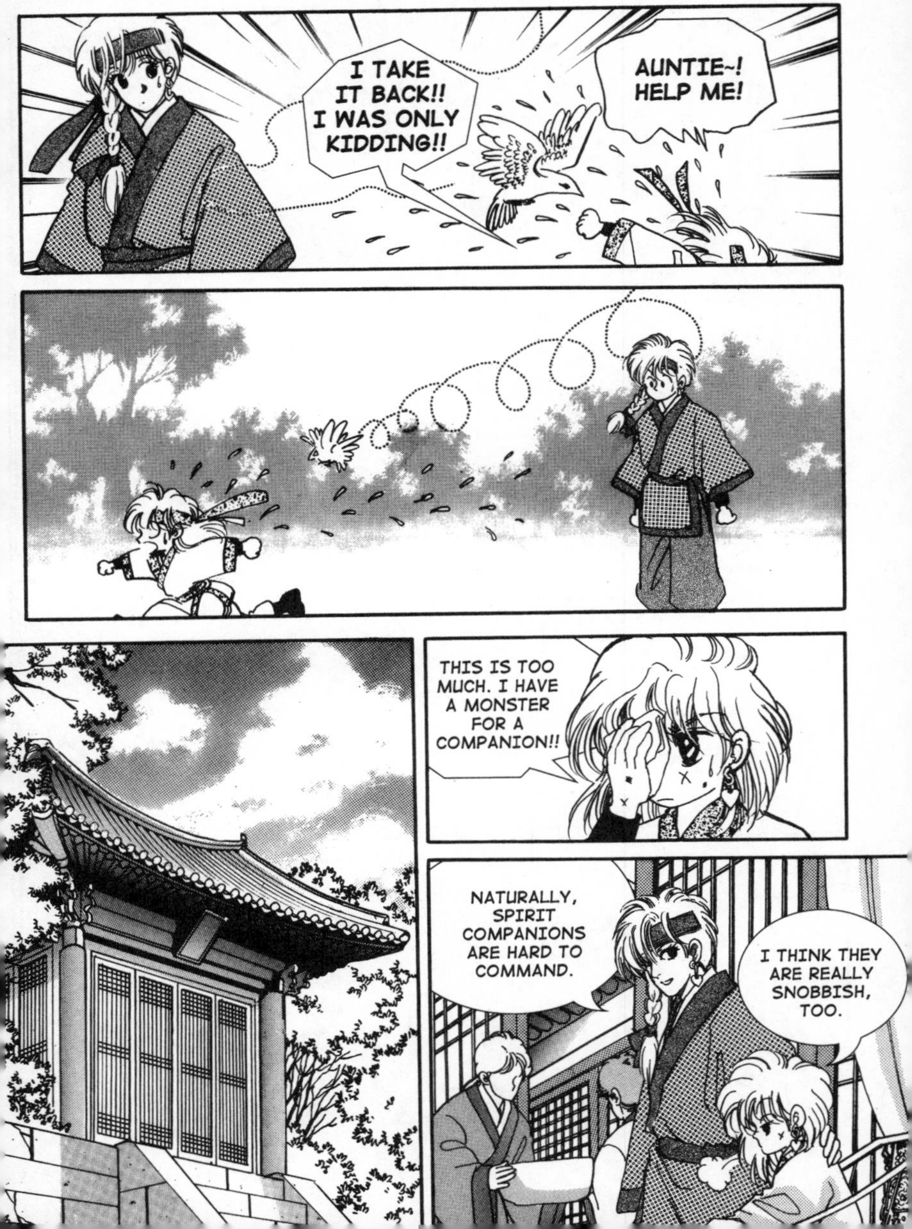
I TAKE IT BACK!! I WAS ONLY KIDDING!!
AUNTIE~! HELP ME!
THIS IS TOO MUCH. I HAVE A MONSTER FOR A COMPANION!!
NATURALLY, SPIRIT COMPANIONS ARE HARD TO COMMAND.
I THINK THEY ARE REALLY SNOBBISH, TOO.

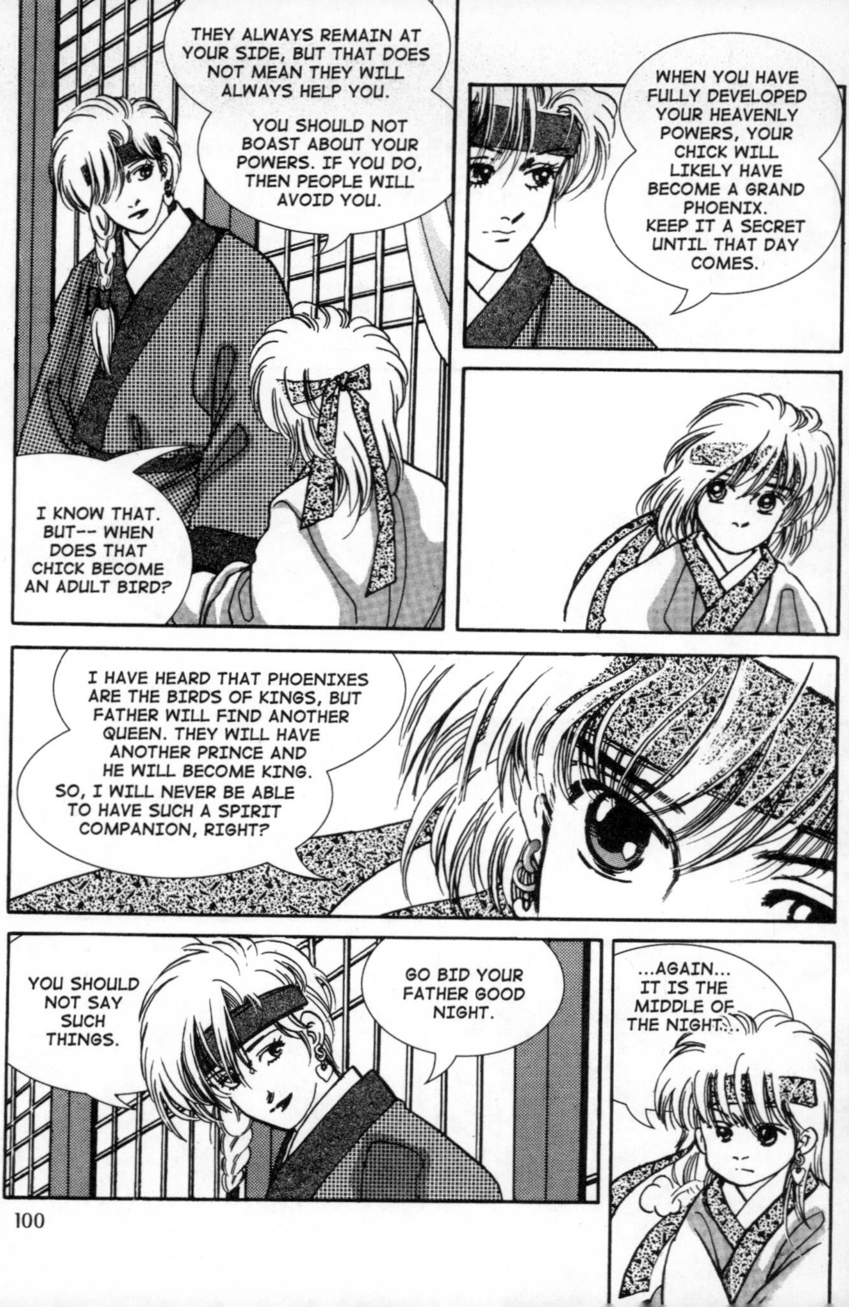
THEY ALWAYS REMAIN AT YOUR SIDE, BUT THAT DOES NOT MEAN THEY WILL ALWAYS HELP YOU.
YOU SHOULD NOT BOAST ABOUT YOUR POWERS. IF YOU DO, THEN PEOPLE WILL AVOID YOU.
I KNOW THAT. BUT-- WHEN DOES THAT CHICK BECOME AN ADULT BIRD?
WHEN YOU HAVE FULLY DEVELOPED YOUR HEAVENLY POWERS, YOUR CHICK WILL LIKELY HAVE BECOME A GRAND PHOENIX. KEEP IT A SECRET UNTIL THAT DAY COMES.
I HAVE HEARD THAT PHOENIXES ARE THE BIRDS OF KINGS, BUT FATHER WILL FIND ANOTHER QUEEN. THEY WILL HAVE ANOTHER PRINCE AND HE WILL BECOME KING. SO, I WILL NEVER BE ABLE TO HAVE SUCH A SPIRIT COMPANION, RIGHT?
YOU SHOULD NOT SAY SUCH THINGS.
GO BID YOUR FATHER GOOD NIGHT.
...AGAIN... IT IS THE MIDDLE OF THE NIGHT...

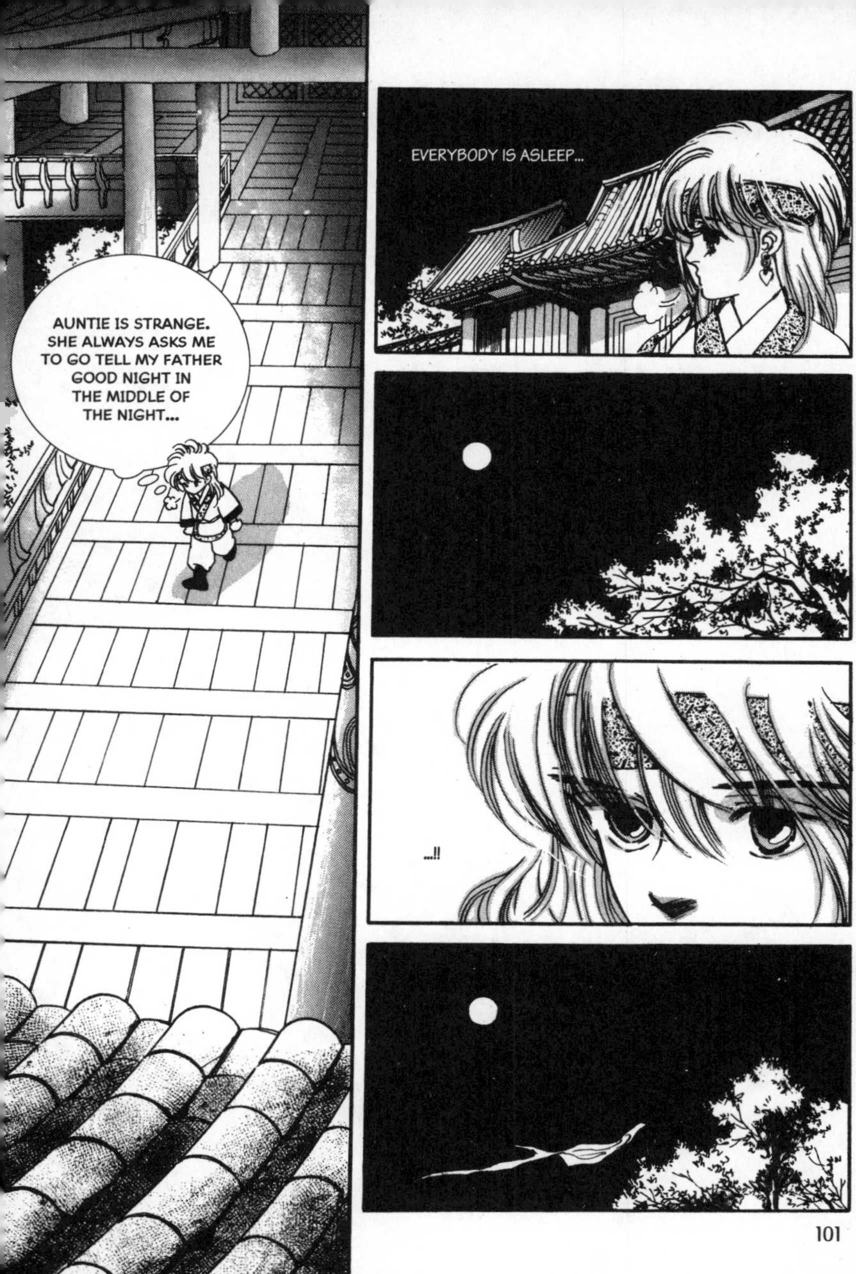
AUNTIE IS STRANGE. SHE ALWAYS ASKS ME TO GO TELL MY FATHER GOOD NIGHT IN THE MIDDLE OF THE NIGHT...
EVERYBODY IS ASLEEP...
...!!

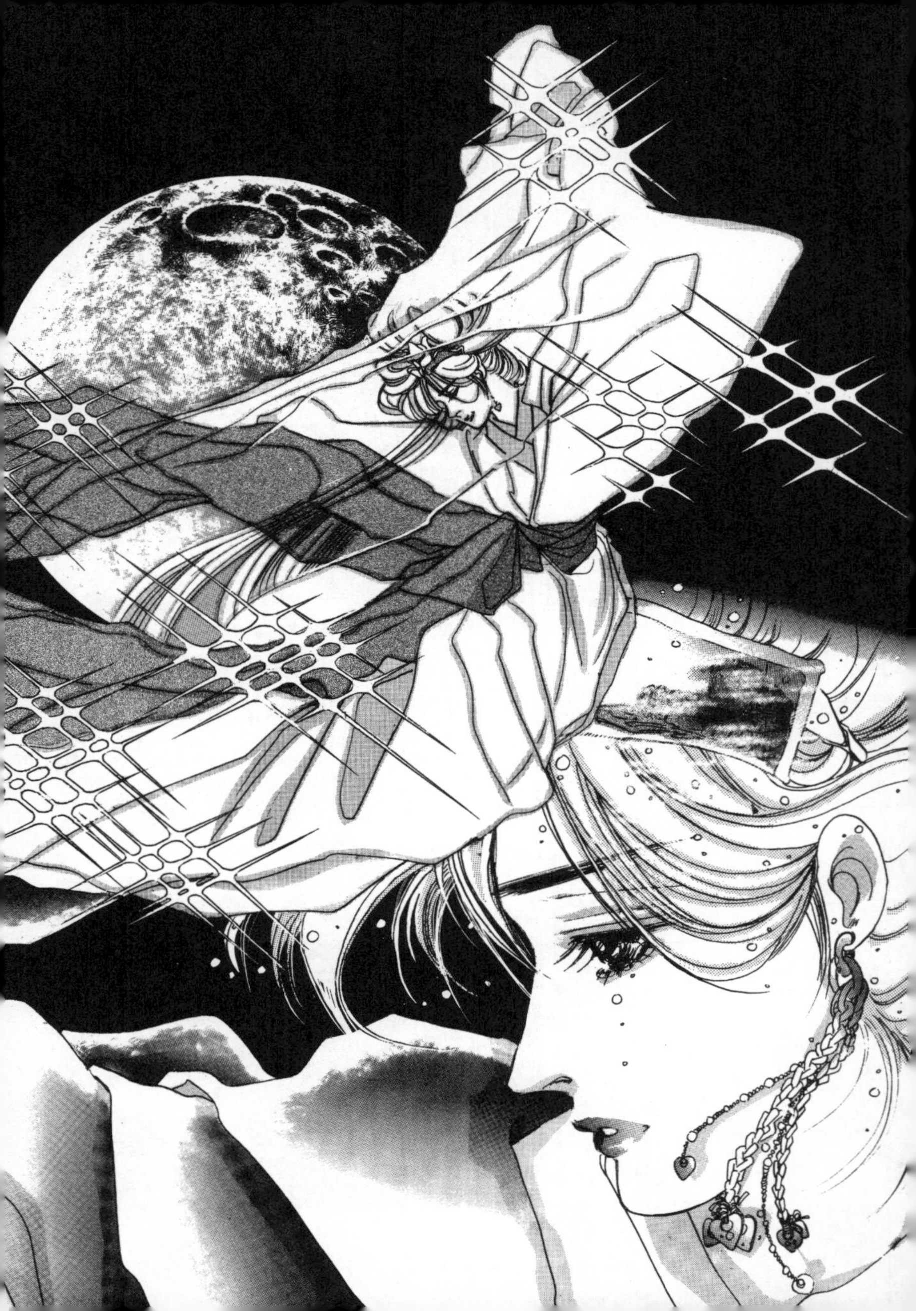

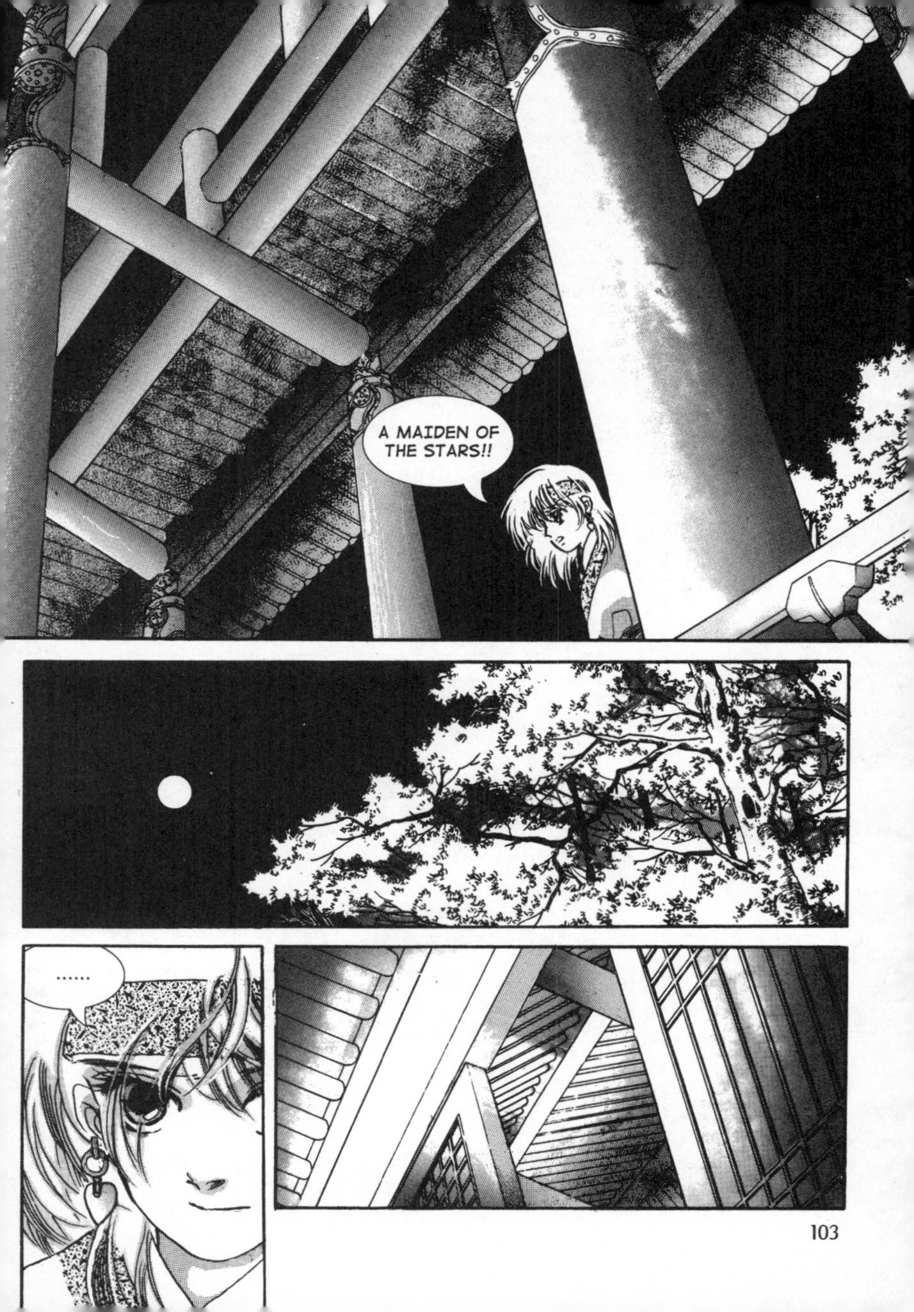
A MAIDEN OF THE STARS!!
......

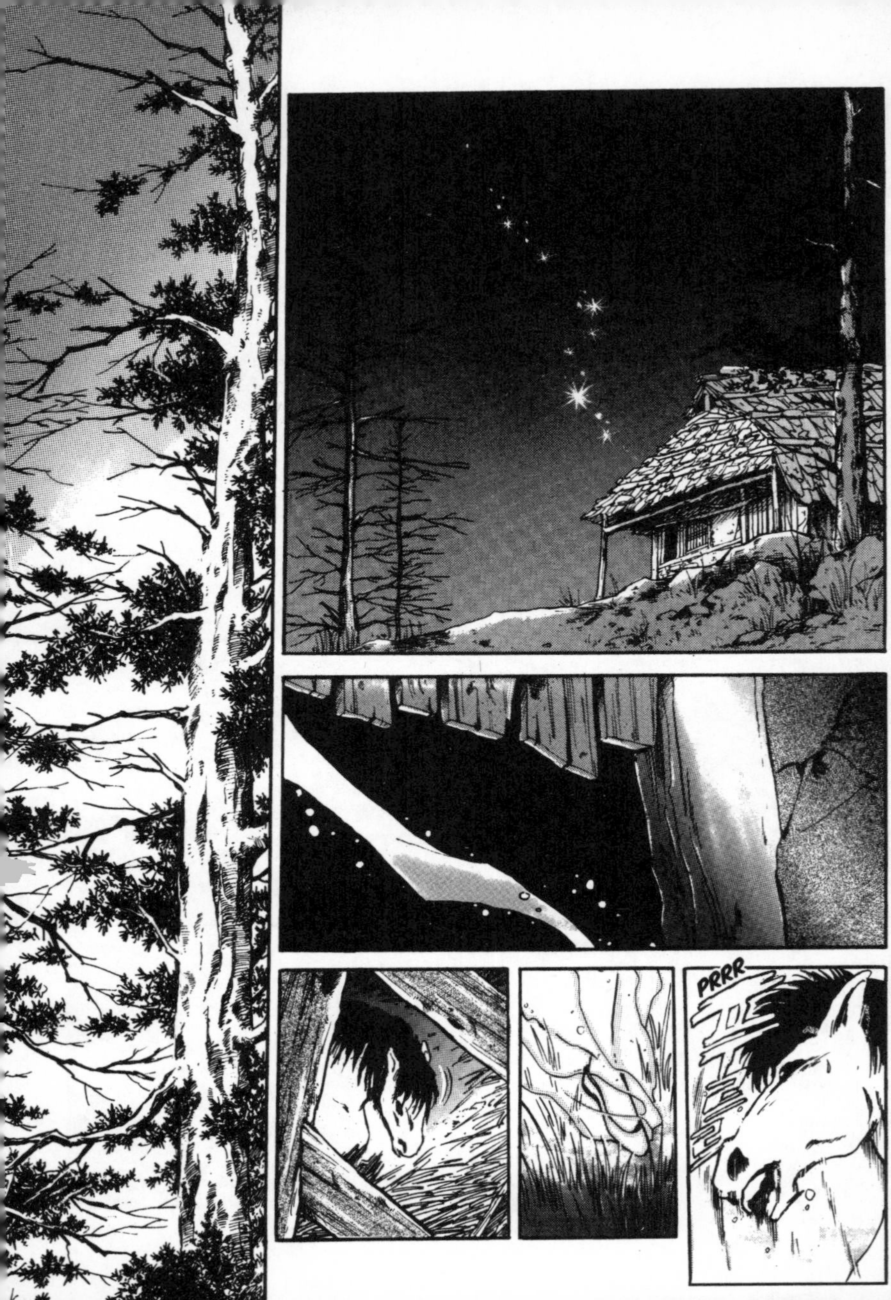
PRRR

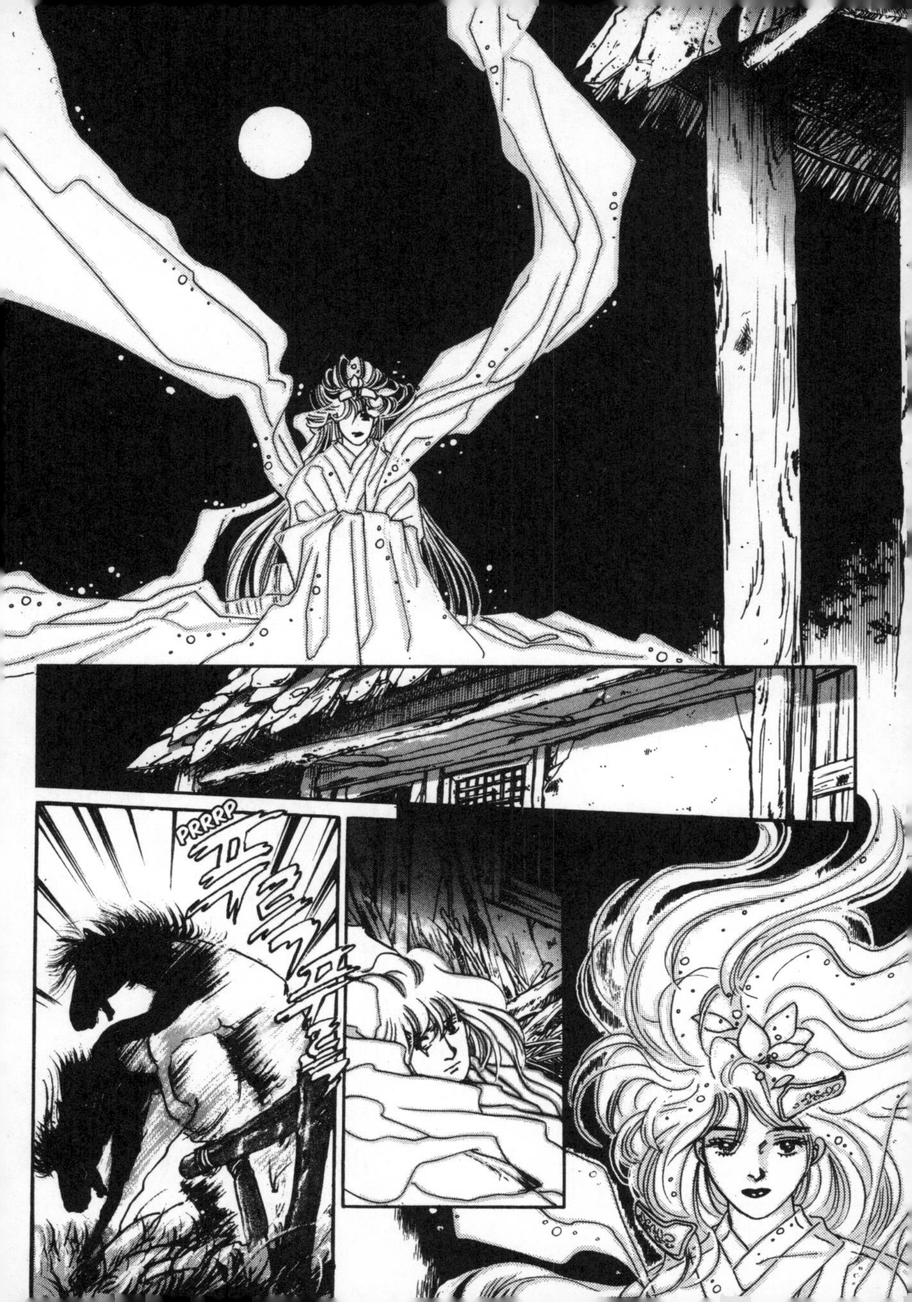
PRRRP

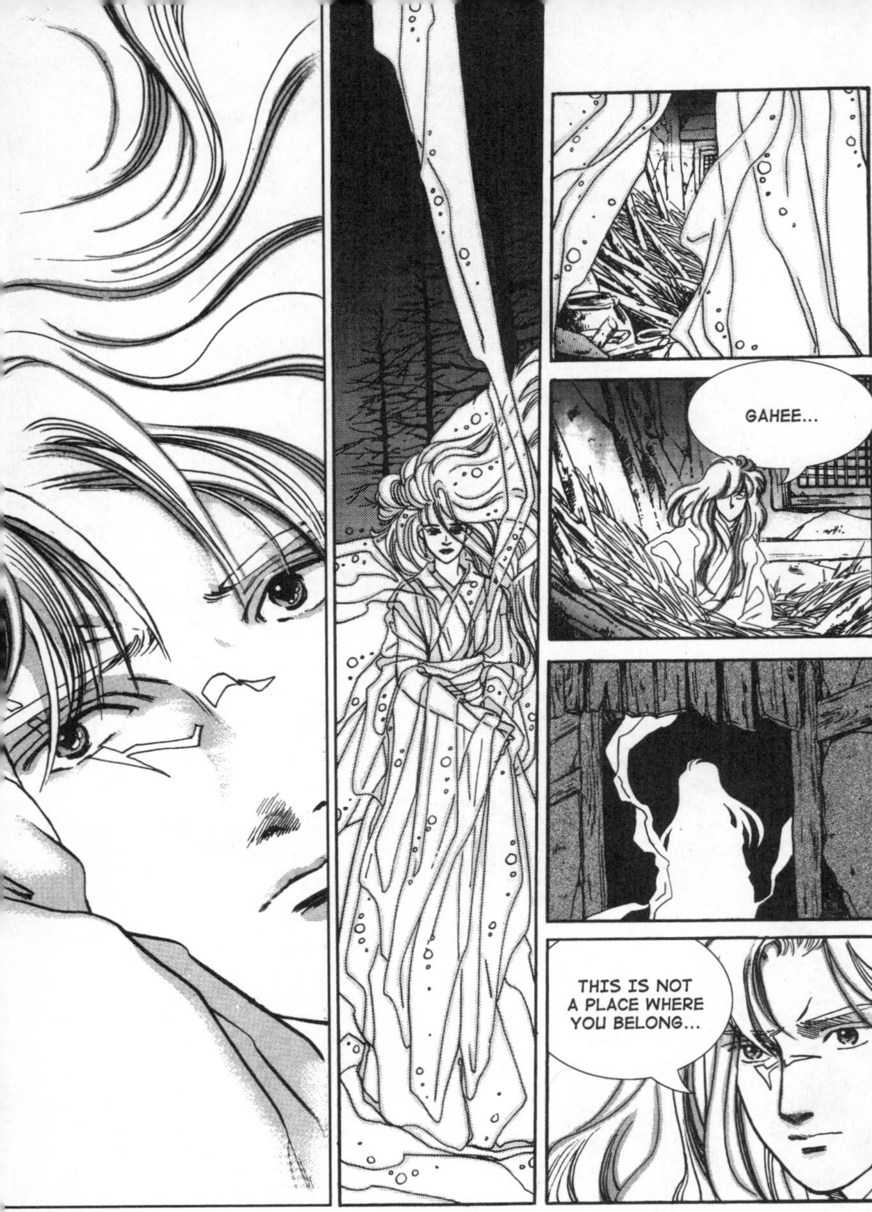
GAHEE...
THIS IS NOT A PLACE WHERE YOU BELONG...

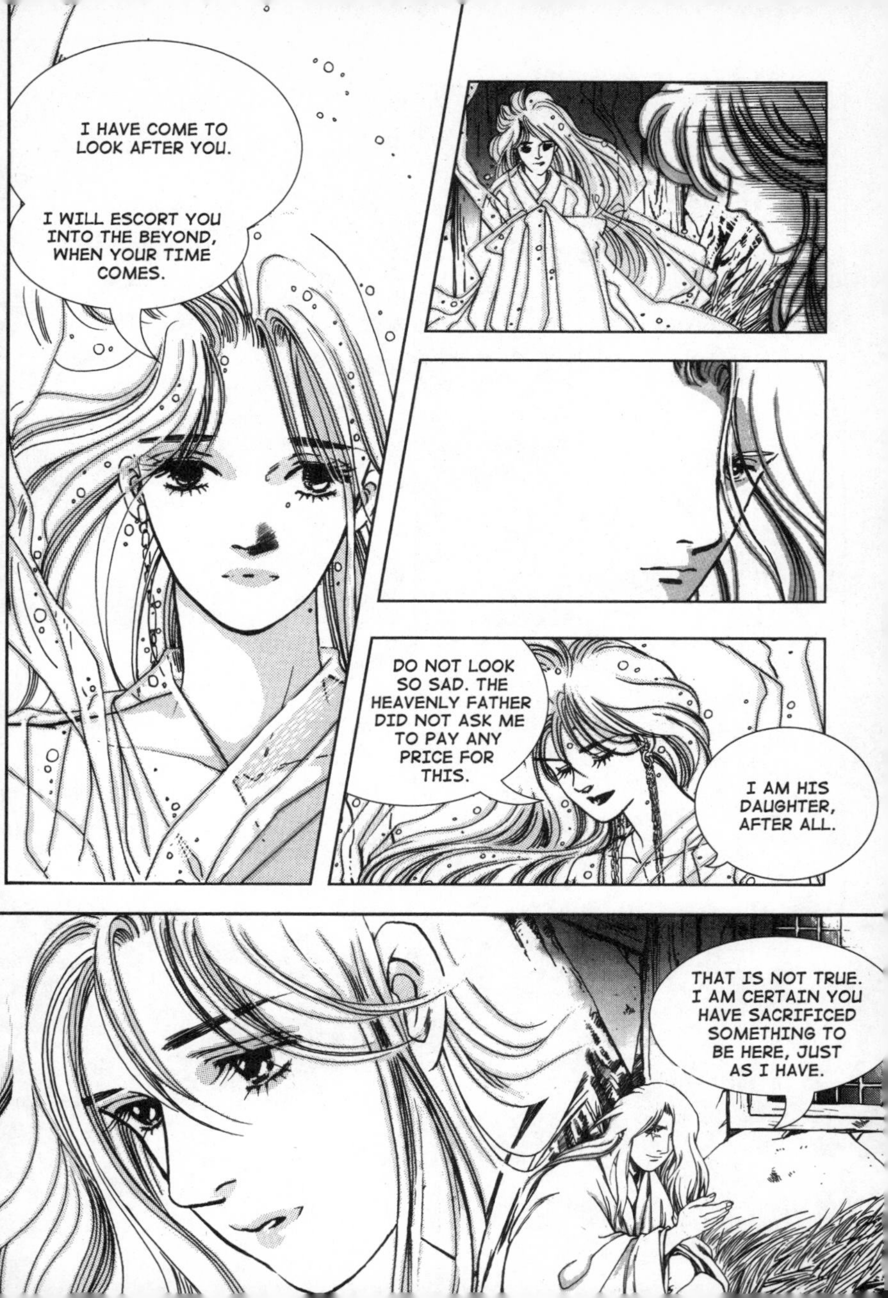
I HAVE COME TO LOOK AFTER YOU.
I WILL ESCORT YOU INTO THE BEYOND, WHEN YOUR TIME COMES.
DO NOT LOOK SO SAD. THE HEAVENLY FATHER DID NOT ASK ME TO PAY ANY PRICE FOR THIS.
I AM HIS DAUGHTER, AFTER ALL.
THAT IS NOT TRUE. I AM CERTAIN YOU HAVE SACRIFICED SOMETHING TO BE HERE, JUST AS I HAVE.

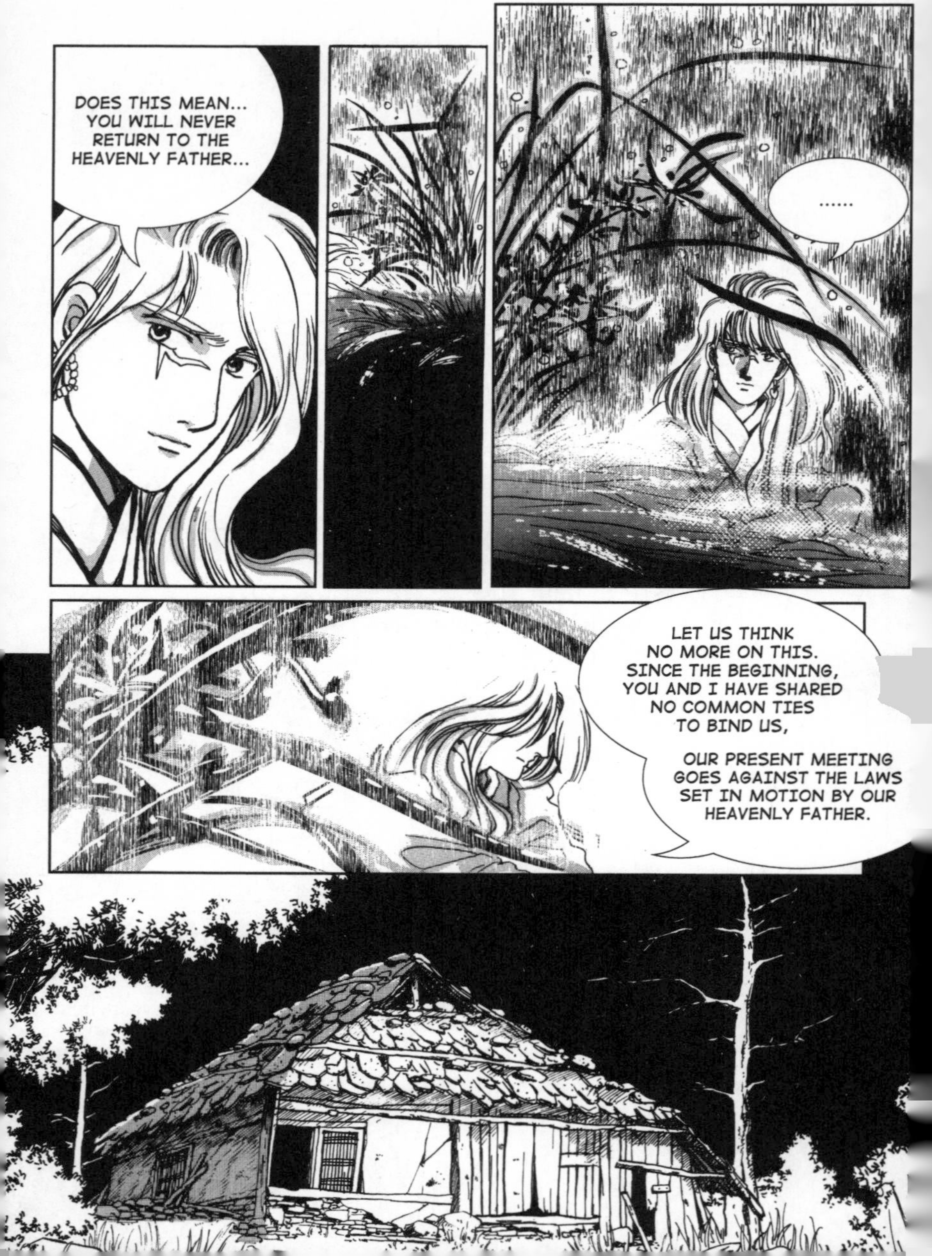
DOES THIS MEAN... YOU WILL NEVER RETURN TO THE HEAVENLY FATHER...
......
LET US THINK NO MORE ON THIS. SINCE THE BEGINNING, YOU AND I HAVE SHARED NO COMMON TIES TO BIND US,
OUR PRESENT MEETING GOES AGAINST THE LAWS SET IN MOTION BY OUR HEAVENLY FATHER.

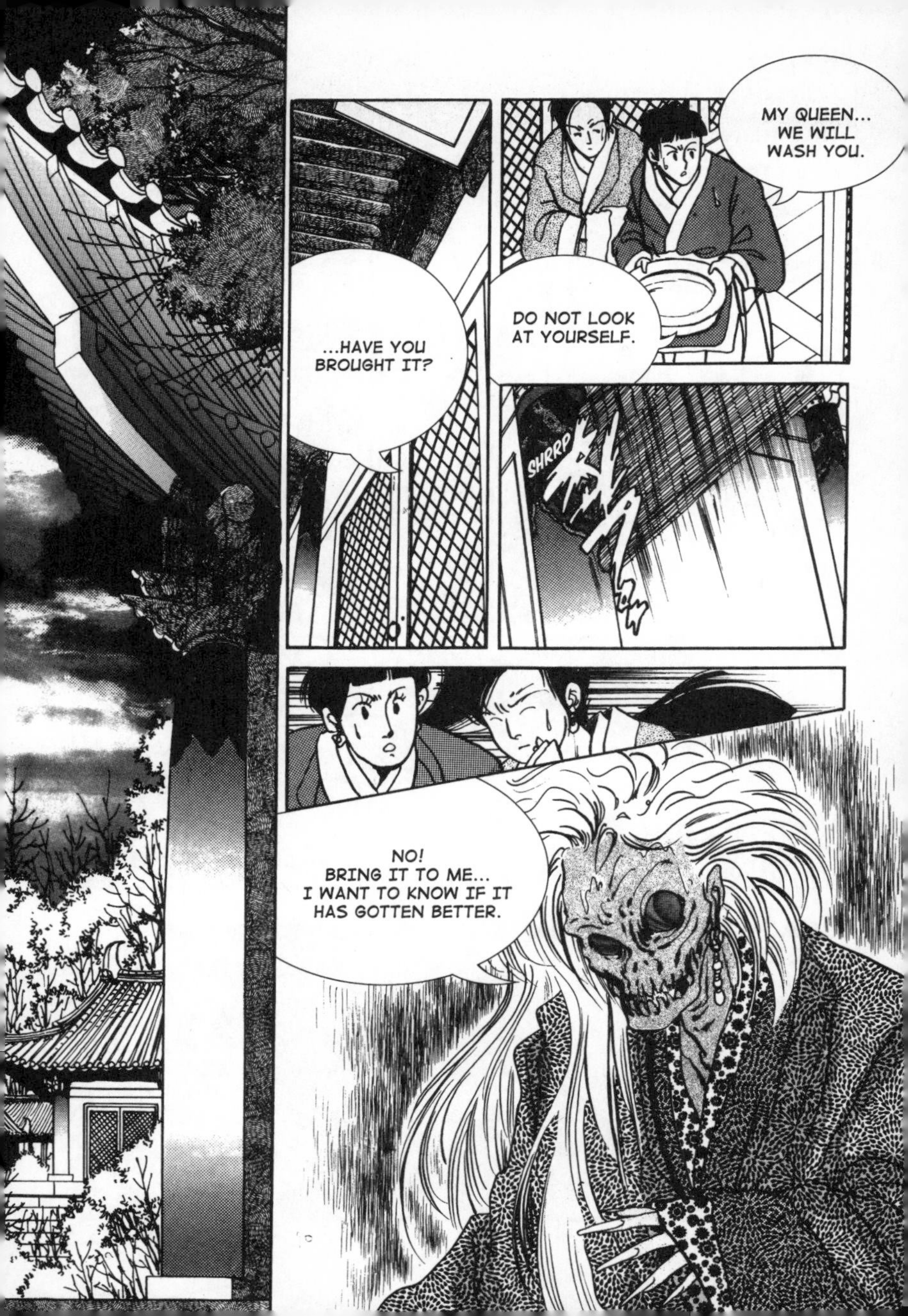
...HAVE YOU BROUGHT IT?
MY QUEEN... WE WILL WASH YOU.
DO NOT LOOK AT YOURSELF.
SHRRP
NO! BRING IT TO ME... I WANT TO KNOW IF IT HAS GOTTEN BETTER.

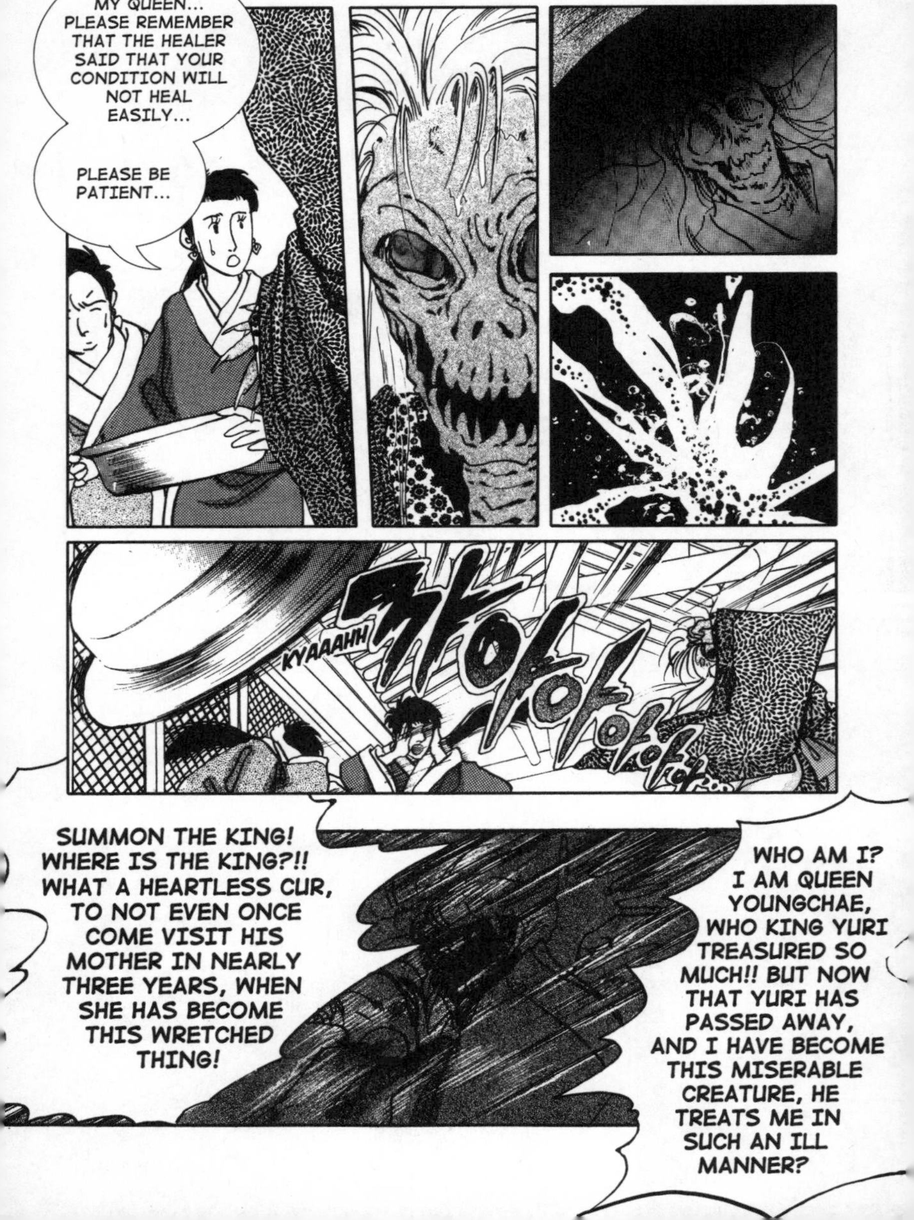
MY QUEEN... PLEASE REMEMBER THAT THE HEALER SAID THAT YOUR CONDITION WILL NOT HEAL EASILY...
PLEASE BE PATIENT...
KYAAAHH
SUMMON THE KING! WHERE IS THE KING?!! WHAT A HEARTLESS CUR, TO NOT EVEN ONCE COME VISIT HIS MOTHER IN NEARLY THREE YEARS, WHEN SHE HAS BECOME THIS WRETCHED THING!
WHO AM I? I AM QUEEN YOUNGCHAE, WHO KING YURI TREASURED SO MUCH!! BUT NOW THAT YURI HAS PASSED AWAY, AND I HAVE BECOME THIS MISERABLE CREATURE, HE TREATS ME IN SUCH AN ILL MANNER?

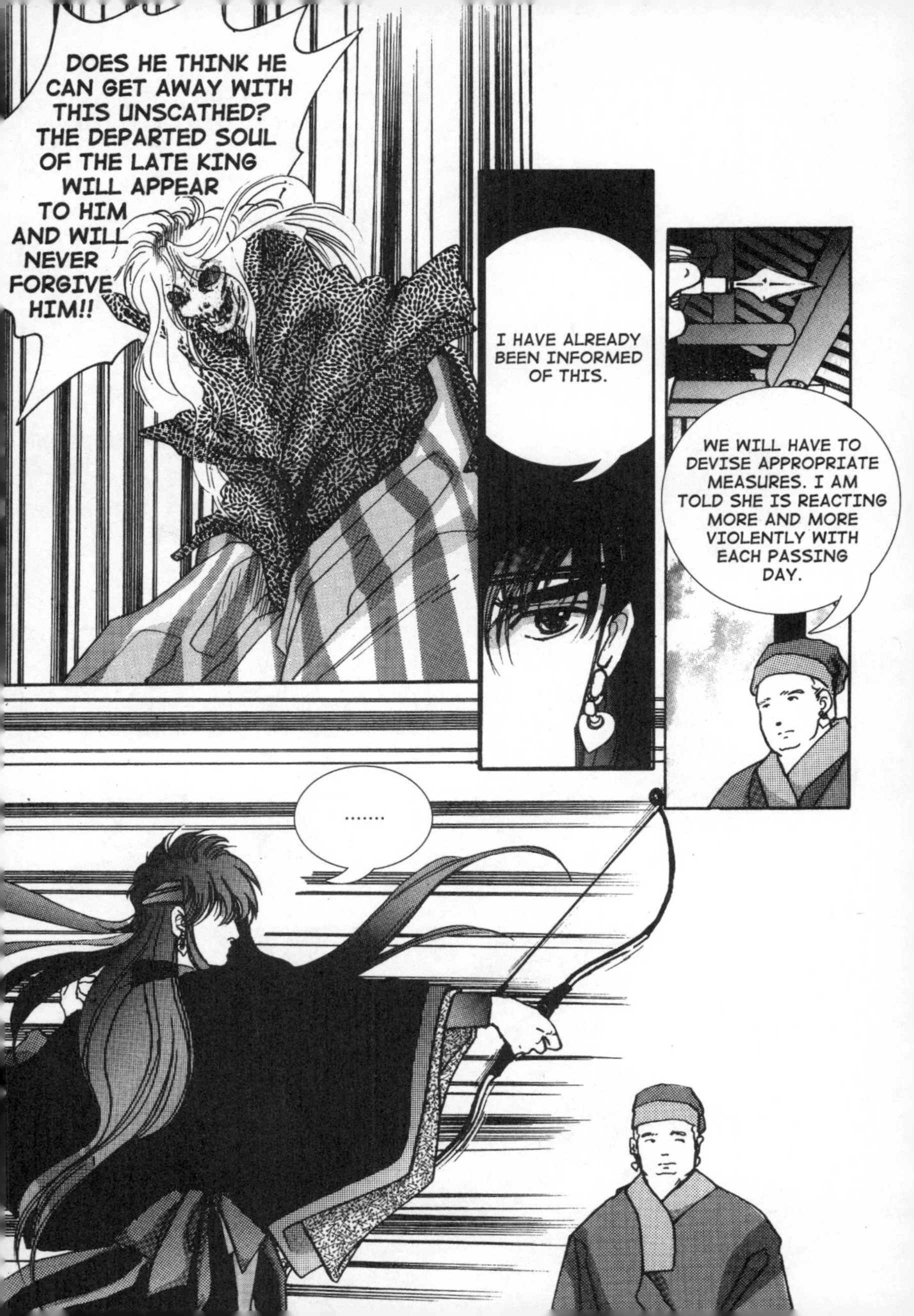
DOES HE THINK HE CAN GET AWAY WITH THIS UNSCATHED? THE DEPARTED SOUL OF THE LATE KING WILL APPEAR TO HIM AND WILL NEVER FORGIVE HIM!!
I HAVE ALREADY BEEN INFORMED OF THIS.
WE WILL HAVE TO DEVISE APPROPRIATE MEASURES. I AM TOLD SHE IS REACTING MORE AND MORE VIOLENTLY WITH EACH PASSING DAY.
....

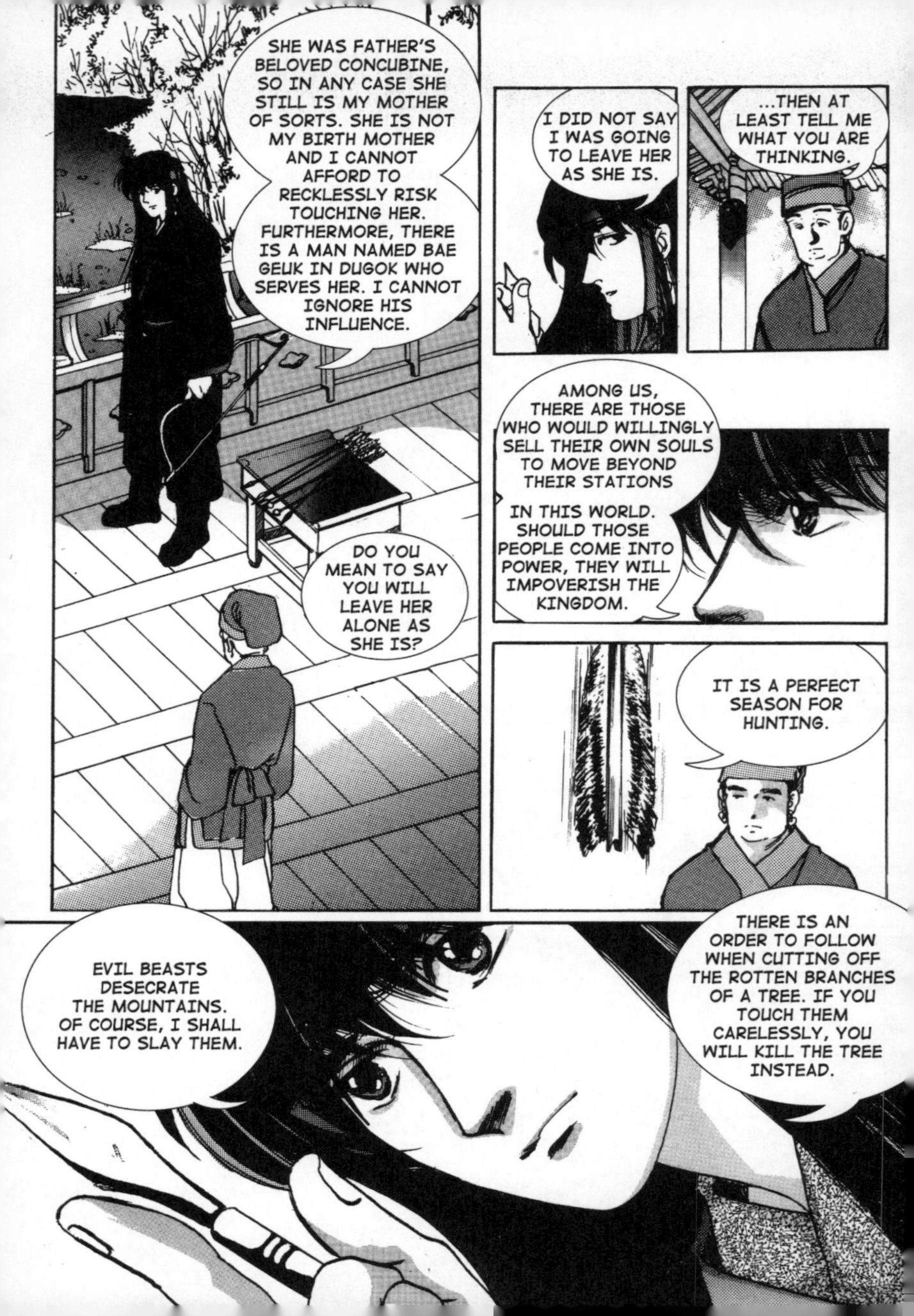
SHE WAS FATHER'S BELOVED CONCUBINE, SO IN ANY CASE SHE STILL IS MY MOTHER OF SORTS. SHE IS NOT MY BIRTH MOTHER AND I CANNOT AFFORD TO RECKLESSLY RISK TOUCHING HER. FURTHERMORE, THERE IS A MAN NAMED BAE GEUK IN DUGOK WHO SERVES HER. I CANNOT IGNORE HIS INFLUENCE.
DO YOU MEAN TO SAY YOU WILL LEAVE HER ALONE AS SHE IS?
I DID NOT SAY I WAS GOING TO LEAVE HER AS SHE IS.
...THEN AT LEAST TELL ME WHAT YOU ARE THINKING.
AMONG US, THERE ARE THOSE WHO WOULD WILLINGLY SELL THEIR OWN SOULS TO MOVE BEYOND THEIR STATIONS
IN THIS WORLD. SHOULD THOSE PEOPLE COME INTO POWER, THEY WILL IMPOVERISH THE KINGDOM.
IT IS A PERFECT SEASON FOR HUNTING.
EVIL BEASTS DESECRATE THE MOUNTAINS. OF COURSE, I SHALL HAVE TO SLAY THEM.
THERE IS AN ORDER TO FOLLOW WHEN CUTTING OFF THE ROTTEN BRANCHES OF A TREE. IF YOU TOUCH THEM CARELESSLY, YOU WILL KILL THE TREE INSTEAD.

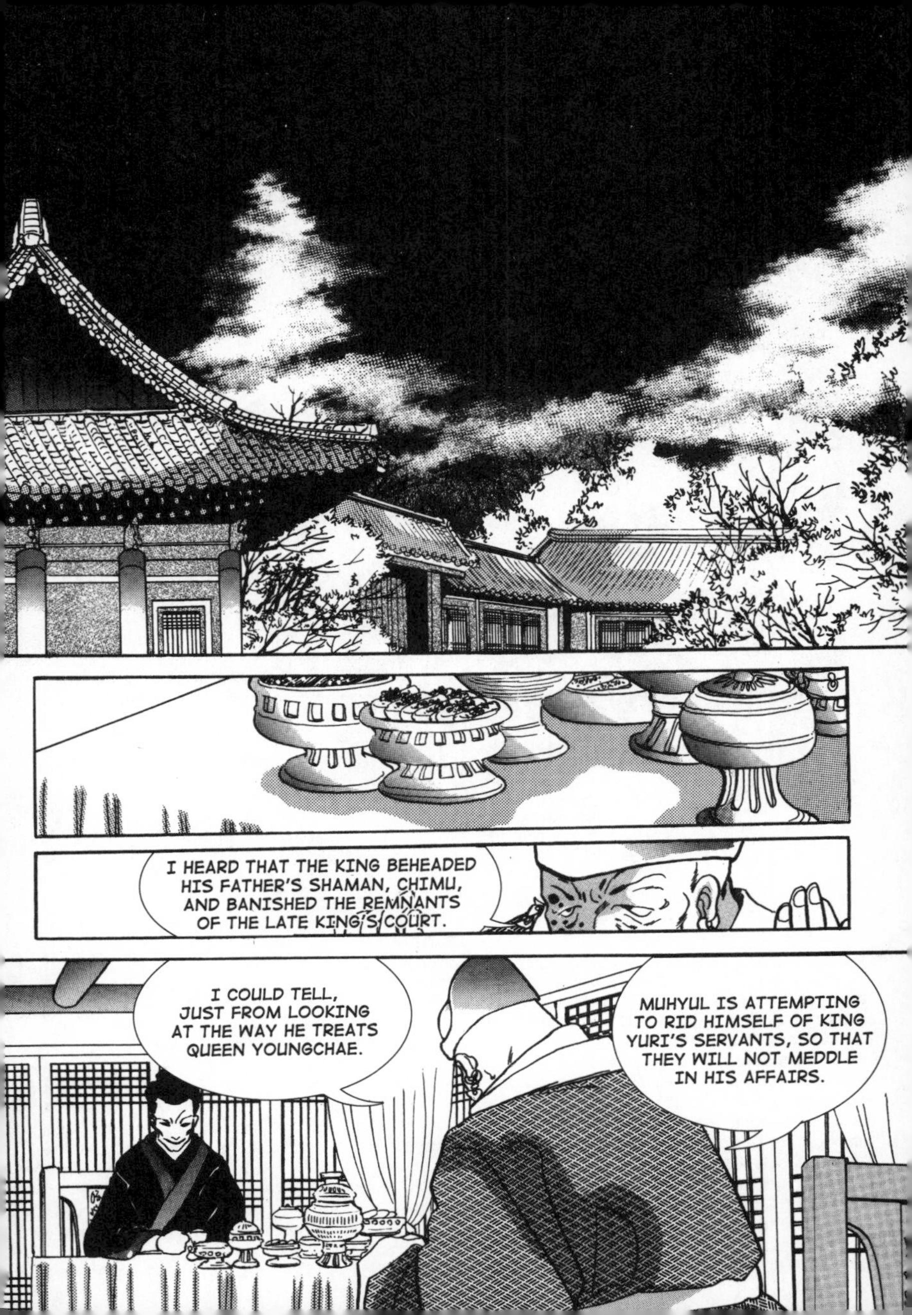
I HEARD THAT THE KING BEHEADED HIS FATHER'S SHAMAN, CHIMU, AND BANISHED THE REMNANTS OF THE LATE KING'S COURT.
I COULD TELL, JUST FROM LOOKING AT THE WAY HE TREATS QUEEN YOUNGCHAE.
MUHYUL IS ATTEMPTING TO RID HIMSELF OF KING YURI'S SERVANTS, SO THAT THEY WILL NOT MEDDLE IN HIS AFFAIRS.

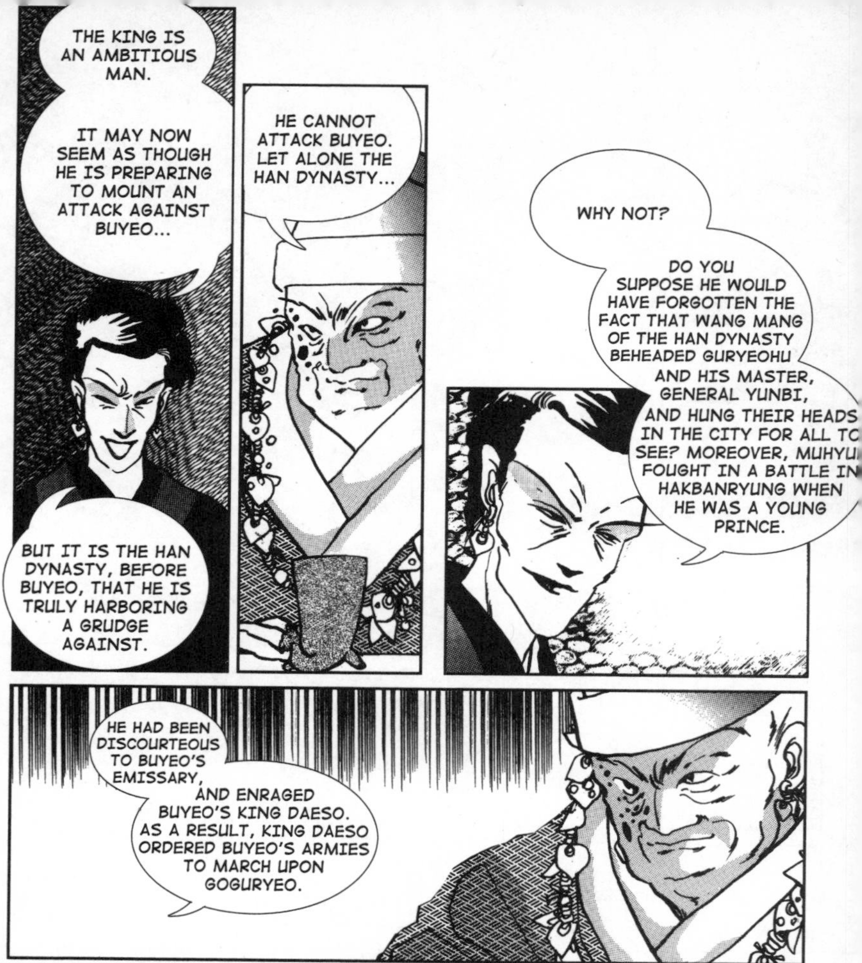
THE KING IS AN AMBITIOUS MAN.
IT MAY NOW SEEM AS THOUGH HE IS PREPARING TO MOUNT AN ATTACK AGAINST BUYEO...
BUT IT IS THE HAN DYNASTY, BEFORE BUYEO, THAT HE IS TRULY HARBORING A GRUDGE AGAINST.
HE CANNOT ATTACK BUYEO. LET ALONE THE HAN DYNASTY...
WHY NOT?
DO YOU SUPPOSE HE WOULD HAVE FORGOTTEN THE FACT THAT WANG MANG OF THE HAN DYNASTY BEHEADED GURYEOHU AND HIS MASTER, GENERAL YUNBI, AND HUNG THEIR HEADS IN THE CITY FOR ALL TO SEE? MOREOVER, MUHYU FOUGHT IN A BATTLE IN HAKBANRYUNG WHEN HE WAS A YOUNG PRINCE.
HE HAD BEEN DISCOURTEOUS TO BUYEO'S EMISSARY, AND ENRAGED BUYEO'S KING DAESO. AS A RESULT, KING DAESO ORDERED BUYEO'S ARMIES TO MARCH UPON GOGURYEO.

Notes: In the winter of King Yuri's 32nd year of reign, Buyeo invades Goguryeo. King Yuri commands his son Muhyul to go forth with Goguryeo's army to stop them.

Notes: In August of King Yuri's 28th year of reign, a messenger of Daeso visits Goguryeo and rebukes King Yuri by saying, "As a rule, there are large and small kingdoms. Likewise, there are young people and elders. It is a proper courtesy for the small to serve the large, and for the young to obey and serve the old." (Omitted). King Yuri opened his mouth to reply to Daeso's messenger, but the Crown Prince Muhyul, at his very young age, answers the messenger himself saying, "Our forefather was a descendant of a divine spirit. He was benevolent and virtuous with many talents. However, your great king Daeso envied my grandfather Jumong. Your king slandered him so that his father Geumwa would disgrace Jumong and make him a horse feeder. Daeso's jealousy is the reason my forefather felt uneasy and finally left Buyeo and headed south. Your great king does not concern himself with his past mistakes, but only with slights he perceives our kingdom is making against him. So, return to Buyeo and report to your great king that there is great peril for him here. If the great king makes no attempt to knock down our fledgling nation, I shall honor him as a great king. If he attempts to do so, I shall not honor him as any king.

- EXCERPT FROM SAMGUK SAGI, BOOK 1 OF GOGURYEO, CHAPTER: KING YURI, CHAPTER: KING DAEMUSHIN.

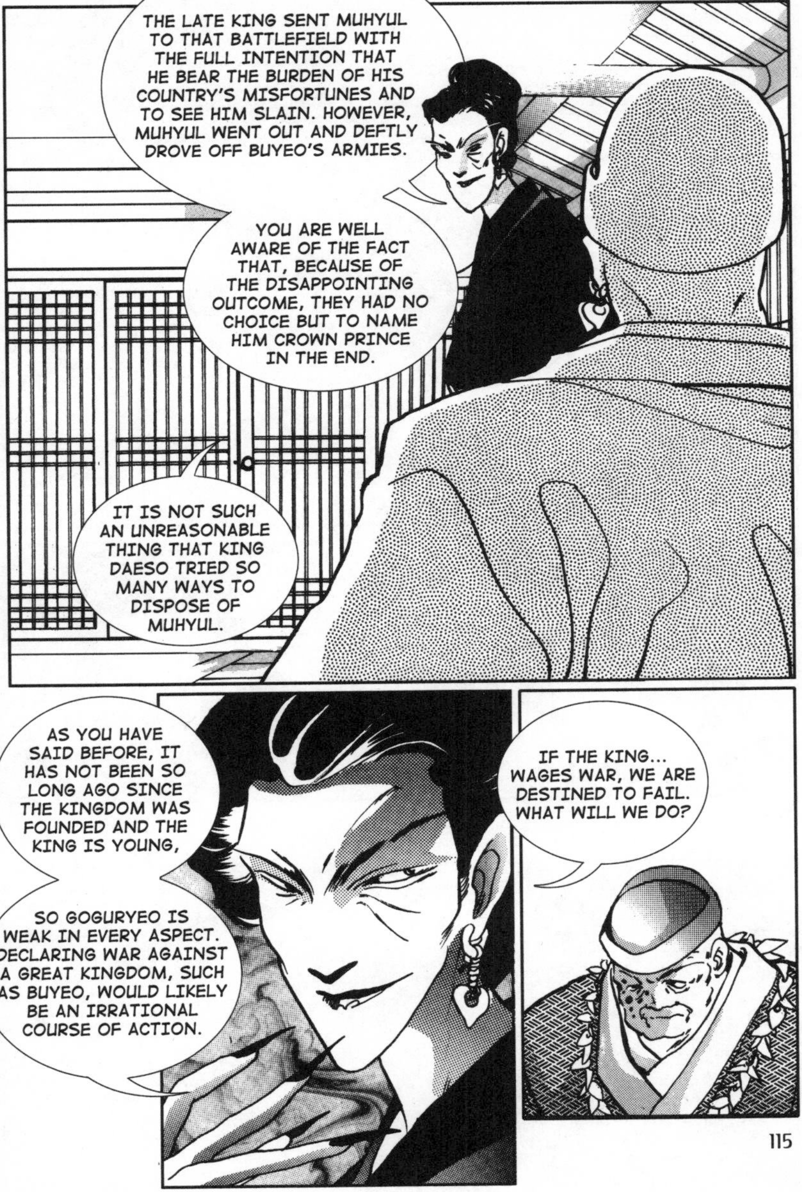
THE LATE KING SENT MUHYUL TO THAT BATTLEFIELD WITH THE FULL INTENTION THAT HE BEAR THE BURDEN OF HIS COUNTRY'S MISFORTUNES AND TO SEE HIM SLAIN. HOWEVER, MUHYUL WENT OUT AND DEFTLY DROVE OFF BUYEO'S ARMIES.
YOU ARE WELL AWARE OF THE FACT THAT, BECAUSE OF THE DISAPPOINTING OUTCOME, THEY HAD NO CHOICE BUT TO NAME HIM CROWN PRINCE IN THE END.
IT IS NOT SUCH AN UNREASONABLE THING THAT KING DAESO TRIED SO MANY WAYS TO DISPOSE OF MUHYUL.
AS YOU HAVE SAID BEFORE, IT HAS NOT BEEN SO LONG AGO SINCE THE KINGDOM WAS FOUNDED AND THE KING IS YOUNG,
SO GOGURYEO IS WEAK IN EVERY ASPECT. DECLARING WAR AGAINST A GREAT KINGDOM, SUCH AS BUYEO, WOULD LIKELY BE AN IRRATIONAL COURSE OF ACTION.
IF THE KING... WAGES WAR, WE ARE DESTINED TO FAIL. WHAT WILL WE DO?

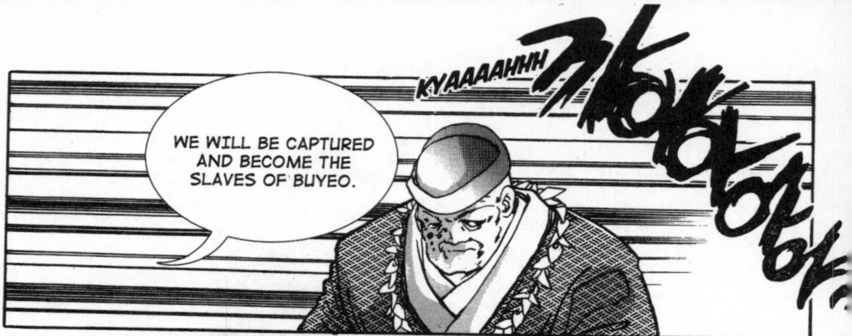
KYAAAAHHH
WE WILL BE CAPTURED AND BECOME THE SLAVES OF BUYEO.

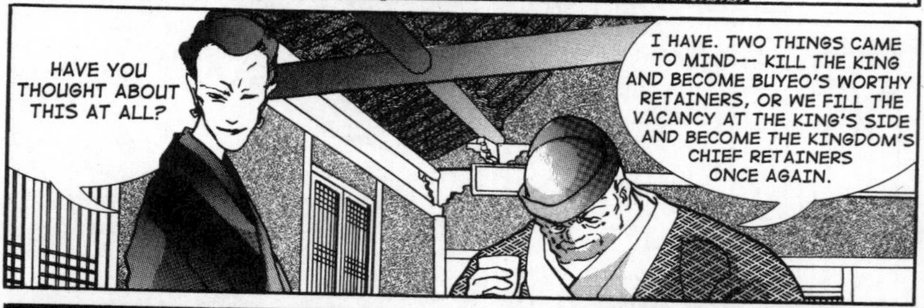
HAVE YOU THOUGHT ABOUT THIS AT ALL?
I HAVE. TWO THINGS CAME TO MIND-- KILL THE KING AND BECOME BUYEO'S WORTHY RETAINERS, OR WE FILL THE VACANCY AT THE KING'S SIDE AND BECOME THE KINGDOM'S CHIEF RETAINERS ONCE AGAIN.

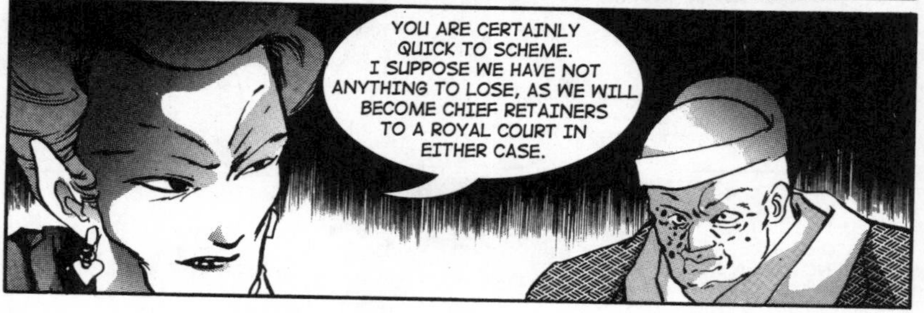
YOU ARE CERTAINLY QUICK TO SCHEME. I SUPPOSE WE HAVE NOT ANYTHING TO LOSE, AS WE WILL BECOME CHIEF RETAINERS TO A ROYAL COURT IN EITHER CASE.

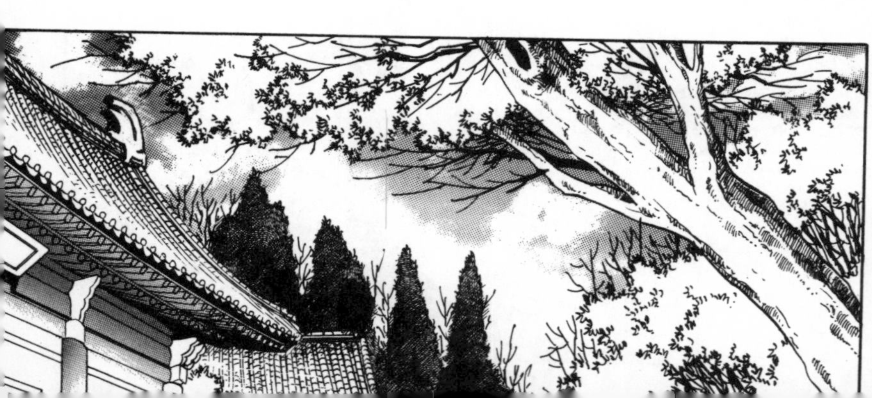

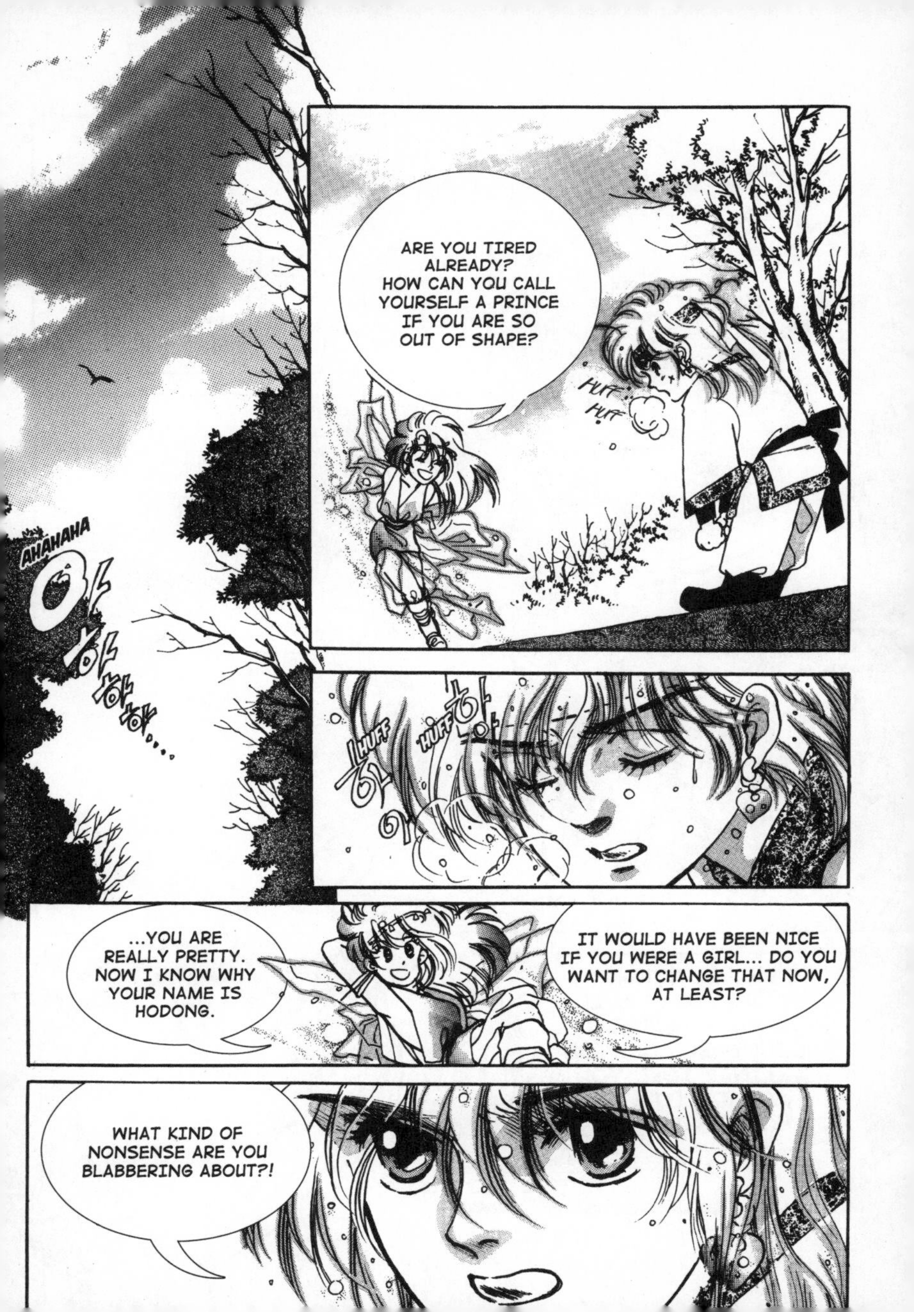
AHAHAHA
아하하하...
ARE YOU TIRED ALREADY? HOW CAN YOU CALL YOURSELF A PRINCE IF YOU ARE SO OUT OF SHAPE?
HUFF HUFF
HUFF HUFF
...YOU ARE REALLY PRETTY. NOW I KNOW WHY YOUR NAME IS HODONG.
IT WOULD HAVE BEEN NICE IF YOU WERE A GIRL... DO YOU WANT TO CHANGE THAT NOW, AT LEAST?
WHAT KIND OF NONSENSE ARE YOU BLABBERING ABOUT?!

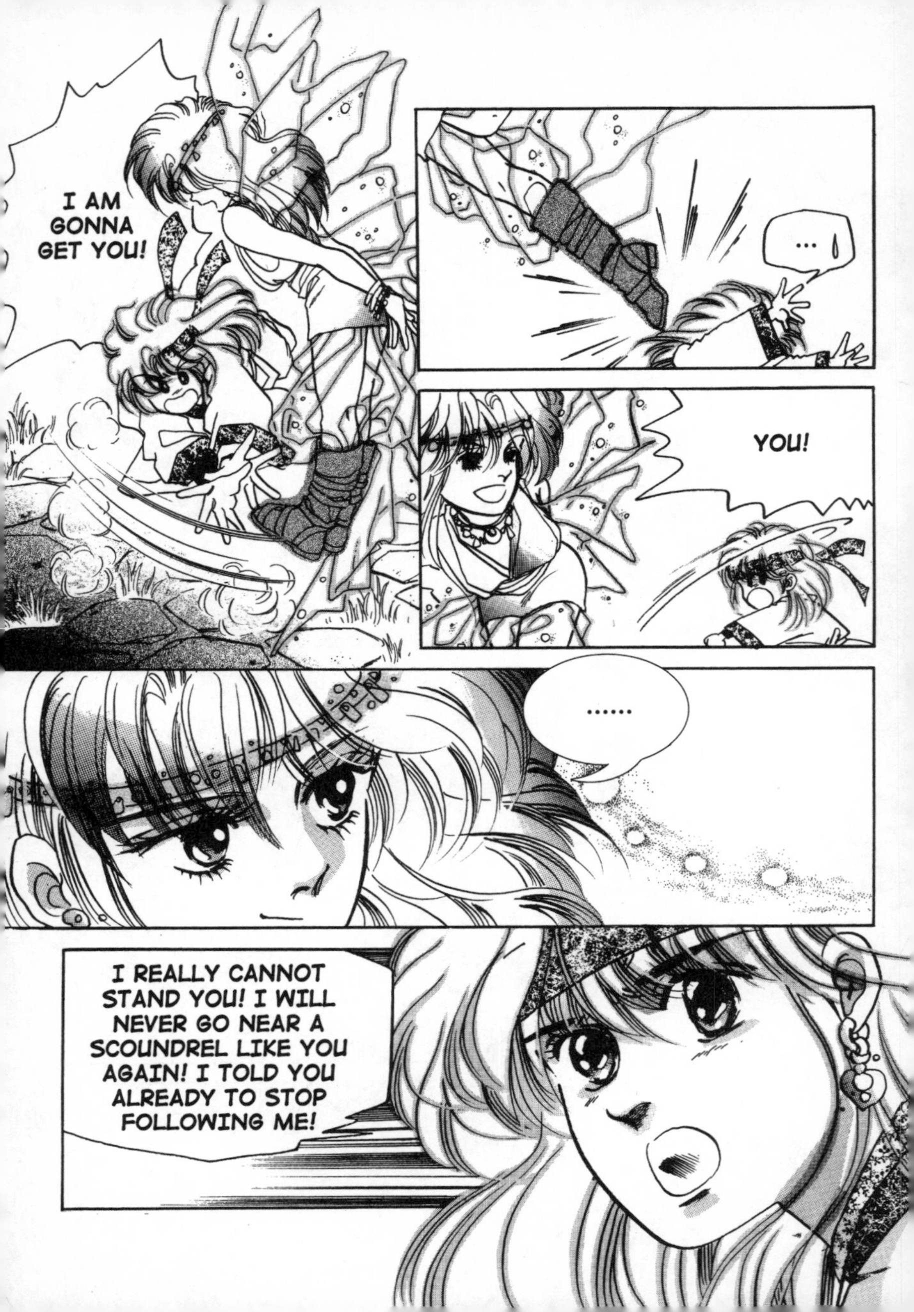
I AM GONNA GET YOU!
...
YOU!
......
I REALLY CANNOT STAND YOU! I WILL NEVER GO NEAR A SCOUNDREL LIKE YOU AGAIN! I TOLD YOU ALREADY TO STOP FOLLOWING ME!

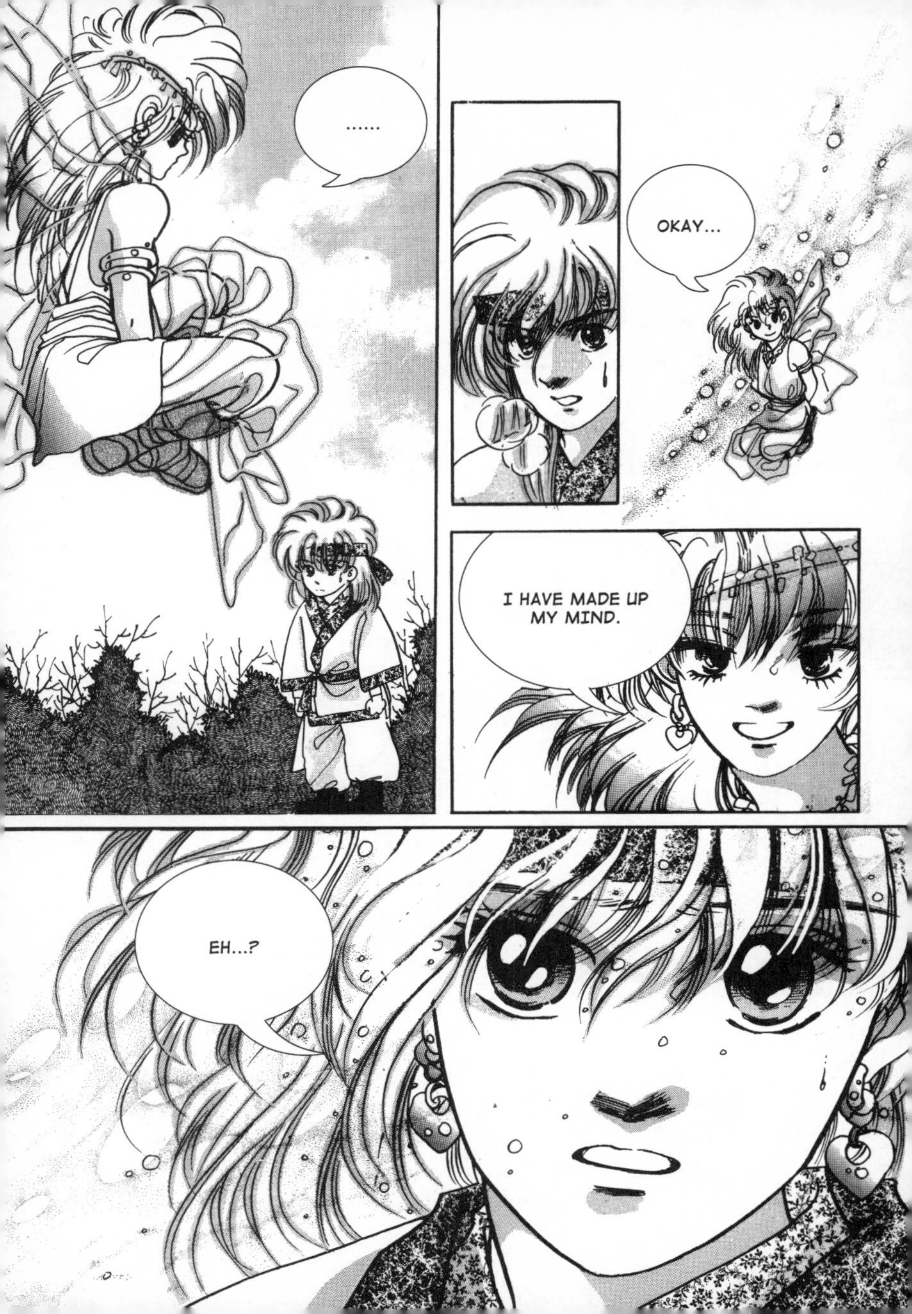
......
OKAY...
I HAVE MADE UP MY MIND.
EH...?

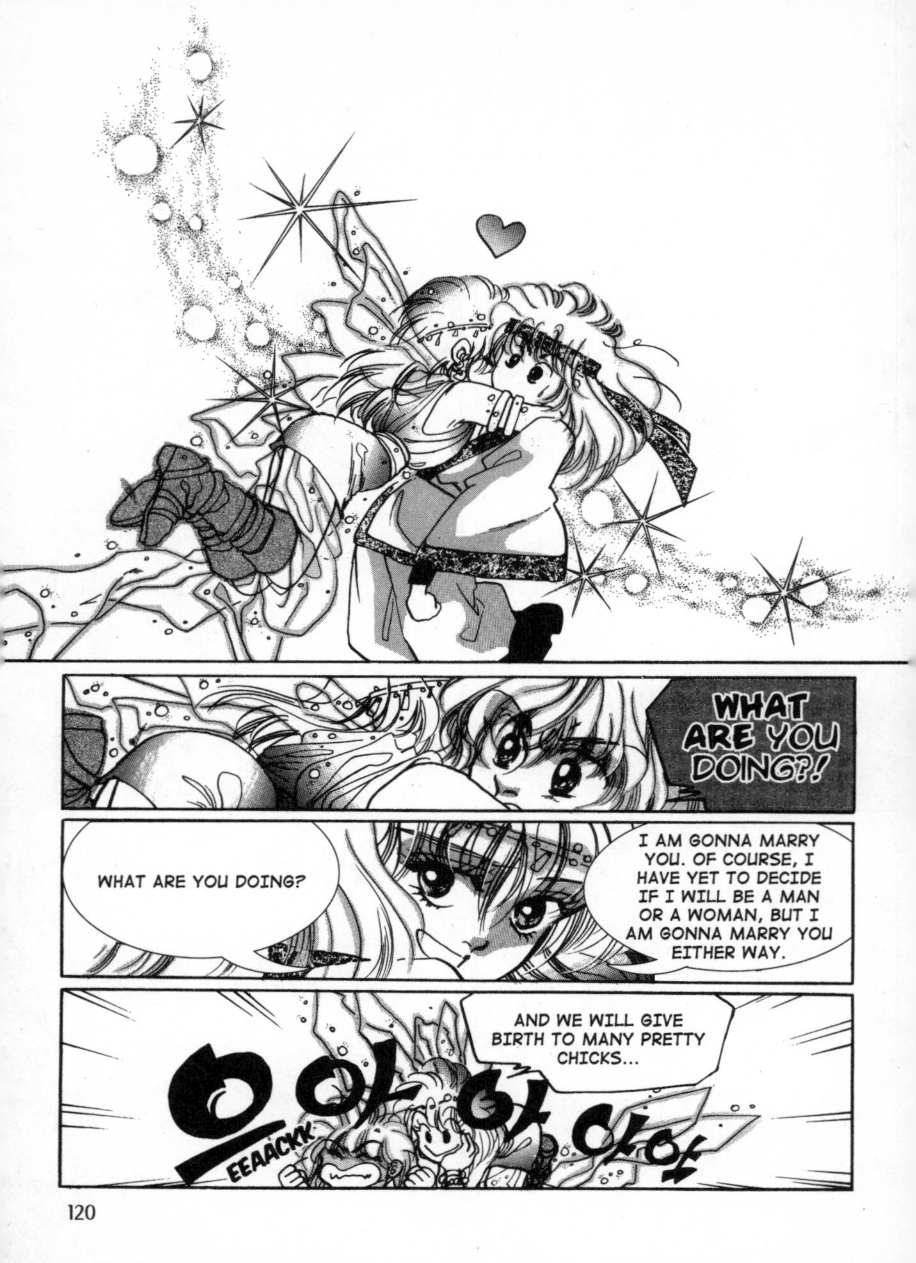
WHAT ARE YOU DOING?!
WHAT ARE YOU DOING?
I AM GONNA MARRY YOU. OF COURSE, I HAVE YET TO DECIDE IF I WILL BE A MAN OR A WOMAN, BUT I AM GONNA MARRY YOU EITHER WAY.
AND WE WILL GIVE BIRTH TO MANY PRETTY CHICKS...
EEAACKK

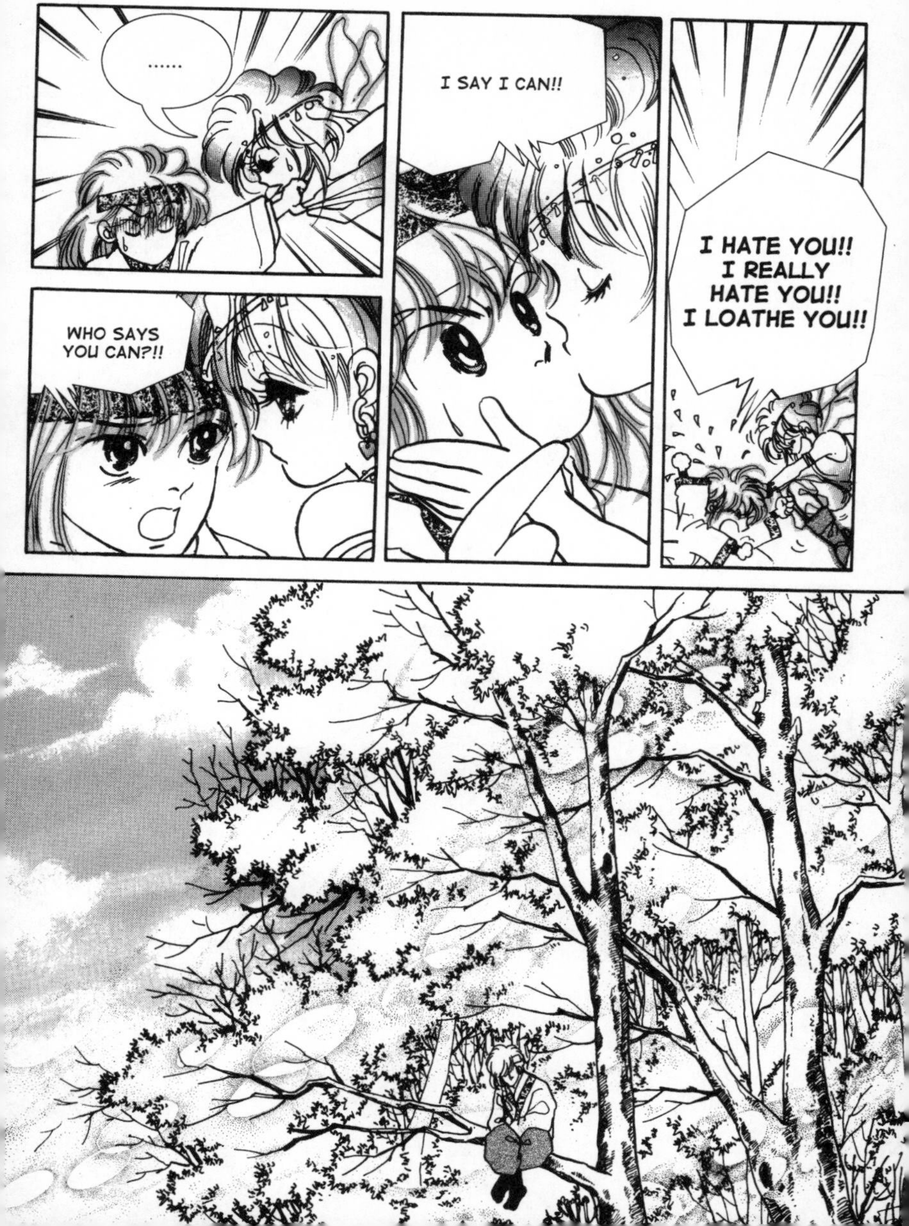
......
WHO SAYS YOU CAN?!!
I SAY I CAN!!
I HATE YOU!! I REALLY HATE YOU!! I LOATHE YOU!!

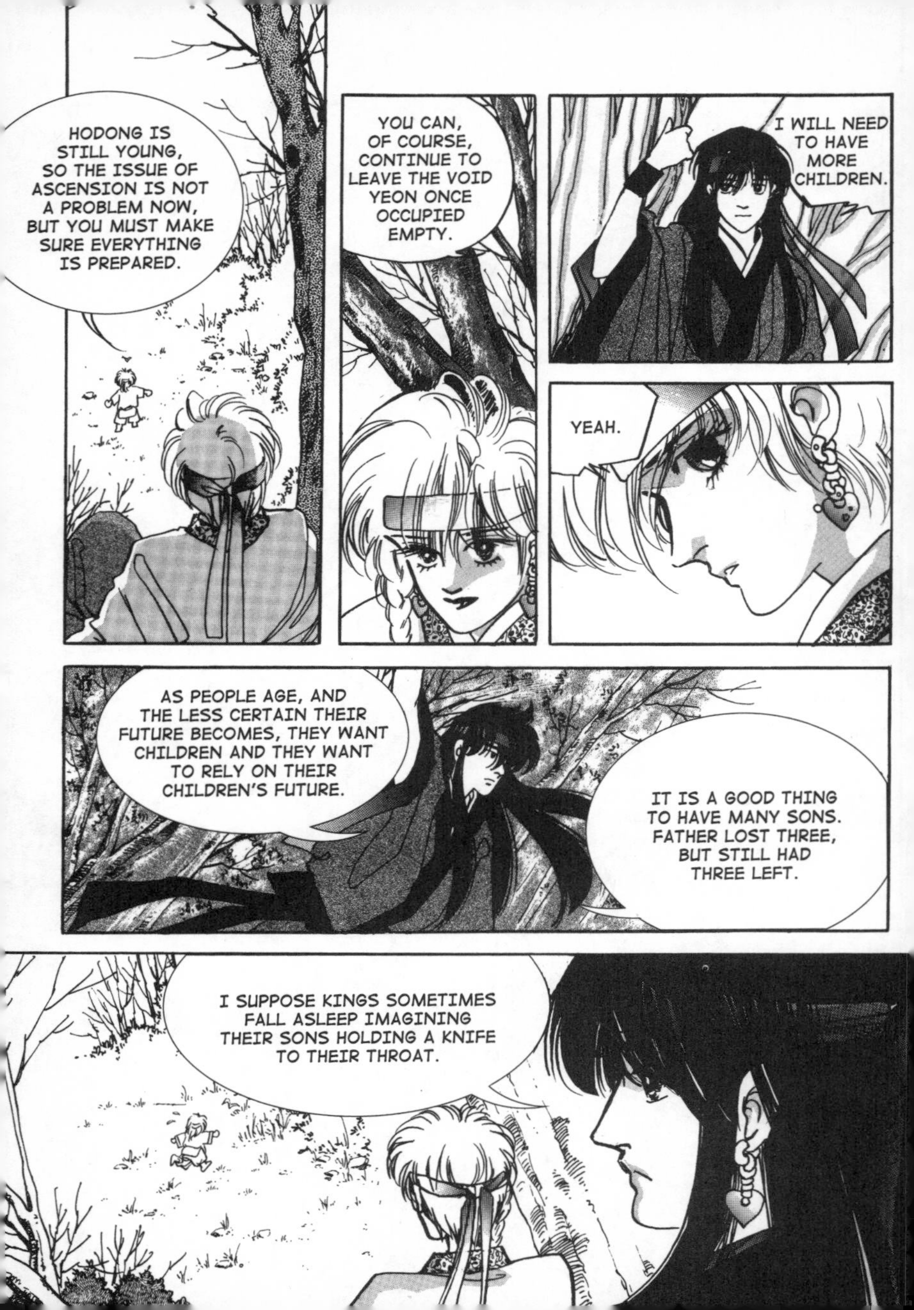
HODONG IS STILL YOUNG, SO THE ISSUE OF ASCENSION IS NOT A PROBLEM NOW, BUT YOU MUST MAKE SURE EVERYTHING IS PREPARED.
YOU CAN, OF COURSE, CONTINUE TO LEAVE THE VOID YEON ONCE OCCUPIED EMPTY.
I WILL NEED TO HAVE MORE CHILDREN.
YEAH.
AS PEOPLE AGE, AND THE LESS CERTAIN THEIR FUTURE BECOMES, THEY WANT CHILDREN AND THEY WANT TO RELY ON THEIR CHILDREN'S FUTURE.
IT IS A GOOD THING TO HAVE MANY SONS. FATHER LOST THREE, BUT STILL HAD THREE LEFT.
I SUPPOSE KINGS SOMETIMES FALL ASLEEP IMAGINING THEIR SONS HOLDING A KNIFE TO THEIR THROAT.

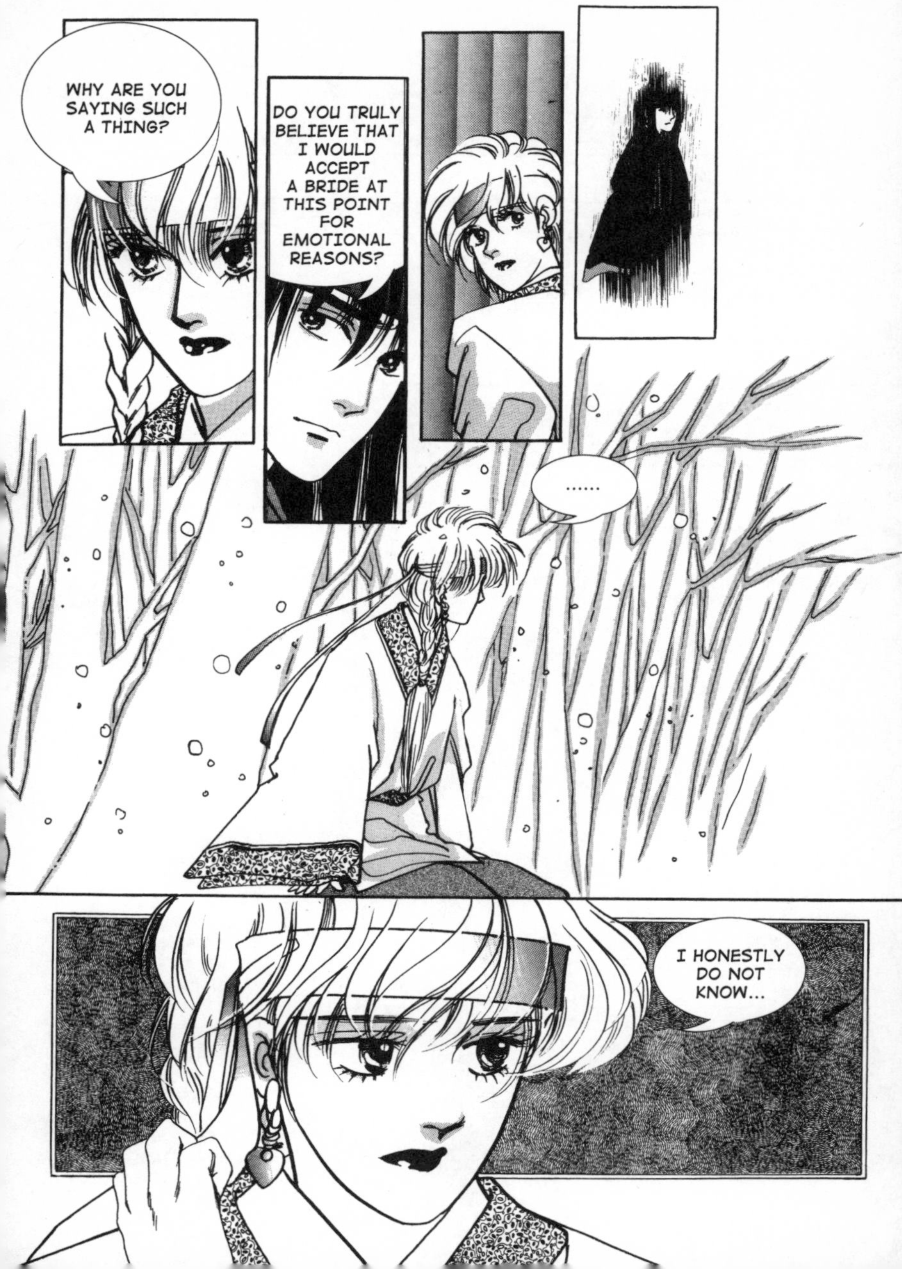
WHY ARE YOU SAYING SUCH A THING?
DO YOU TRULY BELIEVE THAT I WOULD ACCEPT A BRIDE AT THIS POINT FOR EMOTIONAL REASONS?
......
I HONESTLY DO NOT KNOW...

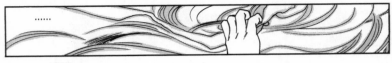

......

YEAH...

EVEN THOUGH YOU SAY THAT... I AM SURE YOU CANNOT DECEIVE YOURSELF.

NO MATTER WHAT YOU SAY NOW, THERE IS ONLY ONE NAME IN YOUR HEART.

I... HAVE SINNED AGAINST YOU.

IF I PUT MY HAIR UP AND ADORN MY FACE WITH MAKEUP

AND LEAVE YOUR SIDE TO SEEK HIM

FOR THE SAME REASON

WOULD YOU UNDERSTAND?

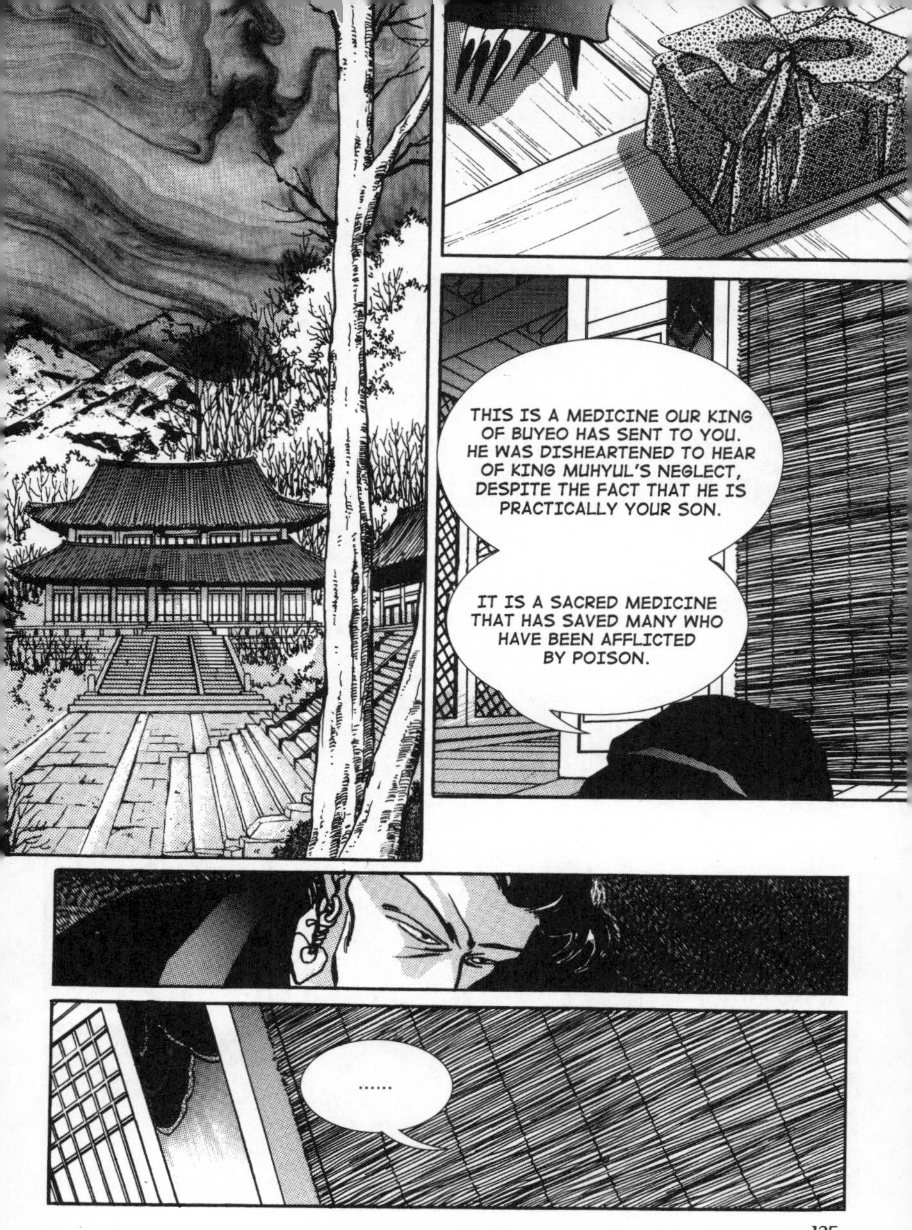
THIS IS A MEDICINE OUR KING OF BUYEO HAS SENT TO YOU. HE WAS DISHEARTENED TO HEAR OF KING MUHYUL'S NEGLECT, DESPITE THE FACT THAT HE IS PRACTICALLY YOUR SON.
IT IS A SACRED MEDICINE THAT HAS SAVED MANY WHO HAVE BEEN AFFLICTED BY POISON.
......

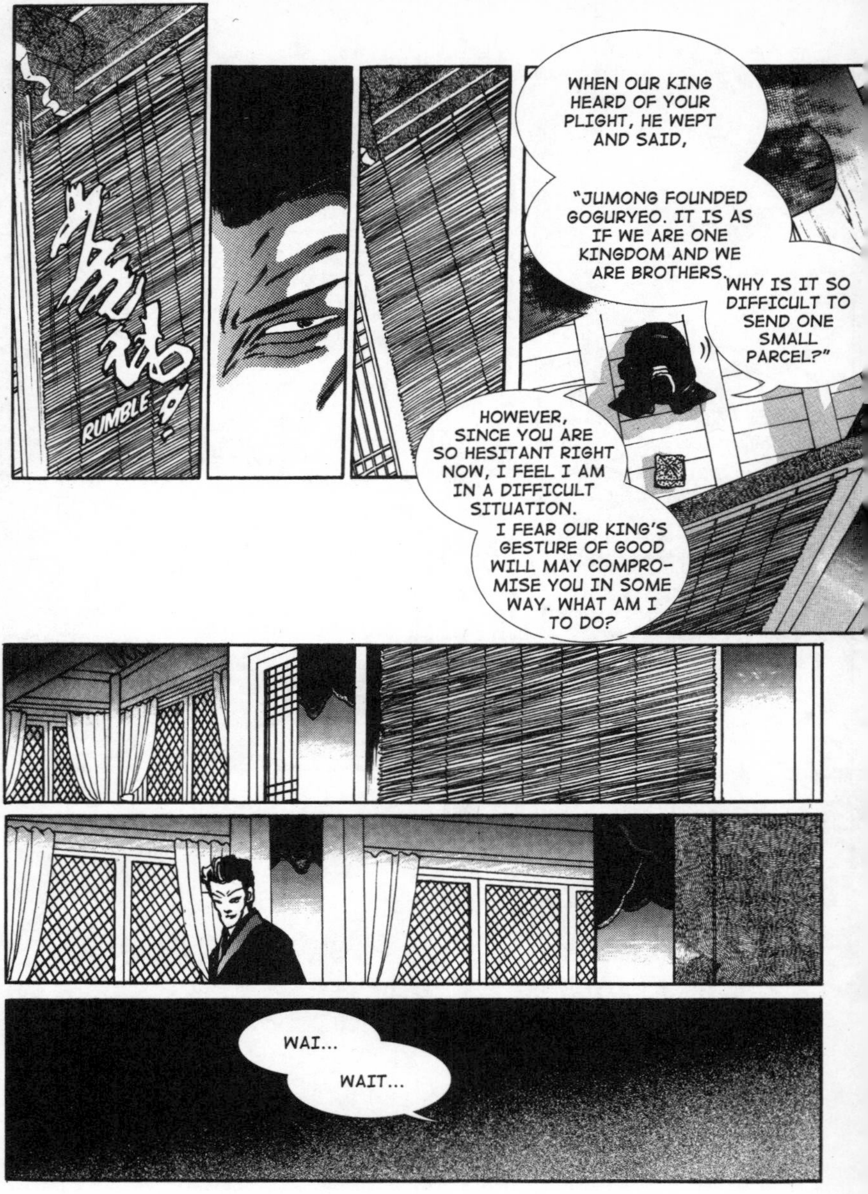
RUMBLE
WHEN OUR KING HEARD OF YOUR PLIGHT, HE WEPT AND SAID,
"JUMONG FOUNDED GOGURYEO. IT IS AS IF WE ARE ONE KINGDOM AND WE ARE BROTHERS.
WHY IS IT SO DIFFICULT TO SEND ONE SMALL PARCEL?"
HOWEVER, SINCE YOU ARE SO HESITANT RIGHT NOW, I FEEL I AM IN A DIFFICULT SITUATION.
I FEAR OUR KING'S GESTURE OF GOOD WILL MAY COMPROMISE YOU IN SOME WAY. WHAT AM I TO DO?
WAI...
WAIT...

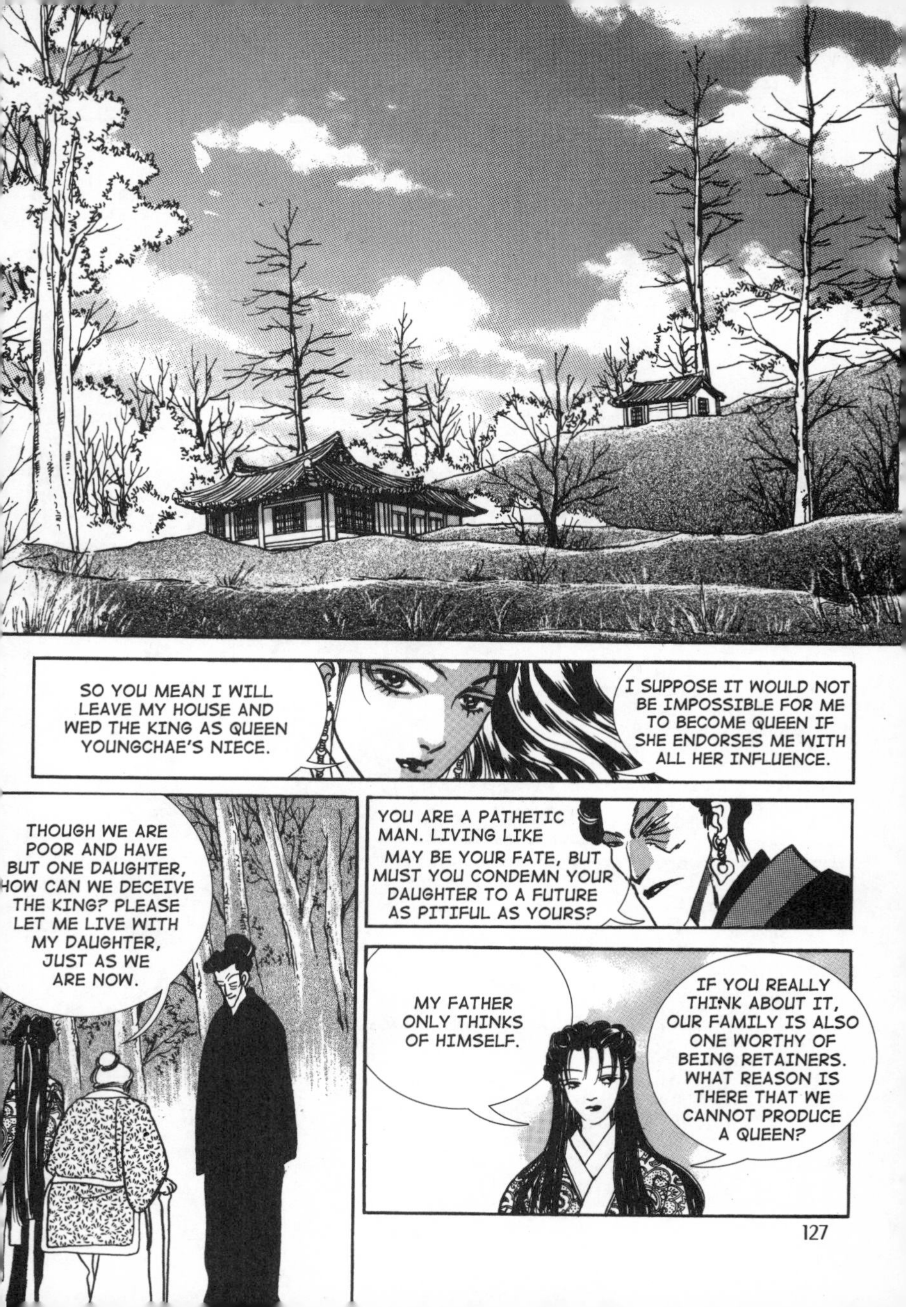

SO YOU MEAN I WILL LEAVE MY HOUSE AND WED THE KING AS QUEEN YOUNGCHAE'S NIECE.
I SUPPOSE IT WOULD NOT BE IMPOSSIBLE FOR ME TO BECOME QUEEN IF SHE ENDORSES ME WITH ALL HER INFLUENCE.
THOUGH WE ARE POOR AND HAVE BUT ONE DAUGHTER, HOW CAN WE DECEIVE THE KING? PLEASE LET ME LIVE WITH MY DAUGHTER, JUST AS WE ARE NOW.
YOU ARE A PATHETIC MAN. LIVING LIKE
MAY BE YOUR FATE, BUT MUST YOU CONDEMN YOUR DAUGHTER TO A FUTURE AS PITIFUL AS YOURS?
MY FATHER ONLY THINKS OF HIMSELF.
IF YOU REALLY THINK ABOUT IT, OUR FAMILY IS ALSO ONE WORTHY OF BEING RETAINERS. WHAT REASON IS THERE THAT WE CANNOT PRODUCE A QUEEN?

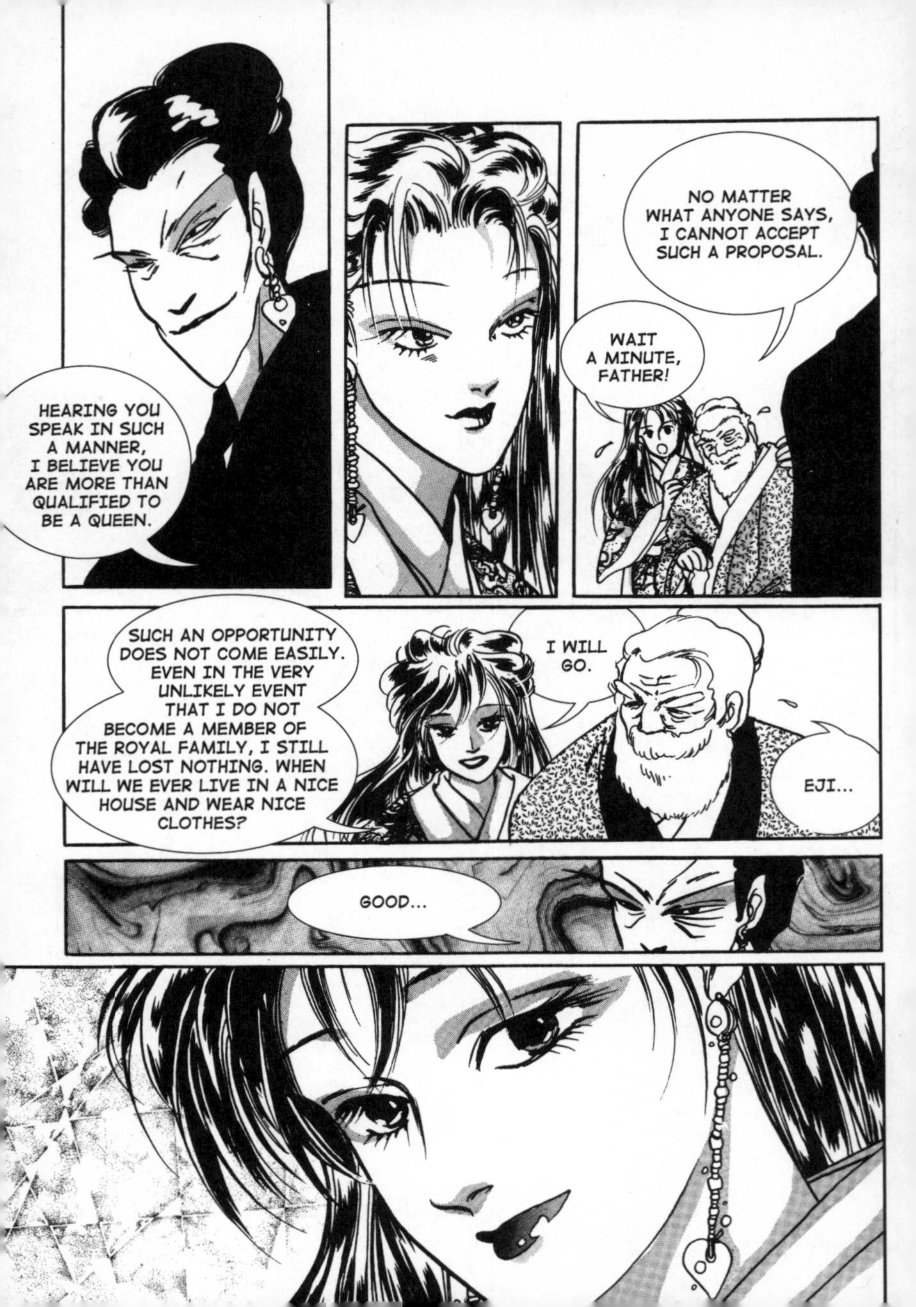
HEARING YOU SPEAK IN SUCH A MANNER, I BELIEVE YOU ARE MORE THAN QUALIFIED TO BE A QUEEN.
NO MATTER WHAT ANYONE SAYS, I CANNOT ACCEPT SUCH A PROPOSAL.
WAIT A MINUTE, FATHER!
SUCH AN OPPORTUNITY DOES NOT COME EASILY. EVEN IN THE VERY UNLIKELY EVENT THAT I DO NOT BECOME A MEMBER OF THE ROYAL FAMILY, I STILL HAVE LOST NOTHING. WHEN WILL WE EVER LIVE IN A NICE HOUSE AND WEAR NICE CLOTHES?
I WILL GO.
EJI...
GOOD...

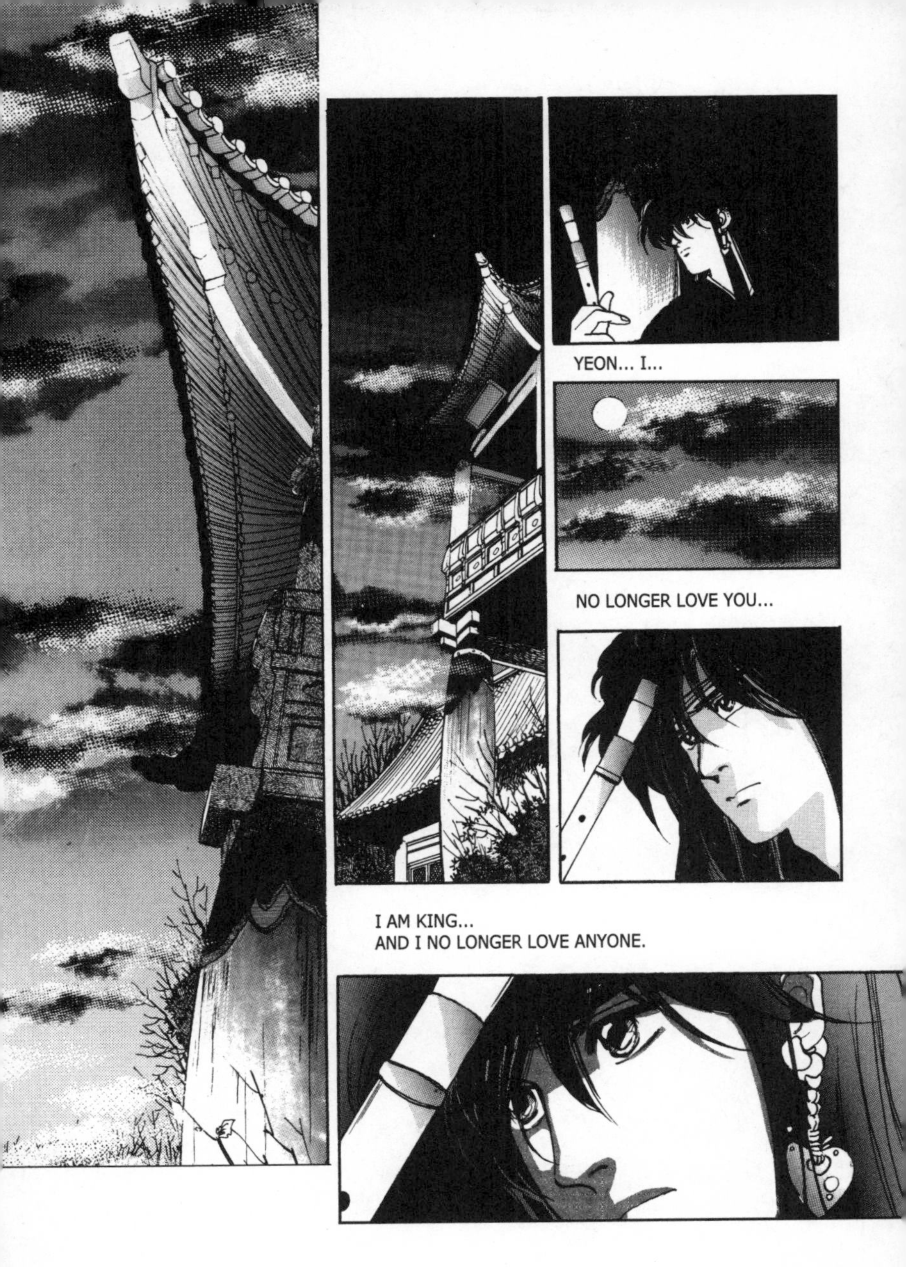
YEON... I...
NO LONGER LOVE YOU...
I AM KING...
AND I NO LONGER LOVE ANYONE.

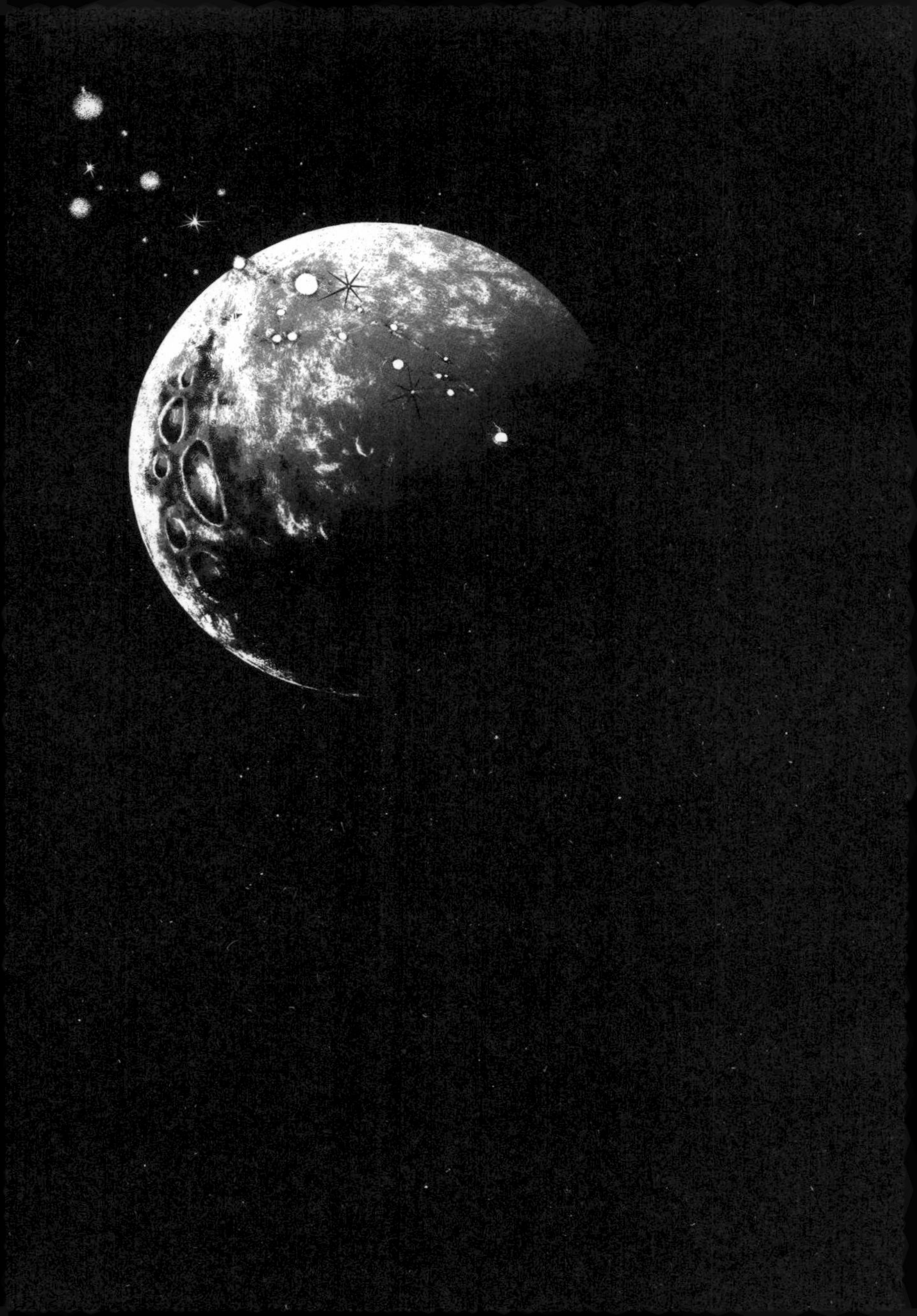

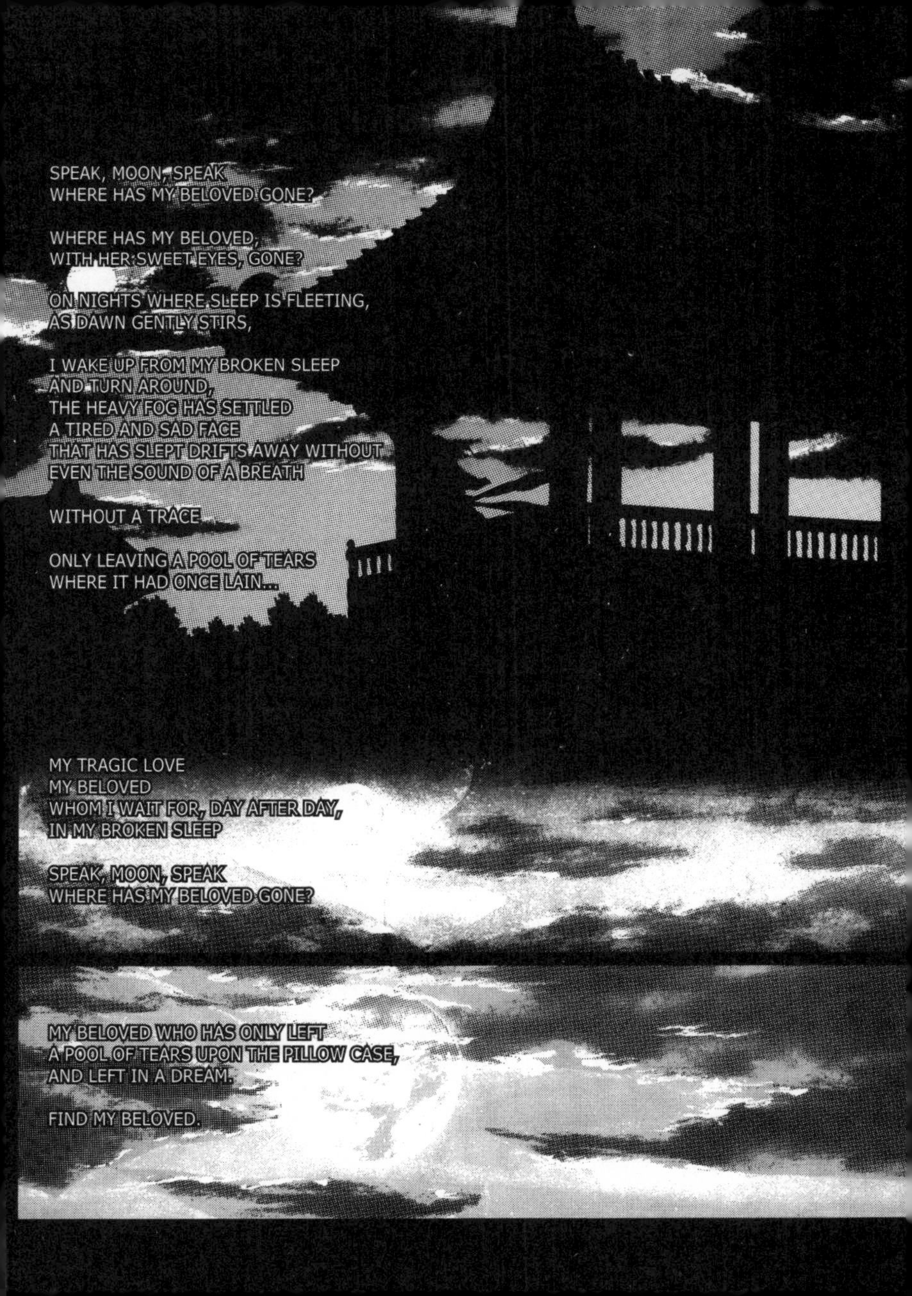
SPEAK, MOON, SPEAK
WHERE HAS MY BELOVED GONE?
WHERE HAS MY BELOVED,
WITH HER SWEET EYES, GONE?
ON NIGHTS WHERE SLEEP IS FLEETING,
AS DAWN GENTLY STIRS,
I WAKE UP FROM MY BROKEN SLEEP
AND TURN AROUND,
THE HEAVY FOG HAS SETTLED
A TIRED AND SAD FACE
THAT HAS SLEPT DRIFTS AWAY WITHOUT
EVEN THE SOUND OF A BREATH
WITHOUT A TRACE
ONLY LEAVING A POOL OF TEARS
WHERE IT HAD ONCE LAIN...
MY TRAGIC LOVE
MY BELOVED
WHOM I WAIT FOR, DAY AFTER DAY,
IN MY BROKEN SLEEP
SPEAK, MOON, SPEAK
WHERE HAS MY BELOVED GONE?
MY BELOVED WHO HAS ONLY LEFT
A POOL OF TEARS UPON THE PILLOW CASE,
AND LEFT IN A DREAM.
FIND MY BELOVED.

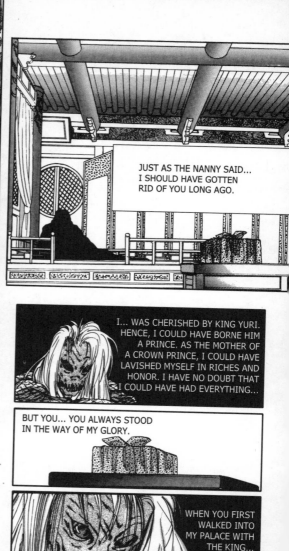

JUST AS THE NANNY SAID...
I SHOULD HAVE GOTTEN
RID OF YOU LONG AGO.

I... WAS CHERISHED BY KING YURI.
HENCE, I COULD HAVE BORNE HIM
A PRINCE. AS THE MOTHER OF
A CROWN PRINCE, I COULD HAVE
LAVISHED MYSELF IN RICHES AND
HONOR. I HAVE NO DOUBT THAT
I COULD HAVE HAD EVERYTHING...

BUT YOU... YOU ALWAYS STOOD
IN THE WAY OF MY GLORY.

WHEN YOU FIRST
WALKED INTO
MY PALACE WITH
THE KING...

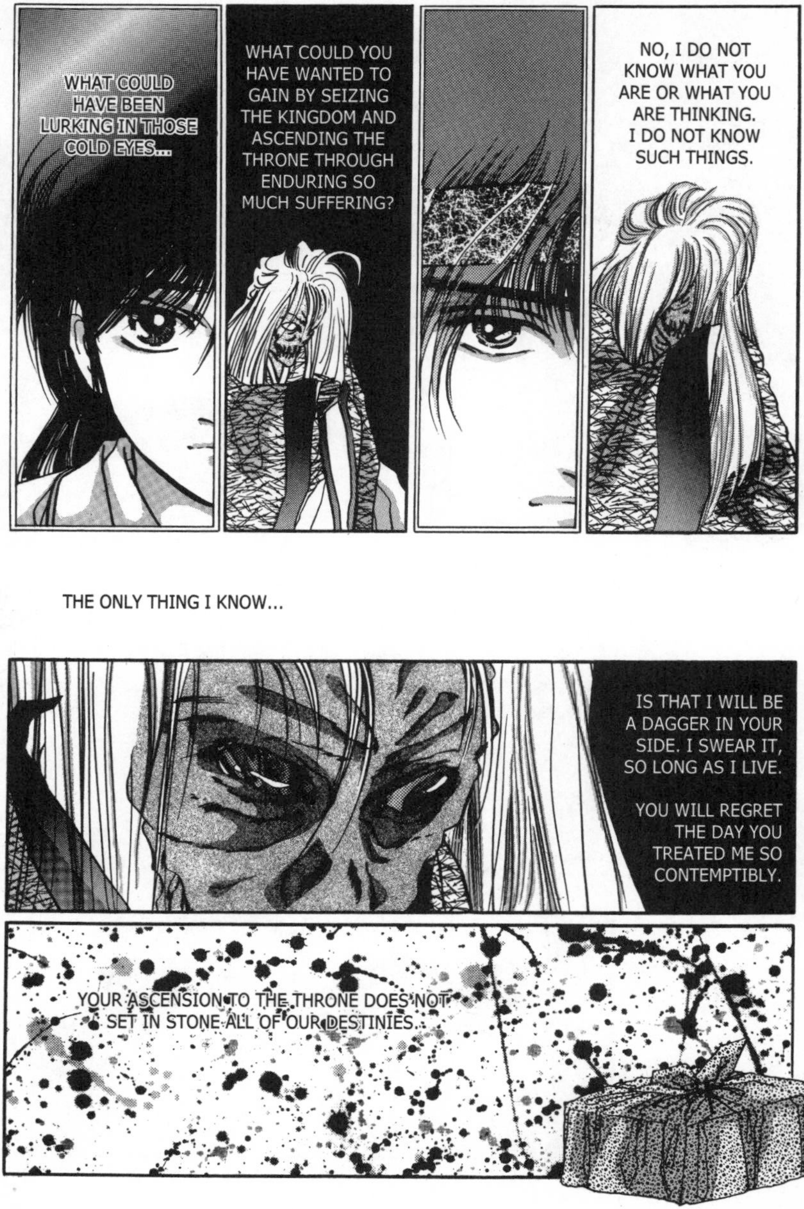
WHAT COULD HAVE BEEN LURKING IN THOSE COLD EYES...
WHAT COULD YOU HAVE WANTED TO GAIN BY SEIZING THE KINGDOM AND ASCENDING THE THRONE THROUGH ENDURING SO MUCH SUFFERING?
NO, I DO NOT KNOW WHAT YOU ARE OR WHAT YOU ARE THINKING. I DO NOT KNOW SUCH THINGS.
THE ONLY THING I KNOW...
IS THAT I WILL BE A DAGGER IN YOUR SIDE. I SWEAR IT, SO LONG AS I LIVE.
YOU WILL REGRET THE DAY YOU TREATED ME SO CONTEMPTIBLY.
YOUR ASCENSION TO THE THRONE DOES NOT SET IN STONE ALL OF OUR DESTINIES.

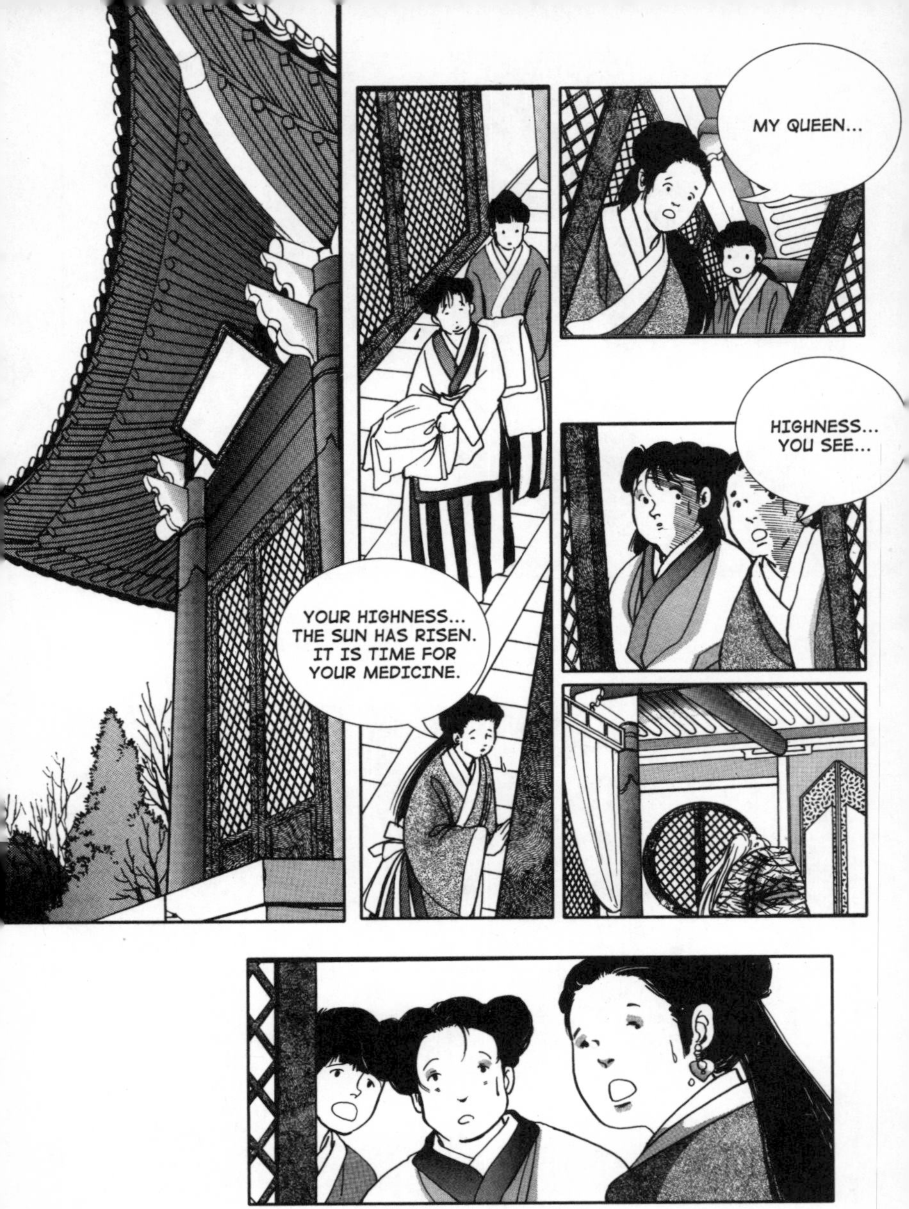
YOUR HIGHNESS... THE SUN HAS RISEN. IT IS TIME FOR YOUR MEDICINE.
MY QUEEN...
HIGHNESS... YOU SEE...

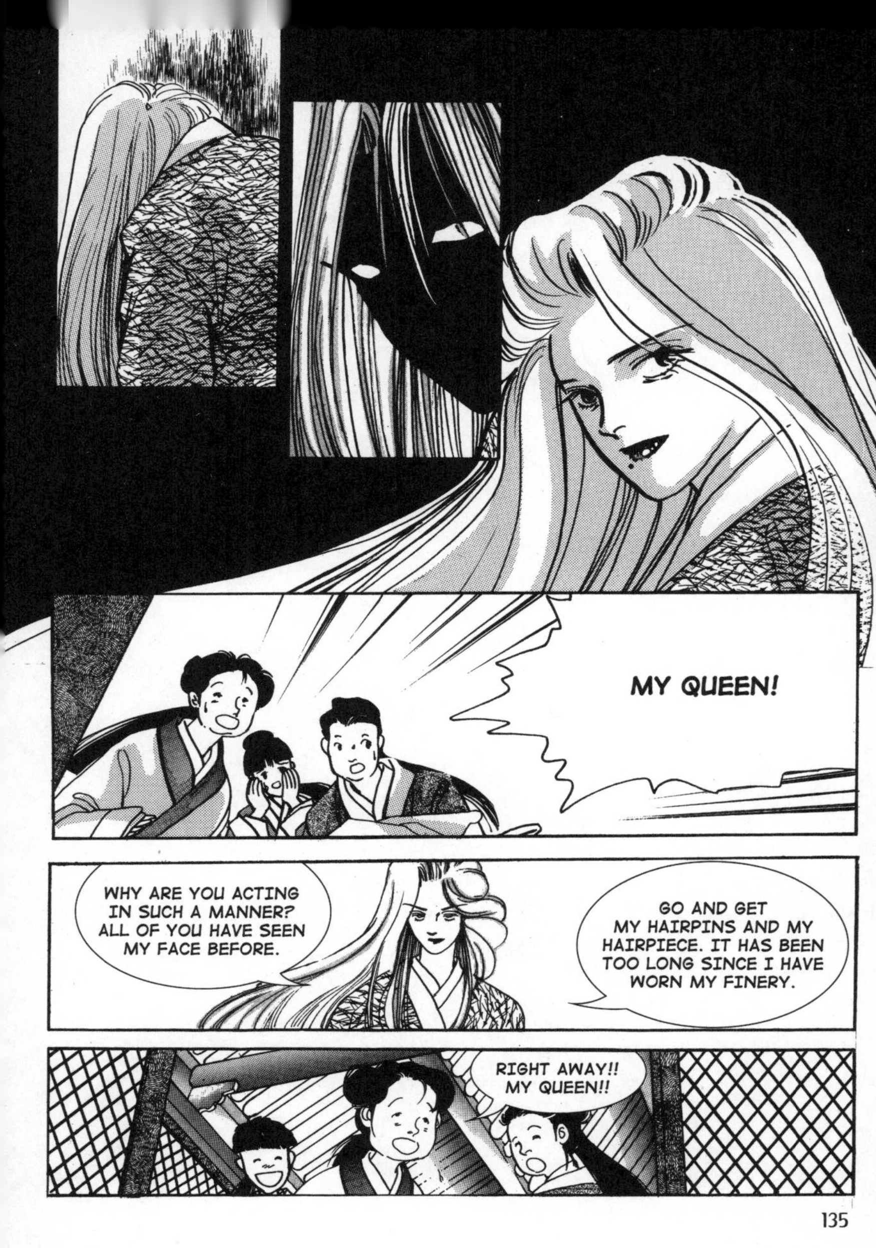
MY QUEEN!
WHY ARE YOU ACTING IN SUCH A MANNER? ALL OF YOU HAVE SEEN MY FACE BEFORE.
GO AND GET MY HAIRPINS AND MY HAIRPIECE. IT HAS BEEN TOO LONG SINCE I HAVE WORN MY FINERY.
RIGHT AWAY!! MY QUEEN!!

Hairpiece: Supplementary hair used in some feminine coiffures. In the Samguk Sagi records, King Kyungmun, Shilla's 48th ruler, sent these extravagant hair extensions of 53 and 59 inches as gifts to the Tang dynasty. The ancient mural paintings in Goguryeo's tombs depict these elaborate hairpieces which were used to enlarge the coiffure and create more commanding impressions.

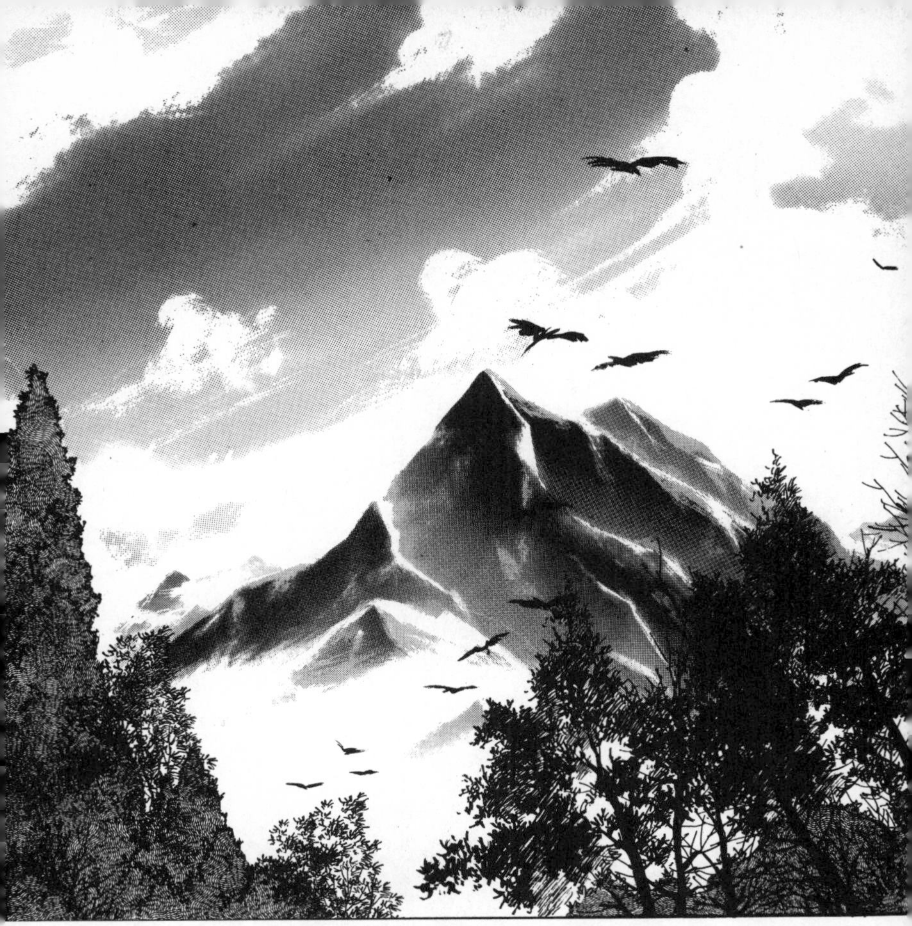

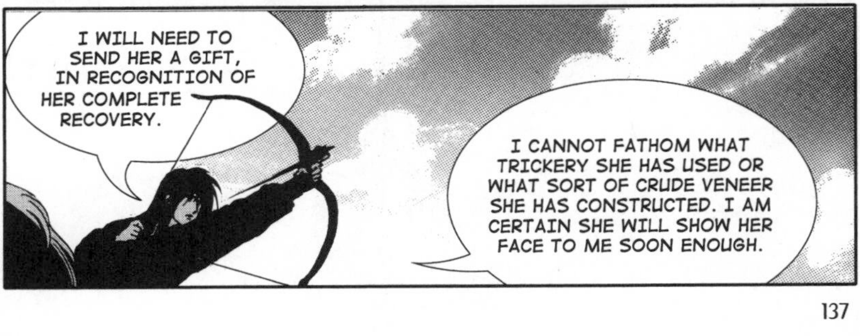
I WILL NEED TO SEND HER A GIFT, IN RECOGNITION OF HER COMPLETE RECOVERY.
I CANNOT FATHOM WHAT TRICKERY SHE HAS USED OR WHAT SORT OF CRUDE VENEER SHE HAS CONSTRUCTED. I AM CERTAIN SHE WILL SHOW HER FACE TO ME SOON ENOUGH.

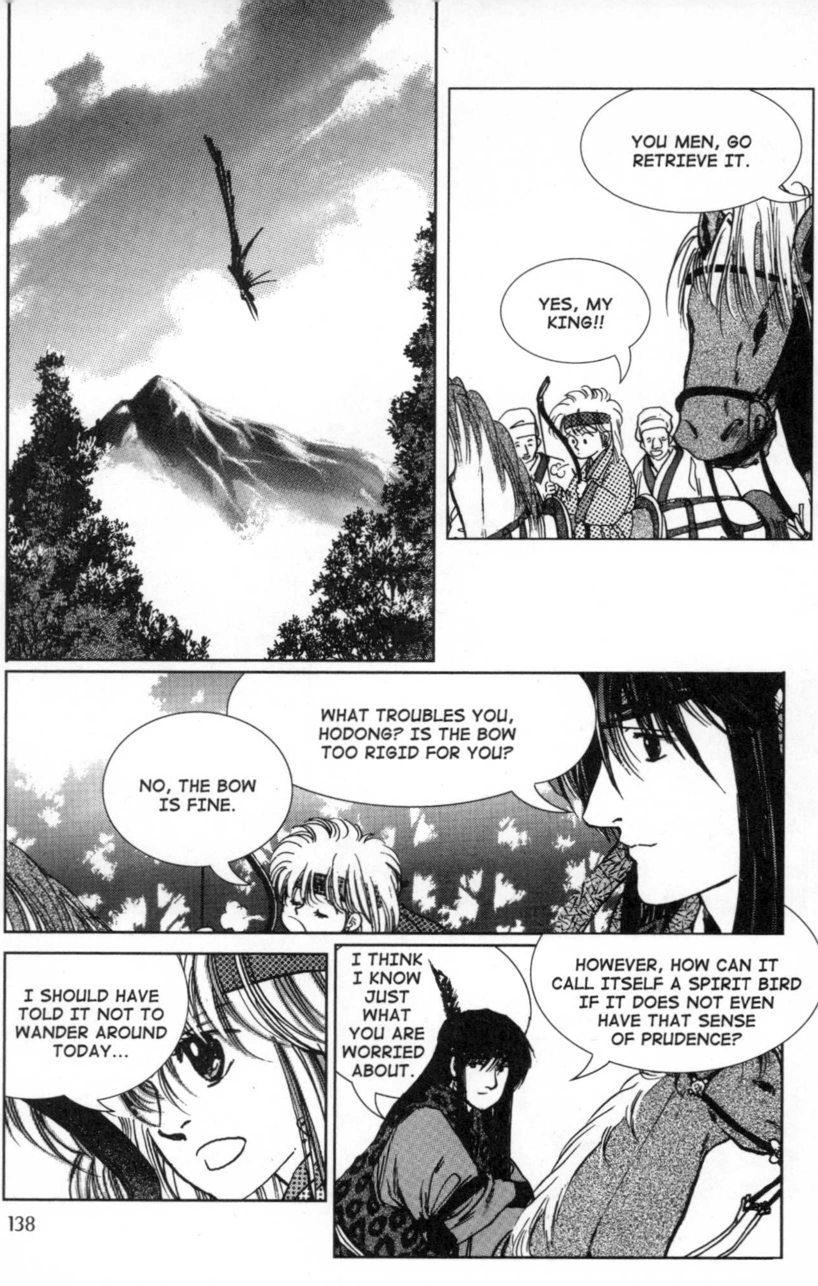
YOU MEN, GO RETRIEVE IT.
YES, MY KING!!
WHAT TROUBLES YOU, HODONG? IS THE BOW TOO RIGID FOR YOU?
NO, THE BOW IS FINE.
I SHOULD HAVE TOLD IT NOT TO WANDER AROUND TODAY...
I THINK I KNOW JUST WHAT YOU ARE WORRIED ABOUT.
HOWEVER, HOW CAN IT CALL ITSELF A SPIRIT BIRD IF IT DOES NOT EVEN HAVE THAT SENSE OF PRUDENCE?

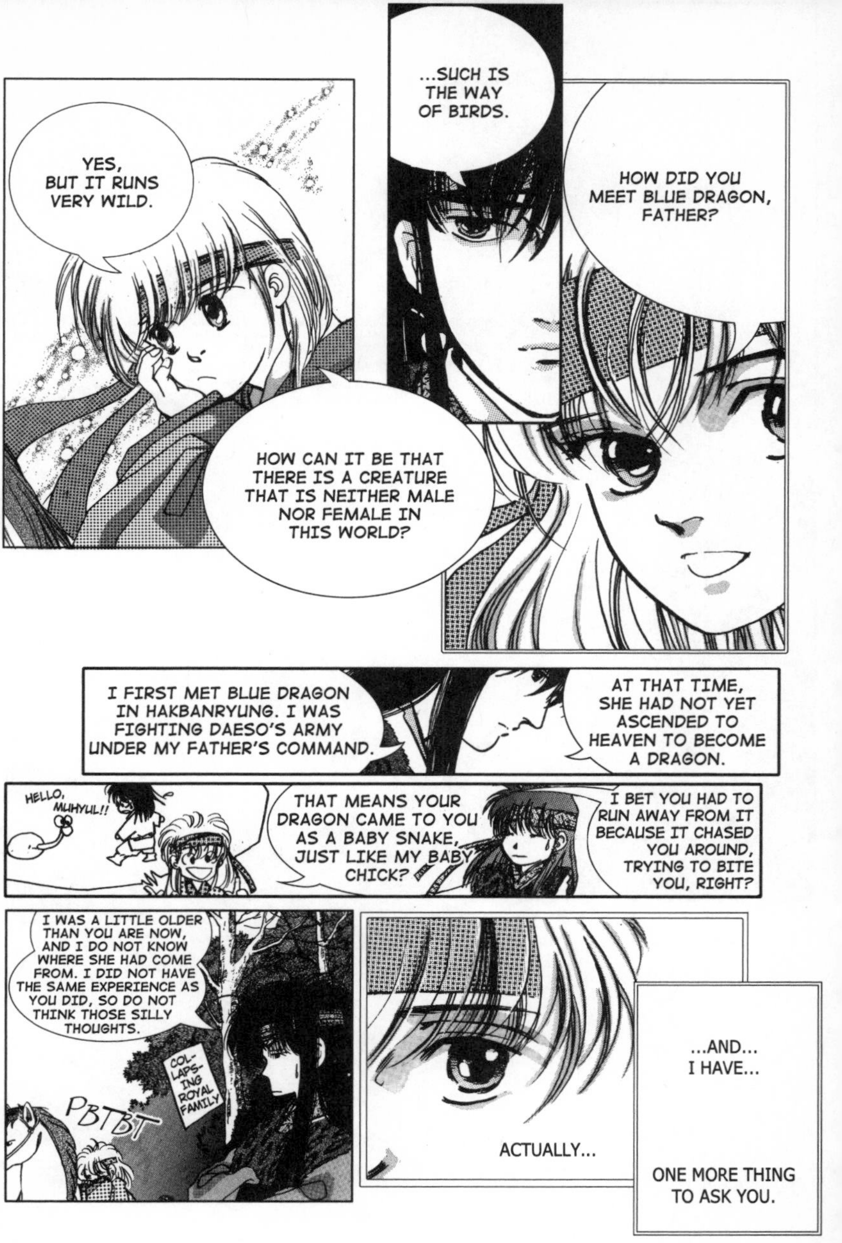
YES, BUT IT RUNS VERY WILD.
HOW CAN IT BE THAT THERE IS A CREATURE THAT IS NEITHER MALE NOR FEMALE IN THIS WORLD?
...SUCH IS THE WAY OF BIRDS.
HOW DID YOU MEET BLUE DRAGON, FATHER?
I FIRST MET BLUE DRAGON IN HAKBANRYUNG. I WAS FIGHTING DAESO'S ARMY UNDER MY FATHER'S COMMAND.
AT THAT TIME, SHE HAD NOT YET ASCENDED TO HEAVEN TO BECOME A DRAGON.
HELLO, MUHYUL!!
THAT MEANS YOUR DRAGON CAME TO YOU AS A BABY SNAKE, JUST LIKE MY BABY CHICK?
I BET YOU HAD TO RUN AWAY FROM IT BECAUSE IT CHASED YOU AROUND, TRYING TO BITE YOU, RIGHT?
I WAS A LITTLE OLDER THAN YOU ARE NOW, AND I DO NOT KNOW WHERE SHE HAD COME FROM. I DID NOT HAVE THE SAME EXPERIENCE AS YOU DID, SO DO NOT THINK THOSE SILLY THOUGHTS.
COL-LAPS-ING ROYAL FAMILY
PBTBT
ACTUALLY...
...AND... I HAVE...
ONE MORE THING TO ASK YOU.

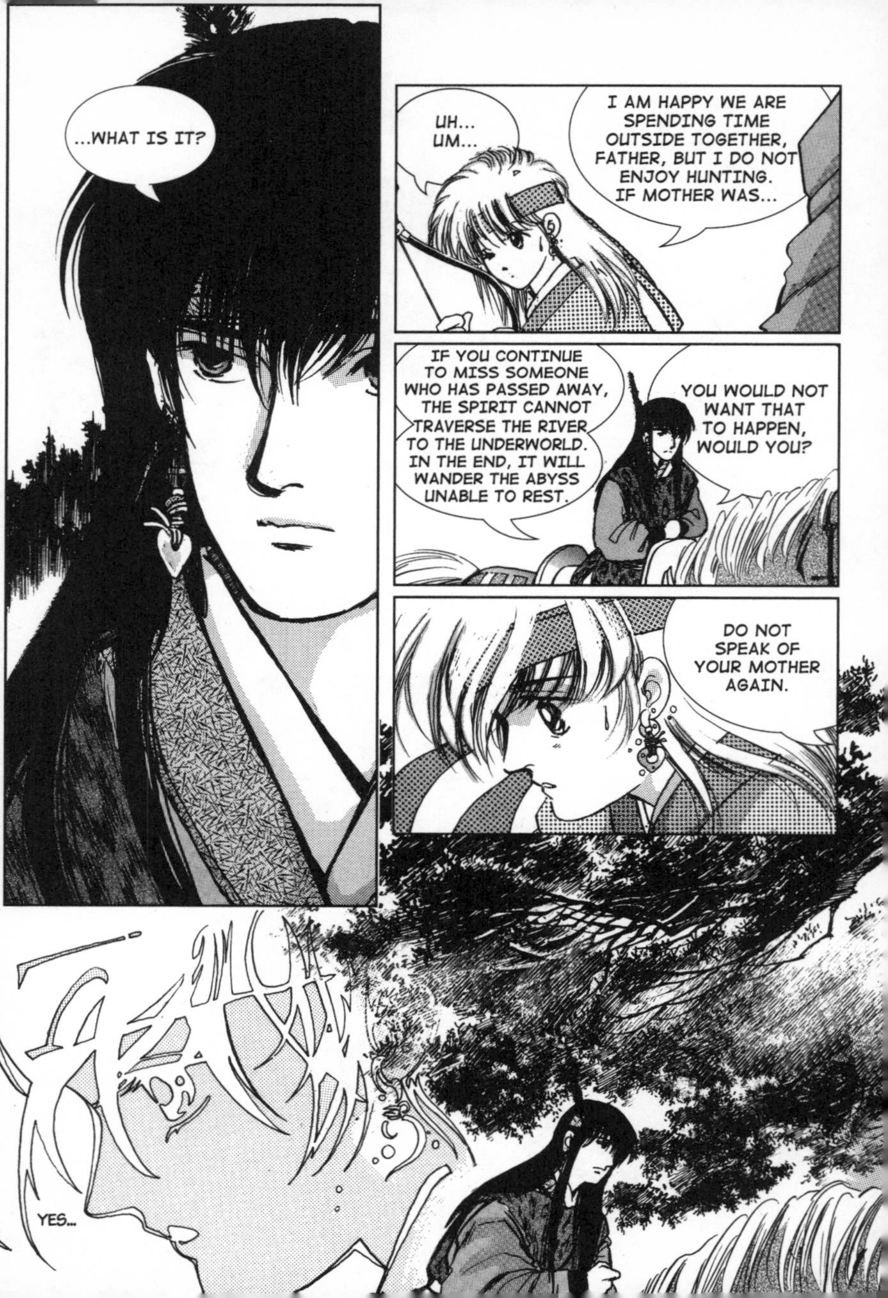
...WHAT IS IT?
UH... UM...
I AM HAPPY WE ARE SPENDING TIME OUTSIDE TOGETHER, FATHER, BUT I DO NOT ENJOY HUNTING. IF MOTHER WAS...
IF YOU CONTINUE TO MISS SOMEONE WHO HAS PASSED AWAY, THE SPIRIT CANNOT TRAVERSE THE RIVER TO THE UNDERWORLD. IN THE END, IT WILL WANDER THE ABYSS UNABLE TO REST.
YOU WOULD NOT WANT THAT TO HAPPEN, WOULD YOU?
DO NOT SPEAK OF YOUR MOTHER AGAIN.
YES...

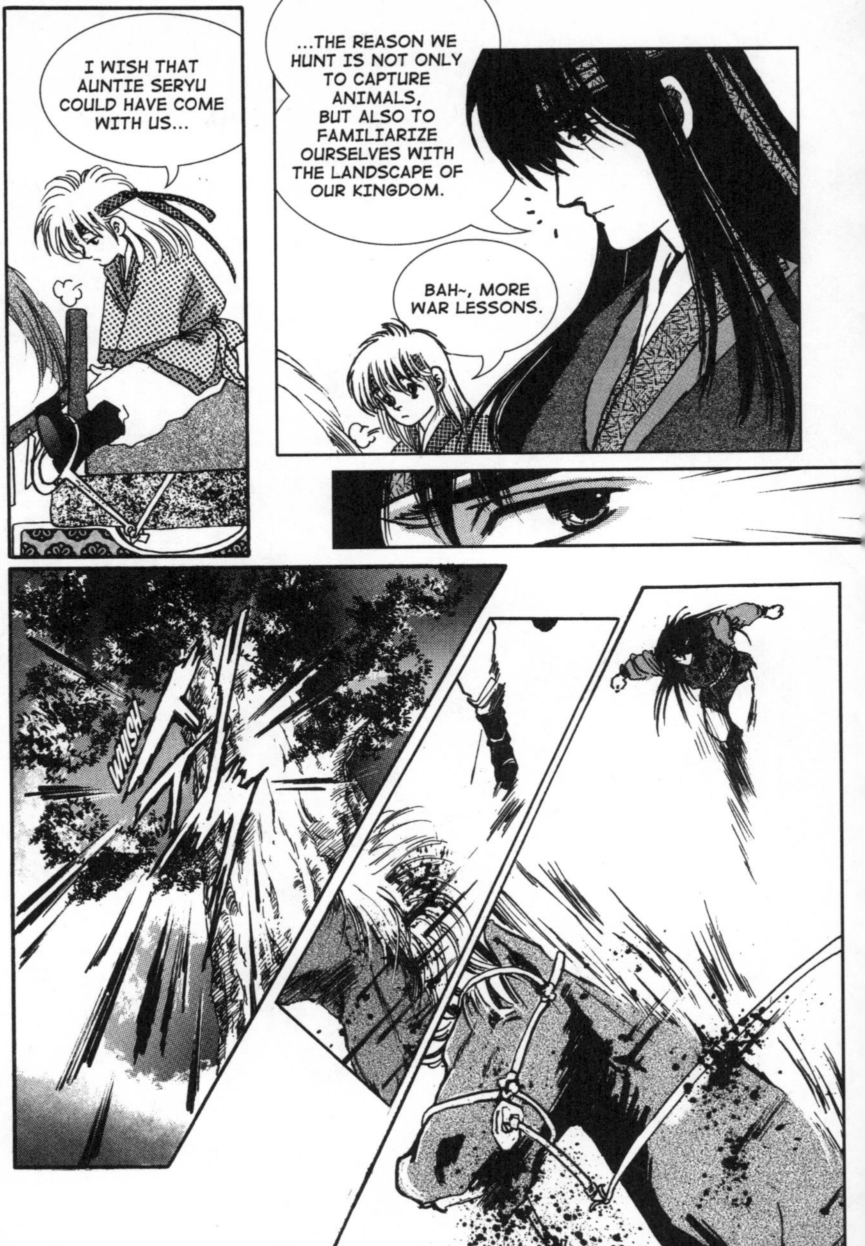
I WISH THAT AUNTIE SERYU COULD HAVE COME WITH US...
...THE REASON WE HUNT IS NOT ONLY TO CAPTURE ANIMALS, BUT ALSO TO FAMILIARIZE OURSELVES WITH THE LANDSCAPE OF OUR KINGDOM.
BAH~, MORE WAR LESSONS.
WHISH

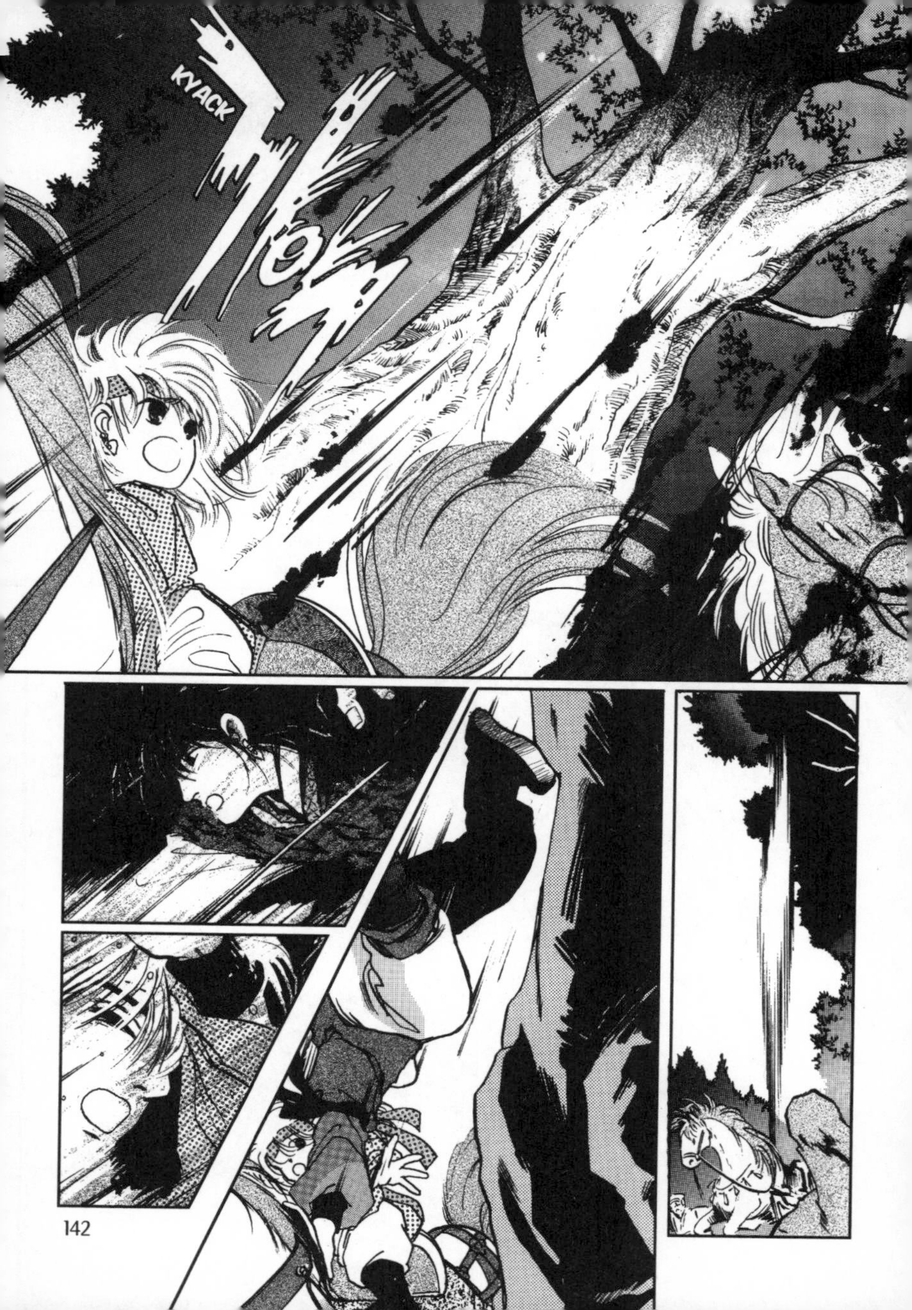
KYACK

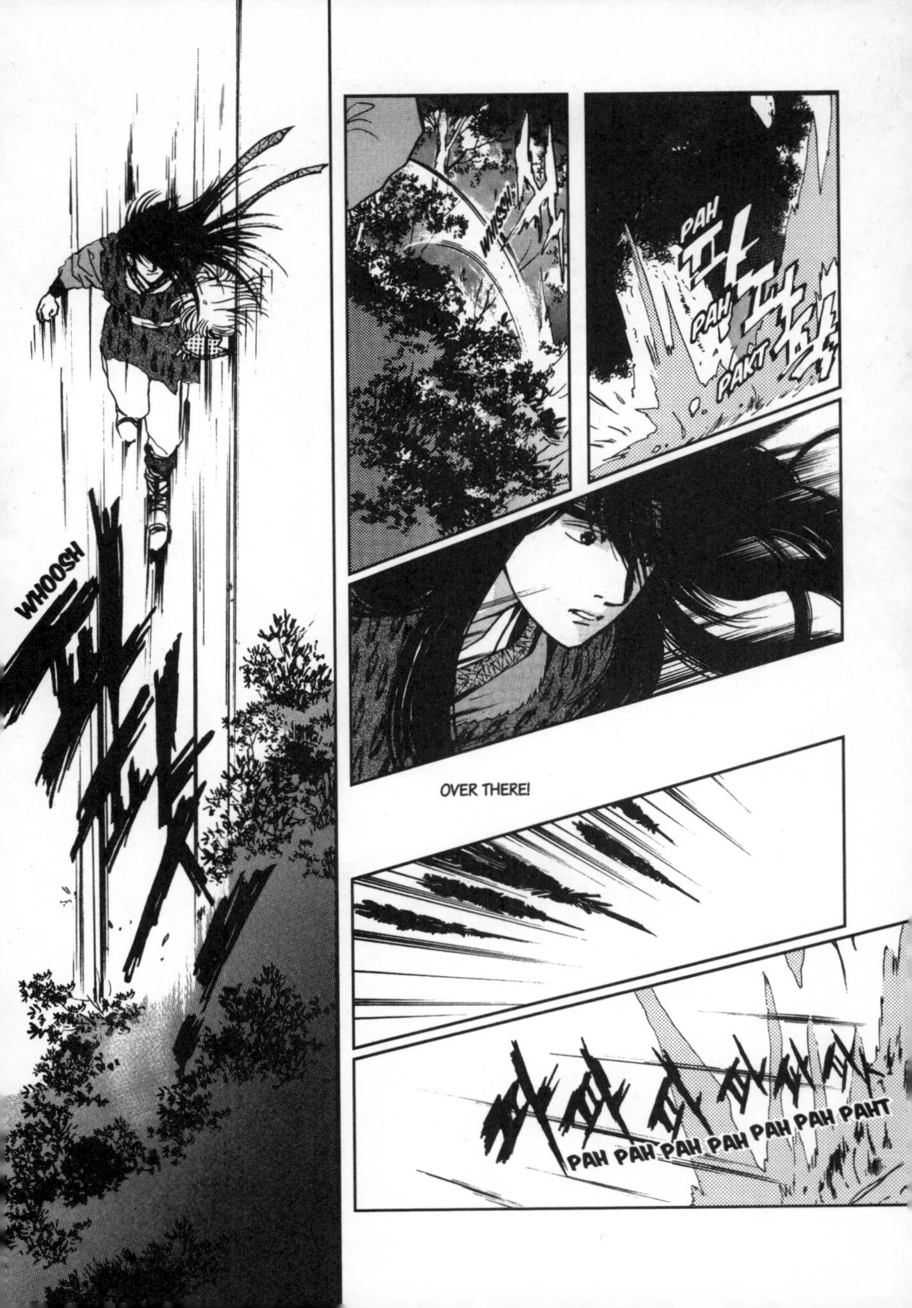
WHOOSH
WHISSH
PAH
PAH
PAKT
OVER THERE!
PAH PAH PAH PAH PAH PAH PAHT

PRAKK

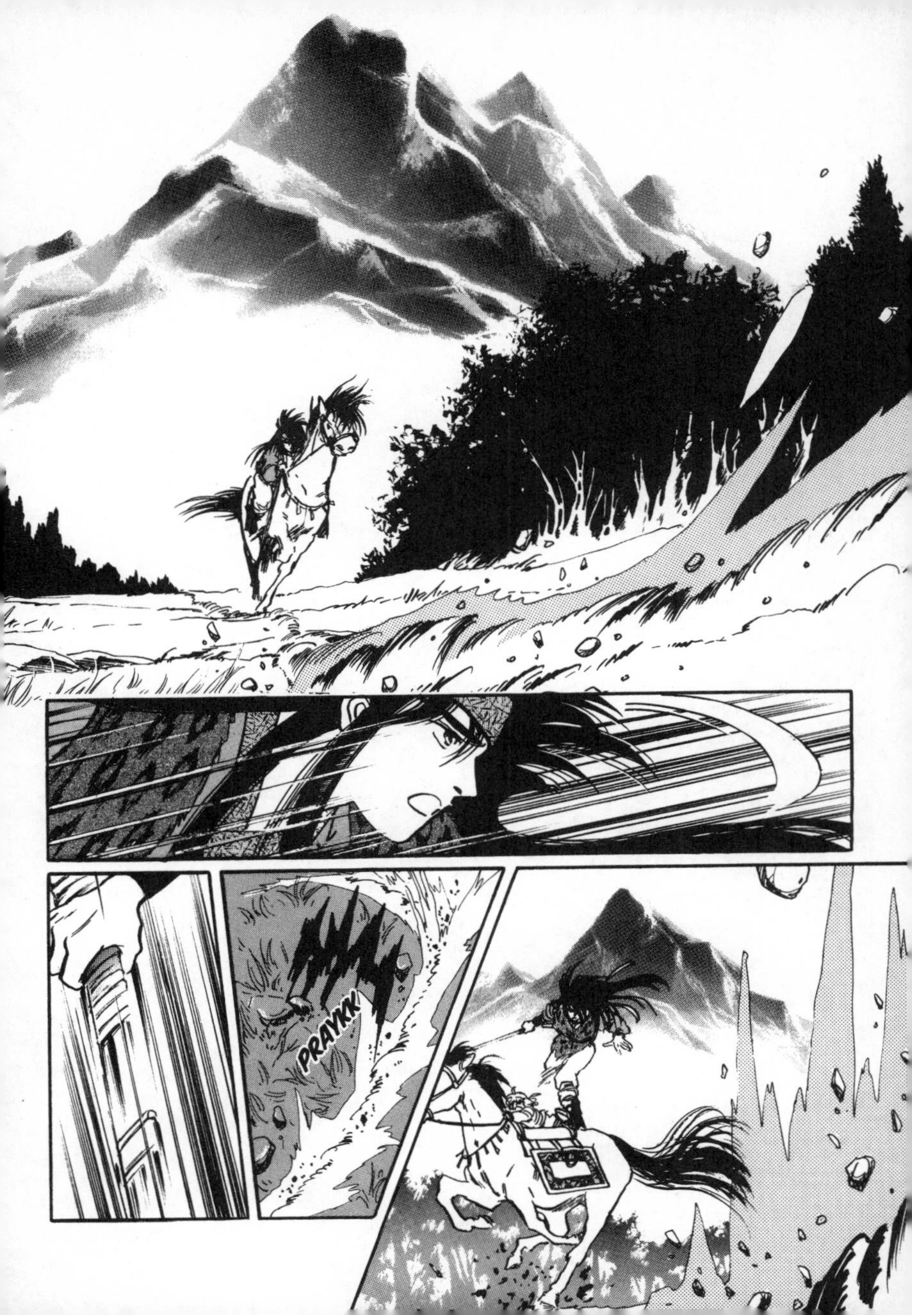
PRAYKK

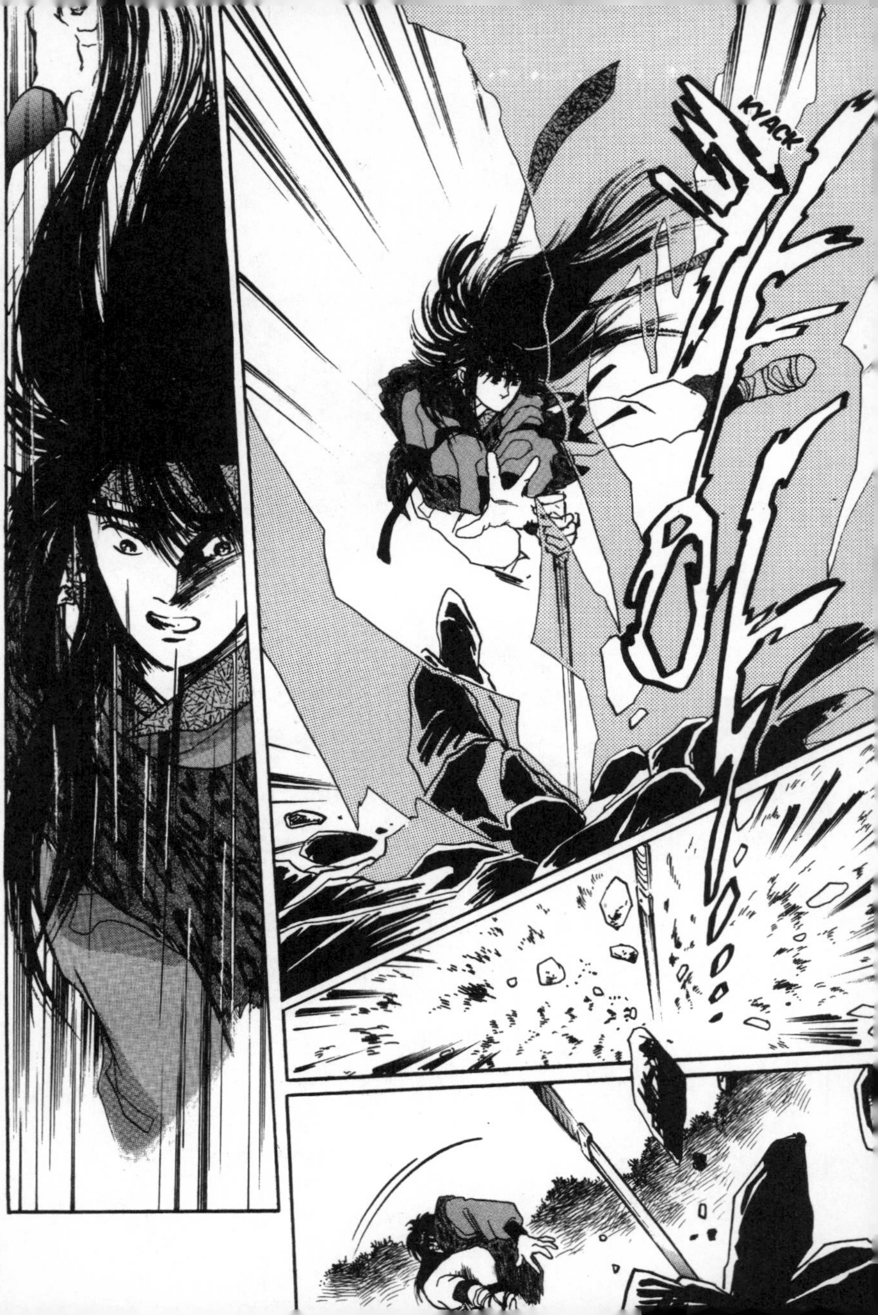
KYACK

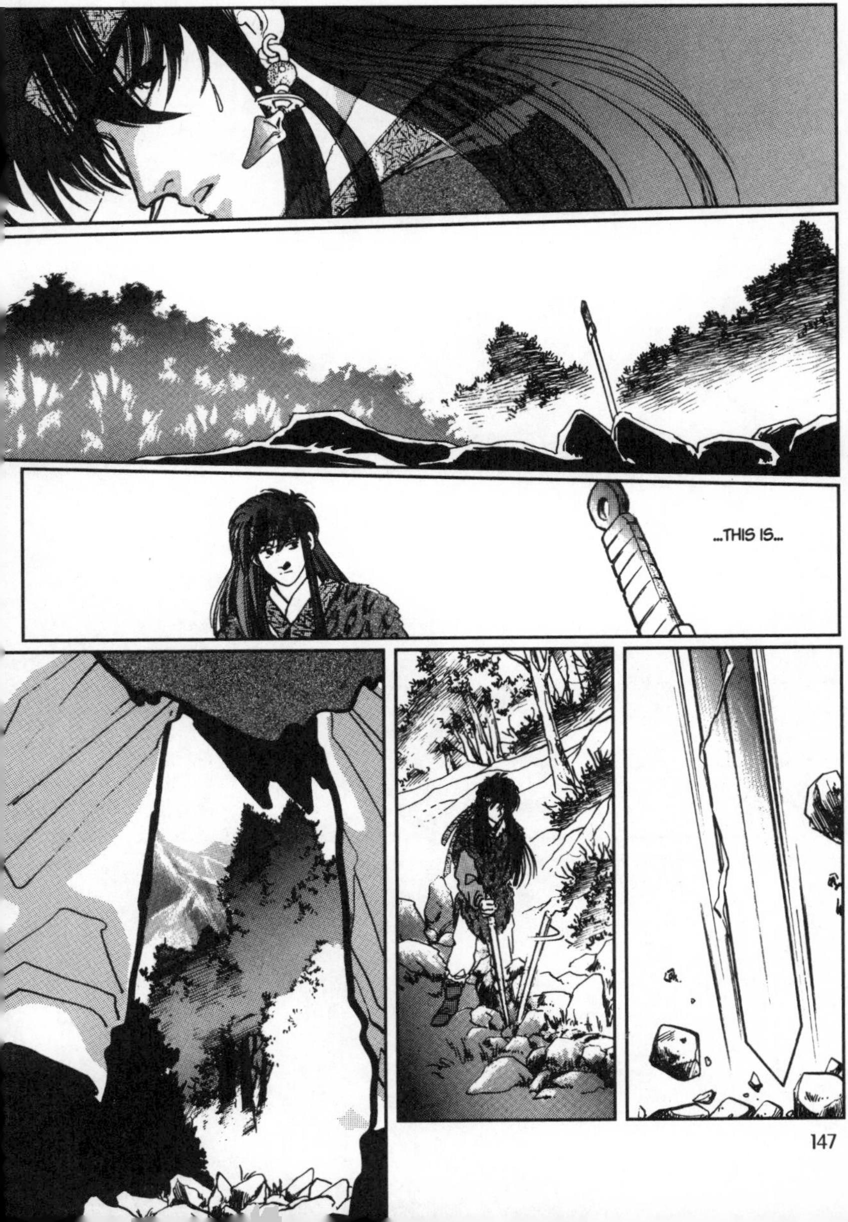
...THIS IS...

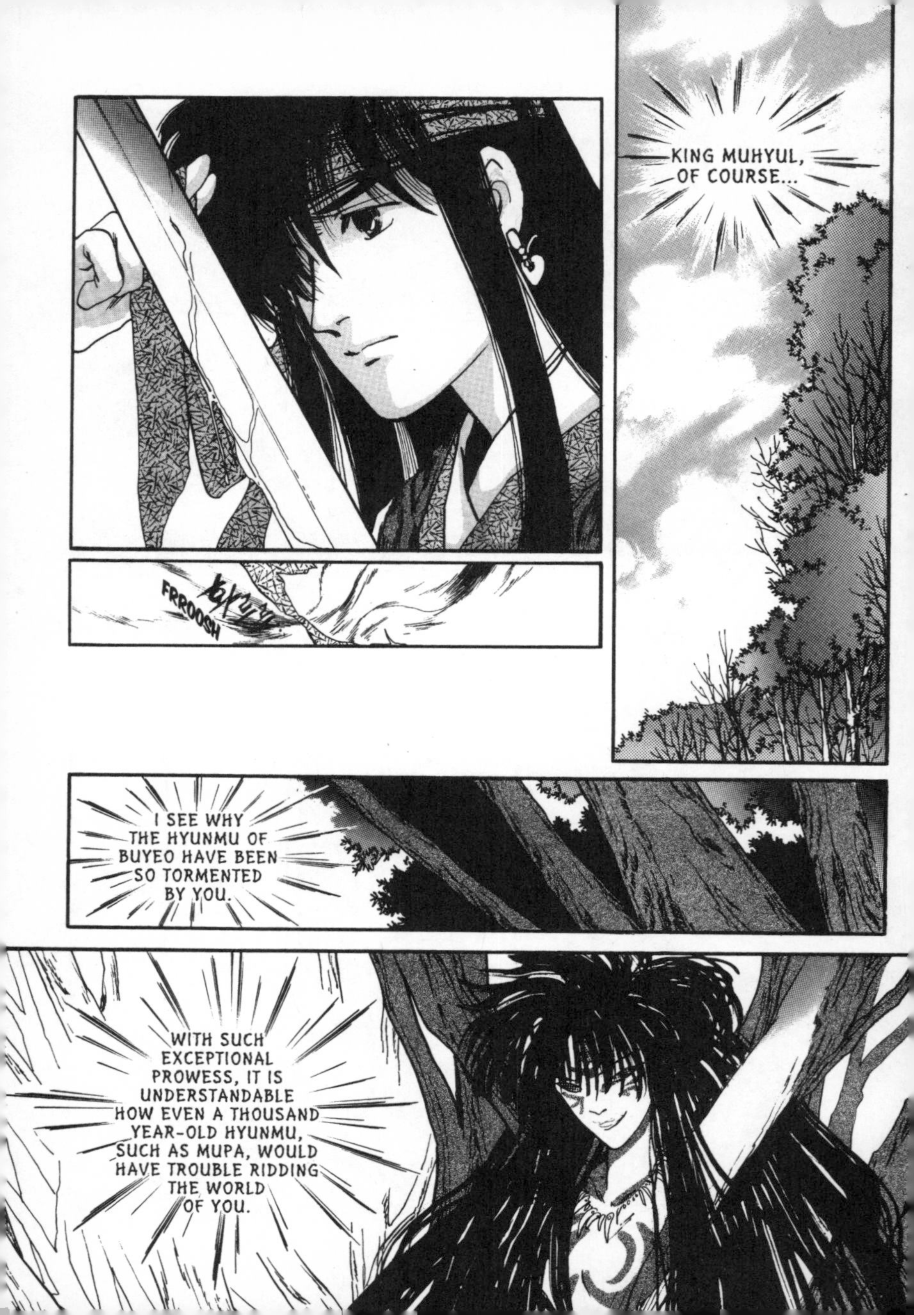
FRROOSH
KING MUHYUL, OF COURSE...
I SEE WHY THE HYUNMU OF BUYEO HAVE BEEN SO TORMENTED BY YOU.
WITH SUCH EXCEPTIONAL PROWESS, IT IS UNDERSTANDABLE HOW EVEN A THOUSAND YEAR-OLD HYUNMU, SUCH AS MUPA, WOULD HAVE TROUBLE RIDDING THE WORLD OF YOU.

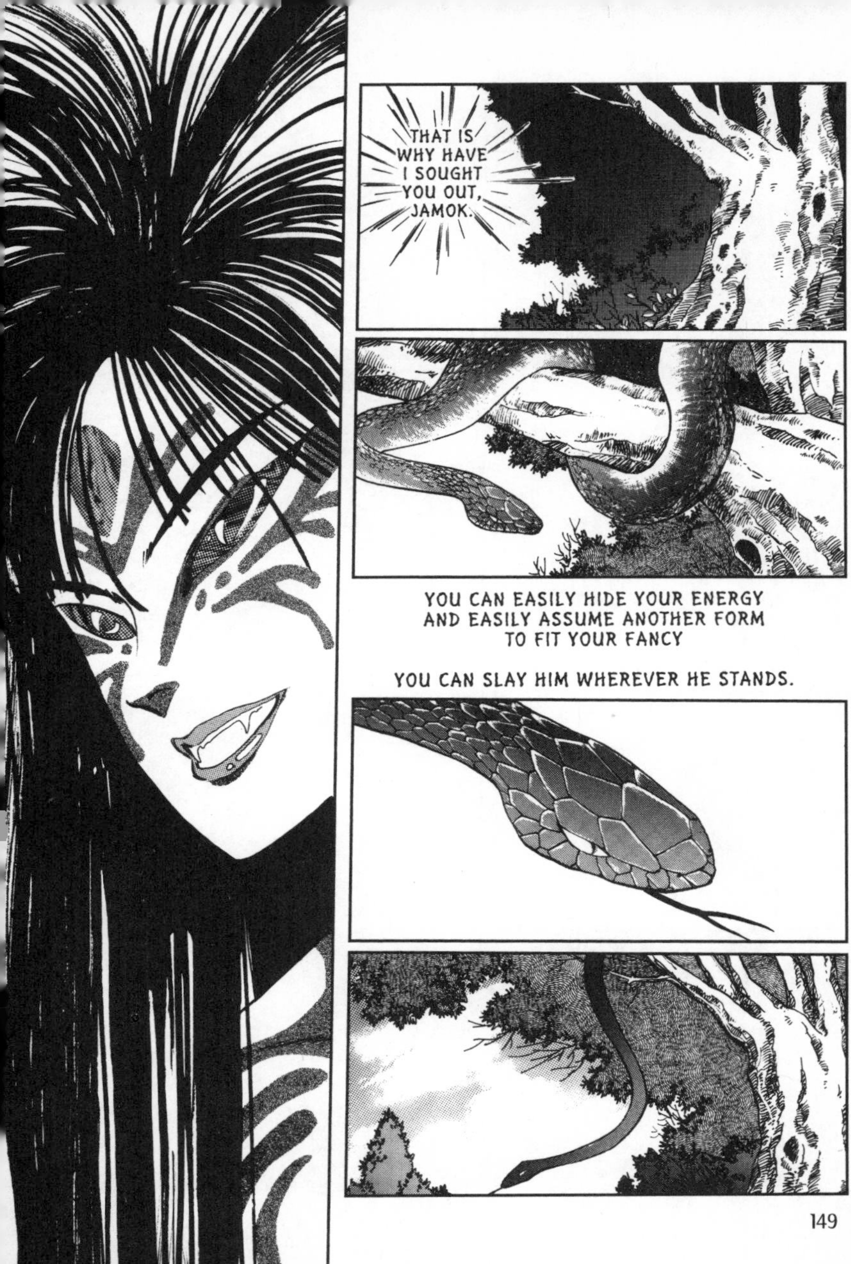
THAT IS WHY HAVE I SOUGHT YOU OUT, JAMOK.
YOU CAN EASILY HIDE YOUR ENERGY AND EASILY ASSUME ANOTHER FORM TO FIT YOUR FANCY
YOU CAN SLAY HIM WHEREVER HE STANDS.

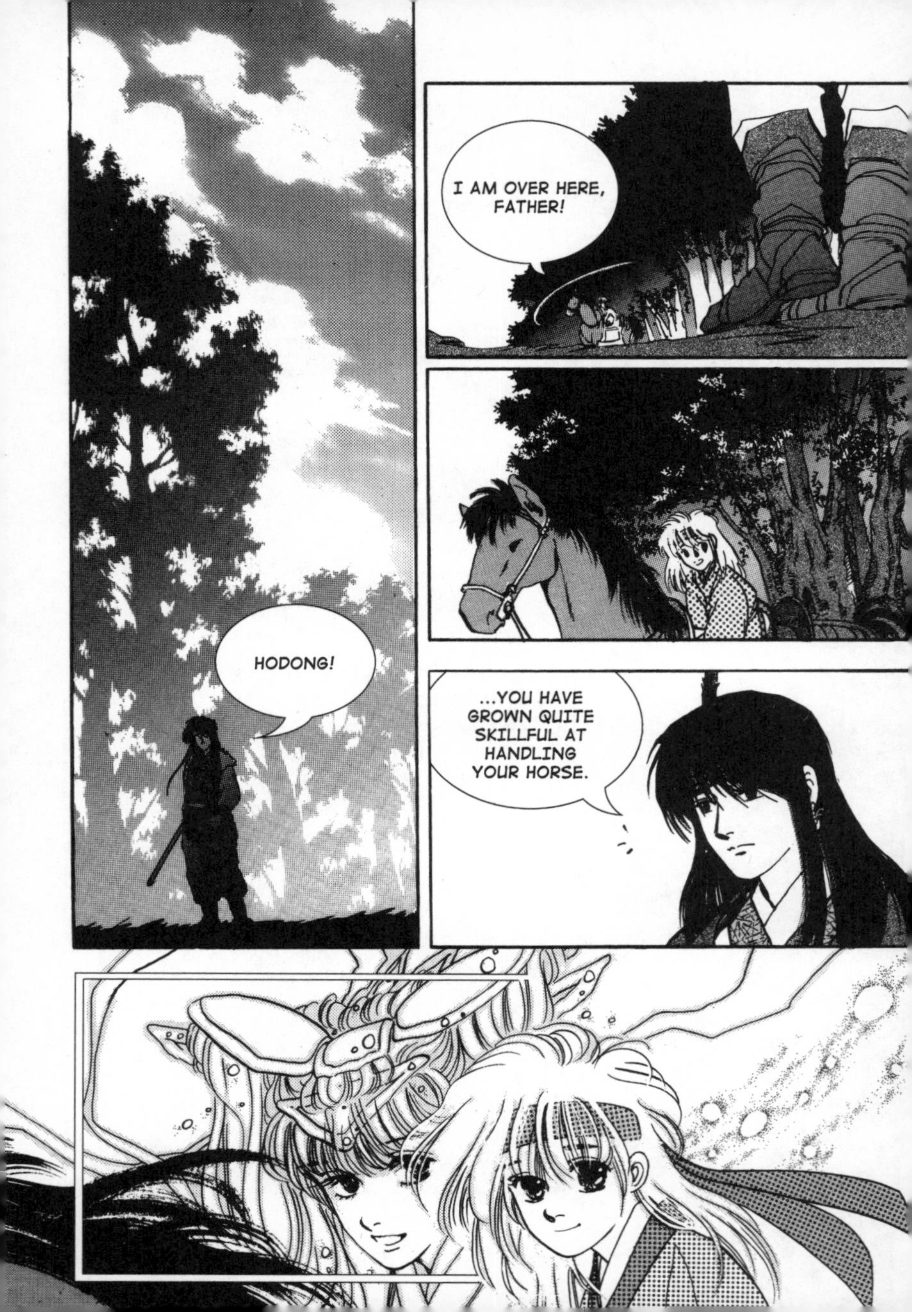
HODONG!
I AM OVER HERE, FATHER!
...YOU HAVE GROWN QUITE SKILLFUL AT HANDLING YOUR HORSE.

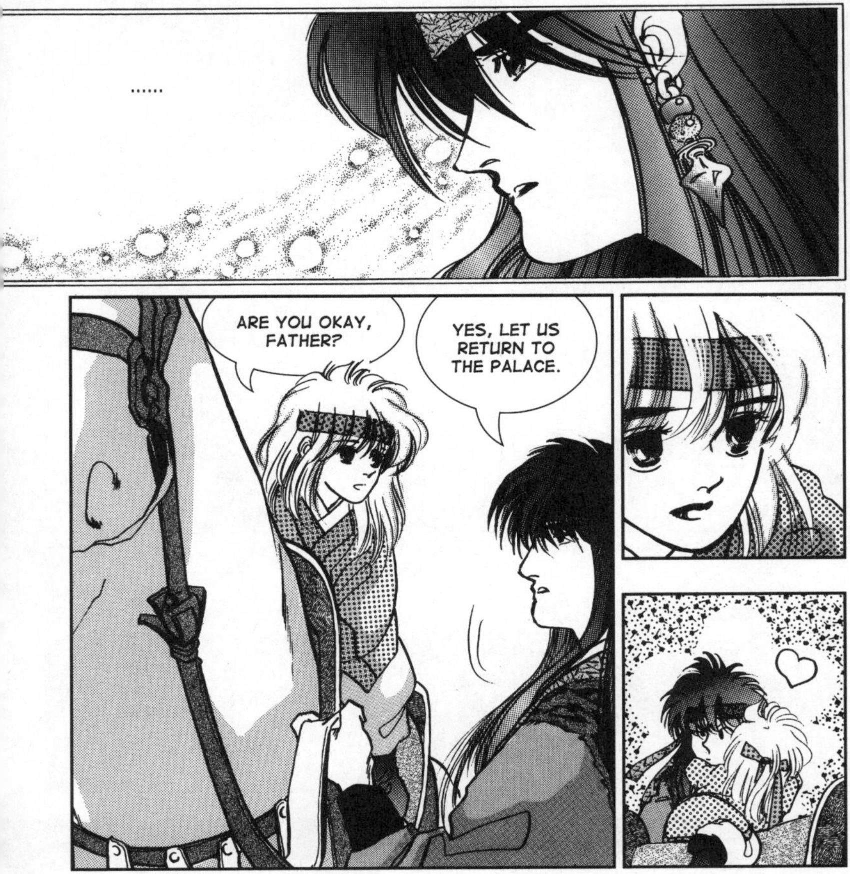
......
ARE YOU OKAY, FATHER?
YES, LET US RETURN TO THE PALACE.

HOWEVER, I MAY HAVE TO RECONSIDER MY FUTURE PLANS FOR YOU.

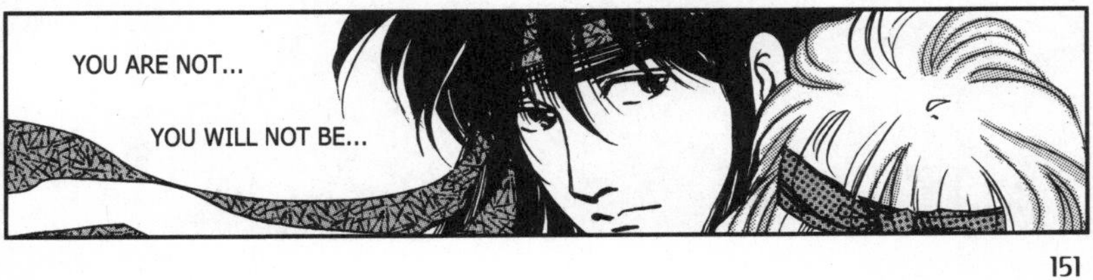
YOU ARE NOT...
YOU WILL NOT BE...

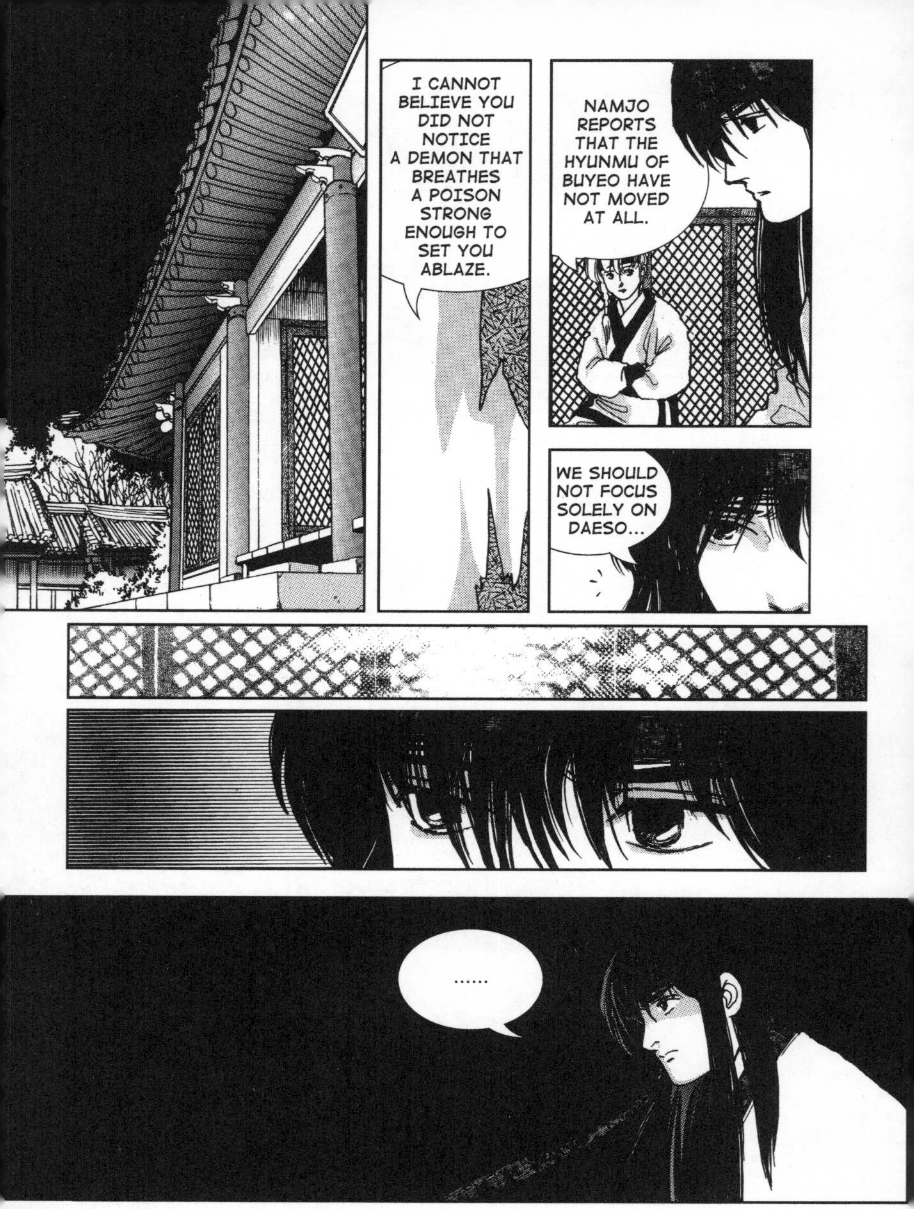
I CANNOT BELIEVE YOU DID NOT NOTICE A DEMON THAT BREATHES A POISON STRONG ENOUGH TO SET YOU ABLAZE.
NAMJO REPORTS THAT THE HYUNMU OF BUYEO HAVE NOT MOVED AT ALL.
WE SHOULD NOT FOCUS SOLELY ON DAESO...
......

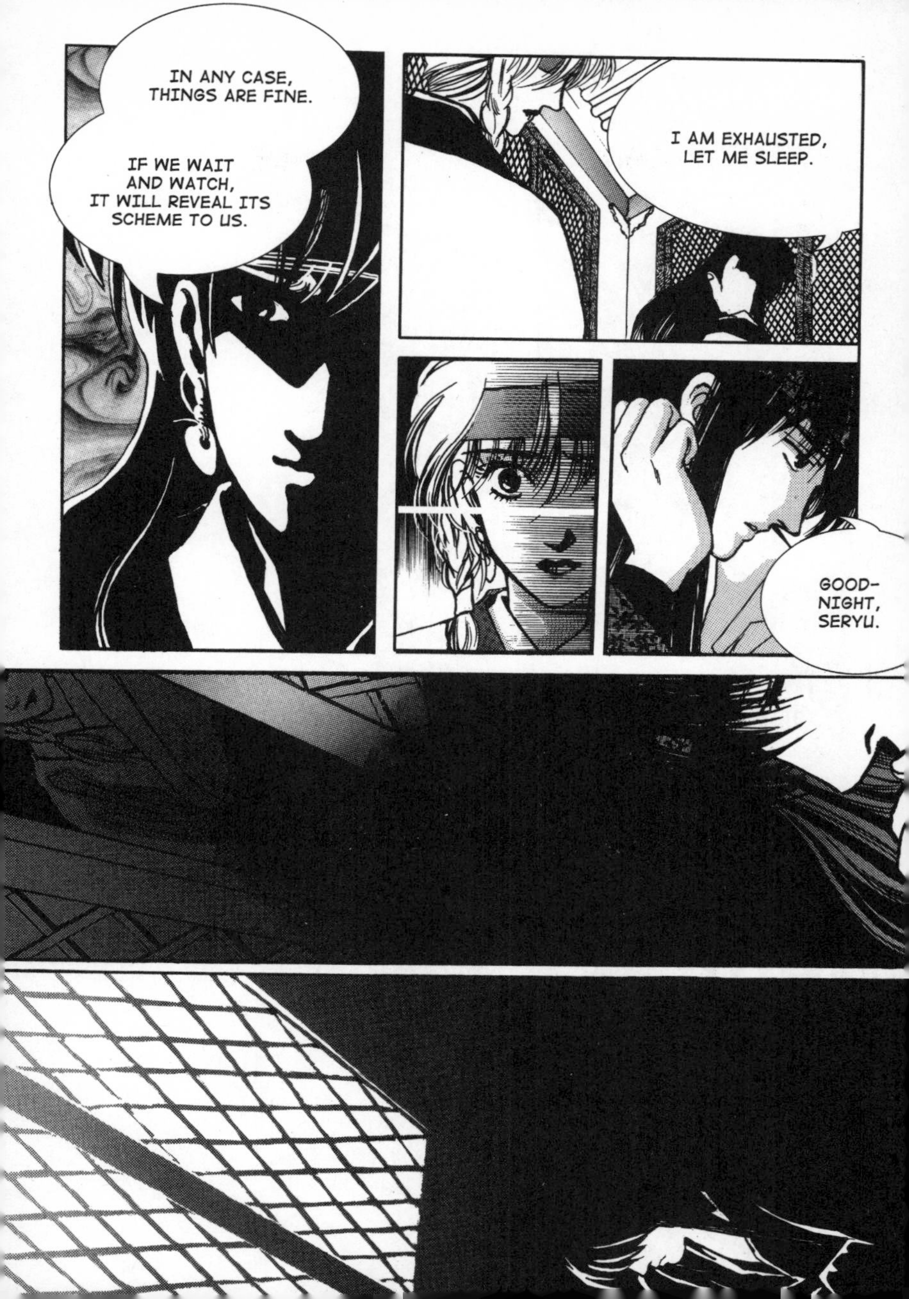
IN ANY CASE, THINGS ARE FINE.
IF WE WAIT AND WATCH, IT WILL REVEAL ITS SCHEME TO US.
I AM EXHAUSTED, LET ME SLEEP.
GOOD-NIGHT, SERYU.

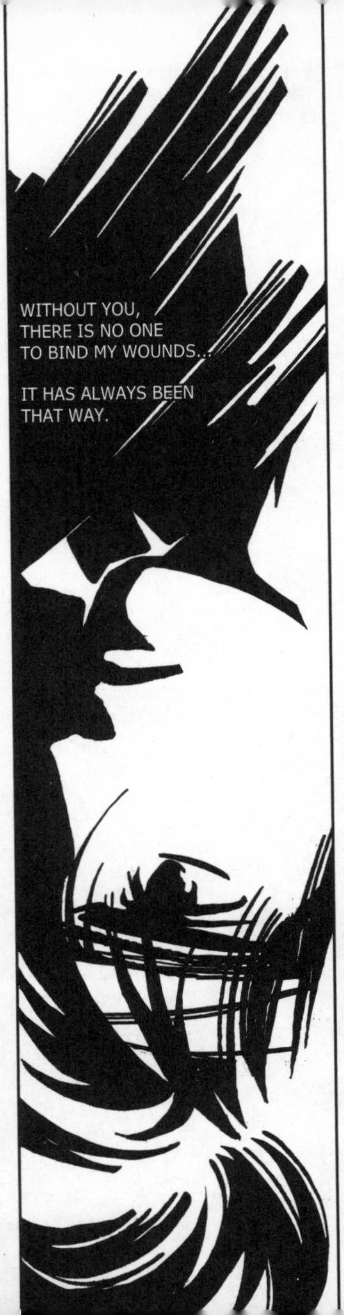
WITHOUT YOU,
THERE IS NO ONE
TO BIND MY WOUNDS...
IT HAS ALWAYS BEEN
THAT WAY.

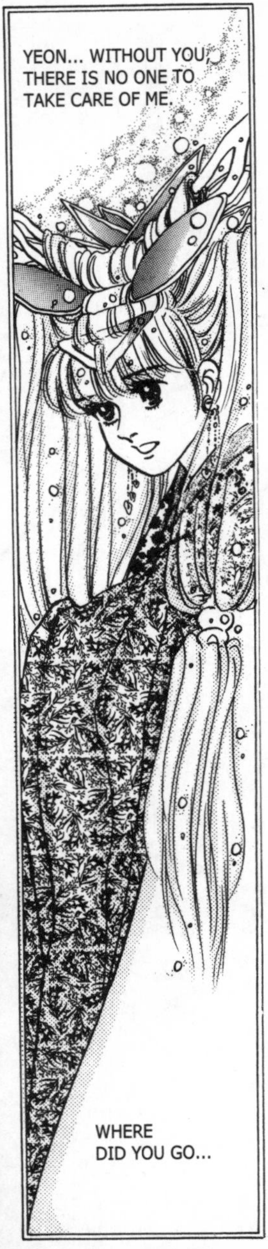
YEON... WITHOUT YOU,
THERE IS NO ONE TO
TAKE CARE OF ME.
WHERE
DID YOU GO...

MY FLOWER...
MY YEON...

WHERE
DID YOU GO...

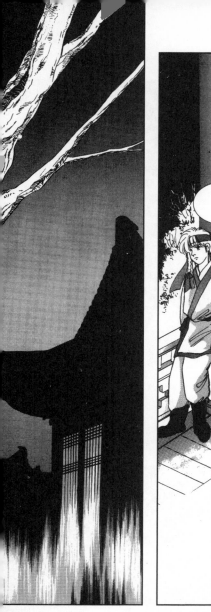

......

THINGS CANNOT CONTINUE ON THIS WAY.

IF I DO NOT TAKE APPROPRIATE MEASURES, THE DEMONS WILL FIND THE CHINKS IN OUR ARMOR, INFILTRATE THE PALACE, AND ONCE AGAIN INFLICT THEIR HORRIBLE DEEDS AS THEY HAVE DONE TO US BEFORE.

...THESE THOUGHTS...

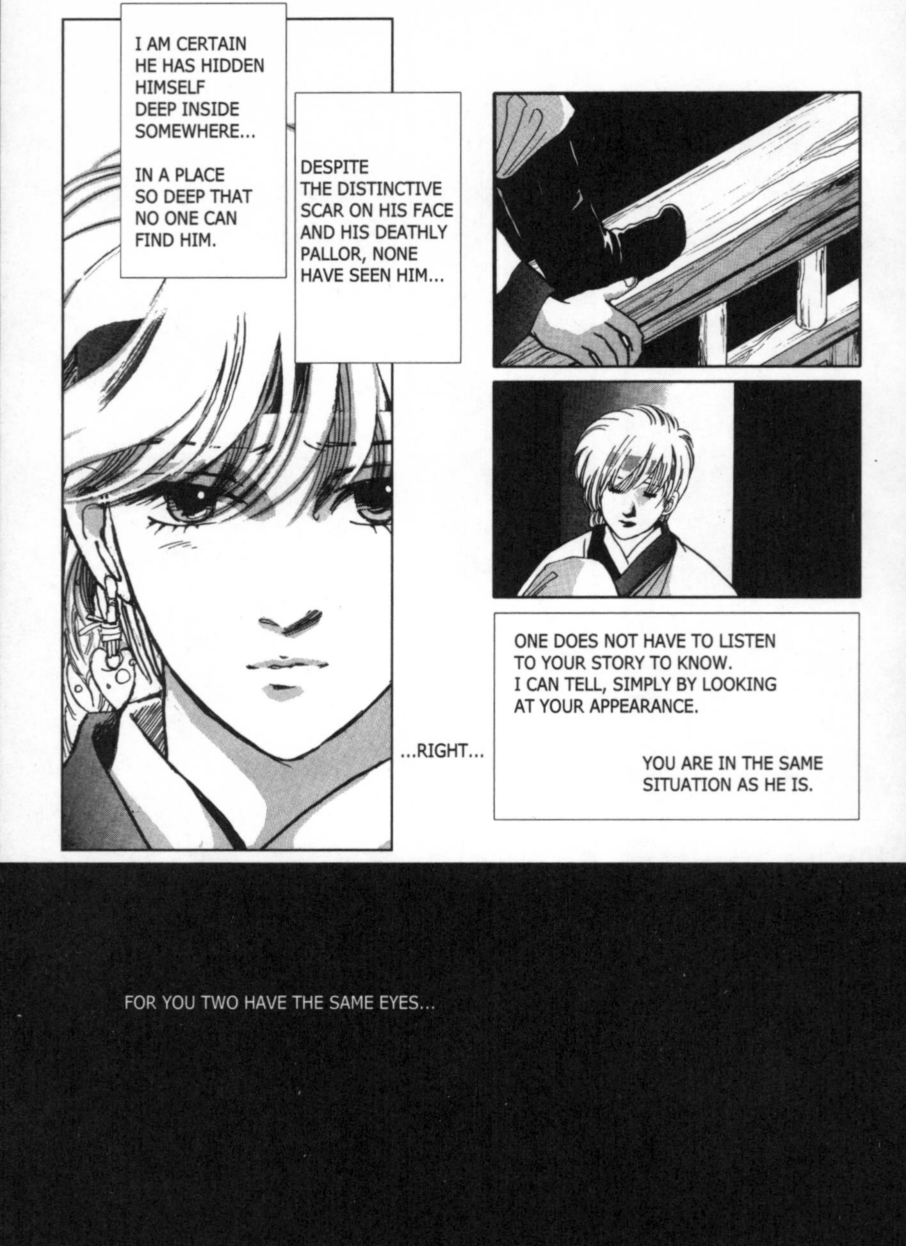
I AM CERTAIN HE HAS HIDDEN HIMSELF DEEP INSIDE SOMEWHERE...
IN A PLACE SO DEEP THAT NO ONE CAN FIND HIM.
DESPITE THE DISTINCTIVE SCAR ON HIS FACE AND HIS DEATHLY PALLOR, NONE HAVE SEEN HIM...
...RIGHT...
ONE DOES NOT HAVE TO LISTEN TO YOUR STORY TO KNOW. I CAN TELL, SIMPLY BY LOOKING AT YOUR APPEARANCE.
YOU ARE IN THE SAME SITUATION AS HE IS.

FOR YOU TWO HAVE THE SAME EYES...

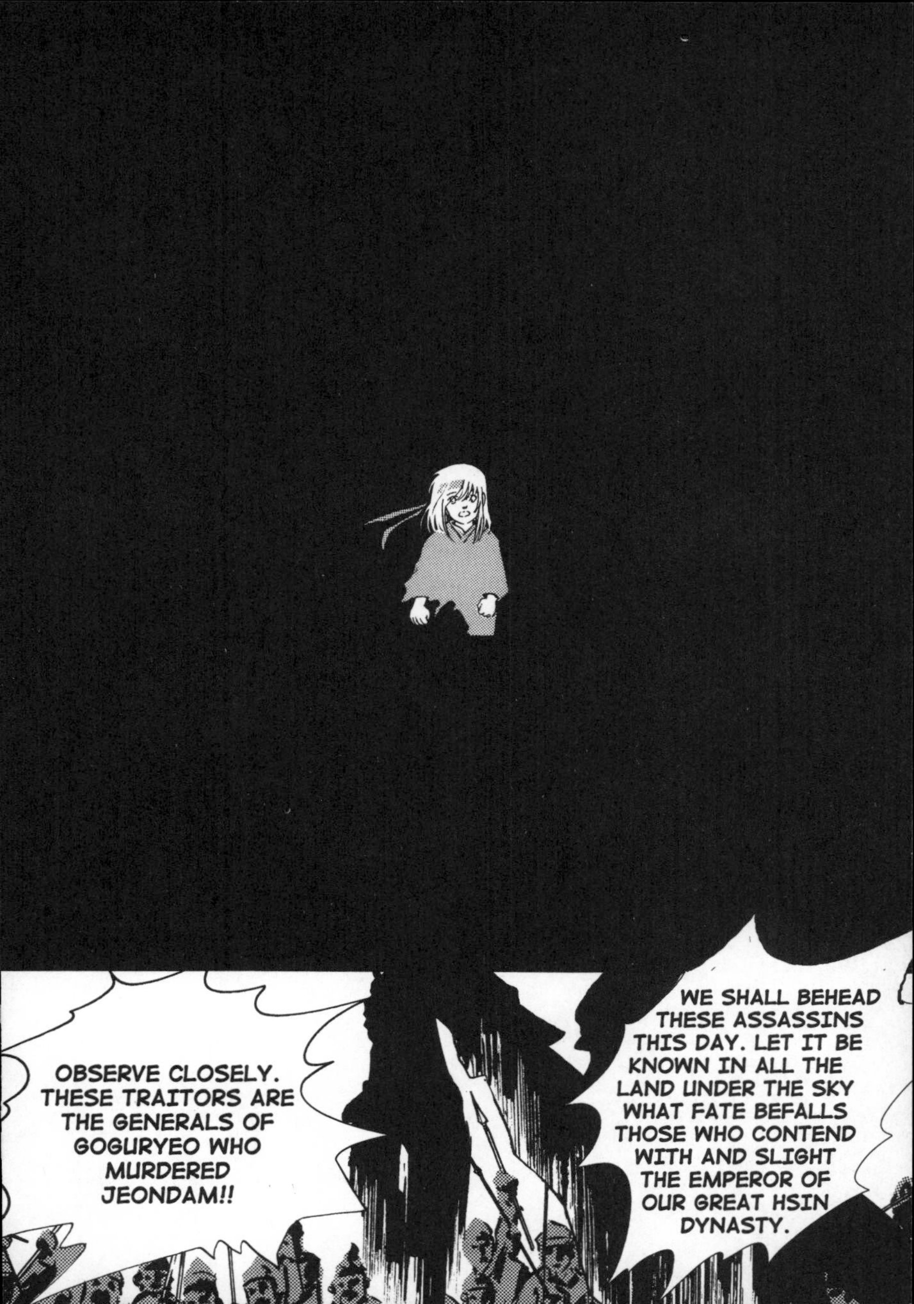
OBSERVE CLOSELY. THESE TRAITORS ARE THE GENERALS OF GOGURYEO WHO MURDERED JEONDAM!!
WE SHALL BEHEAD THESE ASSASSINS THIS DAY. LET IT BE KNOWN IN ALL THE LAND UNDER THE SKY WHAT FATE BEFALLS THOSE WHO CONTEND WITH AND SLIGHT THE EMPEROR OF OUR GREAT HSIN DYNASTY.

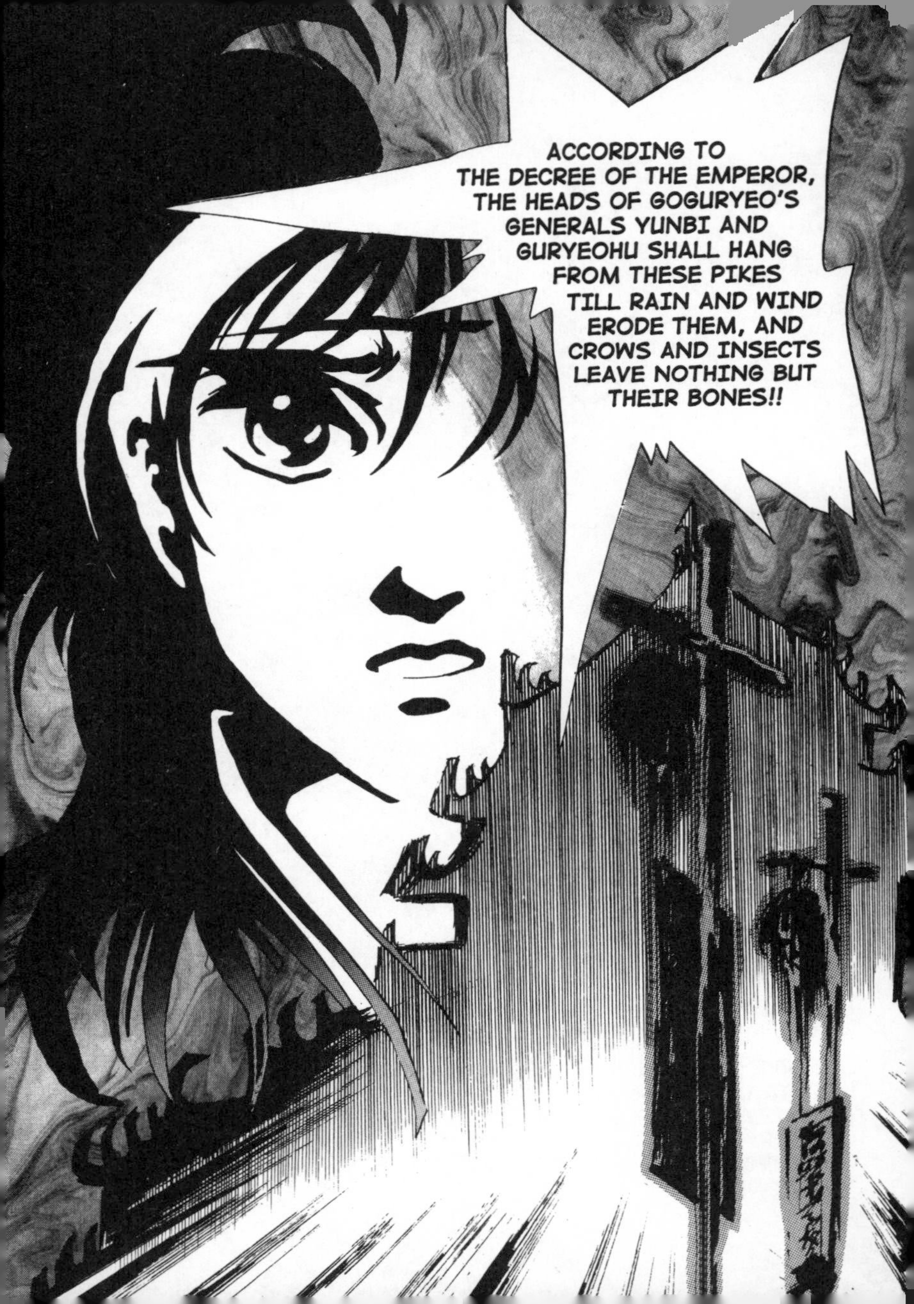
ACCORDING TO THE DECREE OF THE EMPEROR, THE HEADS OF GOGURYEO'S GENERALS YUNBI AND GURYEOHU SHALL HANG FROM THESE PIKES TILL RAIN AND WIND ERODE THEM, AND CROWS AND INSECTS LEAVE NOTHING BUT THEIR BONES!!

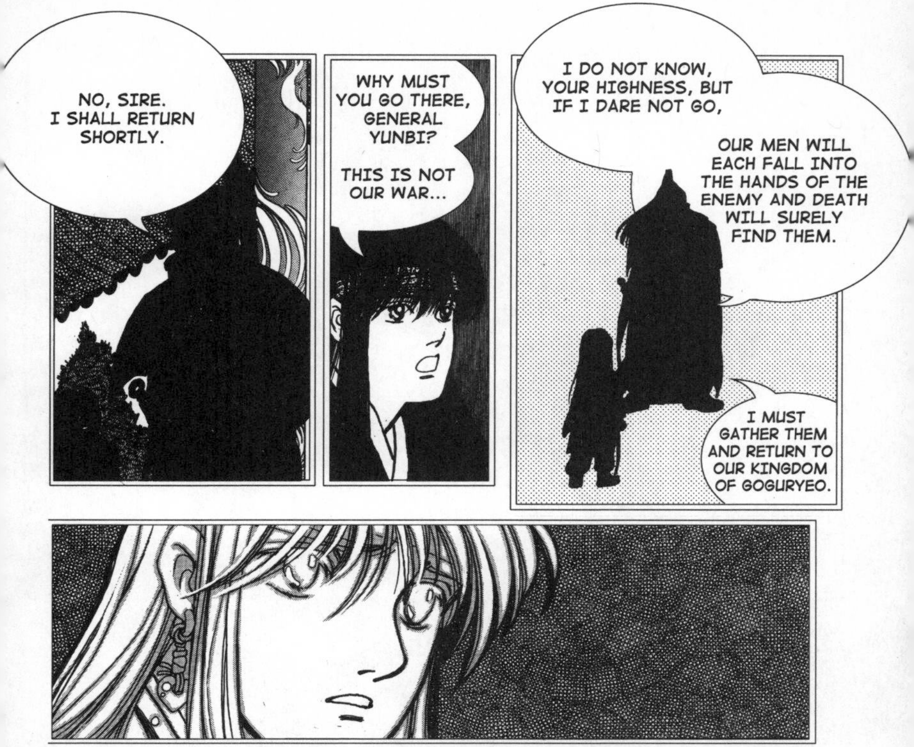
NO, SIRE. I SHALL RETURN SHORTLY.
WHY MUST YOU GO THERE, GENERAL YUNBI?
THIS IS NOT OUR WAR...
I DO NOT KNOW, YOUR HIGHNESS, BUT IF I DARE NOT GO,
OUR MEN WILL EACH FALL INTO THE HANDS OF THE ENEMY AND DEATH WILL SURELY FIND THEM.
I MUST GATHER THEM AND RETURN TO OUR KINGDOM OF GOGURYEO.

Notes: During the 31st year of King Yuri's reign, Wang Mang of the Han dynasty began his campaign against Xiongnu. He tried to requisition the forces of Korean tribes living within the Hsin borders. The Korean tribes refused, and marched out of Hsin borders. The army Wang sent to attack the Korean troops were then defeated. General Wang then sent Yan You who used humble words to trick their leader, Guryeohu Chu, into a meeting with him where he was assassinated. Wang then renamed Goguryeo to the derogatory term "Xiajuli" (gao means "high", while xia means "low"), which further enraged the Koreans, causing them to attack the Hsin northeastern regions with greater ferocity.

Hsin Dynasty: (A.D. 9-23) Dynasty preceded the Eastern Han dynasty.

Wang Mang: (45 B.C.–October 6, 23) A Han Dynasty official who seized the throne from the Liu family and founded the Hsin (or Xin, meaning "new") who ruled between A.D. 9–23. Wang was born into a distinguished family, but his father died when he was young and he held only minor posts until being made a marquess in 16 B.C. In 8 B.C. Wang was appointed regent for Emperor Cheng, but Emperor Cheng died around 7 or 6 B.C. and was succeeded by Emperor Ai. However, in 1 B.C., Emperor Ai died and Wang Mang was reappointed regent for the new Emperor Ping. Wang consolidated his power by marrying his daughter to the Emperor Ping. When Emperor Ping died as a child in A.D. 6, Wang Mang chose an infant successor, the Emperor Ruzi, who had only been born in A.D. 5. Finally, in January of A.D. 9, he ascended the throne himself and declared the Xin Dynasty. In October of A.D. 23, the capital Chang'an was attacked and the imperial palace ransacked. Wang Mang and his 1,000 courtiers made their last stand and fought until they were completely obliterated. Wang Mang died in the battle. The Han dynasty was reestablished in A.D. 25 when Liu Xiu (Emperor Guangwu) took the throne.

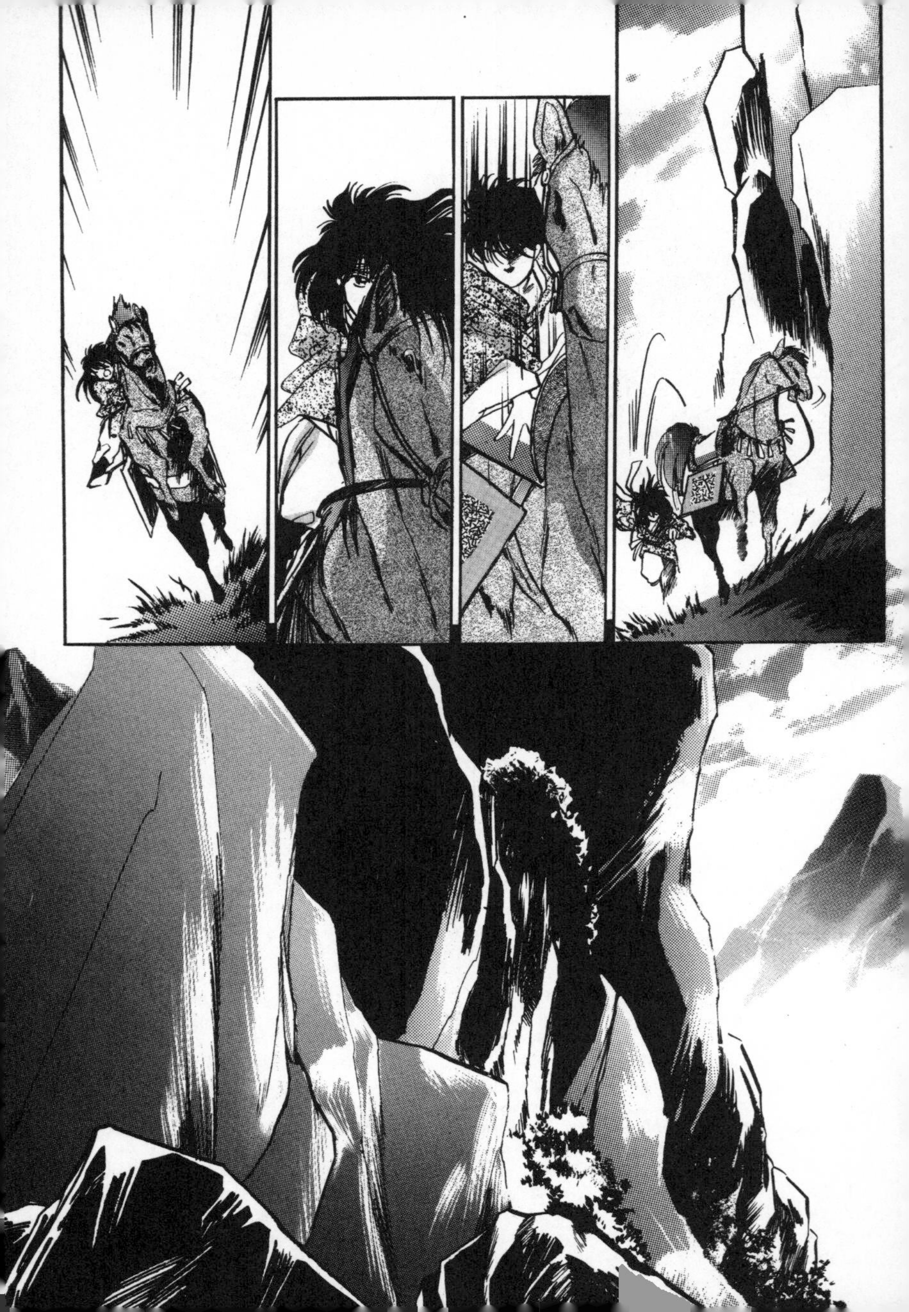

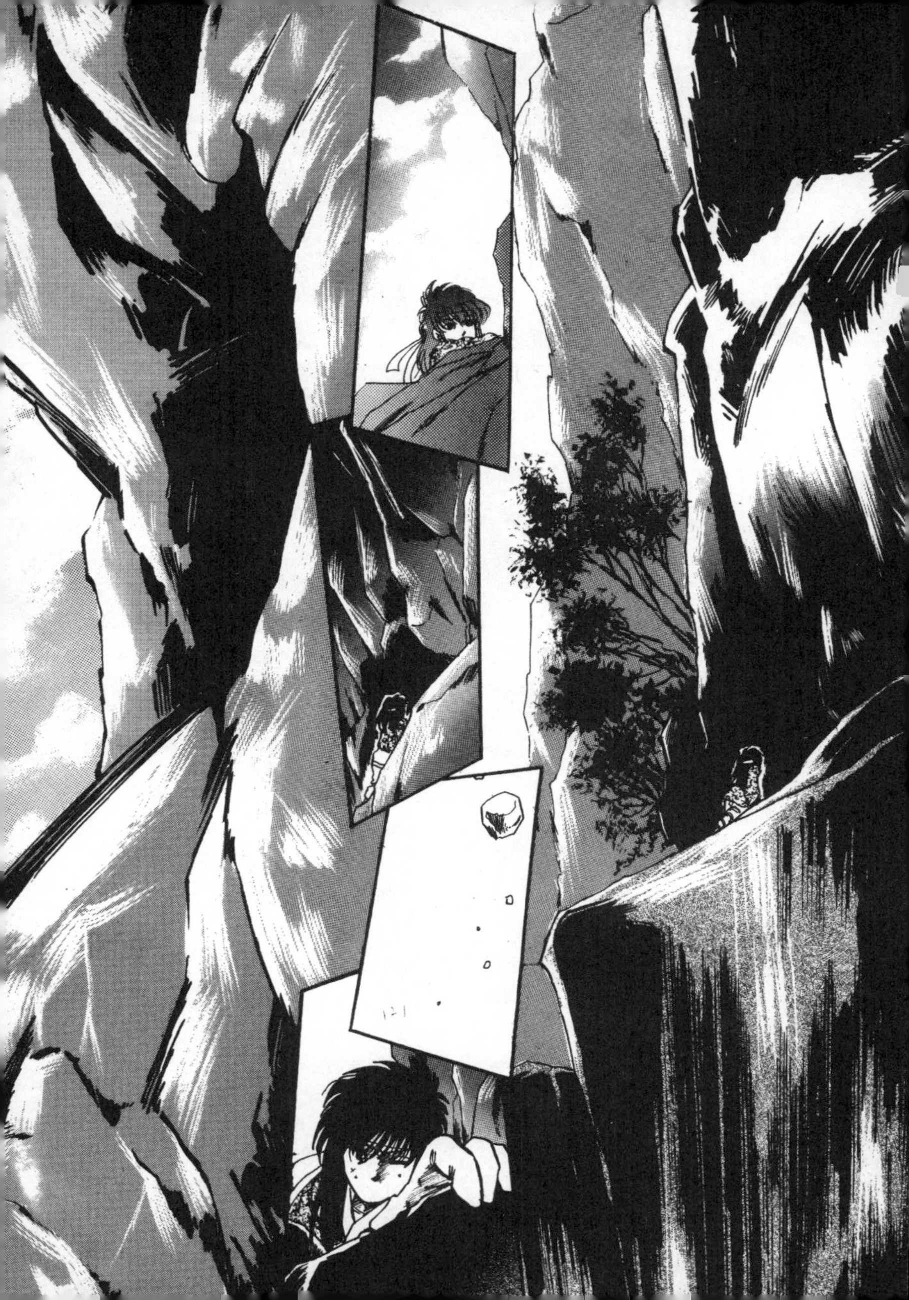

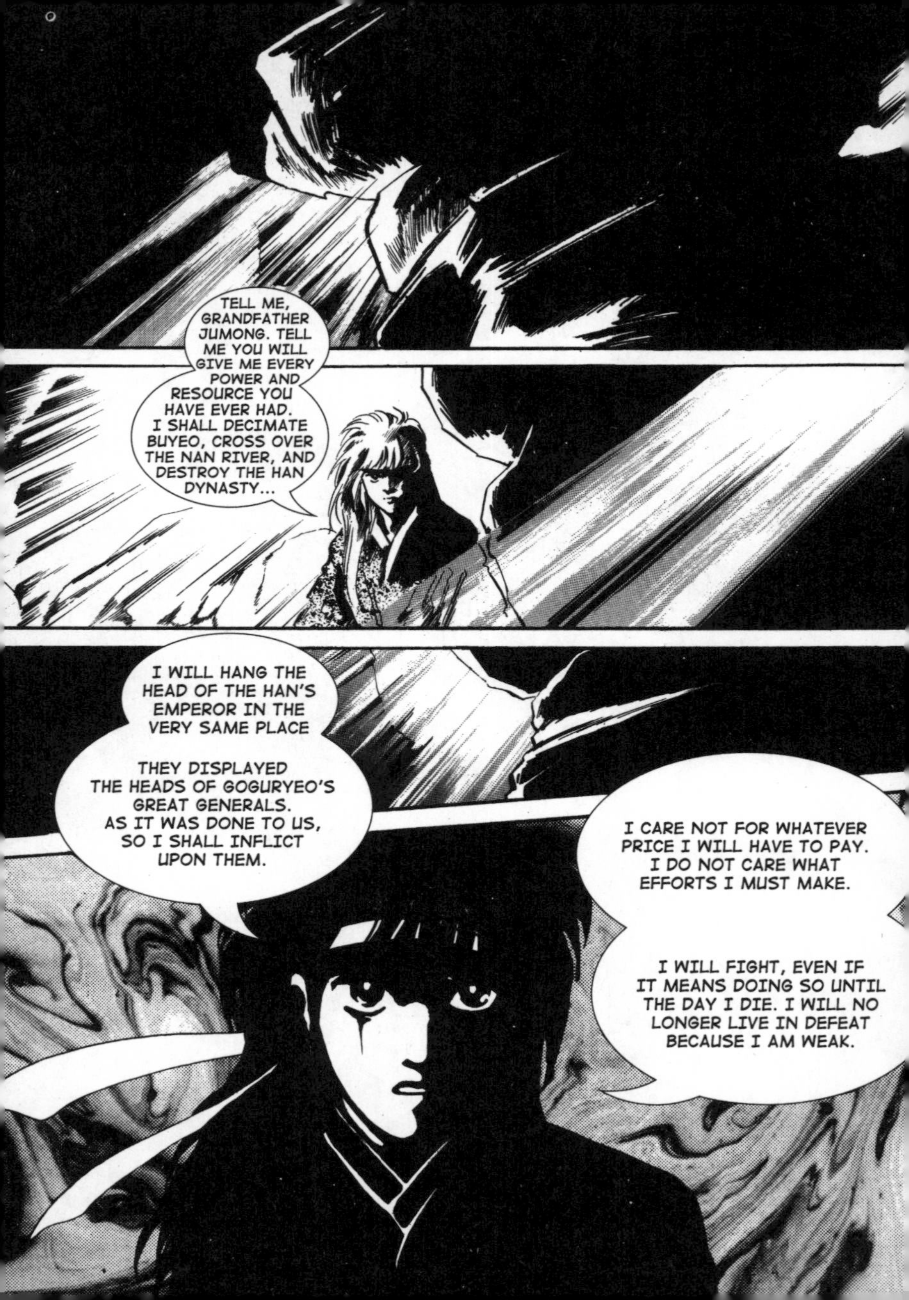
TELL ME, GRANDFATHER JUMONG. TELL ME YOU WILL GIVE ME EVERY POWER AND RESOURCE YOU HAVE EVER HAD. I SHALL DECIMATE BUYEO, CROSS OVER THE NAN RIVER, AND DESTROY THE HAN DYNASTY...
I WILL HANG THE HEAD OF THE HAN'S EMPEROR IN THE VERY SAME PLACE
THEY DISPLAYED THE HEADS OF GOGURYEO'S GREAT GENERALS. AS IT WAS DONE TO US, SO I SHALL INFLICT UPON THEM.
I CARE NOT FOR WHATEVER PRICE I WILL HAVE TO PAY. I DO NOT CARE WHAT EFFORTS I MUST MAKE.
I WILL FIGHT, EVEN IF IT MEANS DOING SO UNTIL THE DAY I DIE. I WILL NO LONGER LIVE IN DEFEAT BECAUSE I AM WEAK.

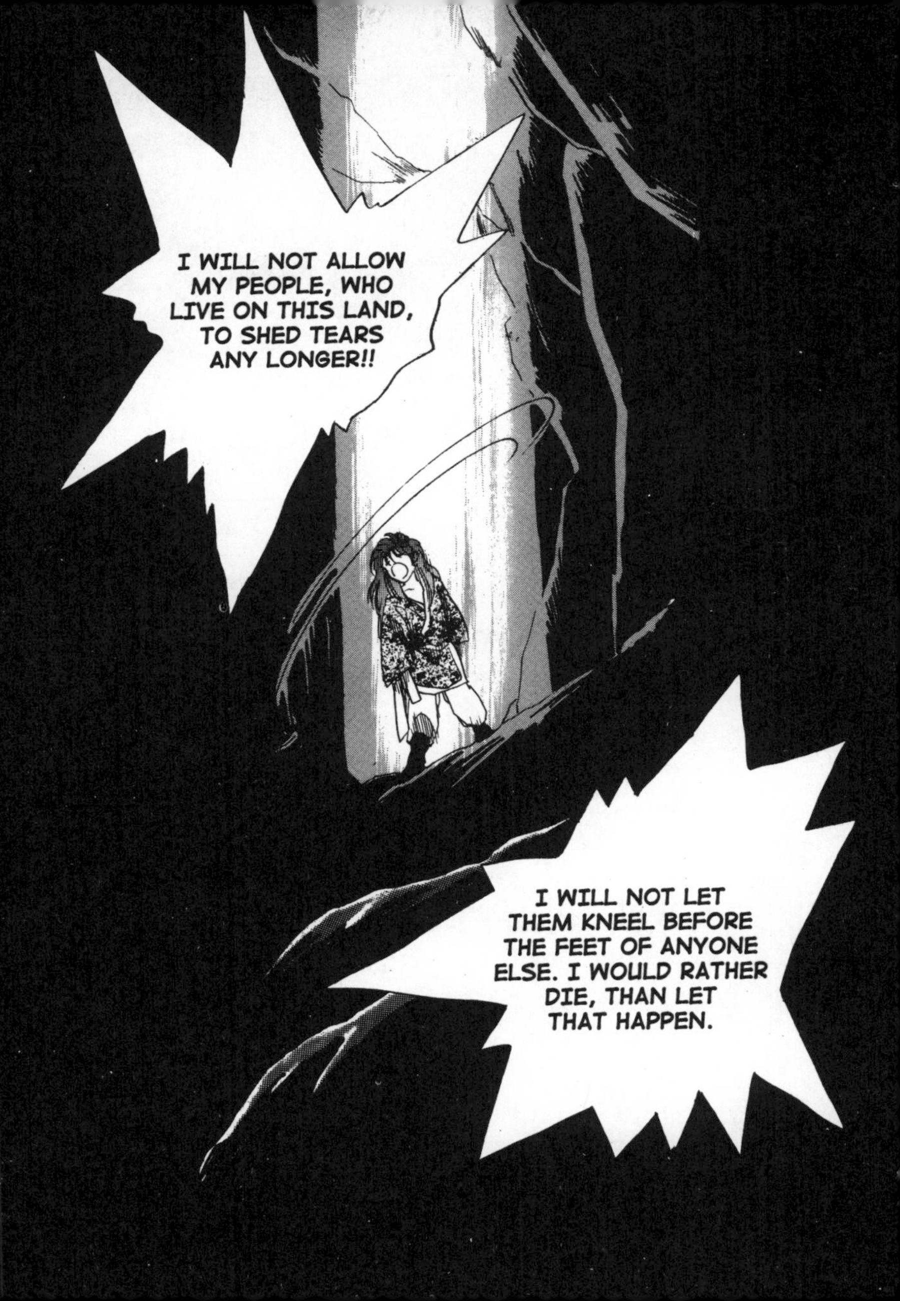
I WILL NOT ALLOW MY PEOPLE, WHO LIVE ON THIS LAND, TO SHED TEARS ANY LONGER!!
I WILL NOT LET THEM KNEEL BEFORE THE FEET OF ANYONE ELSE. I WOULD RATHER DIE, THAN LET THAT HAPPEN.

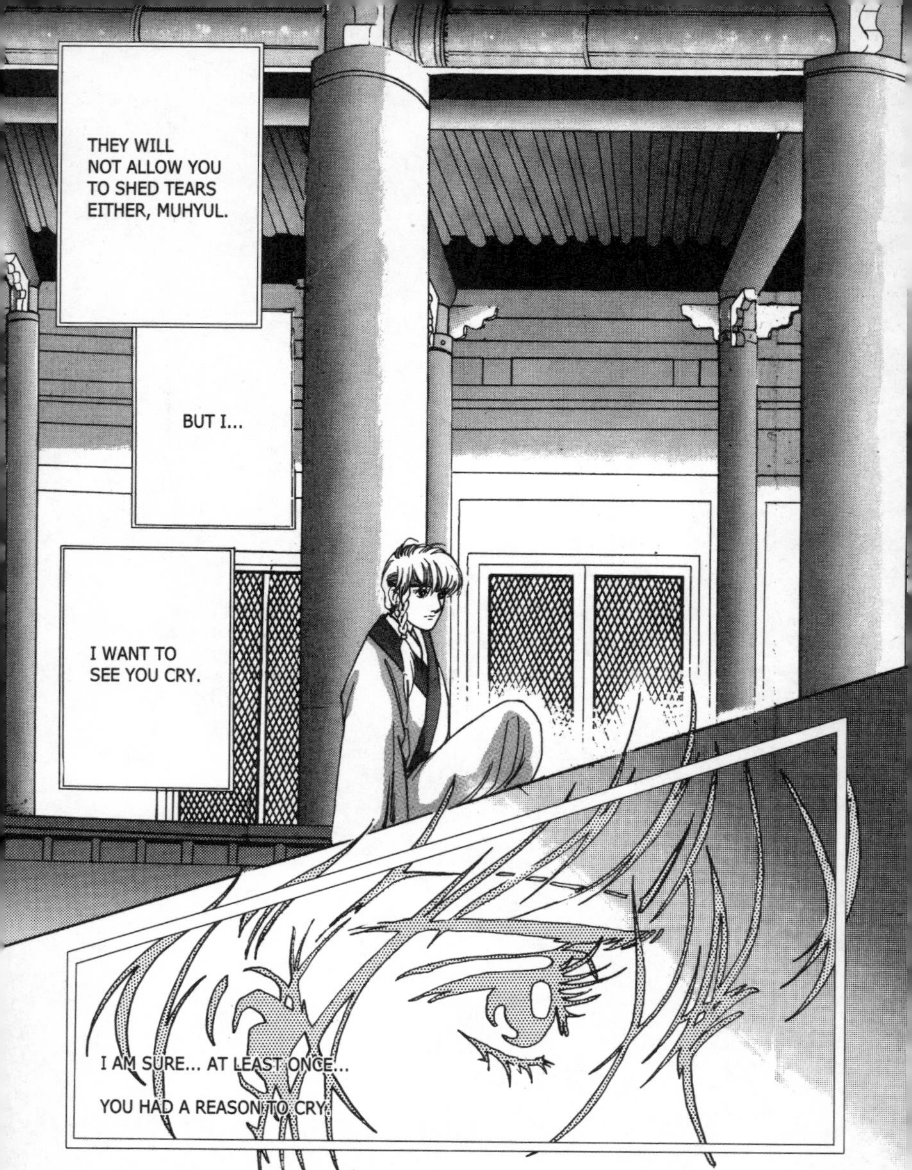
THEY WILL NOT ALLOW YOU TO SHED TEARS EITHER, MUHYUL.
BUT I...
I WANT TO SEE YOU CRY.
I AM SURE... AT LEAST ONCE...
YOU HAD A REASON TO CRY.

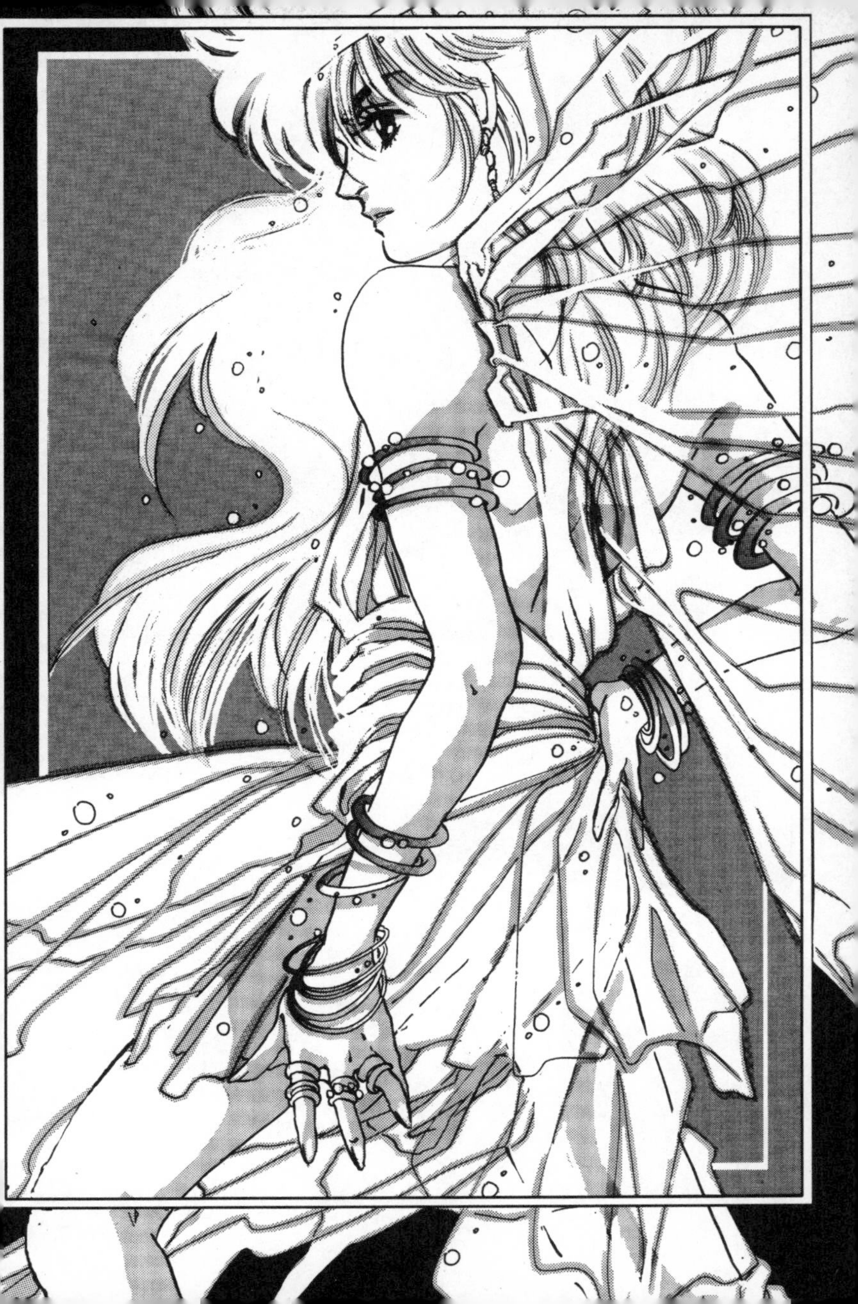

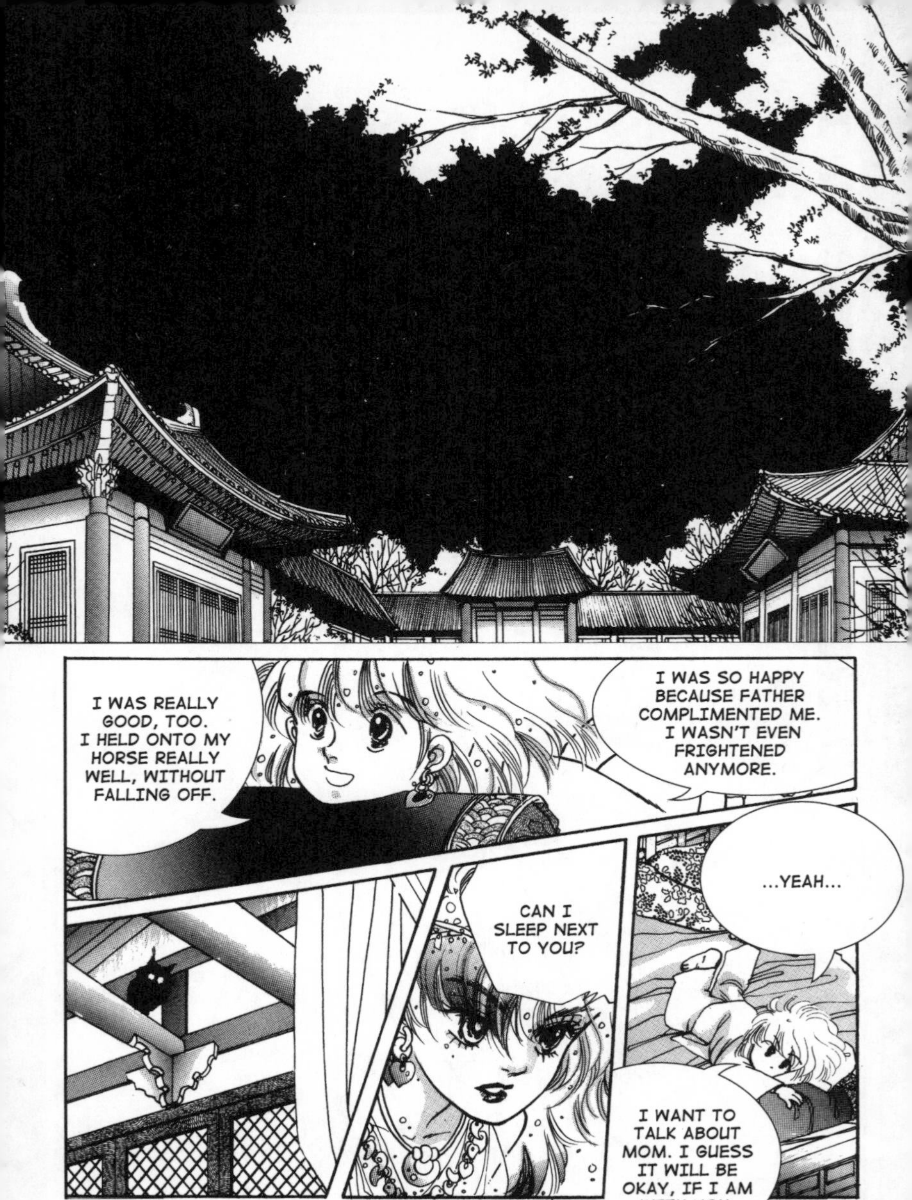
I WAS REALLY GOOD, TOO. I HELD ONTO MY HORSE REALLY WELL, WITHOUT FALLING OFF.
I WAS SO HAPPY BECAUSE FATHER COMPLIMENTED ME. I WASN'T EVEN FRIGHTENED ANYMORE.
CAN I SLEEP NEXT TO YOU?
...YEAH...
I WANT TO TALK ABOUT MOM. I GUESS IT WILL BE OKAY, IF I AM WITH YOU.

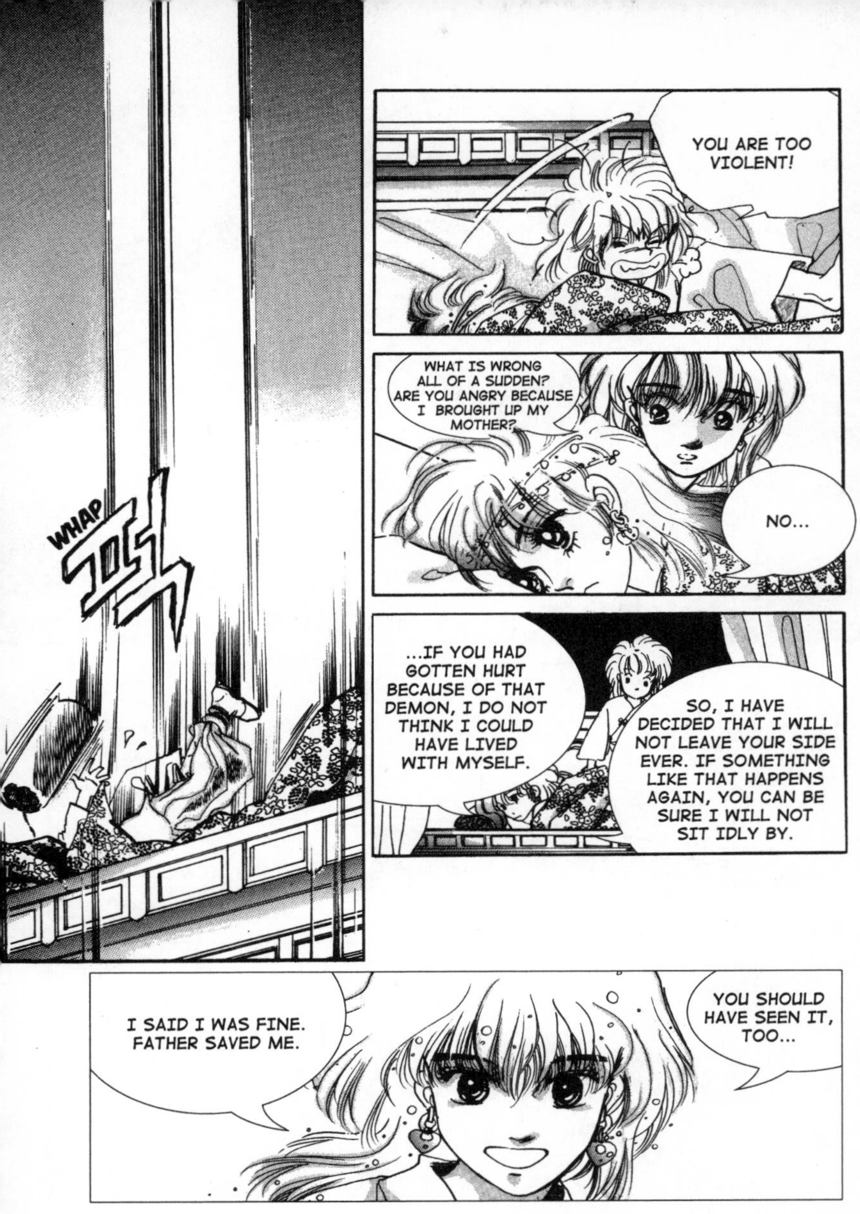
WHAP
퍽
YOU ARE TOO VIOLENT!
WHAT IS WRONG ALL OF A SUDDEN? ARE YOU ANGRY BECAUSE I BROUGHT UP MY MOTHER?
NO...
...IF YOU HAD GOTTEN HURT BECAUSE OF THAT DEMON, I DO NOT THINK I COULD HAVE LIVED WITH MYSELF.
SO, I HAVE DECIDED THAT I WILL NOT LEAVE YOUR SIDE EVER. IF SOMETHING LIKE THAT HAPPENS AGAIN, YOU CAN BE SURE I WILL NOT SIT IDLY BY.
I SAID I WAS FINE. FATHER SAVED ME.
YOU SHOULD HAVE SEEN IT, TOO...

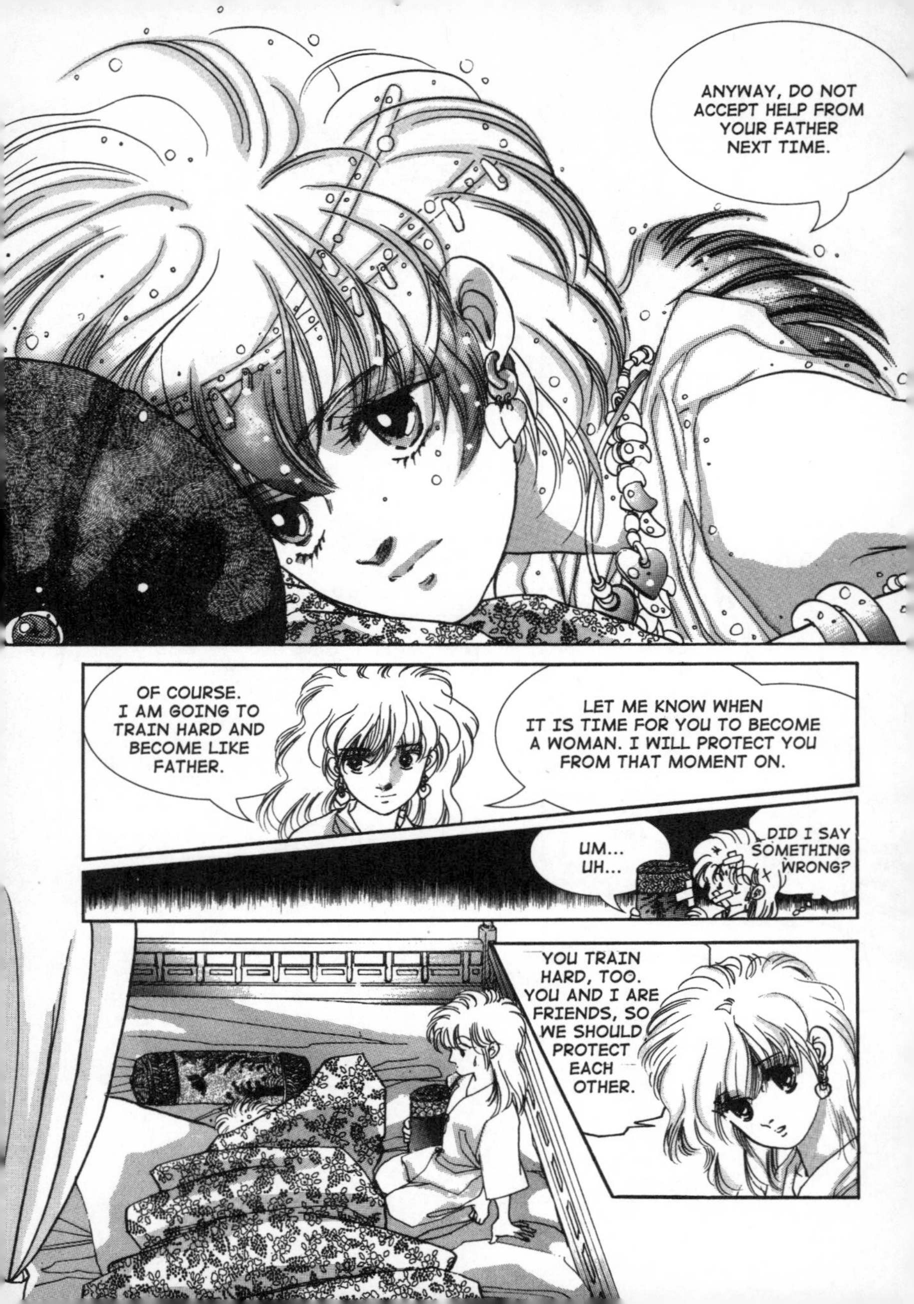
ANYWAY, DO NOT ACCEPT HELP FROM YOUR FATHER NEXT TIME.
OF COURSE. I AM GOING TO TRAIN HARD AND BECOME LIKE FATHER.
LET ME KNOW WHEN IT IS TIME FOR YOU TO BECOME A WOMAN. I WILL PROTECT YOU FROM THAT MOMENT ON.
UM... UH...
DID I SAY SOMETHING WRONG?
YOU TRAIN HARD, TOO. YOU AND I ARE FRIENDS, SO WE SHOULD PROTECT EACH OTHER.

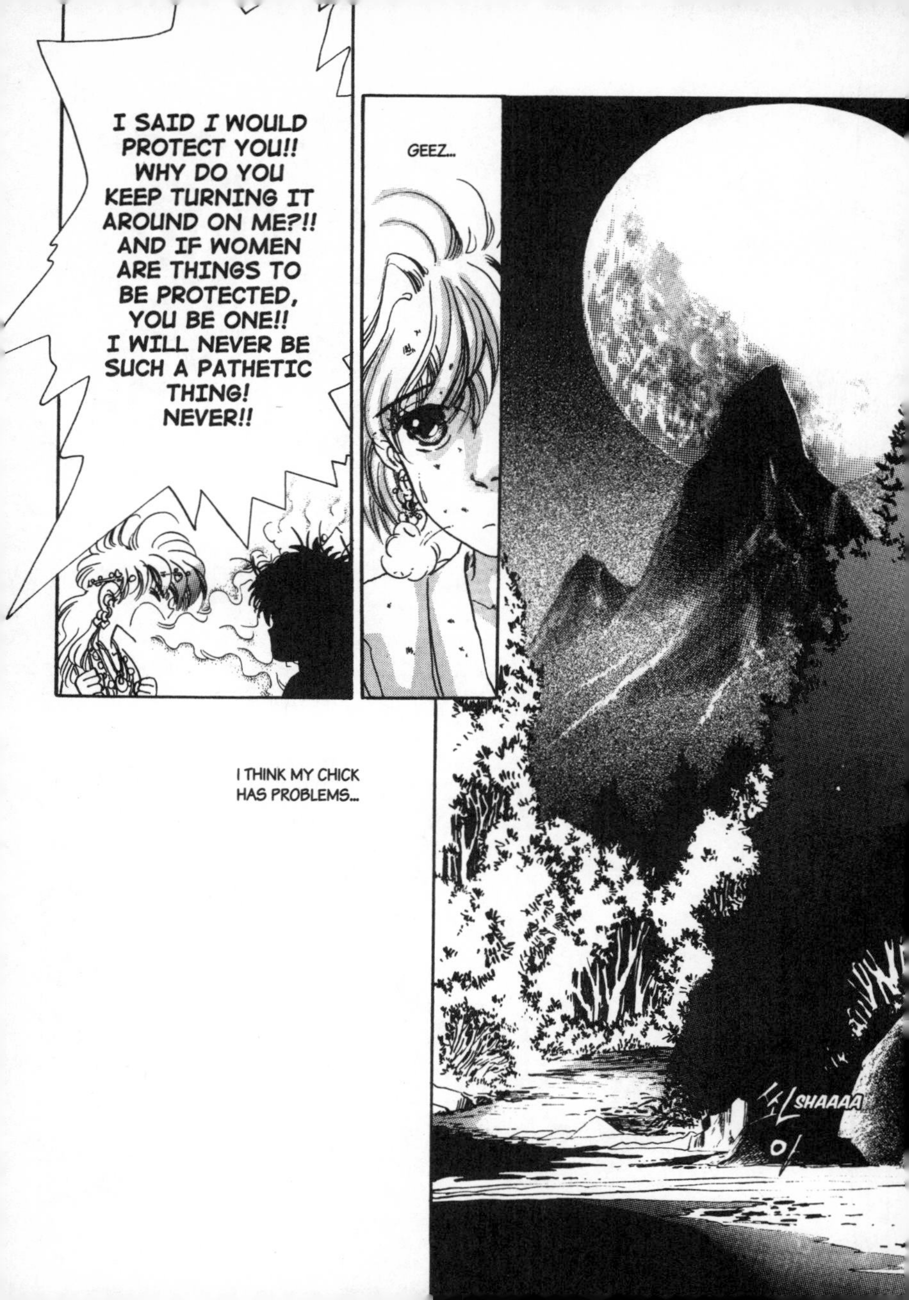
I SAID *I* WOULD PROTECT YOU!! WHY DO YOU KEEP TURNING IT AROUND ON ME?!! AND IF WOMEN ARE THINGS TO BE PROTECTED, YOU BE ONE!! I WILL NEVER BE SUCH A PATHETIC THING! NEVER!!
GEEZ...
I THINK MY CHICK HAS PROBLEMS...
SHAAAA

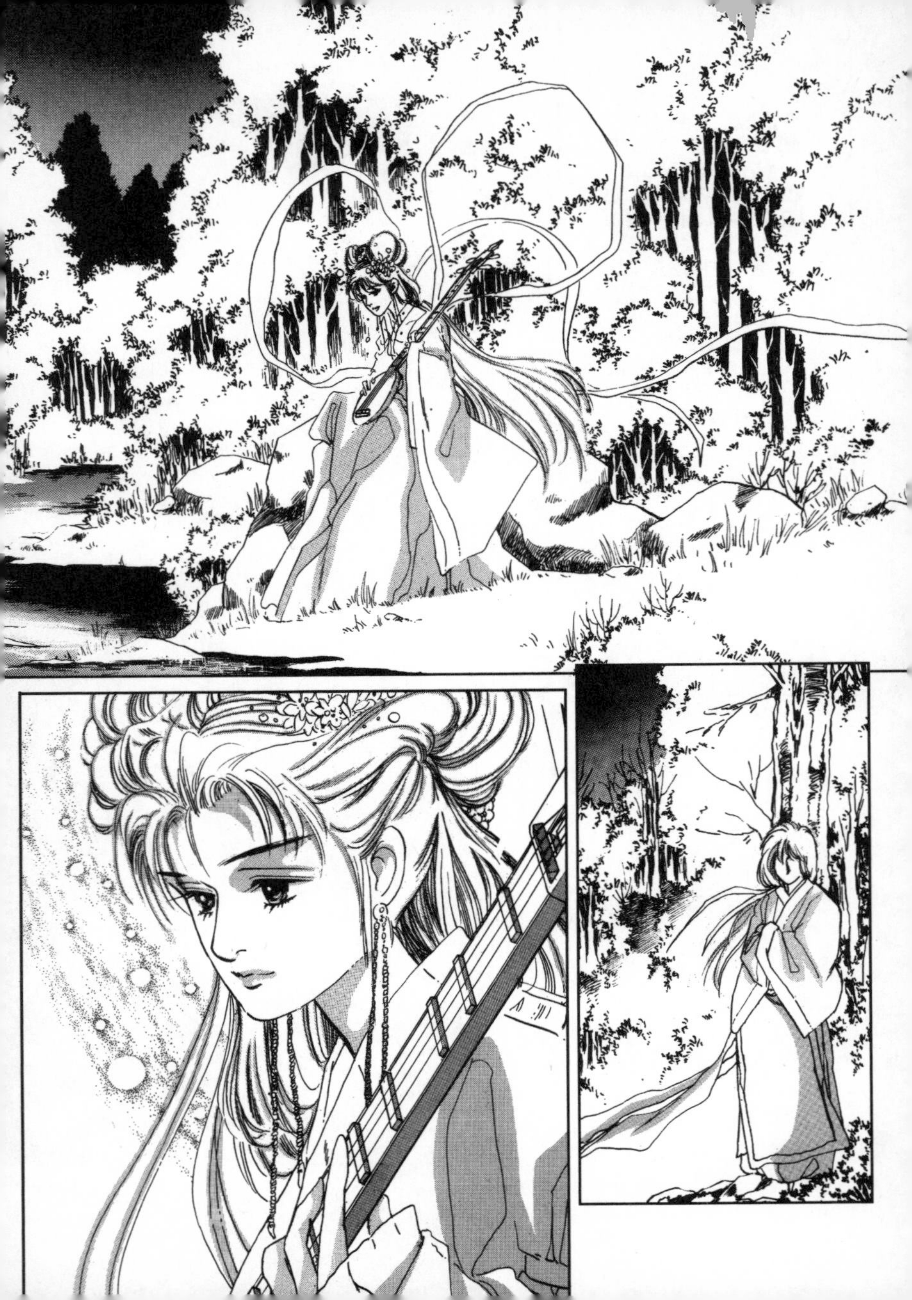

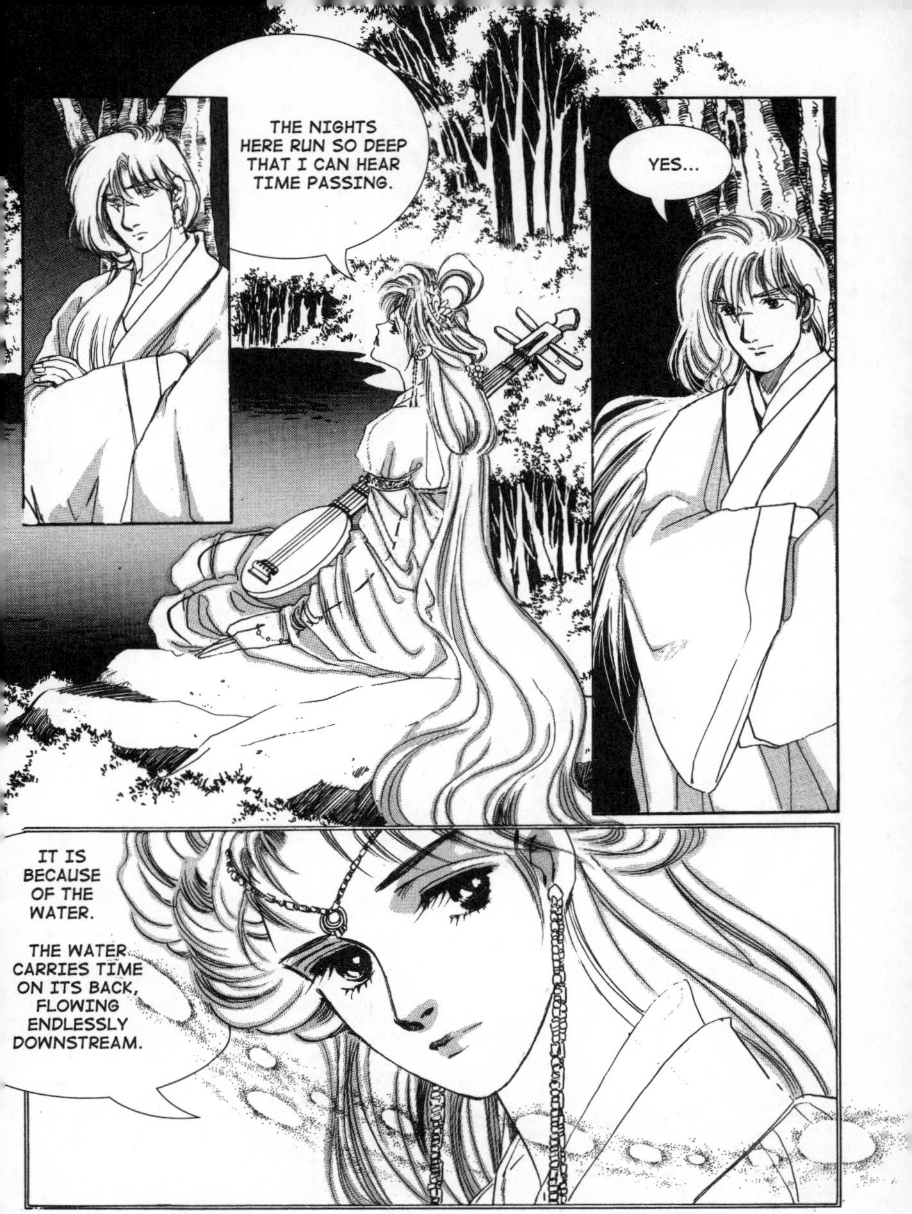
THE NIGHTS HERE RUN SO DEEP THAT I CAN HEAR TIME PASSING.
YES...
IT IS BECAUSE OF THE WATER.
THE WATER CARRIES TIME ON ITS BACK, FLOWING ENDLESSLY DOWNSTREAM.

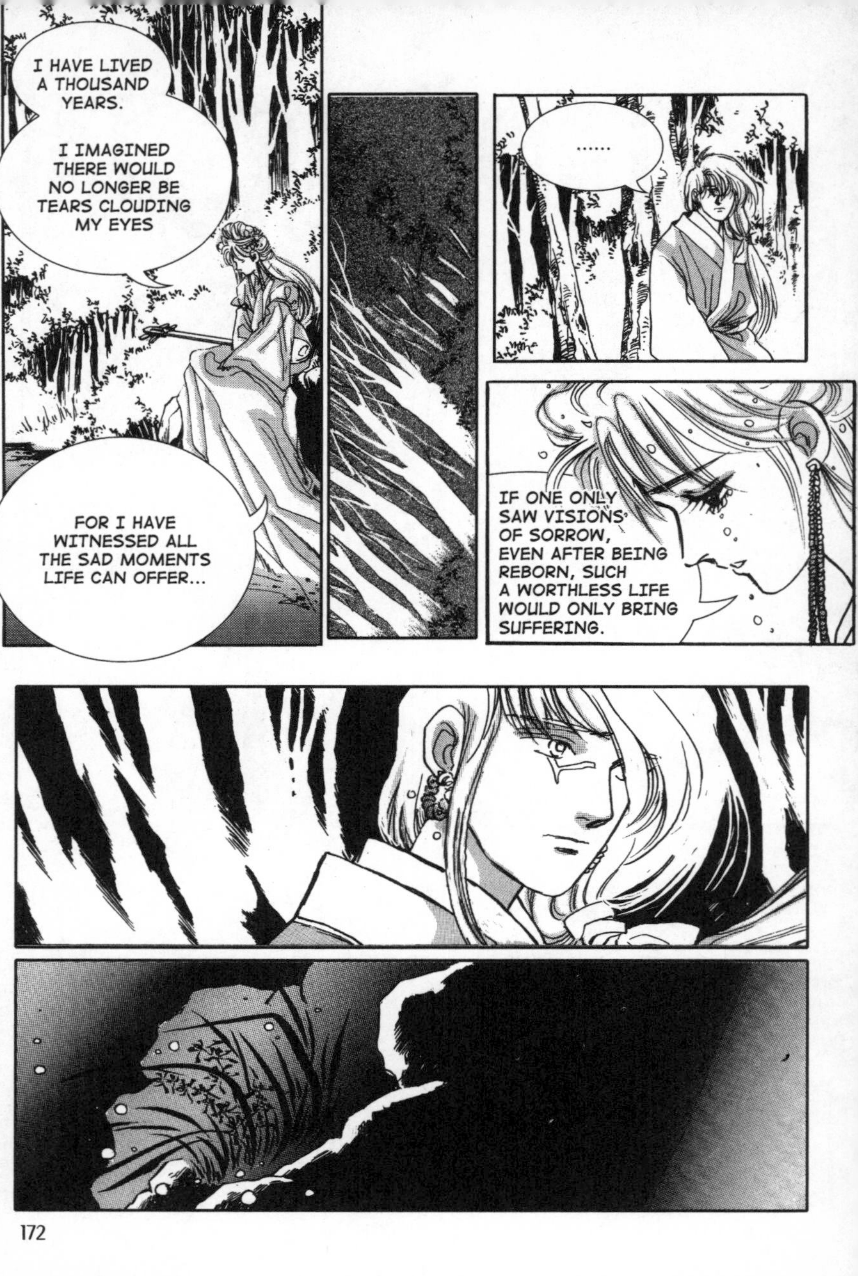
I HAVE LIVED A THOUSAND YEARS.
I IMAGINED THERE WOULD NO LONGER BE TEARS CLOUDING MY EYES
FOR I HAVE WITNESSED ALL THE SAD MOMENTS LIFE CAN OFFER...
......
IF ONE ONLY SAW VISIONS OF SORROW, EVEN AFTER BEING REBORN, SUCH A WORTHLESS LIFE WOULD ONLY BRING SUFFERING.

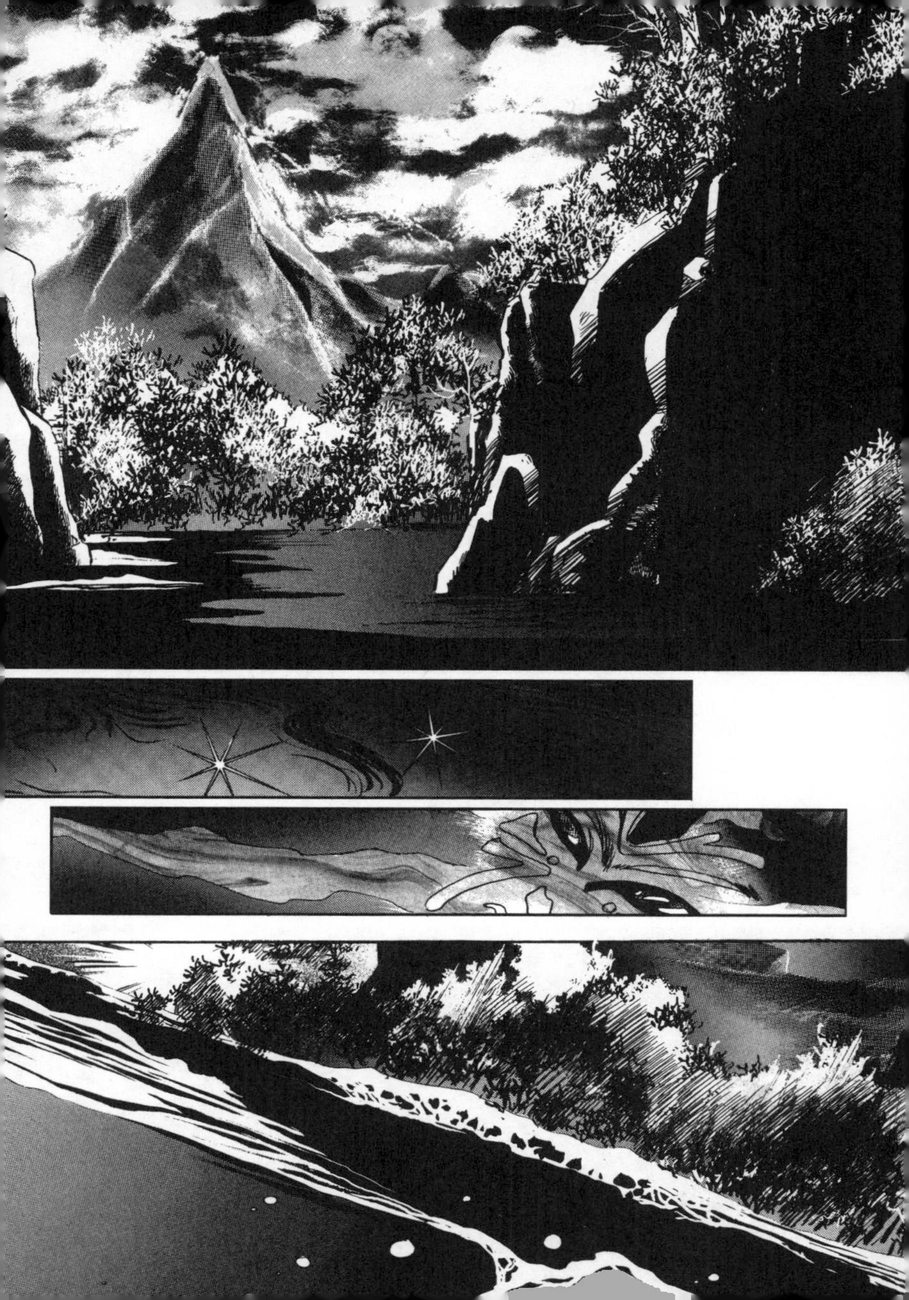

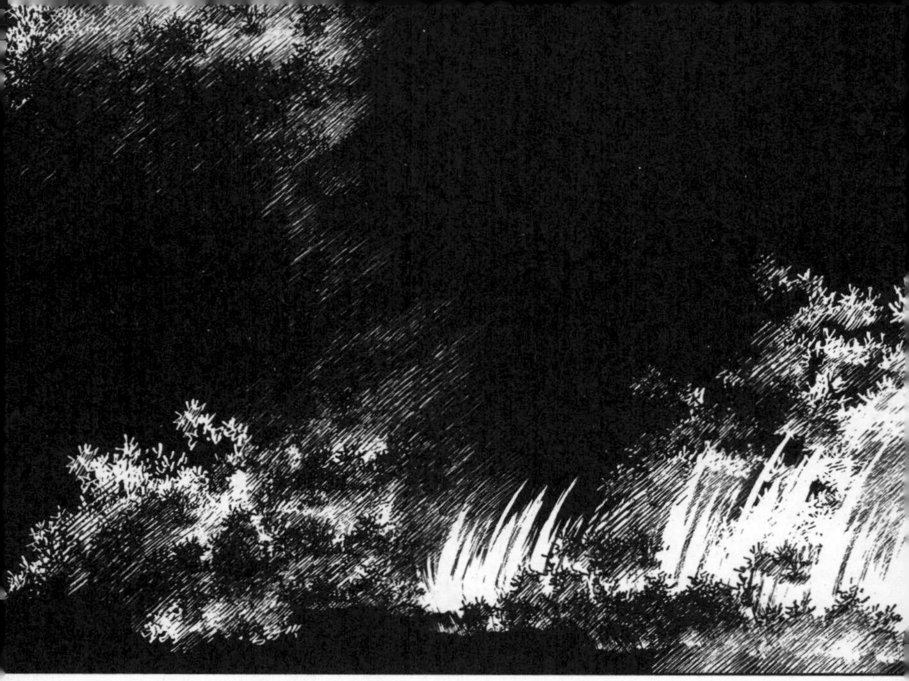

HOW IS IT THAT THE FLOWER OF THE HEAVENLY FATHER
GROWS IN SUCH A PLACE WITH WHITE TIGER...

WHAT IS MORE UNSETTLING, IS THAT THE PALE BOY
WHO POSSESSES THE ENERGY OF WHITE TIGER SEEMS
TO BE FROM THE EUN FAMILY OF BOOKMYUNG...

HOW STRANGE.
THE ENTIRE EUN FAMILY WAS SLAUGHTERED,
AND I BELIEVE NONE ARE STILL LIVING...

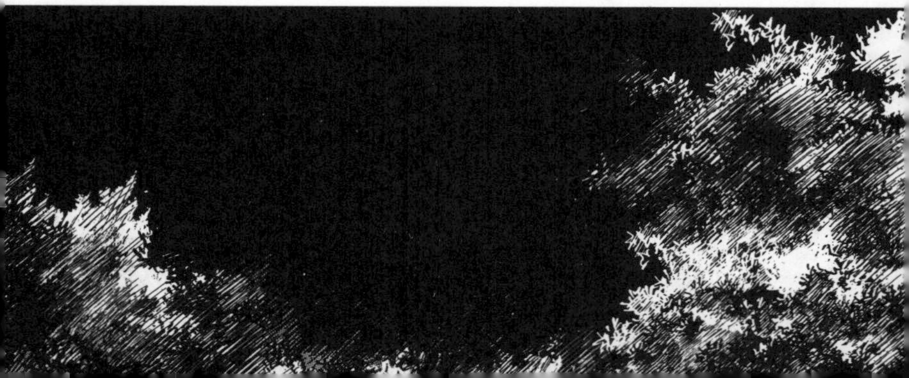

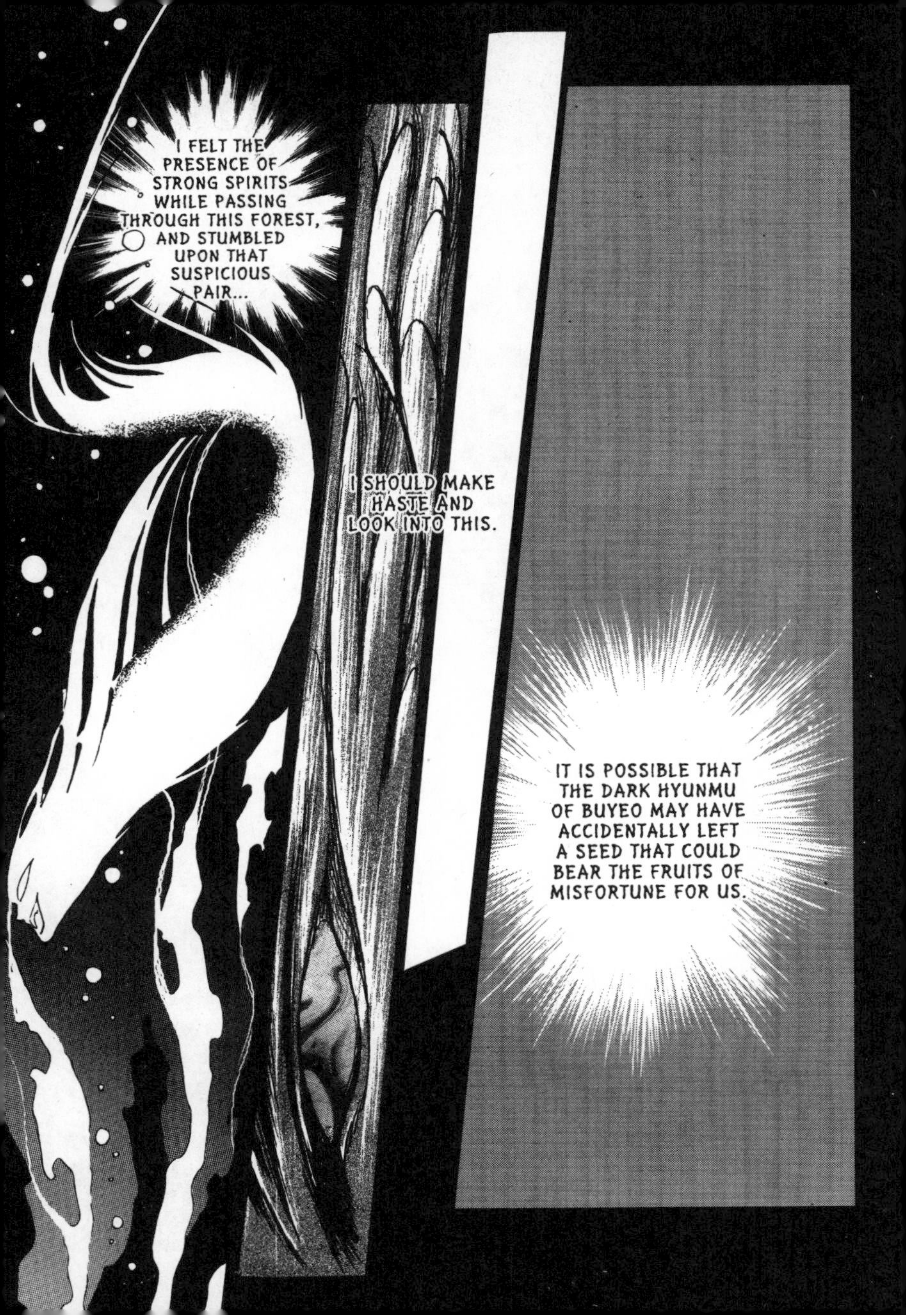
I FELT THE PRESENCE OF STRONG SPIRITS WHILE PASSING THROUGH THIS FOREST, AND STUMBLED UPON THAT SUSPICIOUS PAIR...
I SHOULD MAKE HASTE AND LOOK INTO THIS.
IT IS POSSIBLE THAT THE DARK HYUNMU OF BUYEO MAY HAVE ACCIDENTALLY LEFT A SEED THAT COULD BEAR THE FRUITS OF MISFORTUNE FOR US.

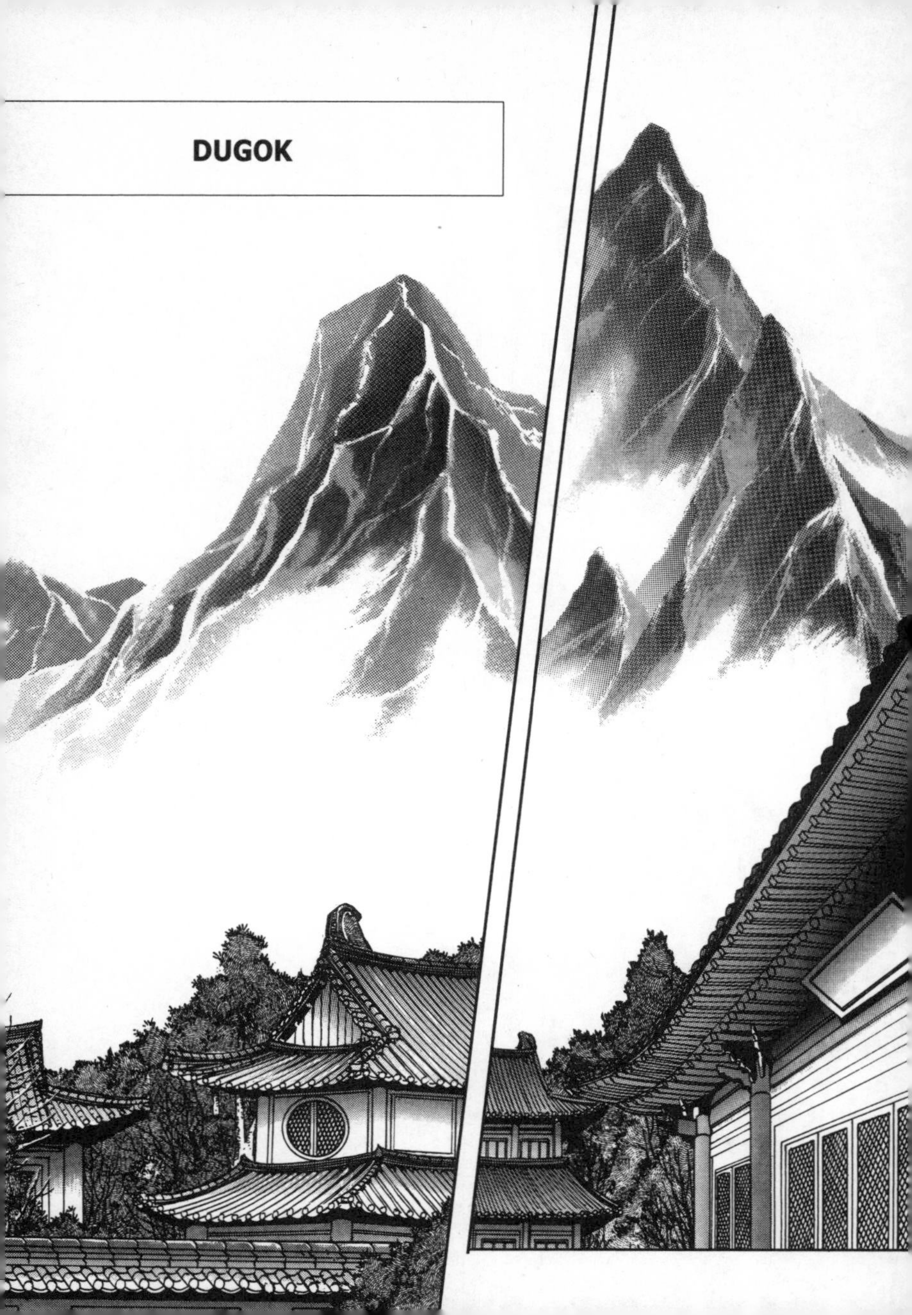
DUGOK

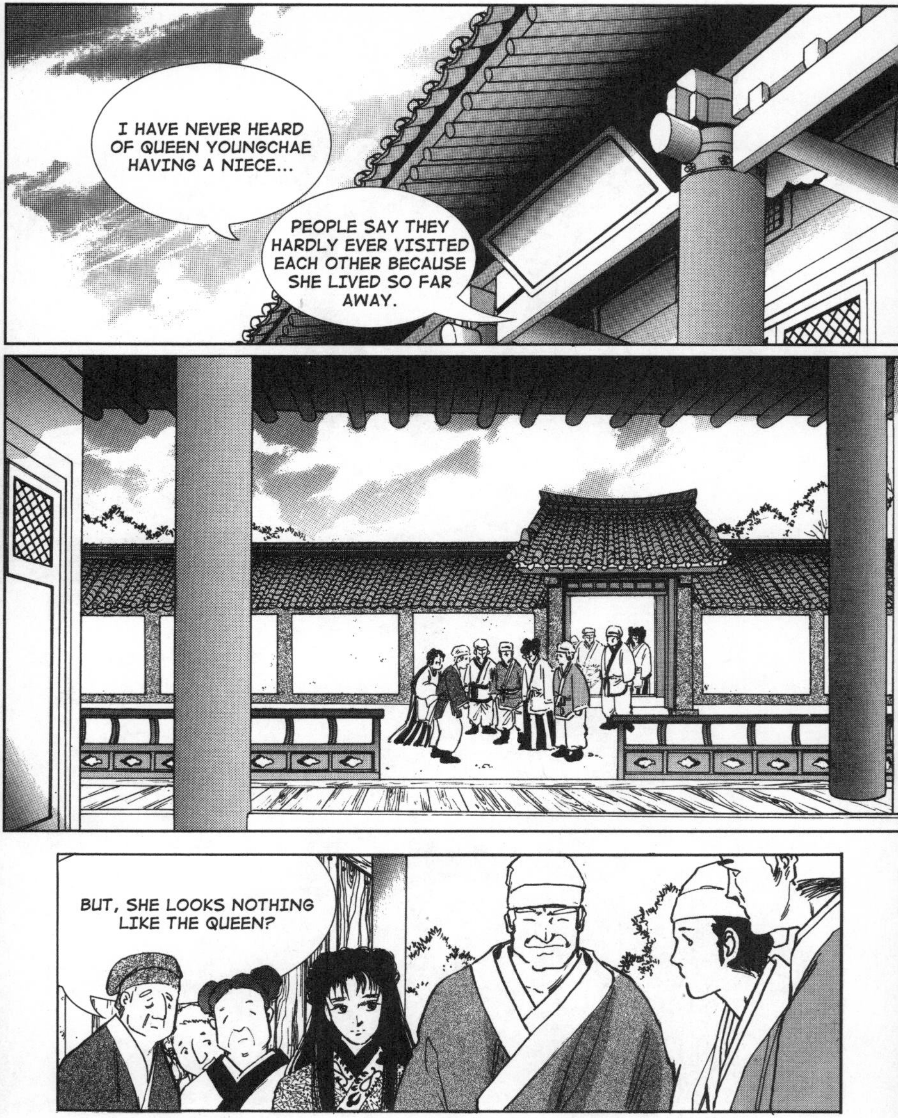
I HAVE NEVER HEARD OF QUEEN YOUNGCHAE HAVING A NIECE...
PEOPLE SAY THEY HARDLY EVER VISITED EACH OTHER BECAUSE SHE LIVED SO FAR AWAY.
BUT, SHE LOOKS NOTHING LIKE THE QUEEN?

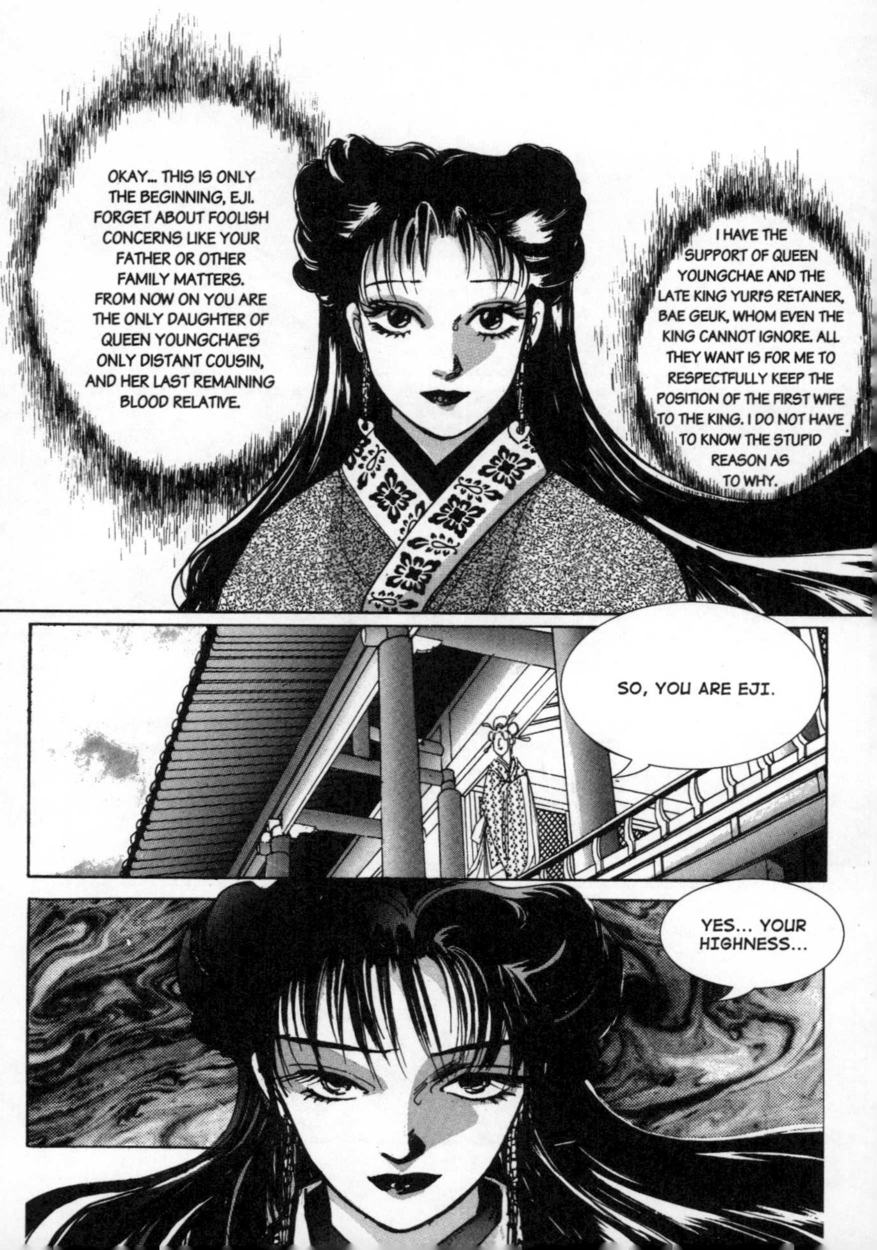
OKAY... THIS IS ONLY THE BEGINNING, EJI. FORGET ABOUT FOOLISH CONCERNS LIKE YOUR FATHER OR OTHER FAMILY MATTERS. FROM NOW ON YOU ARE THE ONLY DAUGHTER OF QUEEN YOUNGCHAE'S ONLY DISTANT COUSIN, AND HER LAST REMAINING BLOOD RELATIVE.
I HAVE THE SUPPORT OF QUEEN YOUNGCHAE AND THE LATE KING YURI'S RETAINER, BAE GEUK, WHOM EVEN THE KING CANNOT IGNORE. ALL THEY WANT IS FOR ME TO RESPECTFULLY KEEP THE POSITION OF THE FIRST WIFE TO THE KING. I DO NOT HAVE TO KNOW THE STUPID REASON AS TO WHY.
SO, YOU ARE EJI.
YES... YOUR HIGHNESS...

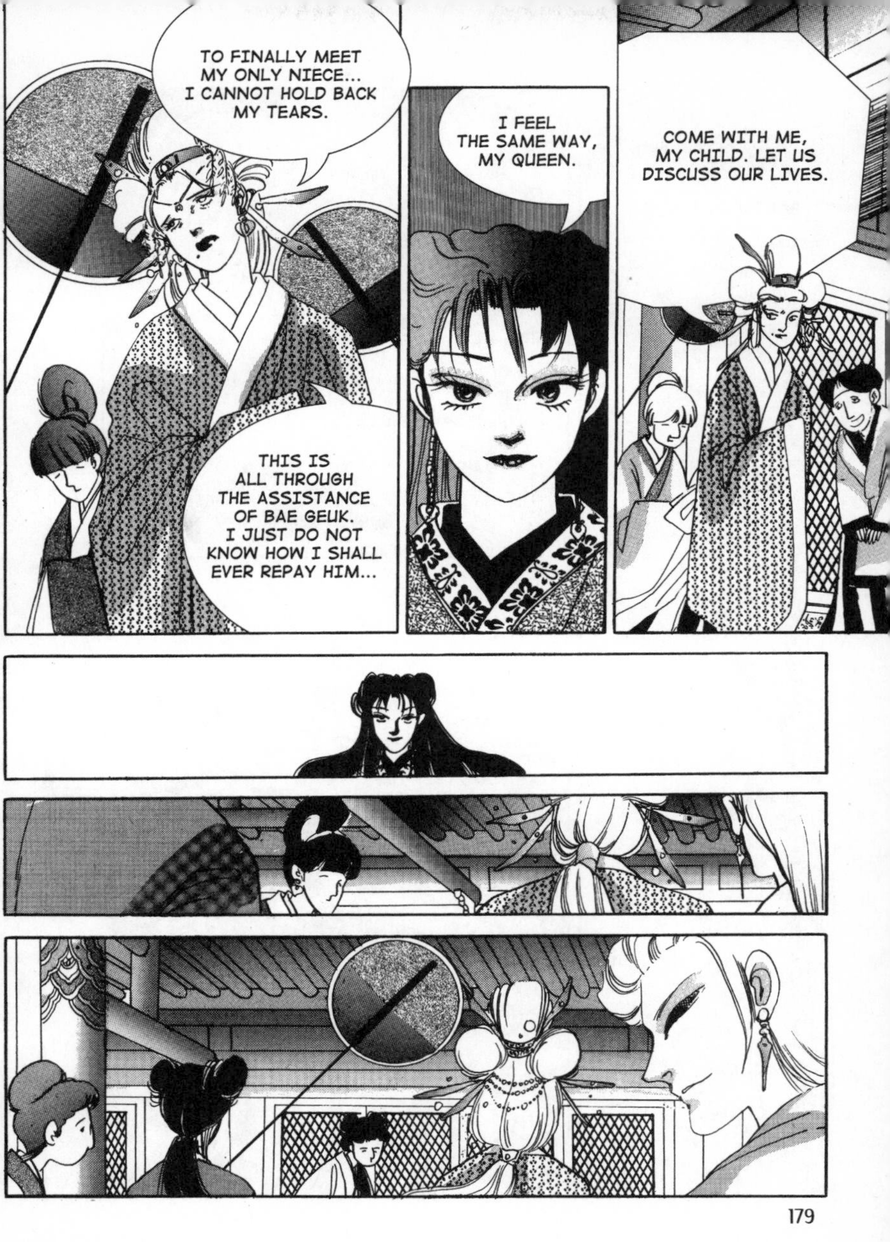
TO FINALLY MEET MY ONLY NIECE... I CANNOT HOLD BACK MY TEARS.
THIS IS ALL THROUGH THE ASSISTANCE OF BAE GEUK. I JUST DO NOT KNOW HOW I SHALL EVER REPAY HIM...
I FEEL THE SAME WAY, MY QUEEN.
COME WITH ME, MY CHILD. LET US DISCUSS OUR LIVES.

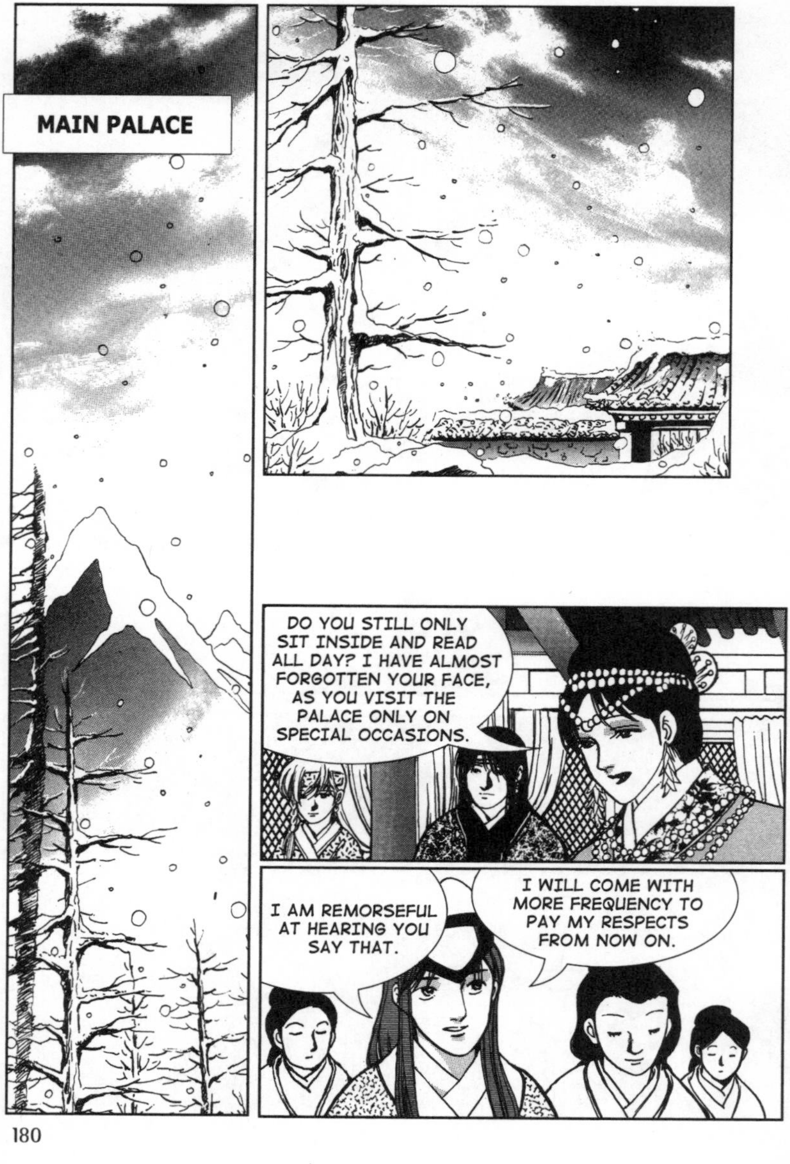
MAIN PALACE
DO YOU STILL ONLY SIT INSIDE AND READ ALL DAY? I HAVE ALMOST FORGOTTEN YOUR FACE, AS YOU VISIT THE PALACE ONLY ON SPECIAL OCCASIONS.
I AM REMORSEFUL AT HEARING YOU SAY THAT.
I WILL COME WITH MORE FREQUENCY TO PAY MY RESPECTS FROM NOW ON.

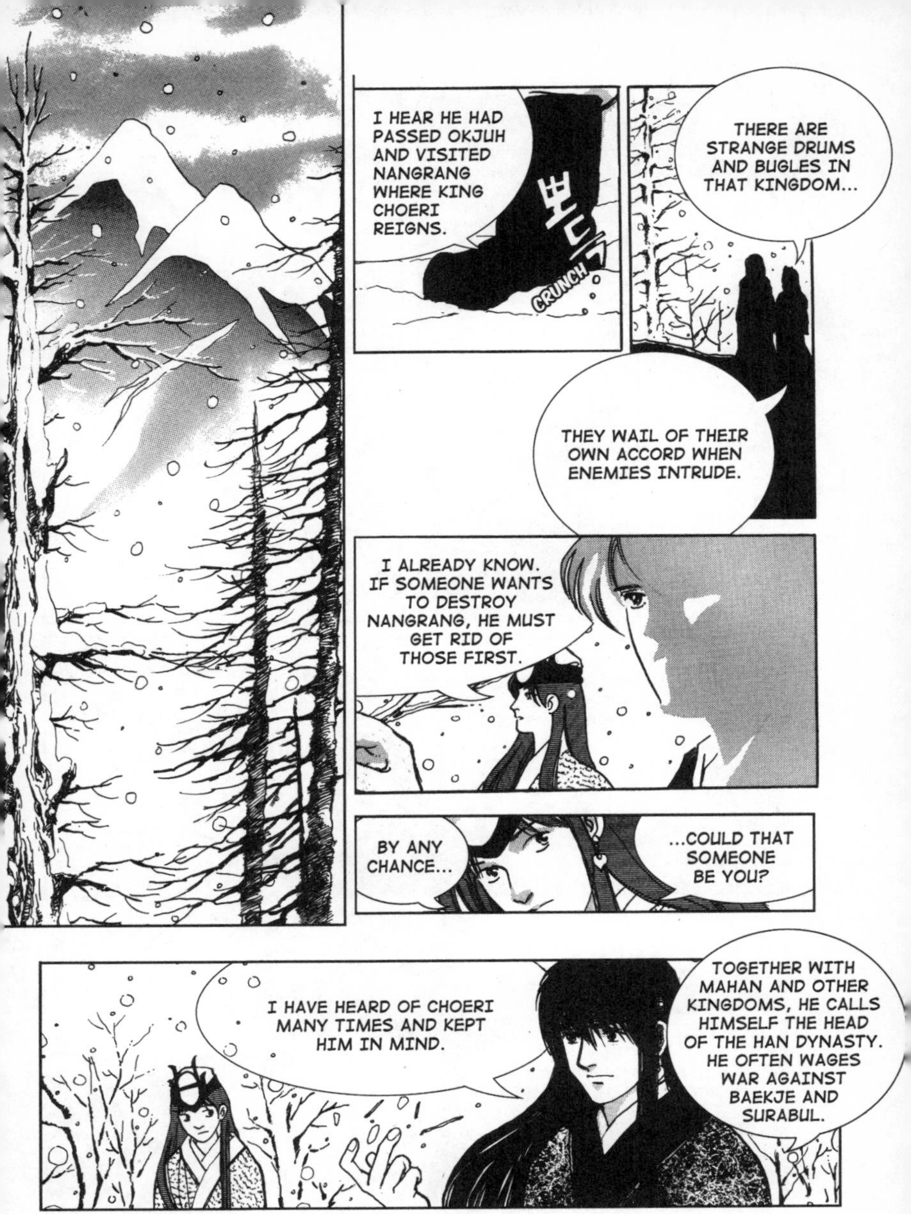

I HEAR HE HAD PASSED OKJUH AND VISITED NANGRANG WHERE KING CHOERI REIGNS.
CRUNCH
THERE ARE STRANGE DRUMS AND BUGLES IN THAT KINGDOM...
THEY WAIL OF THEIR OWN ACCORD WHEN ENEMIES INTRUDE.
I ALREADY KNOW. IF SOMEONE WANTS TO DESTROY NANGRANG, HE MUST GET RID OF THOSE FIRST.
BY ANY CHANCE...
...COULD THAT SOMEONE BE YOU?
I HAVE HEARD OF CHOERI MANY TIMES AND KEPT HIM IN MIND.
TOGETHER WITH MAHAN AND OTHER KINGDOMS, HE CALLS HIMSELF THE HEAD OF THE HAN DYNASTY. HE OFTEN WAGES WAR AGAINST BAEKJE AND SURABUL.

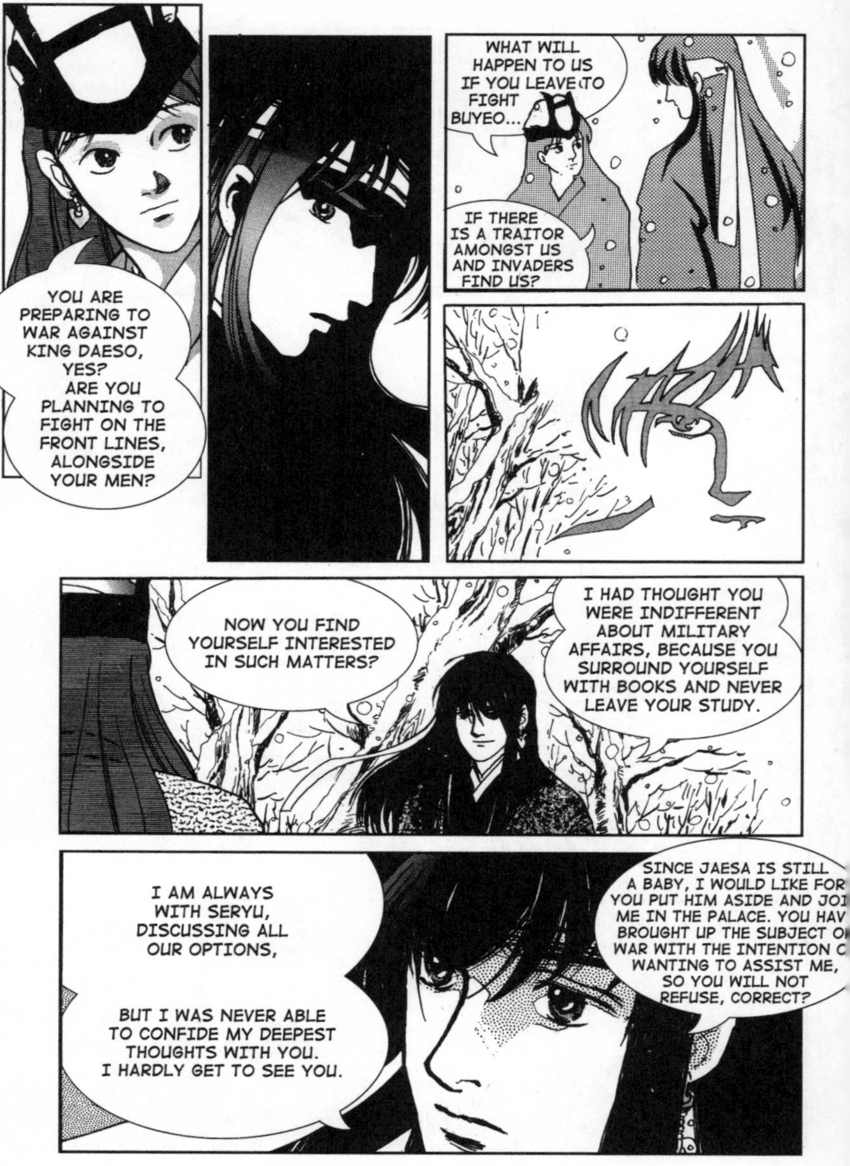
YOU ARE PREPARING TO WAR AGAINST KING DAESO, YES?
ARE YOU PLANNING TO FIGHT ON THE FRONT LINES, ALONGSIDE YOUR MEN?
WHAT WILL HAPPEN TO US IF YOU LEAVE TO FIGHT BUYEO...
IF THERE IS A TRAITOR AMONGST US AND INVADERS FIND US?
I HAD THOUGHT YOU WERE INDIFFERENT ABOUT MILITARY AFFAIRS, BECAUSE YOU SURROUND YOURSELF WITH BOOKS AND NEVER LEAVE YOUR STUDY.
NOW YOU FIND YOURSELF INTERESTED IN SUCH MATTERS?
I AM ALWAYS WITH SERYU, DISCUSSING ALL OUR OPTIONS,
BUT I WAS NEVER ABLE TO CONFIDE MY DEEPEST THOUGHTS WITH YOU. I HARDLY GET TO SEE YOU.
SINCE JAESA IS STILL A BABY, I WOULD LIKE FOR YOU PUT HIM ASIDE AND JOI ME IN THE PALACE. YOU HAV BROUGHT UP THE SUBJECT O WAR WITH THE INTENTION C WANTING TO ASSIST ME, SO YOU WILL NOT REFUSE, CORRECT?

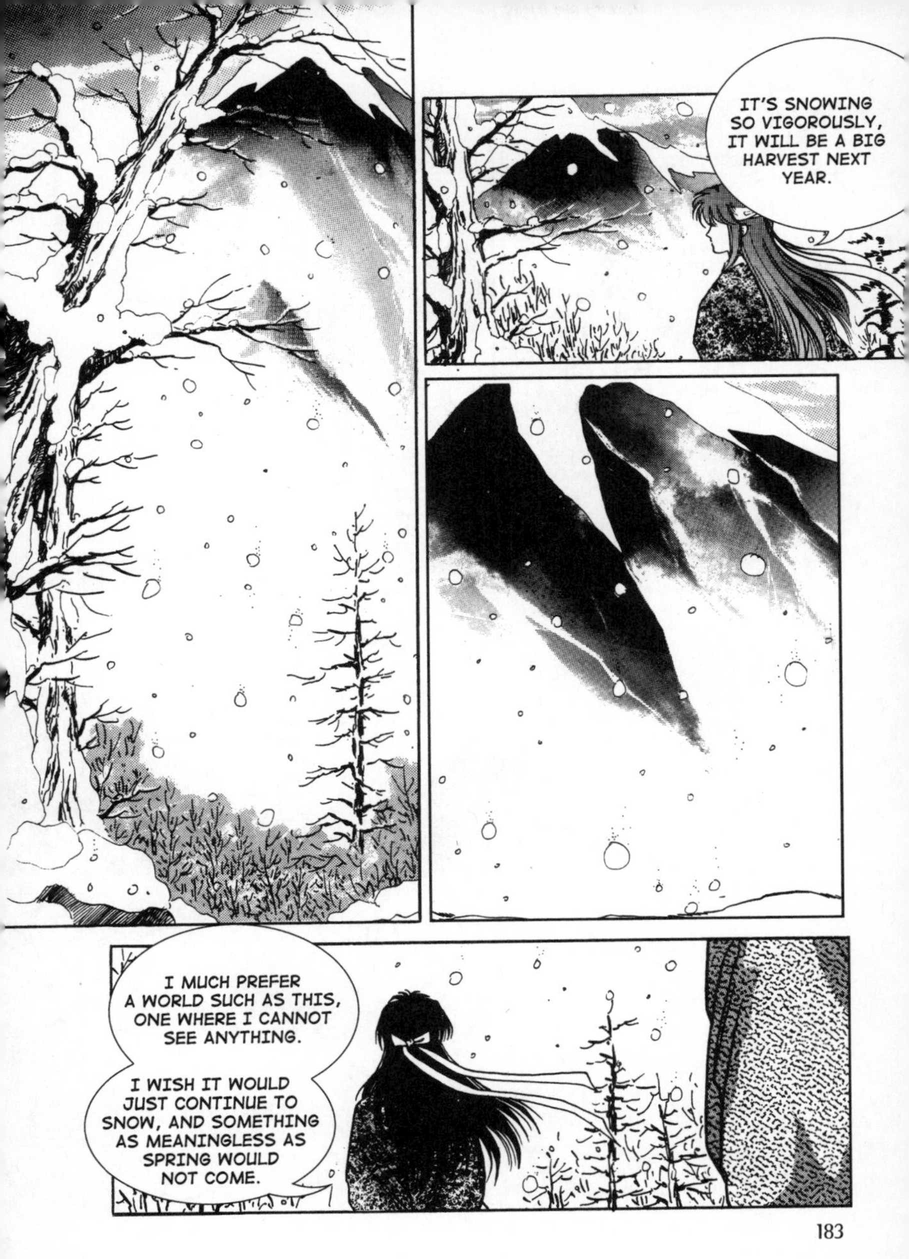
IT'S SNOWING SO VIGOROUSLY, IT WILL BE A BIG HARVEST NEXT YEAR.
I MUCH PREFER A WORLD SUCH AS THIS, ONE WHERE I CANNOT SEE ANYTHING.
I WISH IT WOULD JUST CONTINUE TO SNOW, AND SOMETHING AS MEANINGLESS AS SPRING WOULD NOT COME.

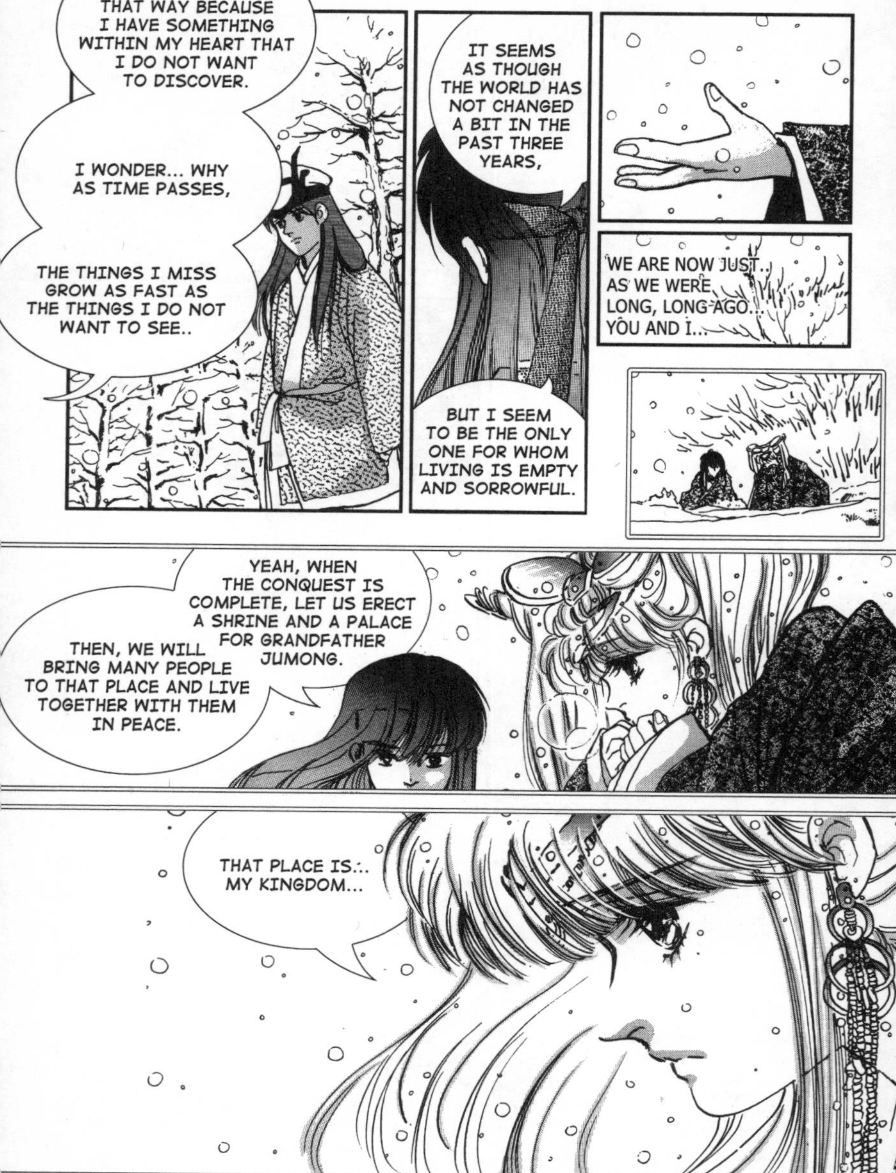
I SUPPOSE I FEEL THAT WAY BECAUSE I HAVE SOMETHING WITHIN MY HEART THAT I DO NOT WANT TO DISCOVER.
I WONDER... WHY AS TIME PASSES,
THE THINGS I MISS GROW AS FAST AS THE THINGS I DO NOT WANT TO SEE..
IT SEEMS AS THOUGH THE WORLD HAS NOT CHANGED A BIT IN THE PAST THREE YEARS,
BUT I SEEM TO BE THE ONLY ONE FOR WHOM LIVING IS EMPTY AND SORROWFUL.
WE ARE NOW JUST.. AS WE WERE, LONG, LONG AGO... YOU AND I...
YEAH, WHEN THE CONQUEST IS COMPLETE, LET US ERECT A SHRINE AND A PALACE FOR GRANDFATHER JUMONG.
THEN, WE WILL BRING MANY PEOPLE TO THAT PLACE AND LIVE TOGETHER WITH THEM IN PEACE.
THAT PLACE IS... MY KINGDOM...

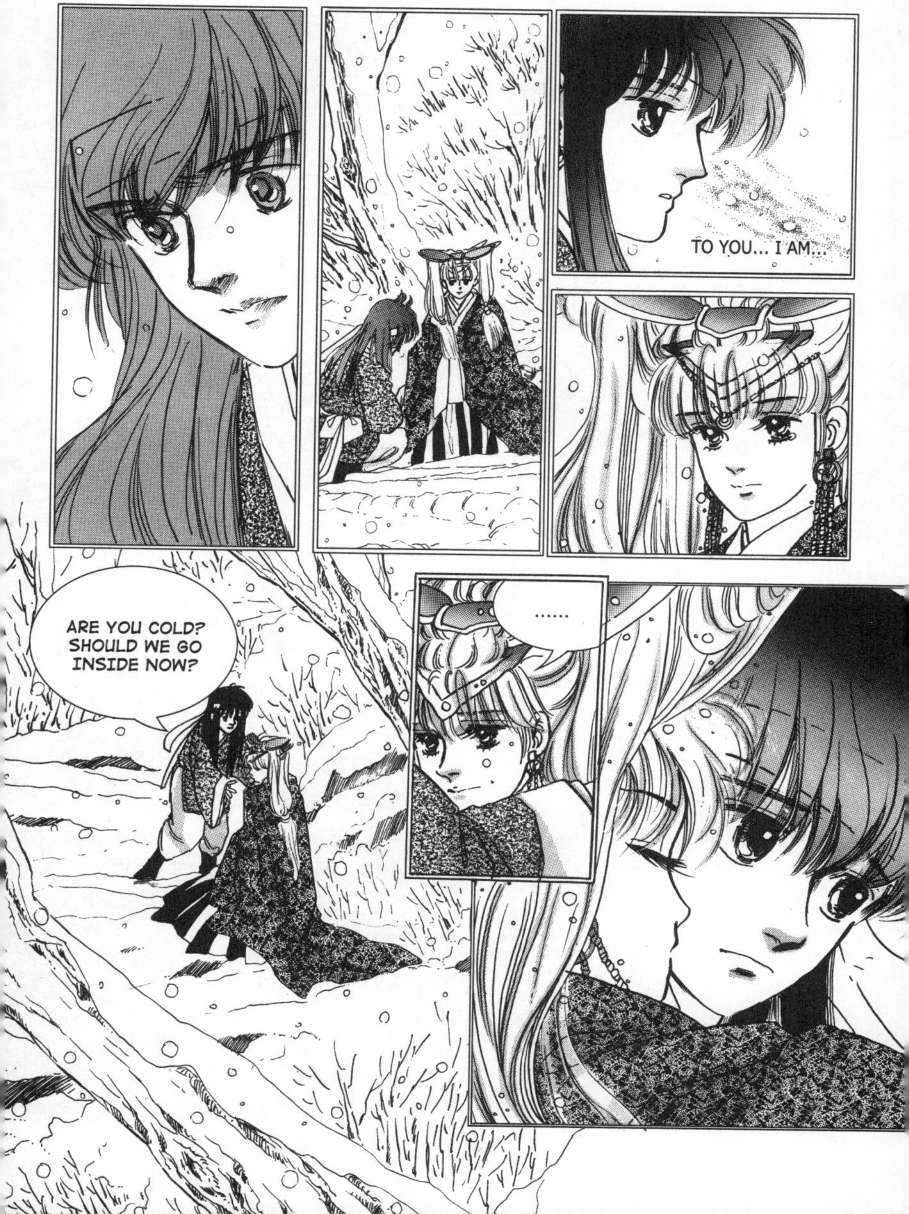
TO YOU... I AM...
ARE YOU COLD? SHOULD WE GO INSIDE NOW?
......

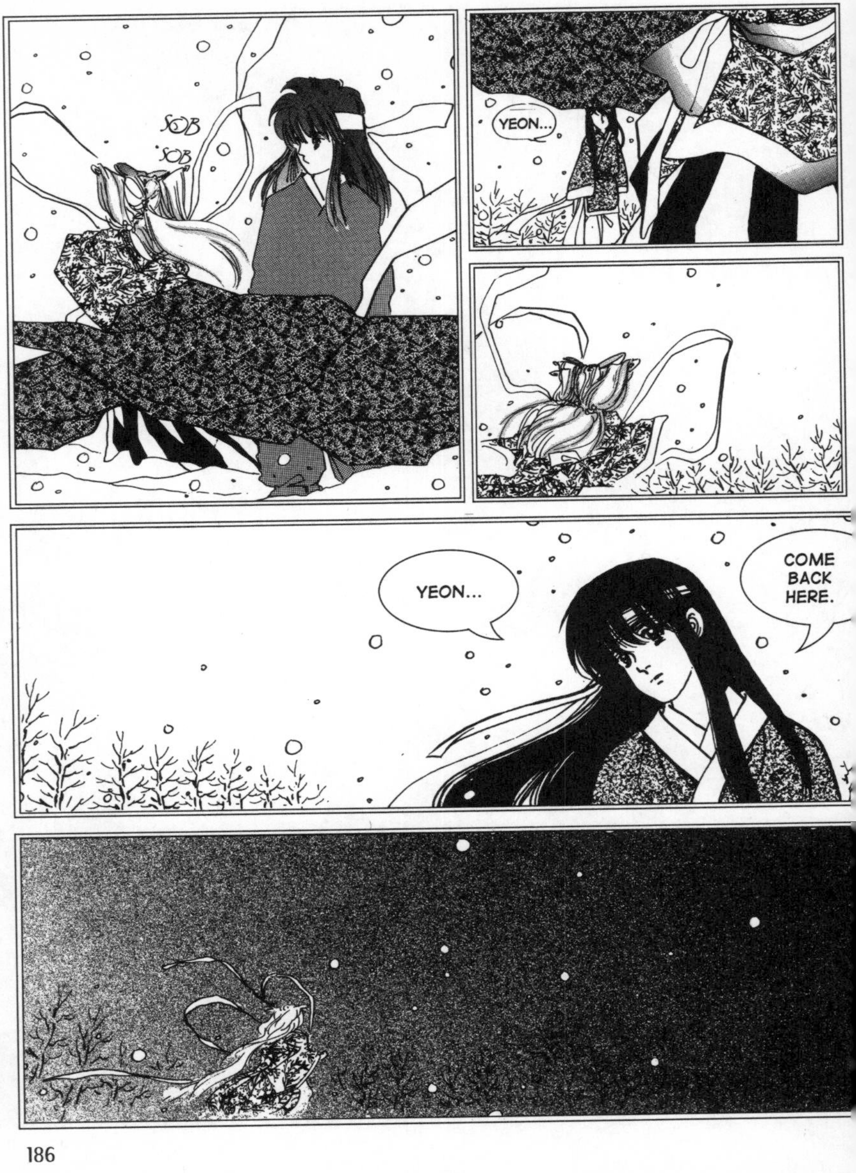
SOB
SOB
YEON...
YEON...
COME BACK HERE.

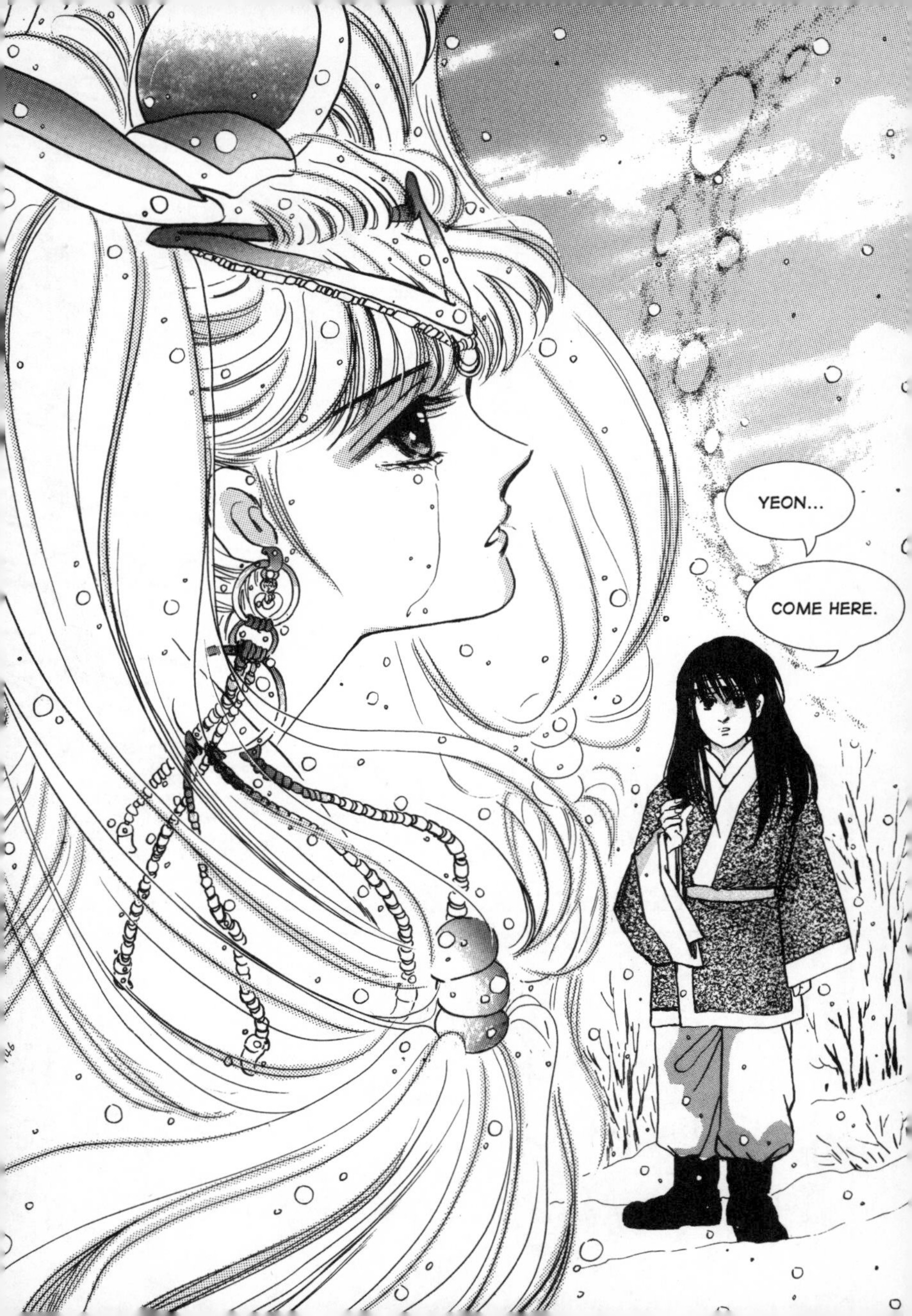
YEON...
COME HERE.

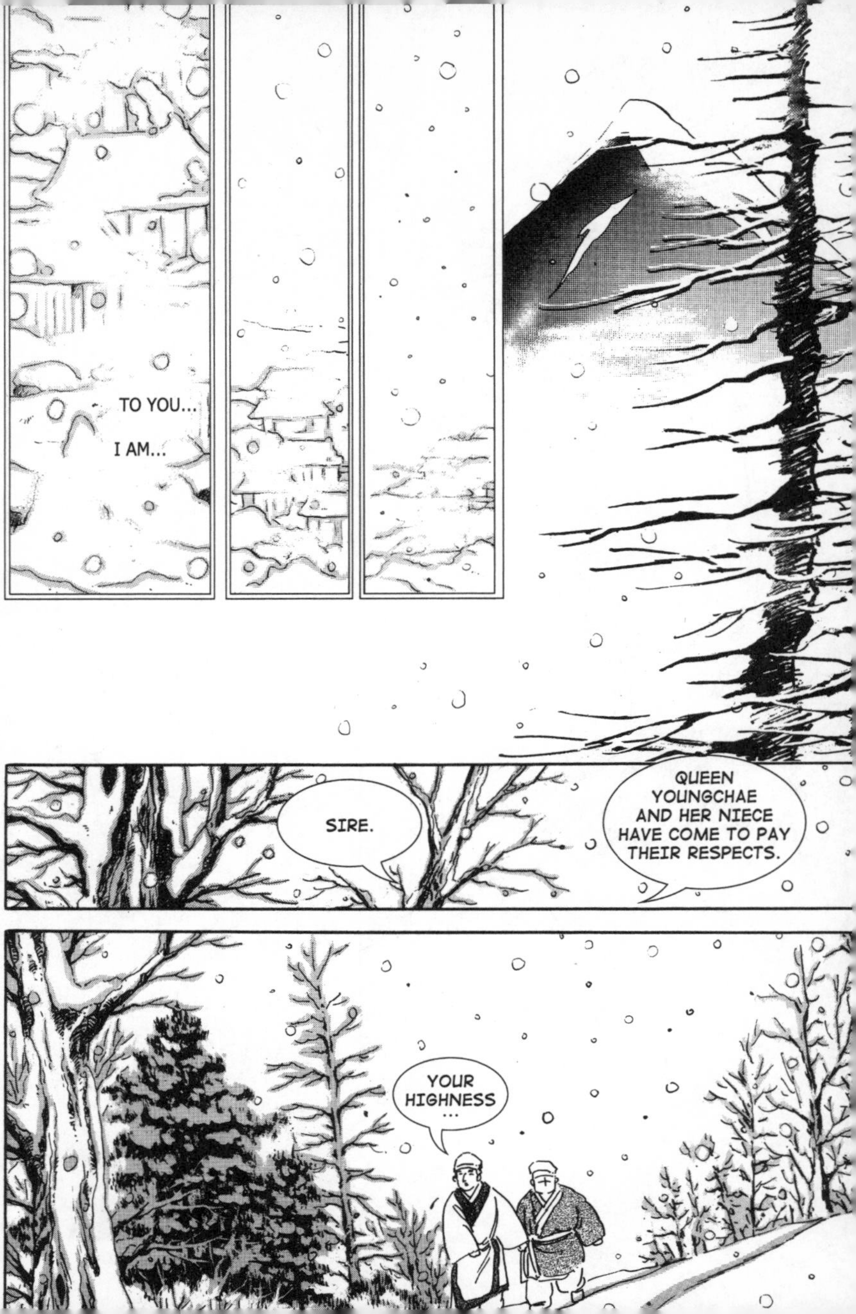
TO YOU...
I AM...
SIRE.
QUEEN YOUNGCHAE AND HER NIECE HAVE COME TO PAY THEIR RESPECTS.
YOUR HIGHNESS ...

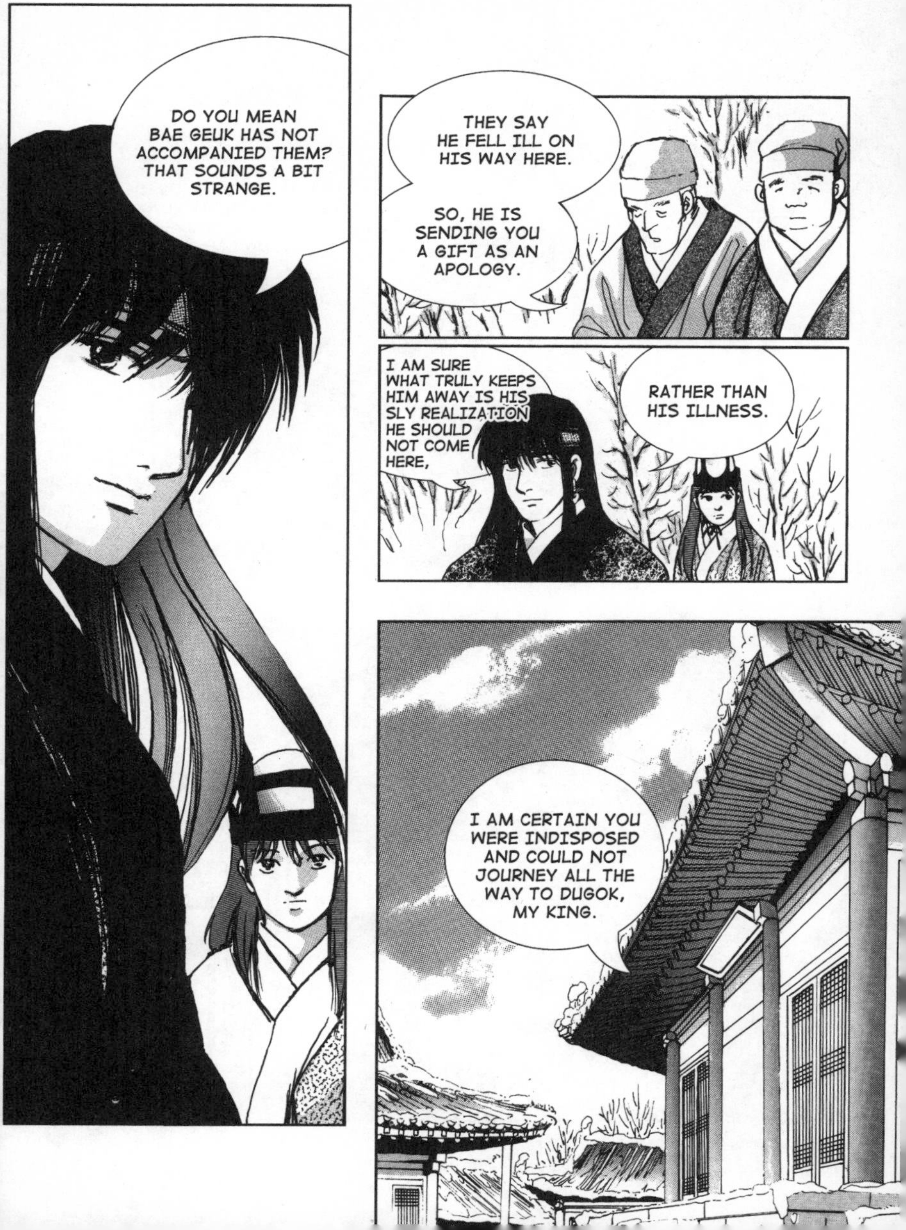
DO YOU MEAN BAE GEUK HAS NOT ACCOMPANIED THEM? THAT SOUNDS A BIT STRANGE.
THEY SAY HE FELL ILL ON HIS WAY HERE.
SO, HE IS SENDING YOU A GIFT AS AN APOLOGY.
I AM SURE WHAT TRULY KEEPS HIM AWAY IS HIS SLY REALIZATION HE SHOULD NOT COME HERE,
RATHER THAN HIS ILLNESS.
I AM CERTAIN YOU WERE INDISPOSED AND COULD NOT JOURNEY ALL THE WAY TO DUGOK, MY KING.

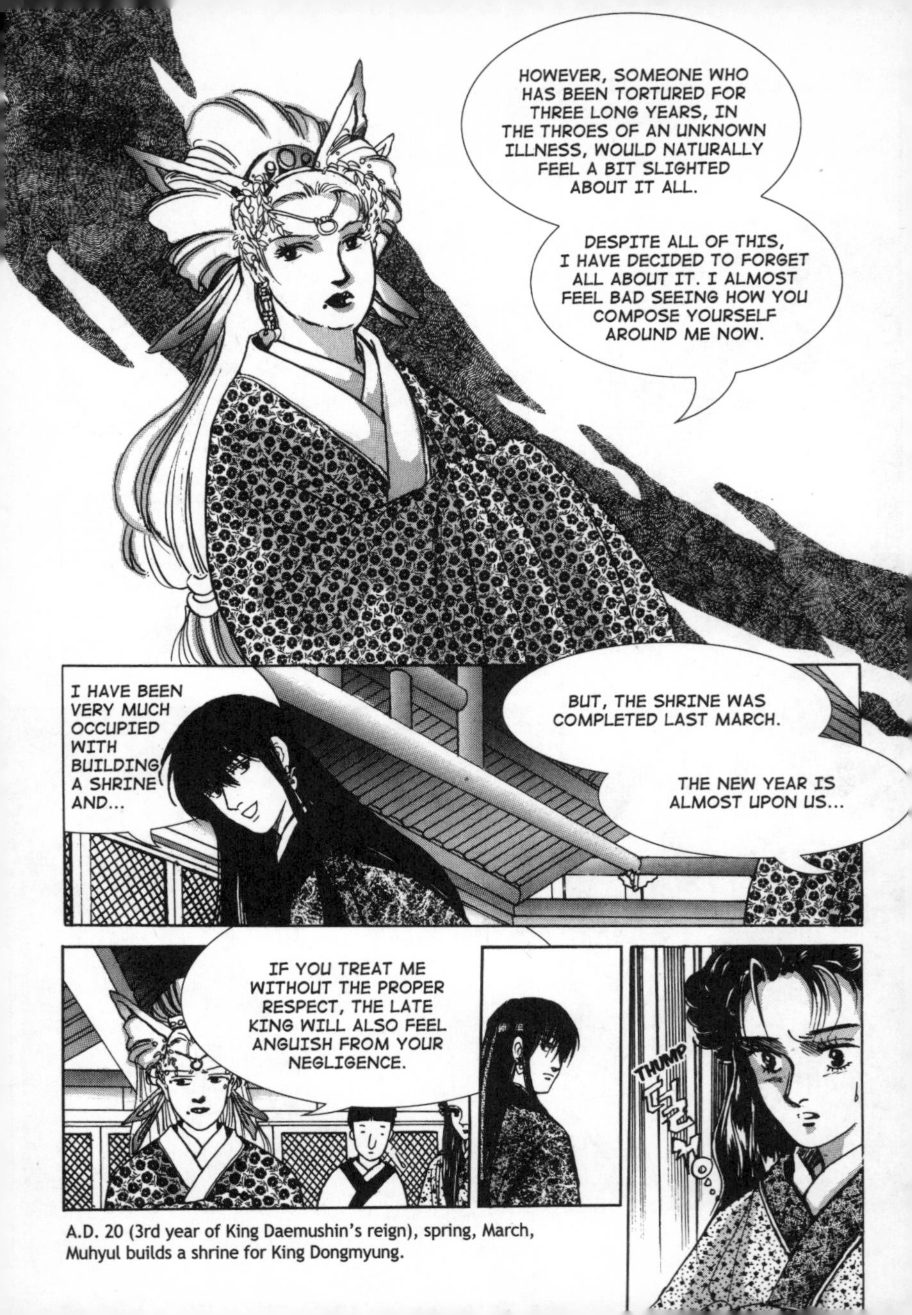
HOWEVER, SOMEONE WHO HAS BEEN TORTURED FOR THREE LONG YEARS, IN THE THROES OF AN UNKNOWN ILLNESS, WOULD NATURALLY FEEL A BIT SLIGHTED ABOUT IT ALL.
DESPITE ALL OF THIS, I HAVE DECIDED TO FORGET ALL ABOUT IT. I ALMOST FEEL BAD SEEING HOW YOU COMPOSE YOURSELF AROUND ME NOW.
I HAVE BEEN VERY MUCH OCCUPIED WITH BUILDING A SHRINE AND...
BUT, THE SHRINE WAS COMPLETED LAST MARCH.
THE NEW YEAR IS ALMOST UPON US...
IF YOU TREAT ME WITHOUT THE PROPER RESPECT, THE LATE KING WILL ALSO FEEL ANGUISH FROM YOUR NEGLIGENCE.
A.D. 20 (3rd year of King Daemushin's reign), spring, March, Muhyul builds a shrine for King Dongmyung.
THUMP

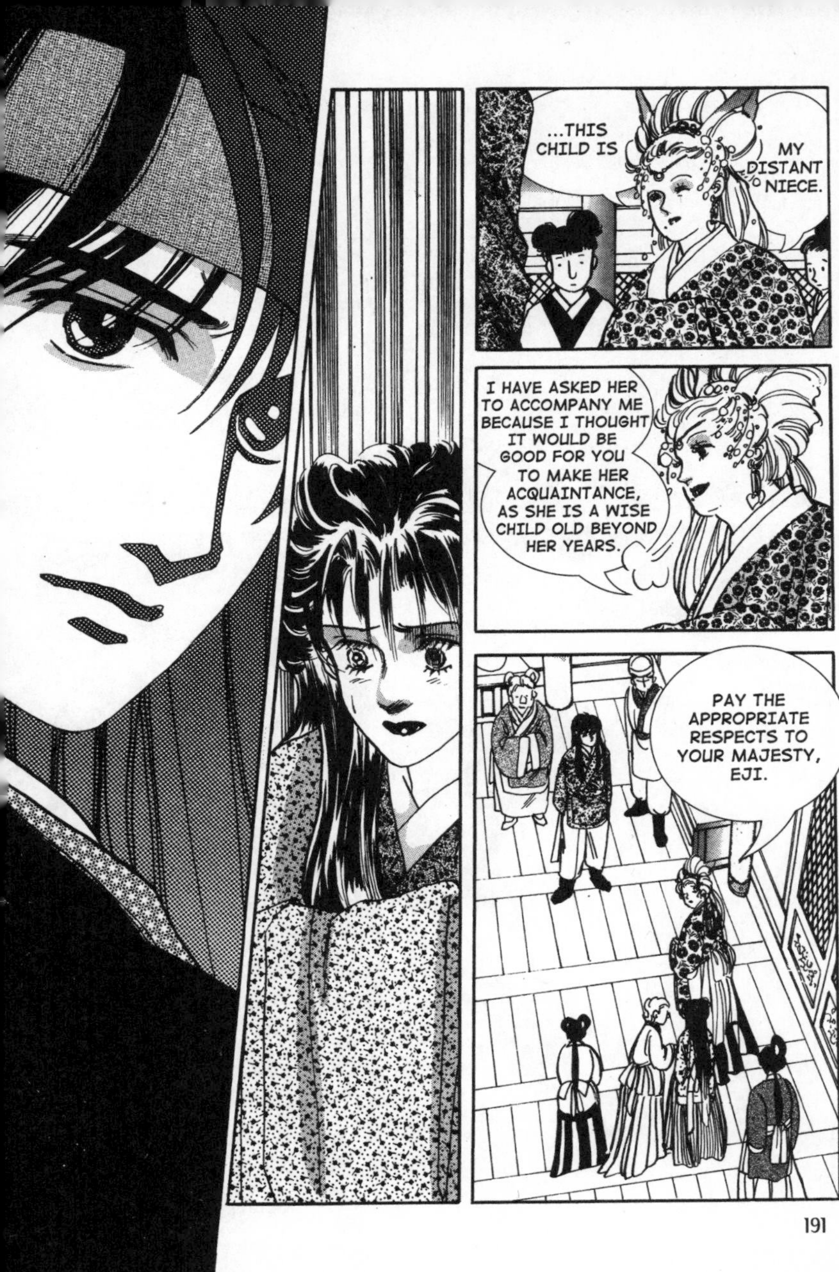
...THIS CHILD IS
MY DISTANT NIECE.
I HAVE ASKED HER TO ACCOMPANY ME BECAUSE I THOUGHT IT WOULD BE GOOD FOR YOU TO MAKE HER ACQUAINTANCE, AS SHE IS A WISE CHILD OLD BEYOND HER YEARS.
PAY THE APPROPRIATE RESPECTS TO YOUR MAJESTY, EJI.

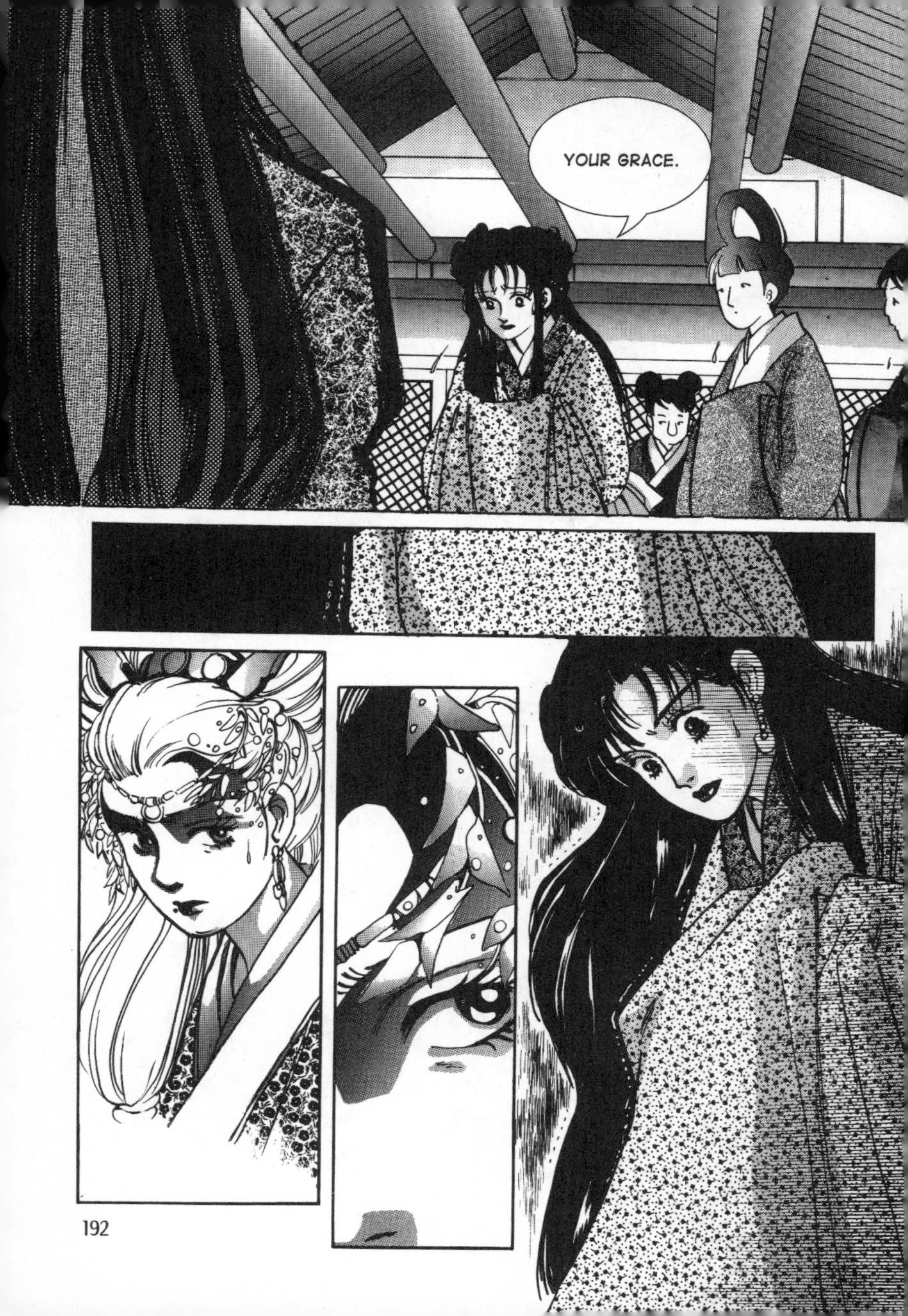
YOUR GRACE.

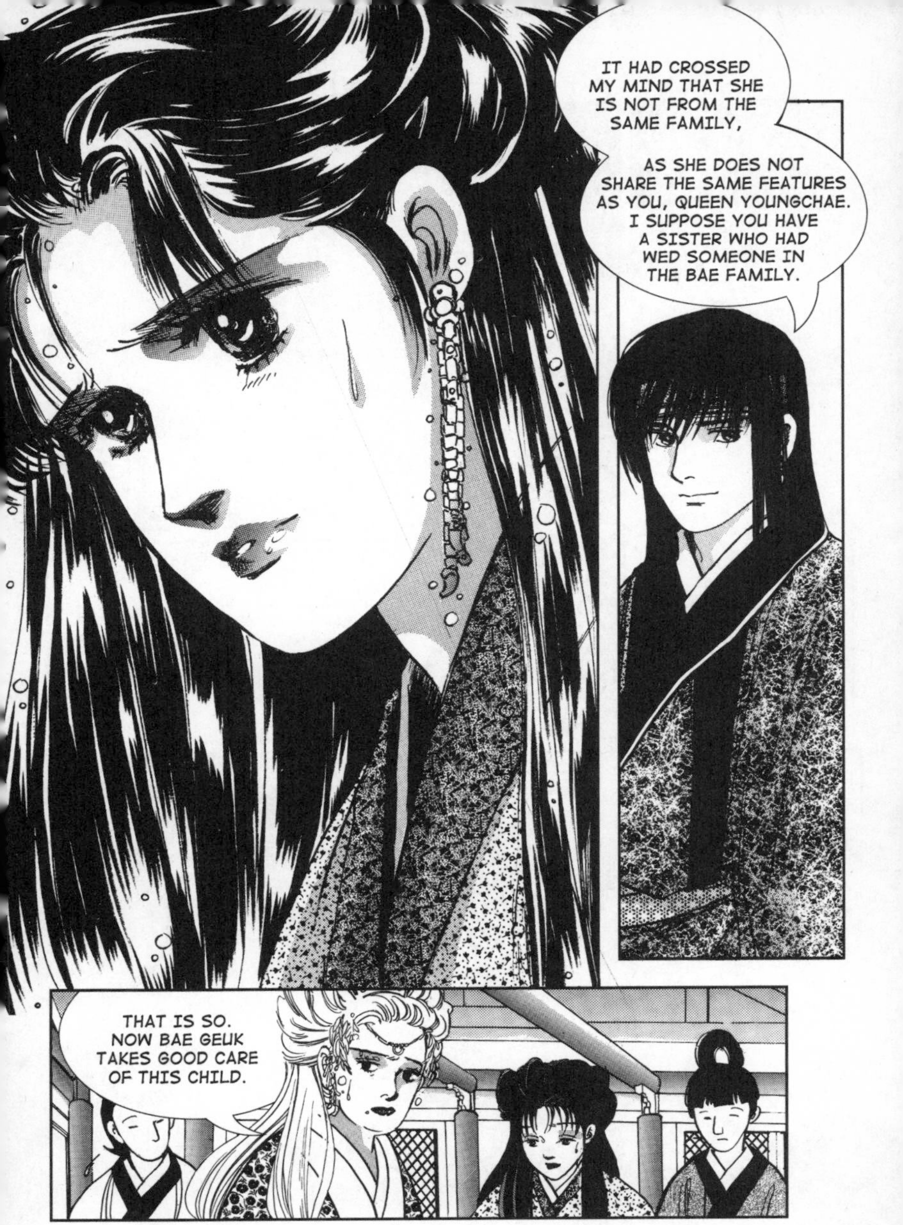
IT HAD CROSSED MY MIND THAT SHE IS NOT FROM THE SAME FAMILY,
AS SHE DOES NOT SHARE THE SAME FEATURES AS YOU, QUEEN YOUNGCHAE. I SUPPOSE YOU HAVE A SISTER WHO HAD WED SOMEONE IN THE BAE FAMILY.
THAT IS SO. NOW BAE GEUK TAKES GOOD CARE OF THIS CHILD.

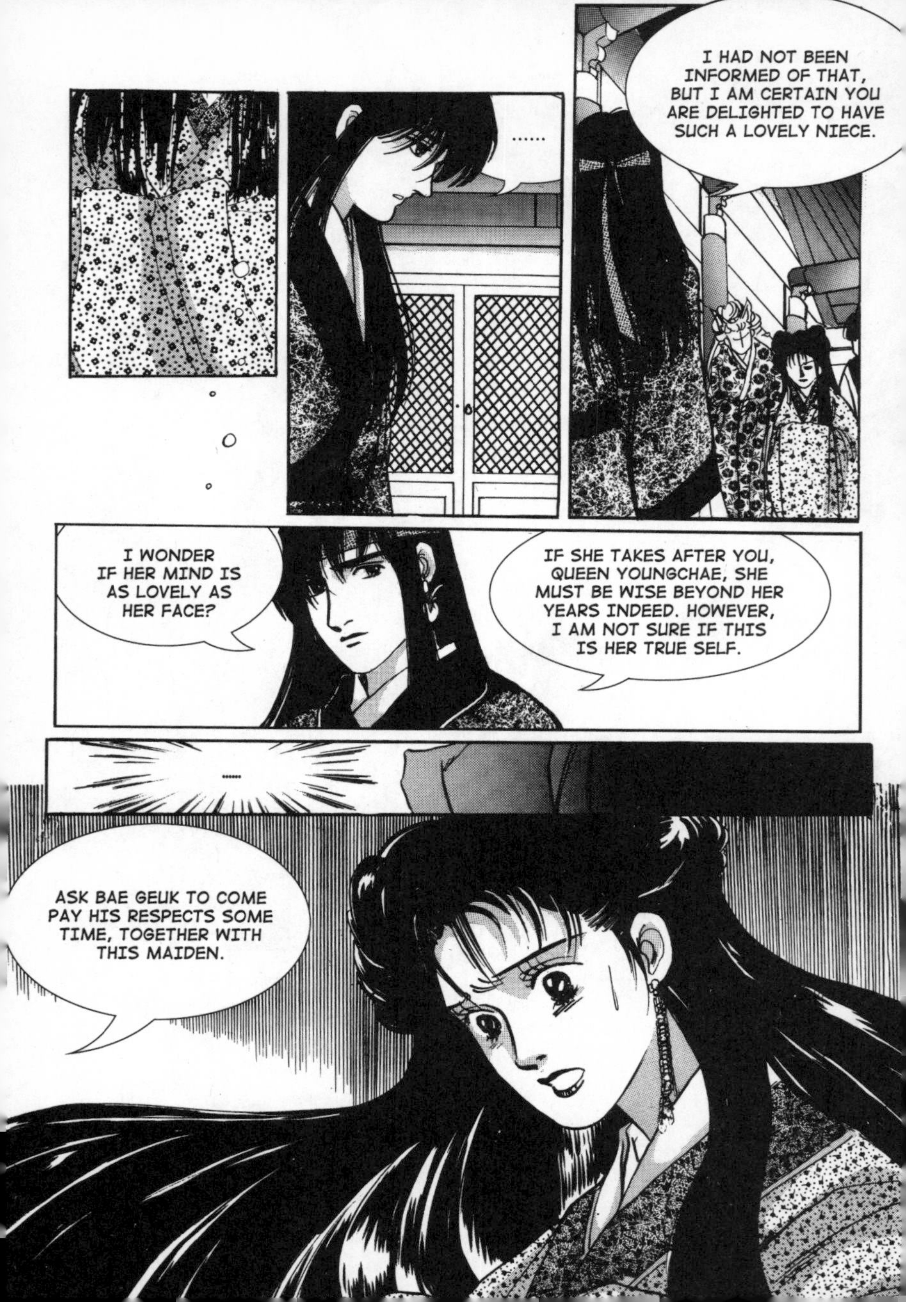
......
I HAD NOT BEEN INFORMED OF THAT, BUT I AM CERTAIN YOU ARE DELIGHTED TO HAVE SUCH A LOVELY NIECE.
I WONDER IF HER MIND IS AS LOVELY AS HER FACE?
IF SHE TAKES AFTER YOU, QUEEN YOUNGCHAE, SHE MUST BE WISE BEYOND HER YEARS INDEED. HOWEVER, I AM NOT SURE IF THIS IS HER TRUE SELF.
......
ASK BAE GEUK TO COME PAY HIS RESPECTS SOME TIME, TOGETHER WITH THIS MAIDEN.

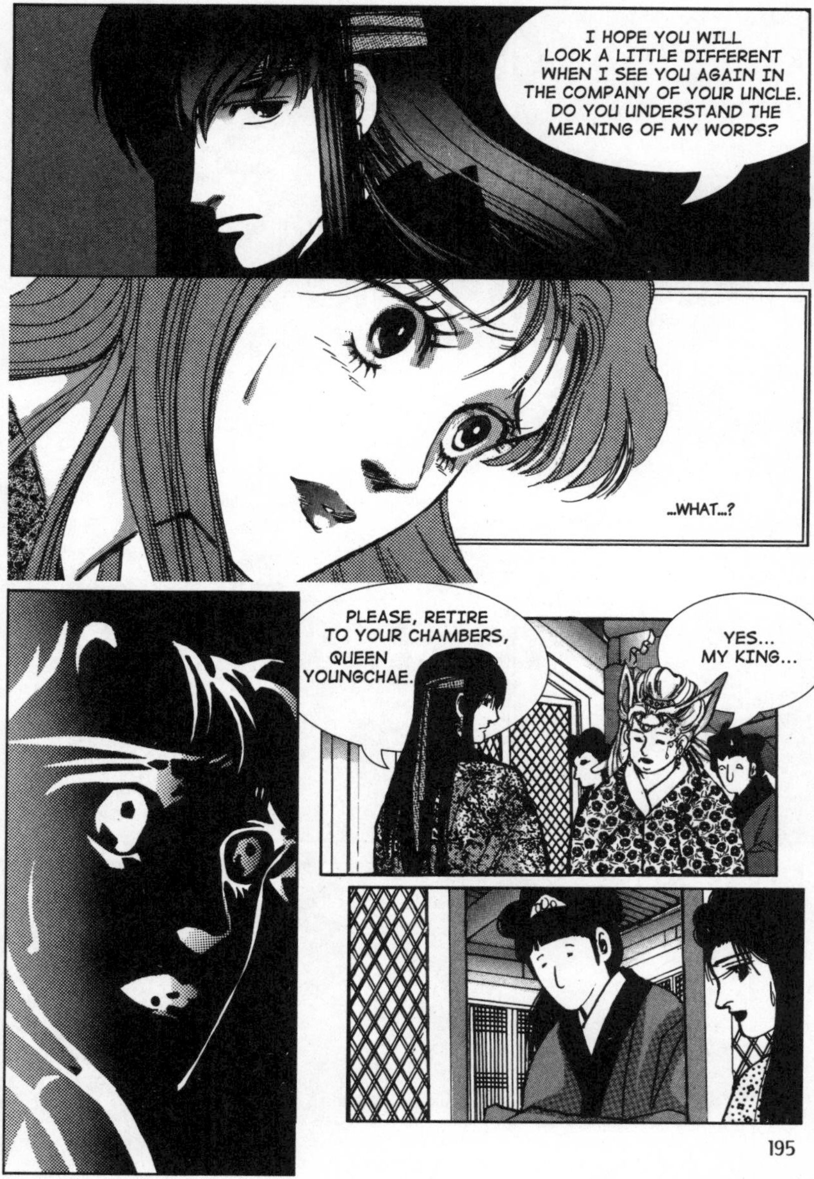
I HOPE YOU WILL LOOK A LITTLE DIFFERENT WHEN I SEE YOU AGAIN IN THE COMPANY OF YOUR UNCLE. DO YOU UNDERSTAND THE MEANING OF MY WORDS?
...WHAT...?
PLEASE, RETIRE TO YOUR CHAMBERS, QUEEN YOUNGCHAE.
YES... MY KING...

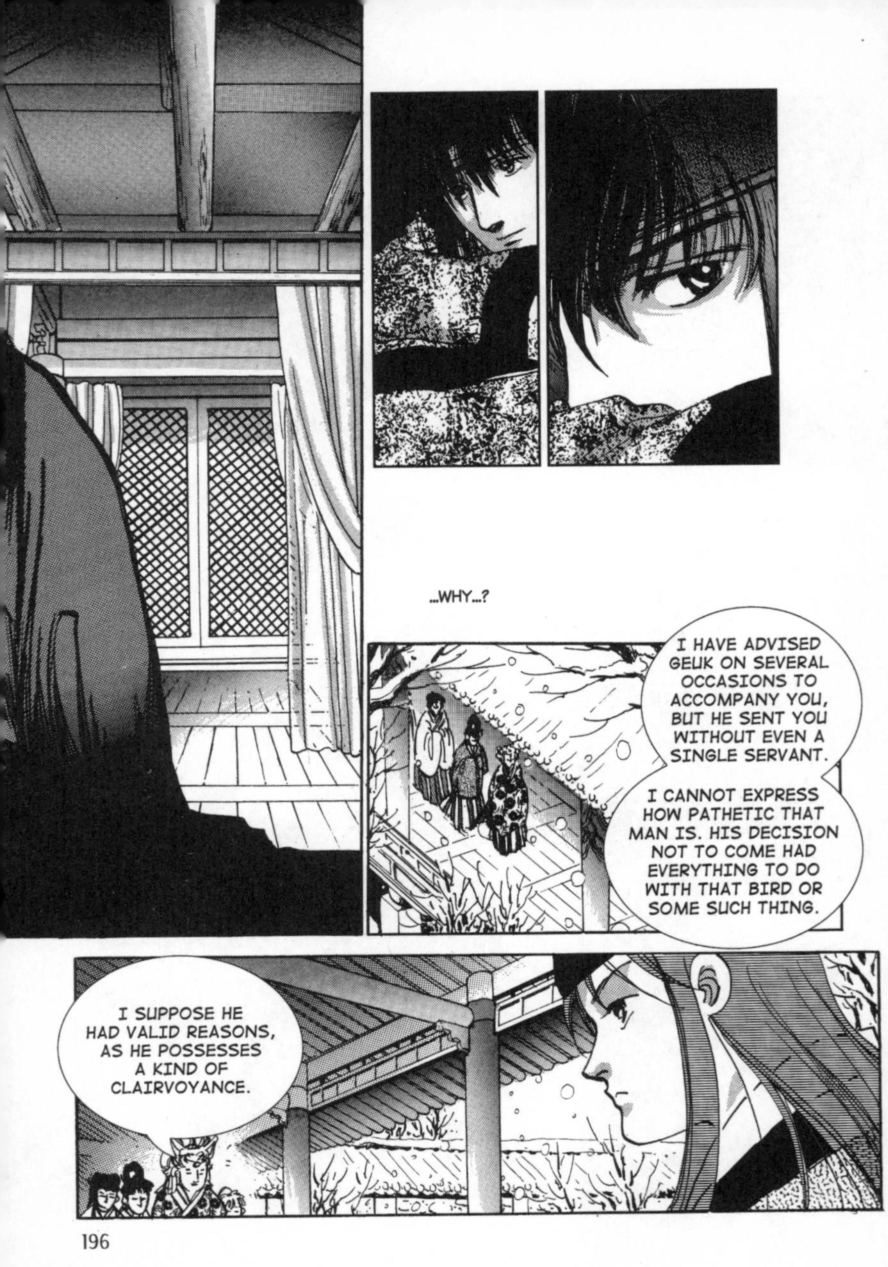
...WHY...?
I HAVE ADVISED GEUK ON SEVERAL OCCASIONS TO ACCOMPANY YOU, BUT HE SENT YOU WITHOUT EVEN A SINGLE SERVANT.
I CANNOT EXPRESS HOW PATHETIC THAT MAN IS. HIS DECISION NOT TO COME HAD EVERYTHING TO DO WITH THAT BIRD OR SOME SUCH THING.
I SUPPOSE HE HAD VALID REASONS, AS HE POSSESSES A KIND OF CLAIRVOYANCE.

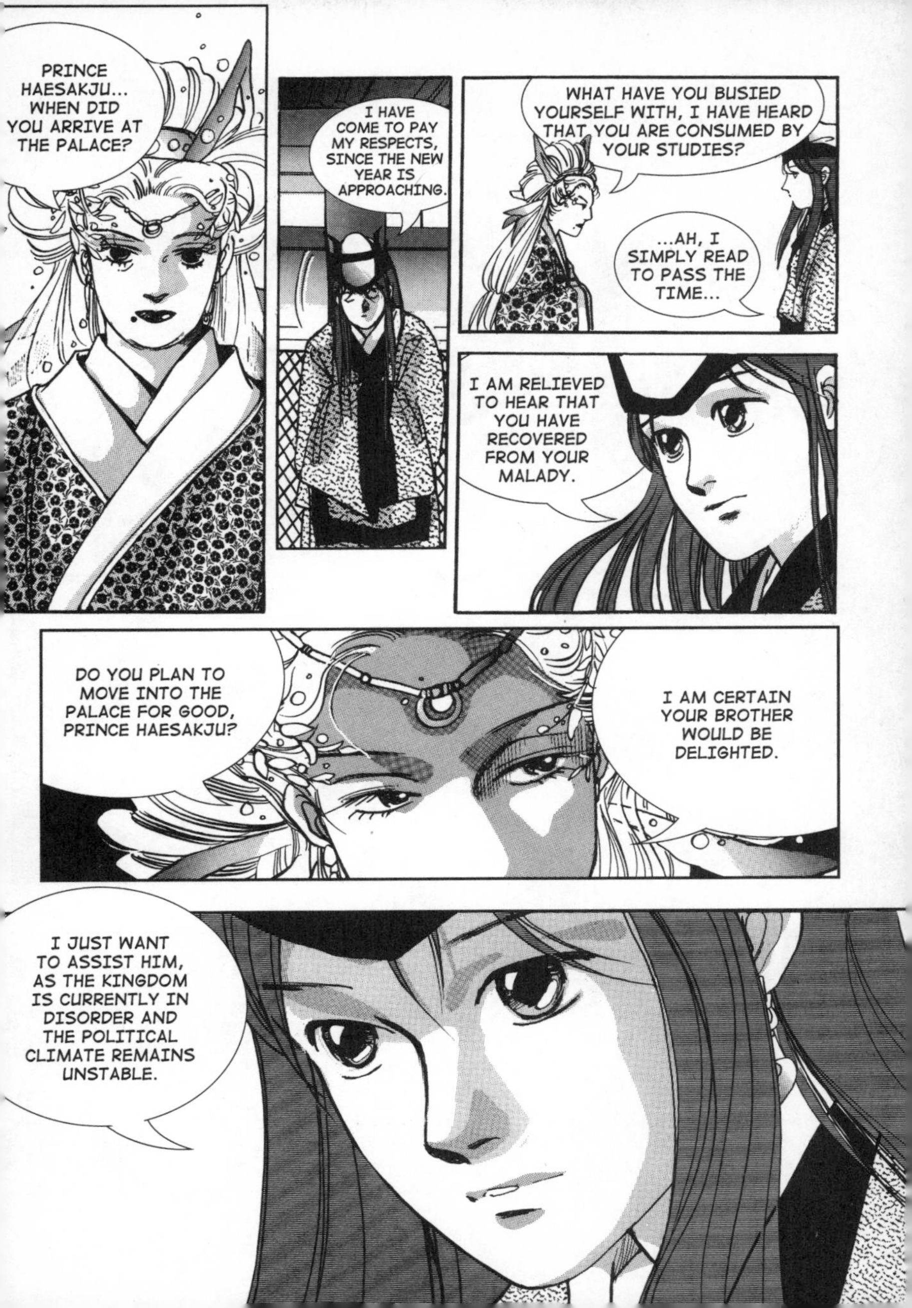
PRINCE HAESAKJU... WHEN DID YOU ARRIVE AT THE PALACE?
I HAVE COME TO PAY MY RESPECTS, SINCE THE NEW YEAR IS APPROACHING.
WHAT HAVE YOU BUSIED YOURSELF WITH, I HAVE HEARD THAT YOU ARE CONSUMED BY YOUR STUDIES?
...AH, I SIMPLY READ TO PASS THE TIME...
I AM RELIEVED TO HEAR THAT YOU HAVE RECOVERED FROM YOUR MALADY.
DO YOU PLAN TO MOVE INTO THE PALACE FOR GOOD, PRINCE HAESAKJU?
I AM CERTAIN YOUR BROTHER WOULD BE DELIGHTED.
I JUST WANT TO ASSIST HIM, AS THE KINGDOM IS CURRENTLY IN DISORDER AND THE POLITICAL CLIMATE REMAINS UNSTABLE.

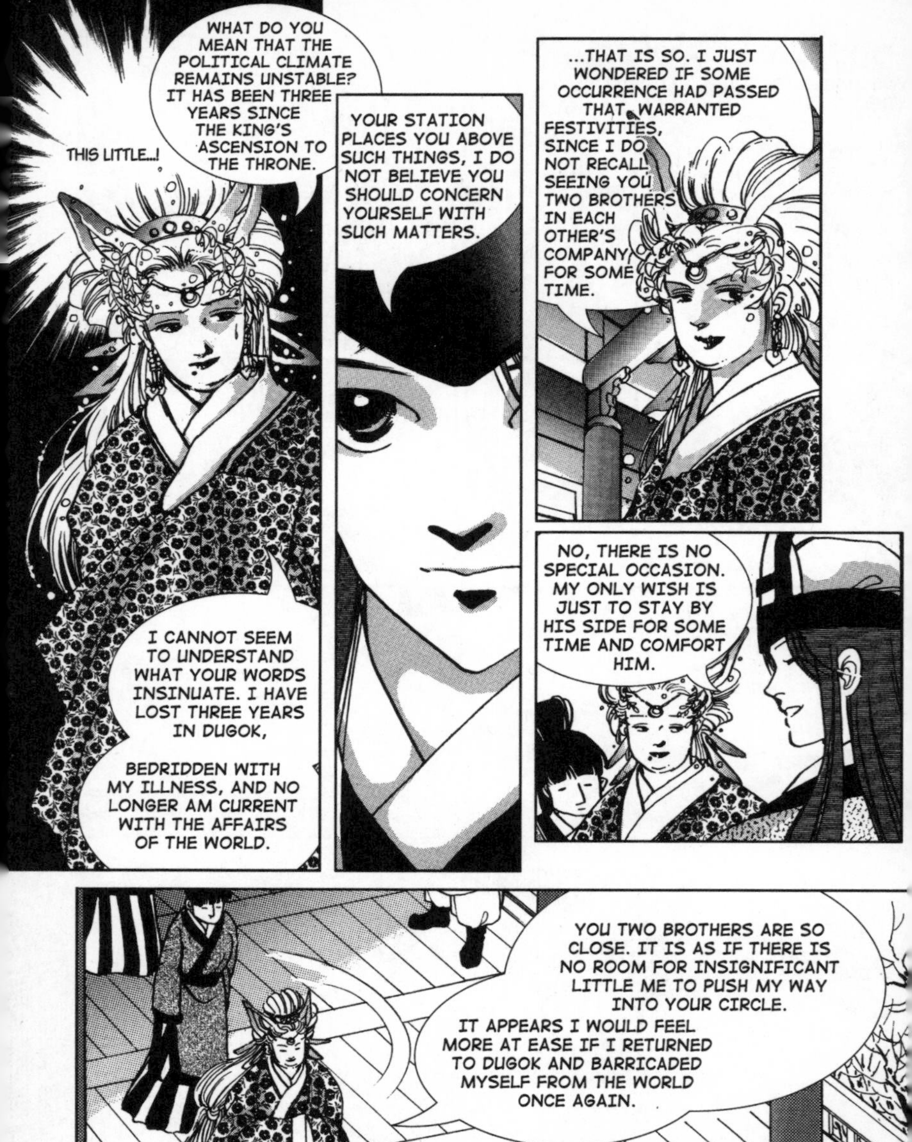
WHAT DO YOU MEAN THAT THE POLITICAL CLIMATE REMAINS UNSTABLE? IT HAS BEEN THREE YEARS SINCE THE KING'S ASCENSION TO THE THRONE.
THIS LITTLE...!
I CANNOT SEEM TO UNDERSTAND WHAT YOUR WORDS INSINUATE. I HAVE LOST THREE YEARS IN DUGOK,
BEDRIDDEN WITH MY ILLNESS, AND NO LONGER AM CURRENT WITH THE AFFAIRS OF THE WORLD.
YOUR STATION PLACES YOU ABOVE SUCH THINGS, I DO NOT BELIEVE YOU SHOULD CONCERN YOURSELF WITH SUCH MATTERS.
...THAT IS SO. I JUST WONDERED IF SOME OCCURRENCE HAD PASSED THAT WARRANTED FESTIVITIES, SINCE I DO NOT RECALL SEEING YOU TWO BROTHERS IN EACH OTHER'S COMPANY FOR SOME TIME.
NO, THERE IS NO SPECIAL OCCASION. MY ONLY WISH IS JUST TO STAY BY HIS SIDE FOR SOME TIME AND COMFORT HIM.
YOU TWO BROTHERS ARE SO CLOSE. IT IS AS IF THERE IS NO ROOM FOR INSIGNIFICANT LITTLE ME TO PUSH MY WAY INTO YOUR CIRCLE.
IT APPEARS I WOULD FEEL MORE AT EASE IF I RETURNED TO DUGOK AND BARRICADED MYSELF FROM THE WORLD ONCE AGAIN.

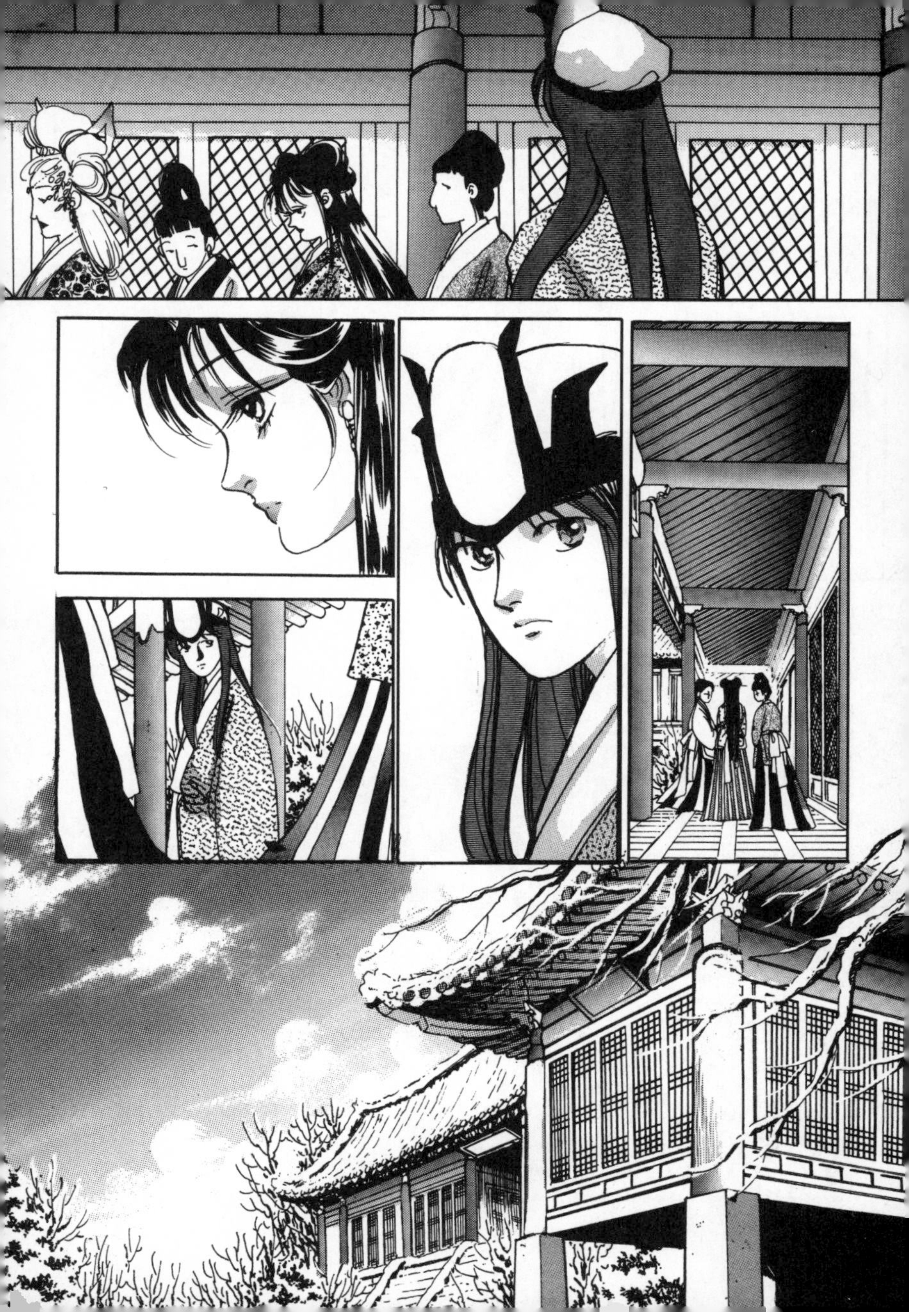

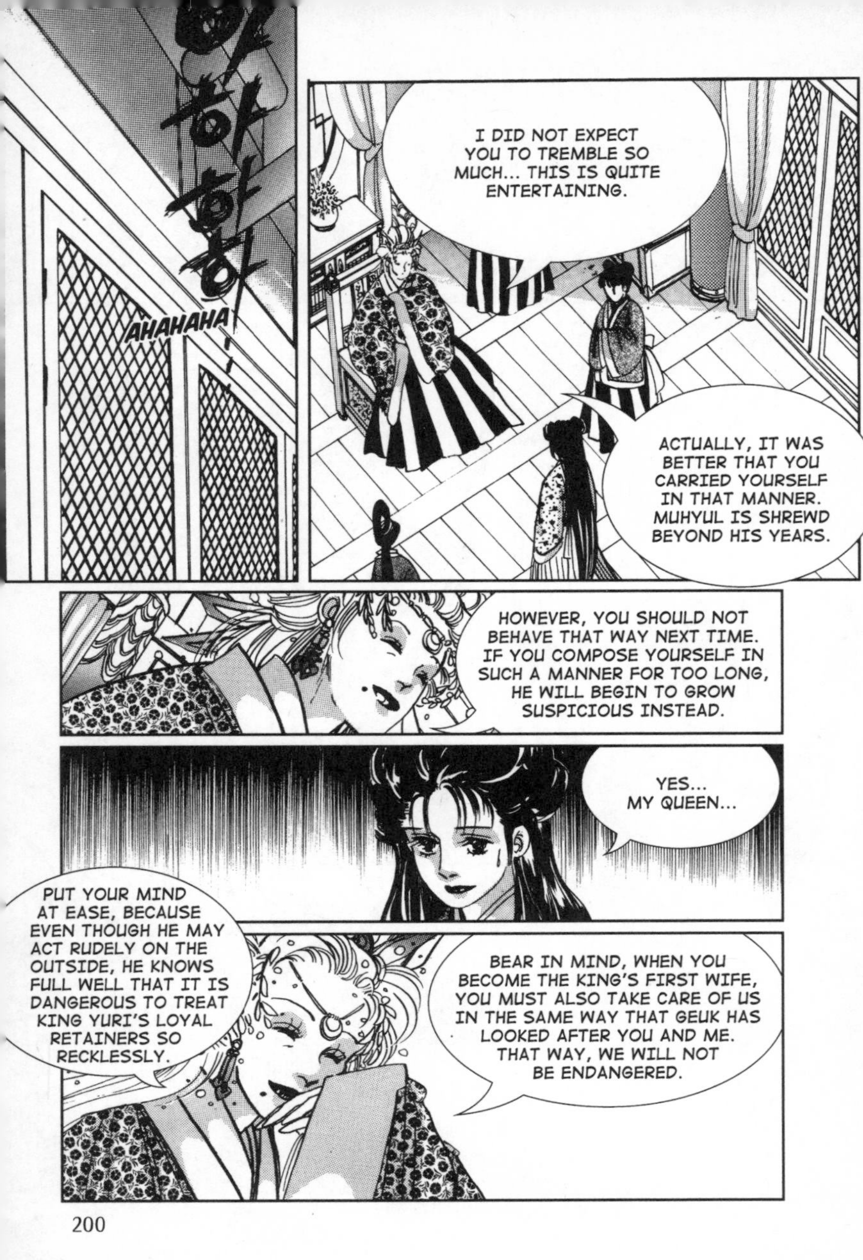
AHAHAHA
I DID NOT EXPECT YOU TO TREMBLE SO MUCH... THIS IS QUITE ENTERTAINING.
ACTUALLY, IT WAS BETTER THAT YOU CARRIED YOURSELF IN THAT MANNER. MUHYUL IS SHREWD BEYOND HIS YEARS.
HOWEVER, YOU SHOULD NOT BEHAVE THAT WAY NEXT TIME. IF YOU COMPOSE YOURSELF IN SUCH A MANNER FOR TOO LONG, HE WILL BEGIN TO GROW SUSPICIOUS INSTEAD.
YES... MY QUEEN...
PUT YOUR MIND AT EASE, BECAUSE EVEN THOUGH HE MAY ACT RUDELY ON THE OUTSIDE, HE KNOWS FULL WELL THAT IT IS DANGEROUS TO TREAT KING YURI'S LOYAL RETAINERS SO RECKLESSLY.
BEAR IN MIND, WHEN YOU BECOME THE KING'S FIRST WIFE, YOU MUST ALSO TAKE CARE OF US IN THE SAME WAY THAT GEUK HAS LOOKED AFTER YOU AND ME. THAT WAY, WE WILL NOT BE ENDANGERED.

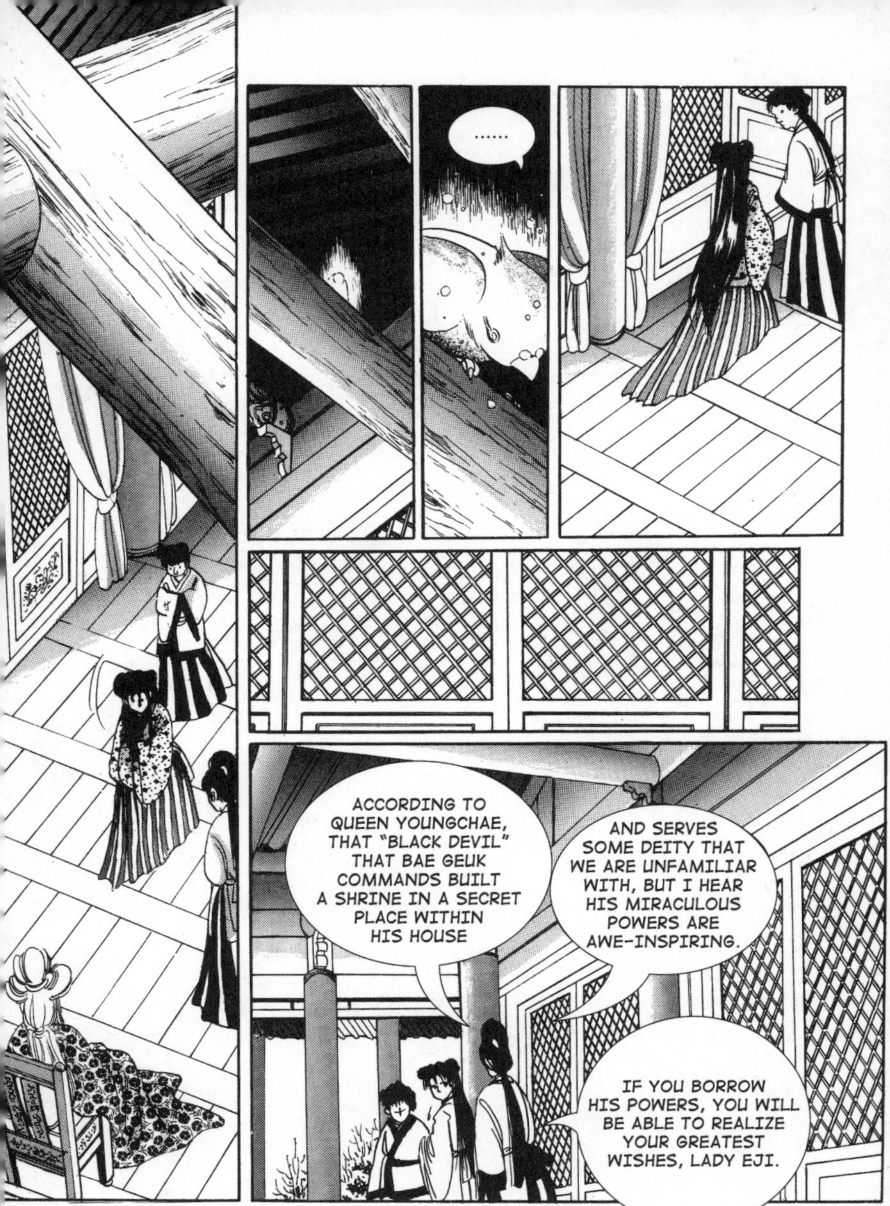
......
ACCORDING TO QUEEN YOUNGCHAE, THAT "BLACK DEVIL" THAT BAE GEUK COMMANDS BUILT A SHRINE IN A SECRET PLACE WITHIN HIS HOUSE
AND SERVES SOME DEITY THAT WE ARE UNFAMILIAR WITH, BUT I HEAR HIS MIRACULOUS POWERS ARE AWE-INSPIRING.
IF YOU BORROW HIS POWERS, YOU WILL BE ABLE TO REALIZE YOUR GREATEST WISHES, LADY EJI.

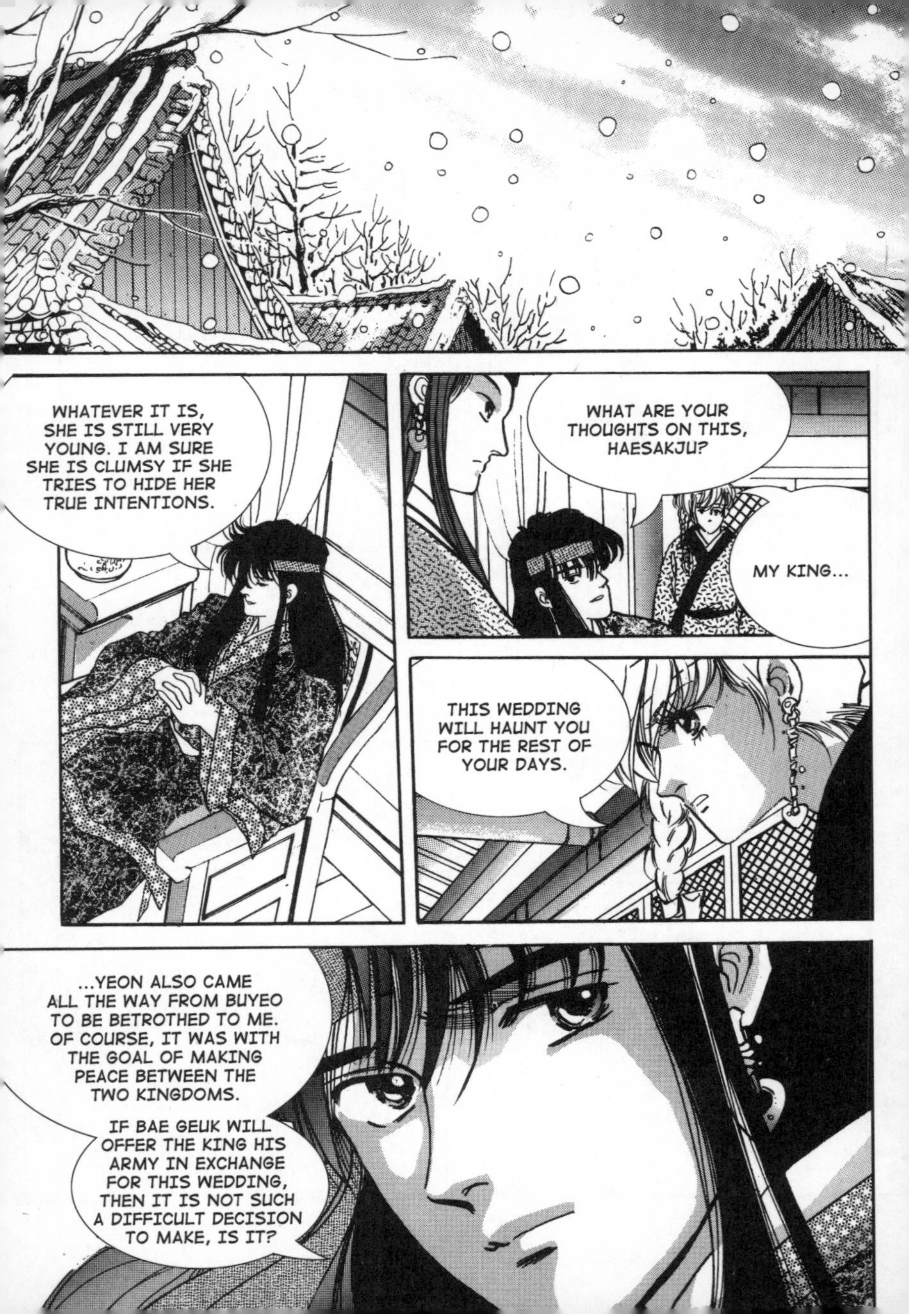
WHATEVER IT IS, SHE IS STILL VERY YOUNG. I AM SURE SHE IS CLUMSY IF SHE TRIES TO HIDE HER TRUE INTENTIONS.
WHAT ARE YOUR THOUGHTS ON THIS, HAESAKJU?
MY KING...
THIS WEDDING WILL HAUNT YOU FOR THE REST OF YOUR DAYS.
...YEON ALSO CAME ALL THE WAY FROM BUYEO TO BE BETROTHED TO ME. OF COURSE, IT WAS WITH THE GOAL OF MAKING PEACE BETWEEN THE TWO KINGDOMS.
IF BAE GEUK WILL OFFER THE KING HIS ARMY IN EXCHANGE FOR THIS WEDDING, THEN IT IS NOT SUCH A DIFFICULT DECISION TO MAKE, IS IT?

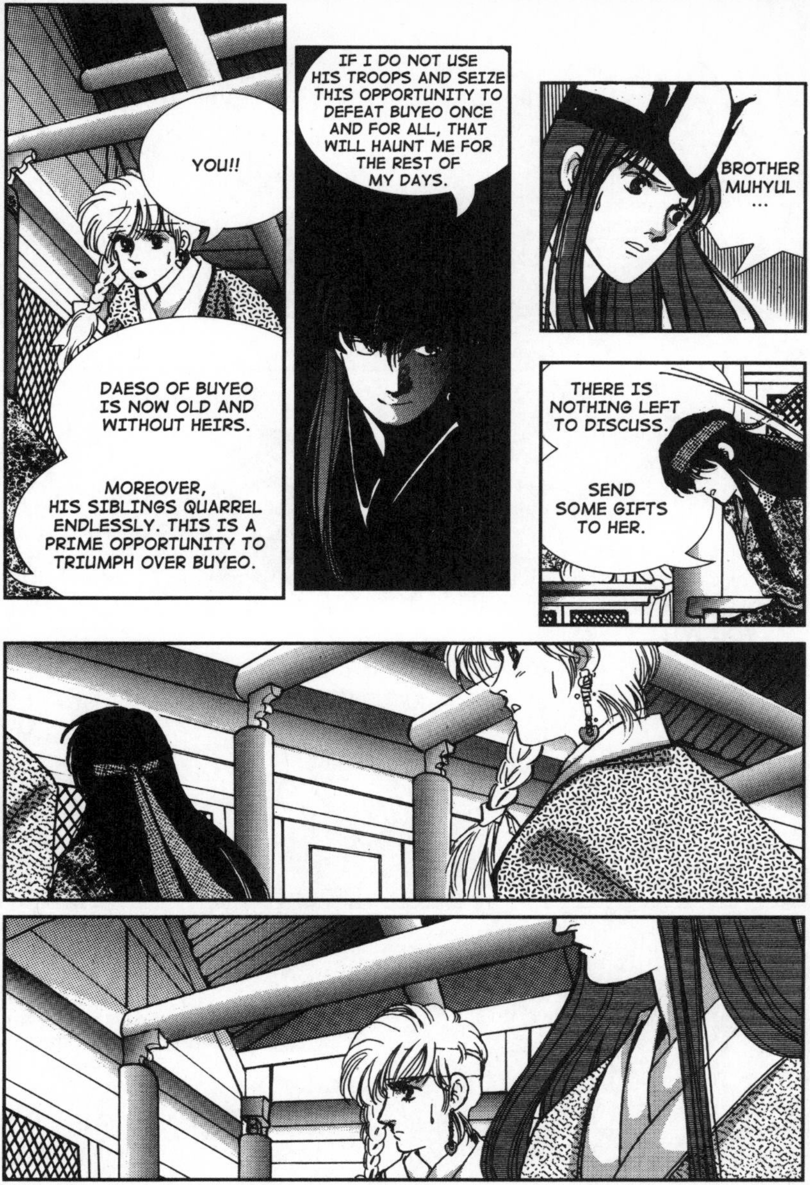
YOU!!
DAESO OF BUYEO IS NOW OLD AND WITHOUT HEIRS.
MOREOVER, HIS SIBLINGS QUARREL ENDLESSLY. THIS IS A PRIME OPPORTUNITY TO TRIUMPH OVER BUYEO.
IF I DO NOT USE HIS TROOPS AND SEIZE THIS OPPORTUNITY TO DEFEAT BUYEO ONCE AND FOR ALL, THAT WILL HAUNT ME FOR THE REST OF MY DAYS.
BROTHER MUHYUL ...
THERE IS NOTHING LEFT TO DISCUSS.
SEND SOME GIFTS TO HER.

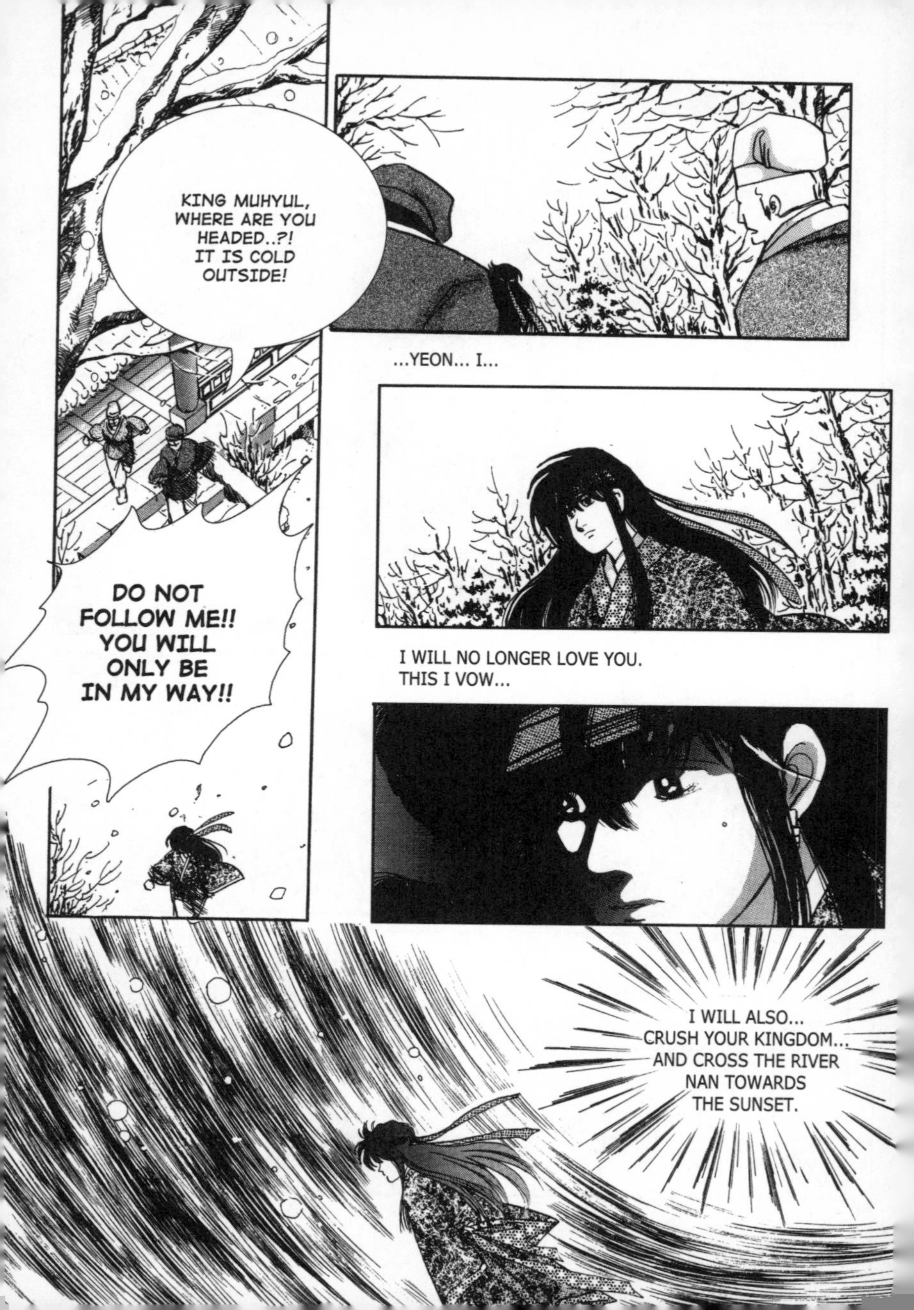
KING MUHYUL, WHERE ARE YOU HEADED..?! IT IS COLD OUTSIDE!
DO NOT FOLLOW ME!! YOU WILL ONLY BE IN MY WAY!!
...YEON... I...
I WILL NO LONGER LOVE YOU. THIS I VOW...
I WILL ALSO... CRUSH YOUR KINGDOM... AND CROSS THE RIVER NAN TOWARDS THE SUNSET.

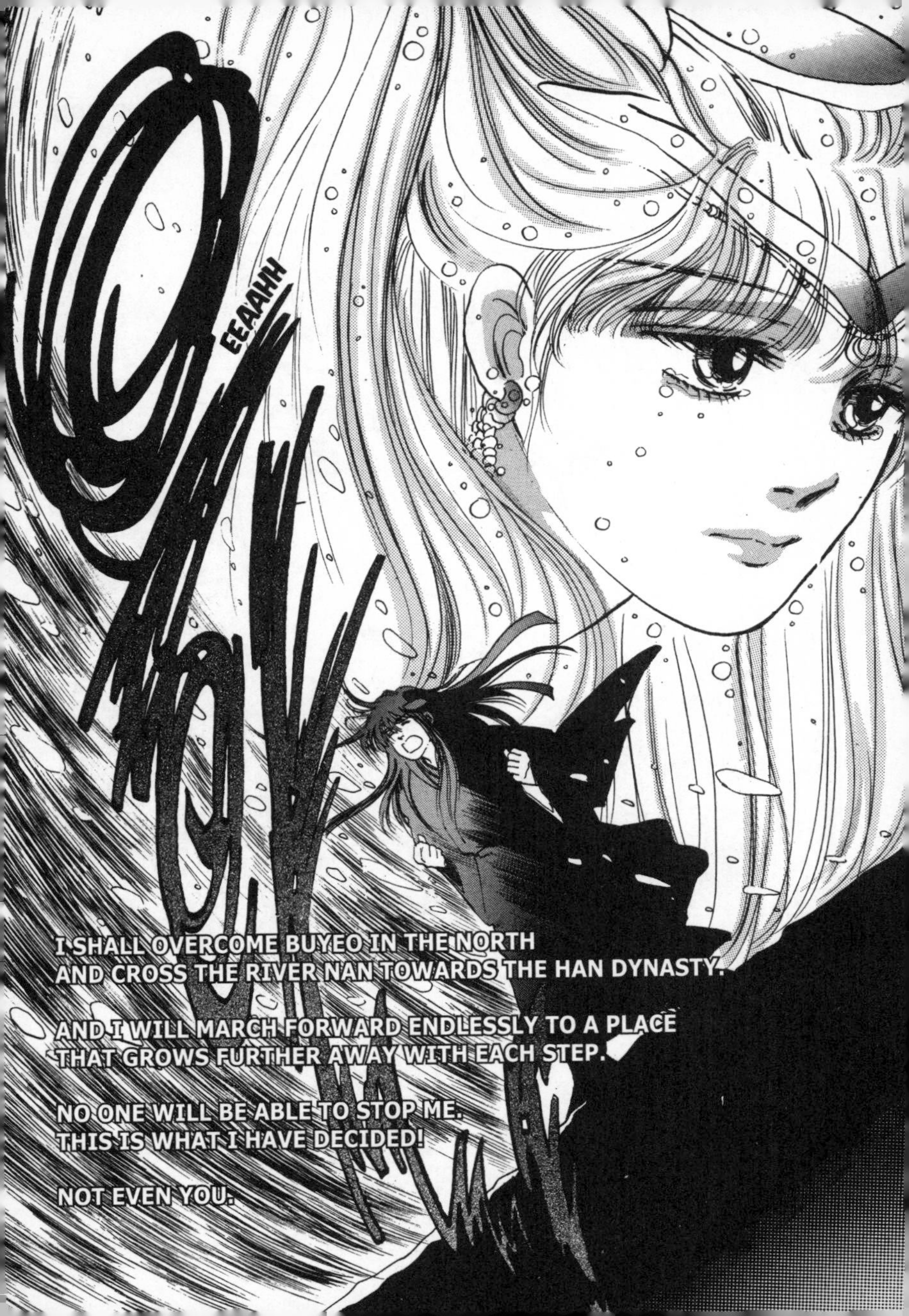
EEAAHH
I SHALL OVERCOME BUYEO IN THE NORTH
AND CROSS THE RIVER NAN TOWARDS THE HAN DYNASTY.
AND I WILL MARCH FORWARD ENDLESSLY TO A PLACE
THAT GROWS FURTHER AWAY WITH EACH STEP.
NO ONE WILL BE ABLE TO STOP ME.
THIS IS WHAT I HAVE DECIDED!
NOT EVEN YOU.

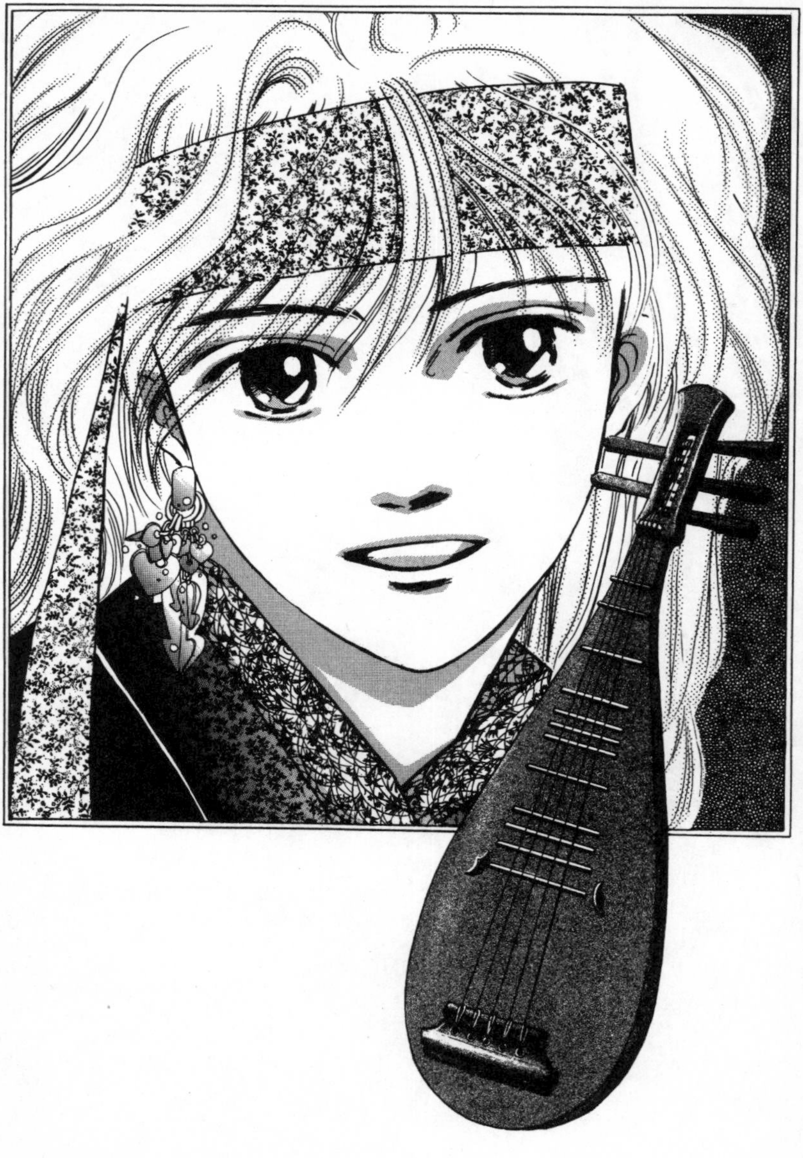

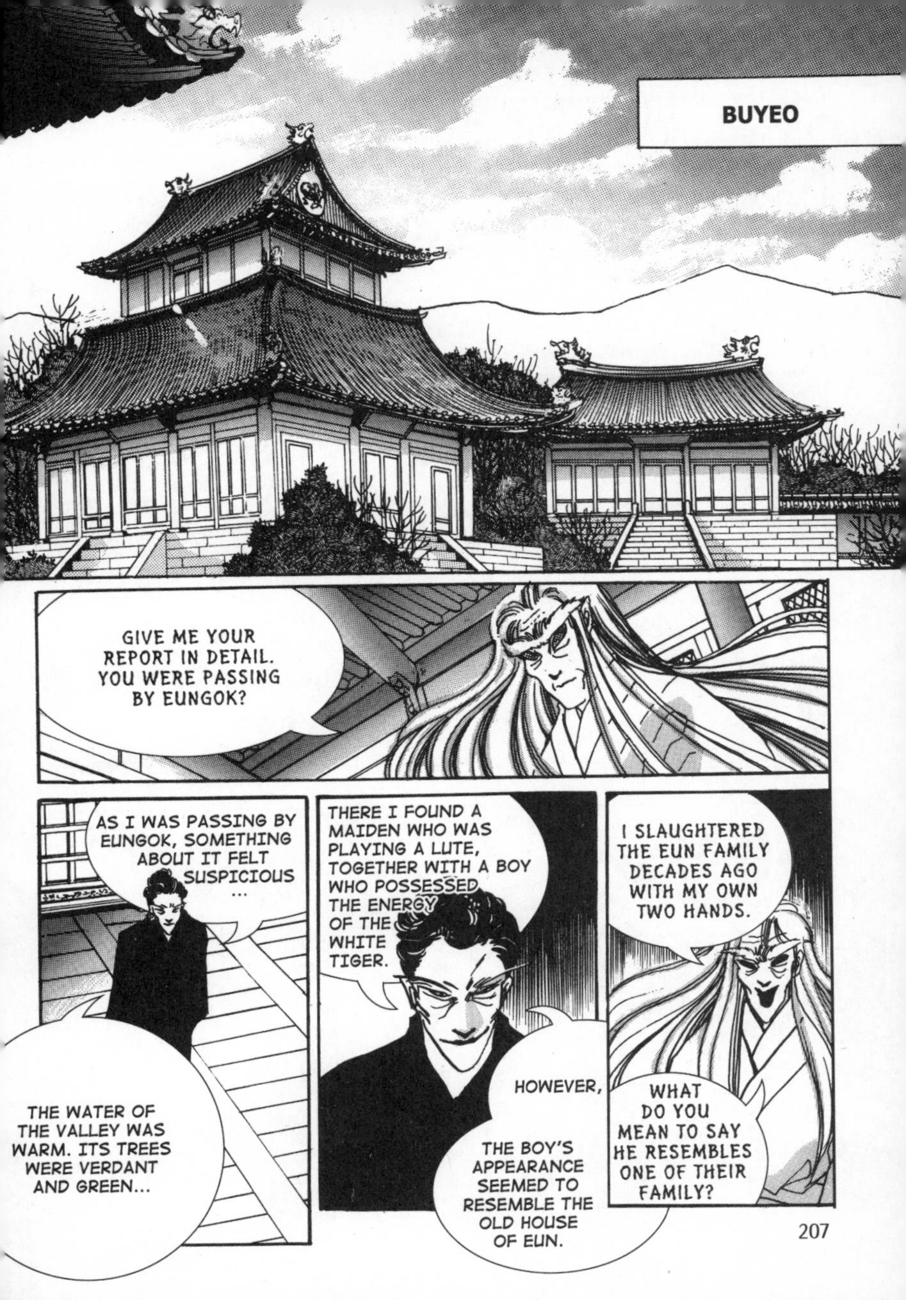
BUYEO
GIVE ME YOUR REPORT IN DETAIL. YOU WERE PASSING BY EUNGOK?
AS I WAS PASSING BY EUNGOK, SOMETHING ABOUT IT FELT SUSPICIOUS ...
THE WATER OF THE VALLEY WAS WARM. ITS TREES WERE VERDANT AND GREEN...
THERE I FOUND A MAIDEN WHO WAS PLAYING A LUTE, TOGETHER WITH A BOY WHO POSSESSED THE ENERGY OF THE WHITE TIGER.
HOWEVER,
THE BOY'S APPEARANCE SEEMED TO RESEMBLE THE OLD HOUSE OF EUN.
I SLAUGHTERED THE EUN FAMILY DECADES AGO WITH MY OWN TWO HANDS.
WHAT DO YOU MEAN TO SAY HE RESEMBLES ONE OF THEIR FAMILY?

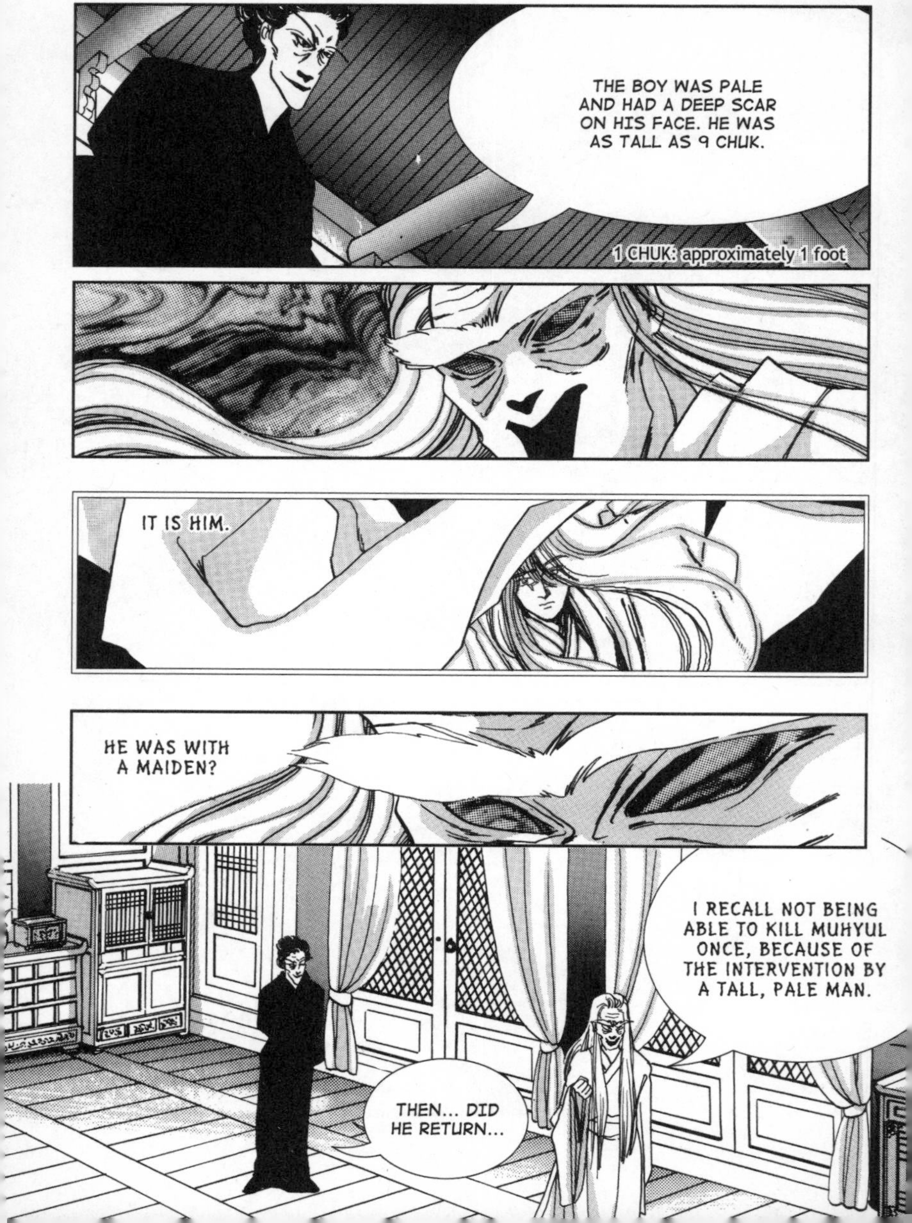

THE BOY WAS PALE AND HAD A DEEP SCAR ON HIS FACE. HE WAS AS TALL AS 9 CHUK.
1 CHUK: approximately 1 foot
IT IS HIM.
HE WAS WITH A MAIDEN?
I RECALL NOT BEING ABLE TO KILL MUHYUL ONCE, BECAUSE OF THE INTERVENTION BY A TALL, PALE MAN.
THEN... DID HE RETURN...

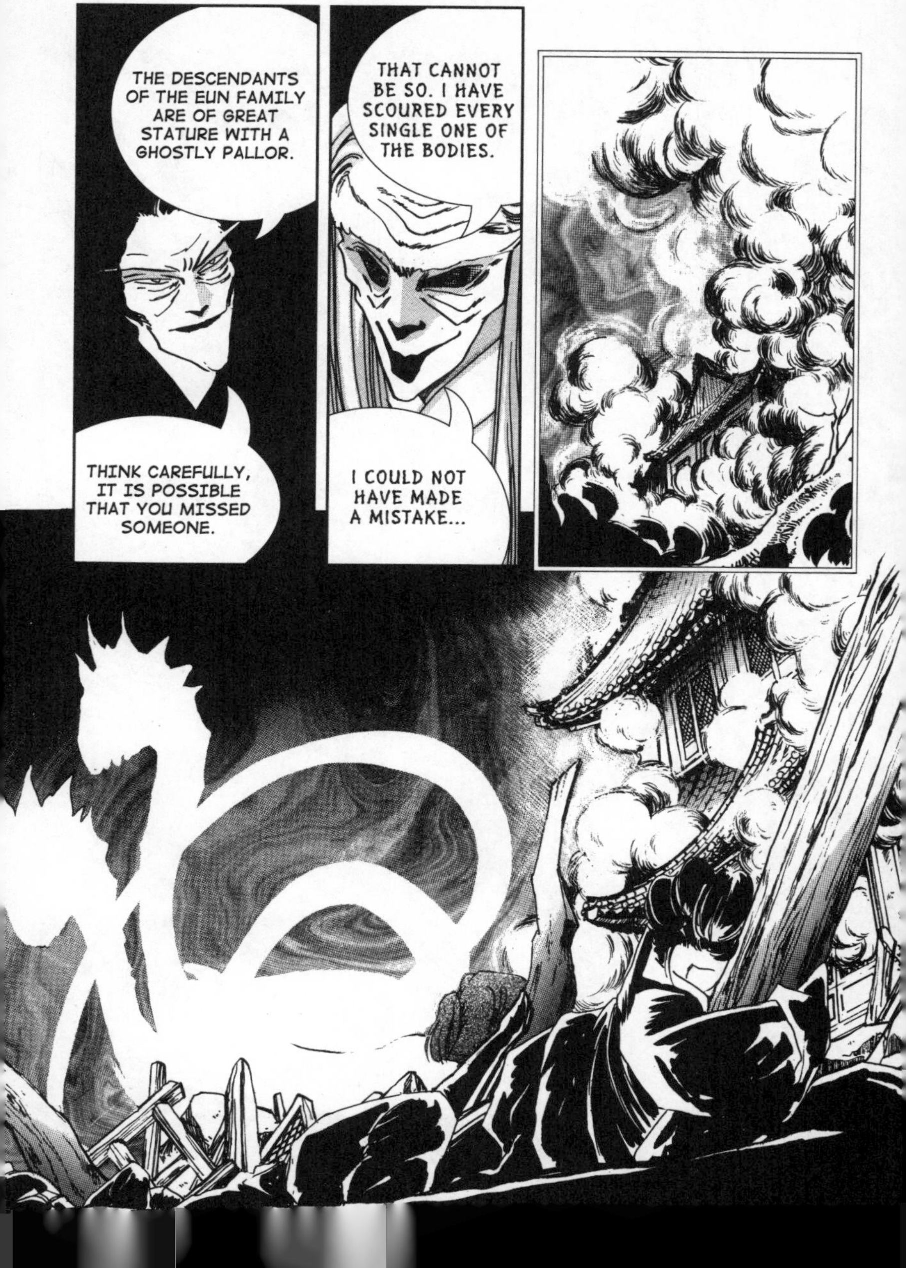
THE DESCENDANTS OF THE EUN FAMILY ARE OF GREAT STATURE WITH A GHOSTLY PALLOR.
THINK CAREFULLY, IT IS POSSIBLE THAT YOU MISSED SOMEONE.
THAT CANNOT BE SO. I HAVE SCOURED EVERY SINGLE ONE OF THE BODIES.
I COULD NOT HAVE MADE A MISTAKE...

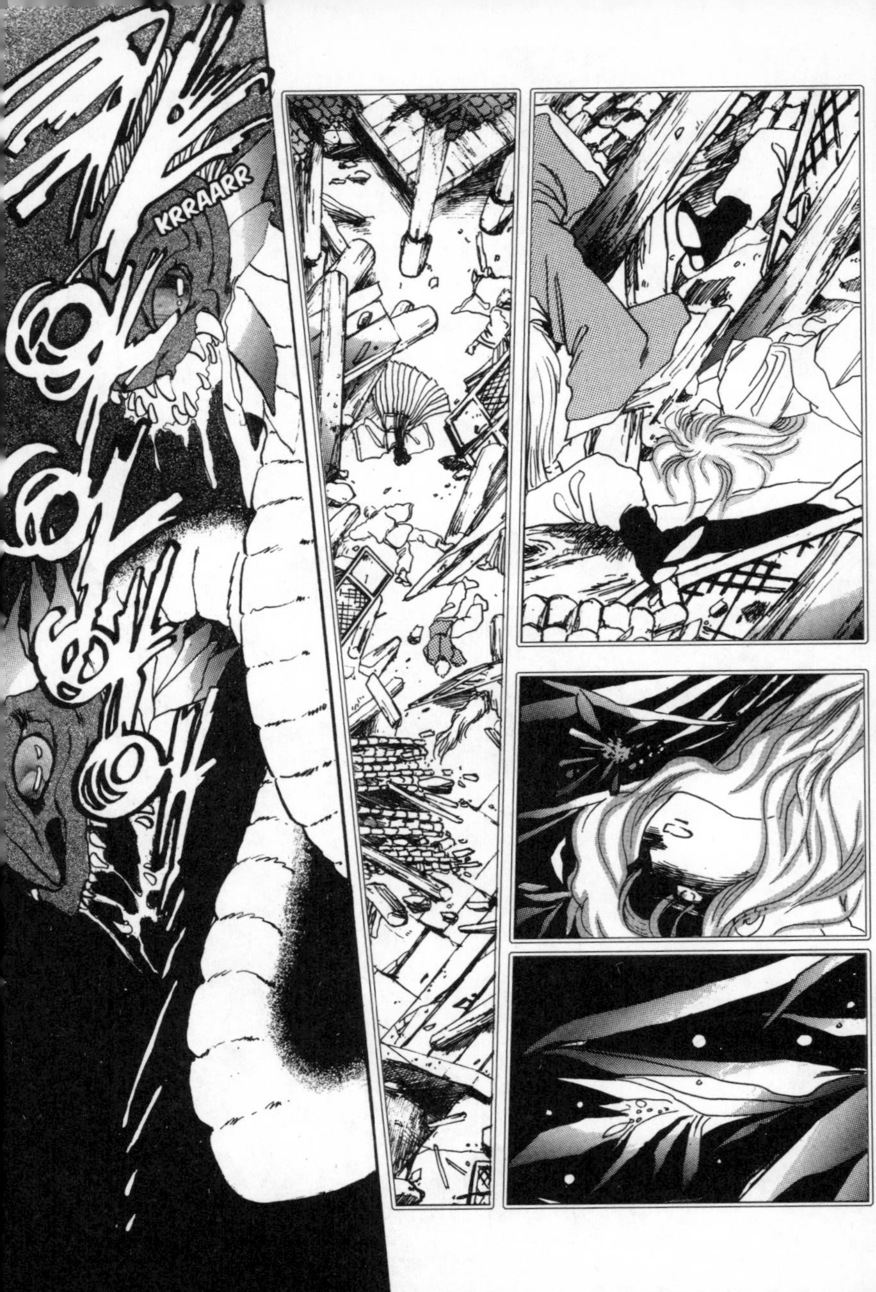
KRRAARR

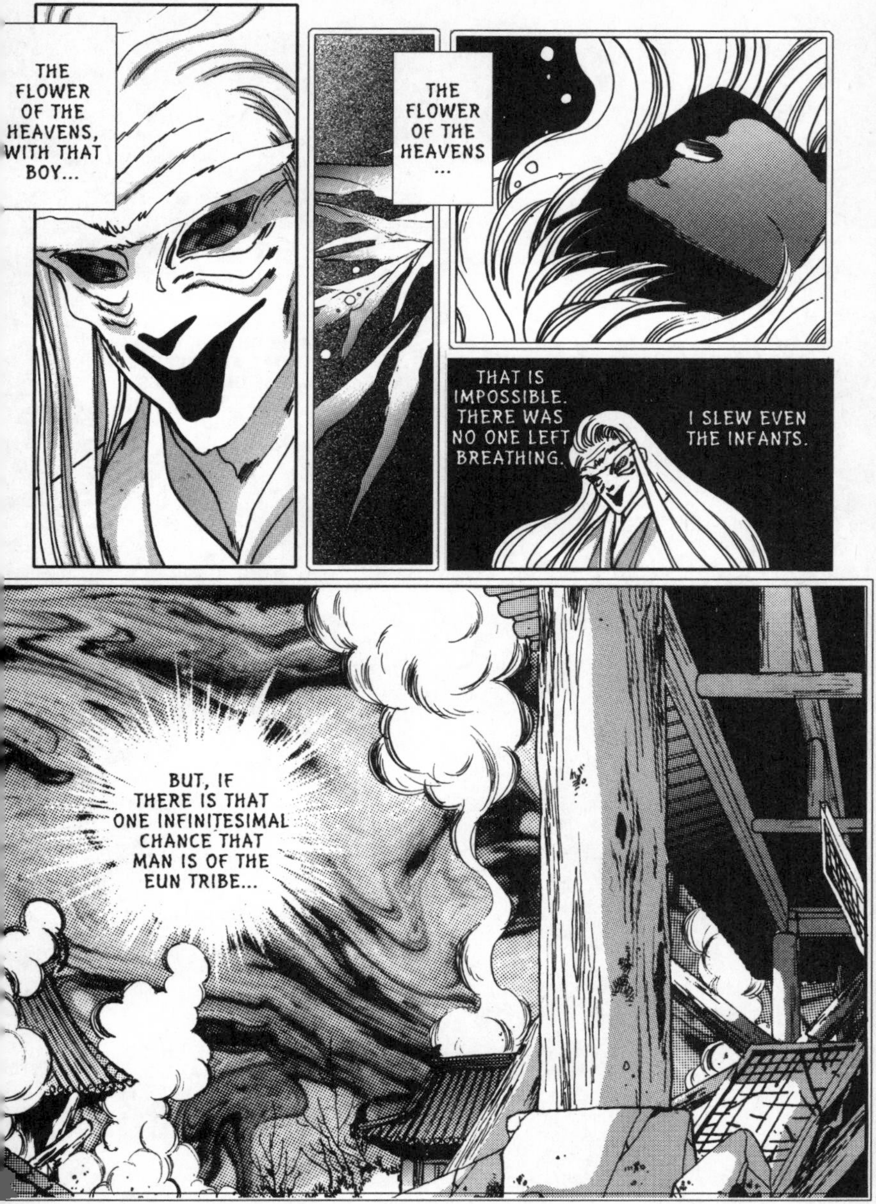
THE FLOWER OF THE HEAVENS, WITH THAT BOY...
THE FLOWER OF THE HEAVENS ...
THAT IS IMPOSSIBLE. THERE WAS NO ONE LEFT BREATHING.
I SLEW EVEN THE INFANTS.
BUT, IF THERE IS THAT ONE INFINITESIMAL CHANCE THAT MAN IS OF THE EUN TRIBE...

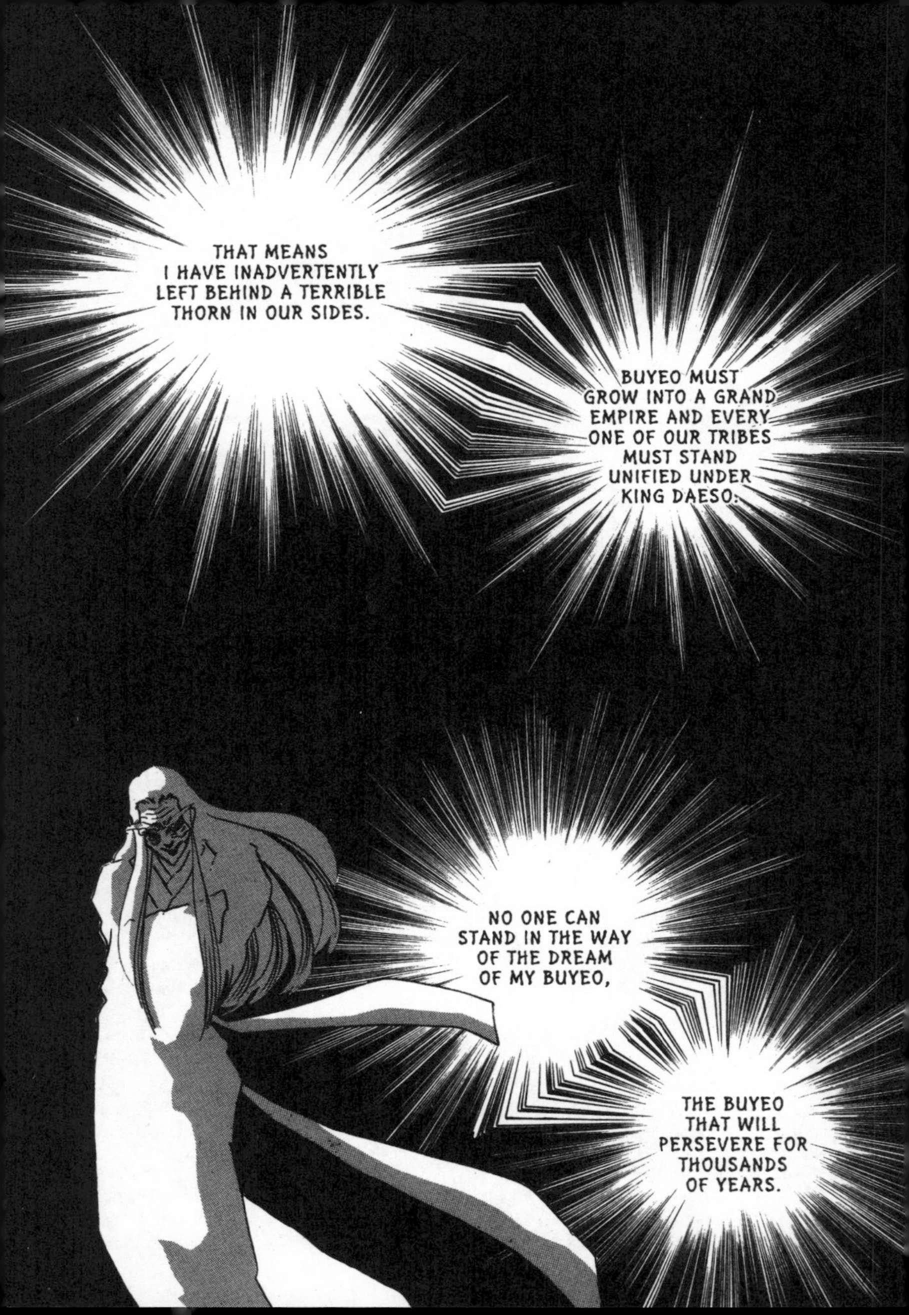
THAT MEANS I HAVE INADVERTENTLY LEFT BEHIND A TERRIBLE THORN IN OUR SIDES.
BUYEO MUST GROW INTO A GRAND EMPIRE AND EVERY ONE OF OUR TRIBES MUST STAND UNIFIED UNDER KING DAESO.
NO ONE CAN STAND IN THE WAY OF THE DREAM OF MY BUYEO,
THE BUYEO THAT WILL PERSEVERE FOR THOUSANDS OF YEARS.

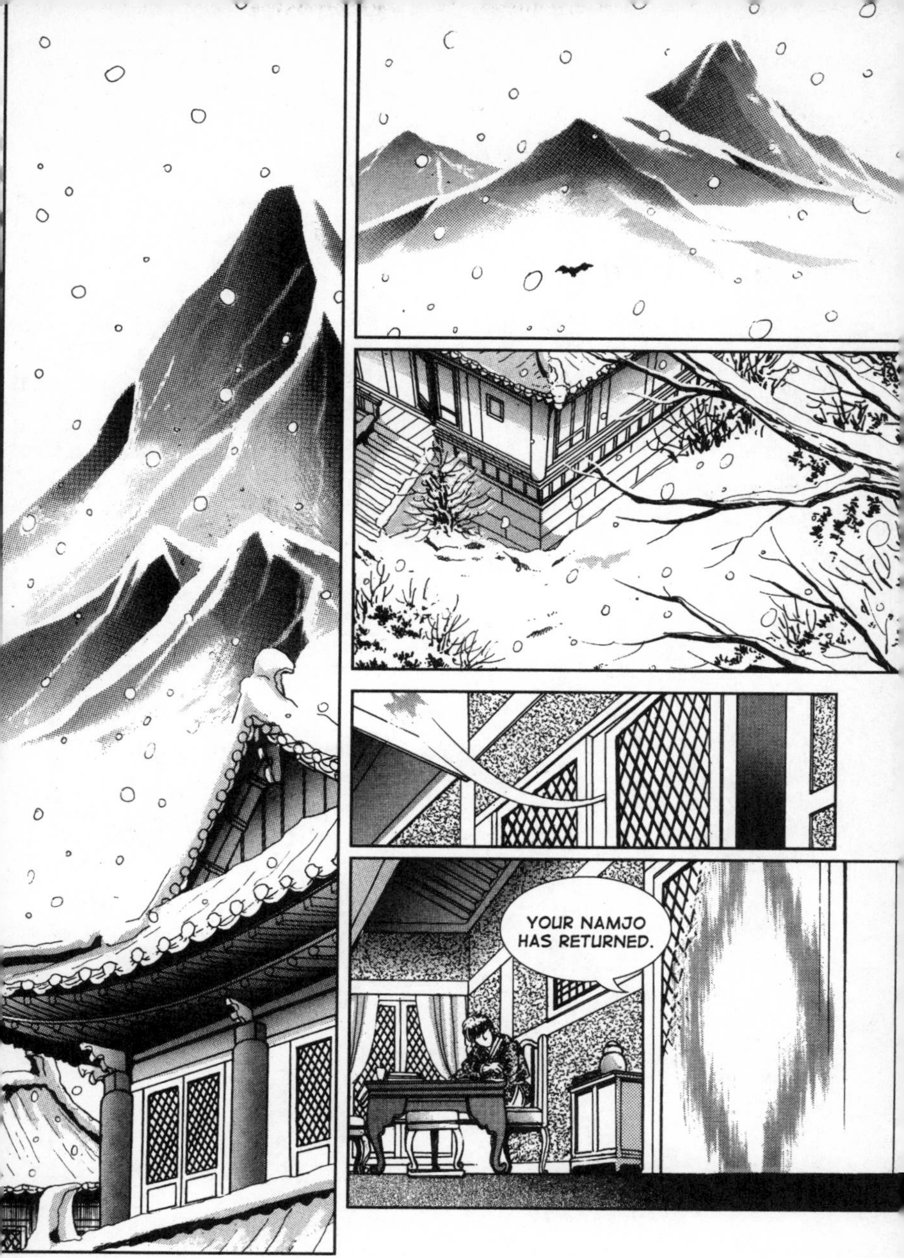
YOUR NAMJO HAS RETURNED.

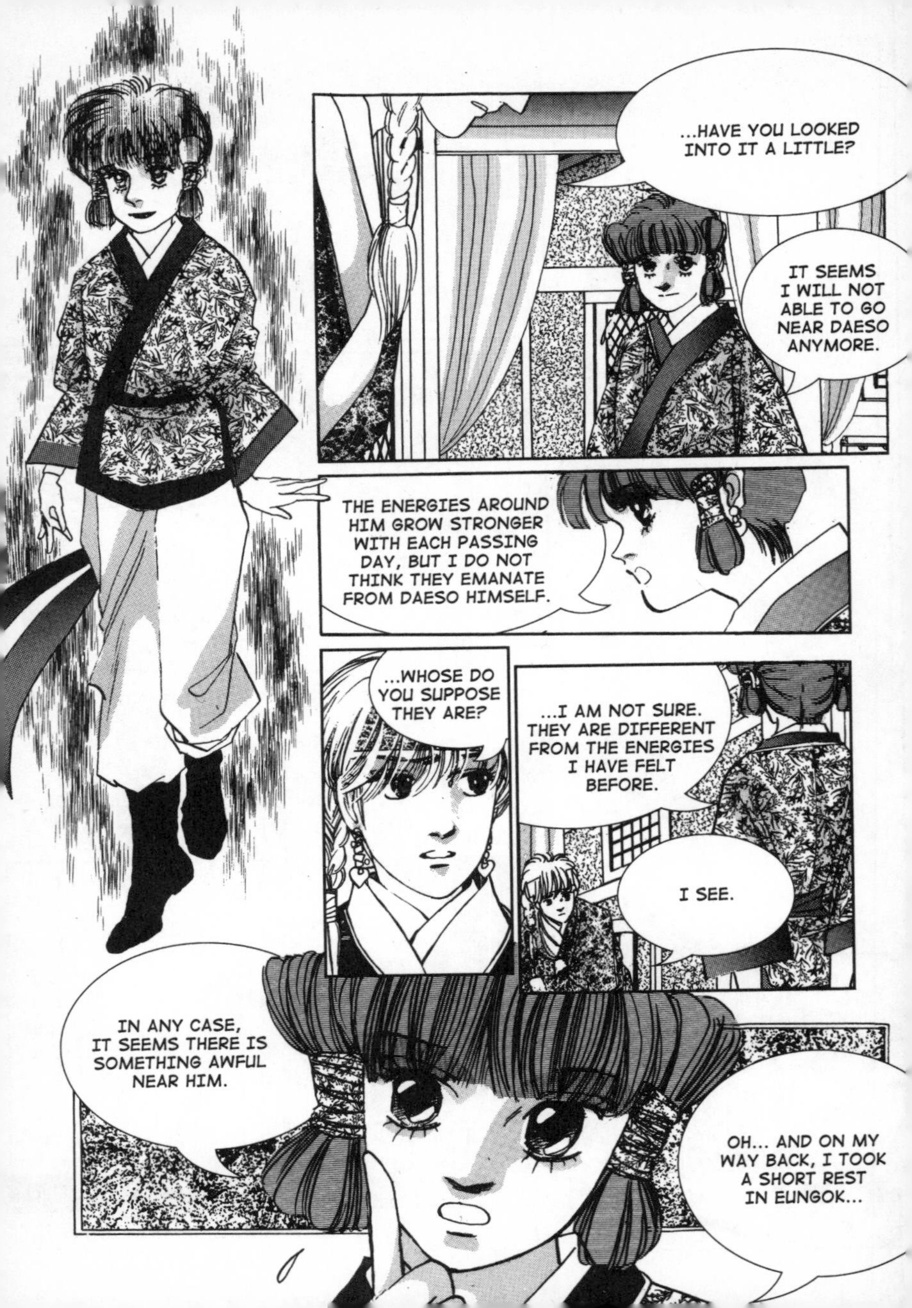
...HAVE YOU LOOKED INTO IT A LITTLE?
IT SEEMS I WILL NOT ABLE TO GO NEAR DAESO ANYMORE.
THE ENERGIES AROUND HIM GROW STRONGER WITH EACH PASSING DAY, BUT I DO NOT THINK THEY EMANATE FROM DAESO HIMSELF.
...WHOSE DO YOU SUPPOSE THEY ARE?
...I AM NOT SURE. THEY ARE DIFFERENT FROM THE ENERGIES I HAVE FELT BEFORE.
I SEE.
IN ANY CASE, IT SEEMS THERE IS SOMETHING AWFUL NEAR HIM.
OH... AND ON MY WAY BACK, I TOOK A SHORT REST IN EUNGOK...

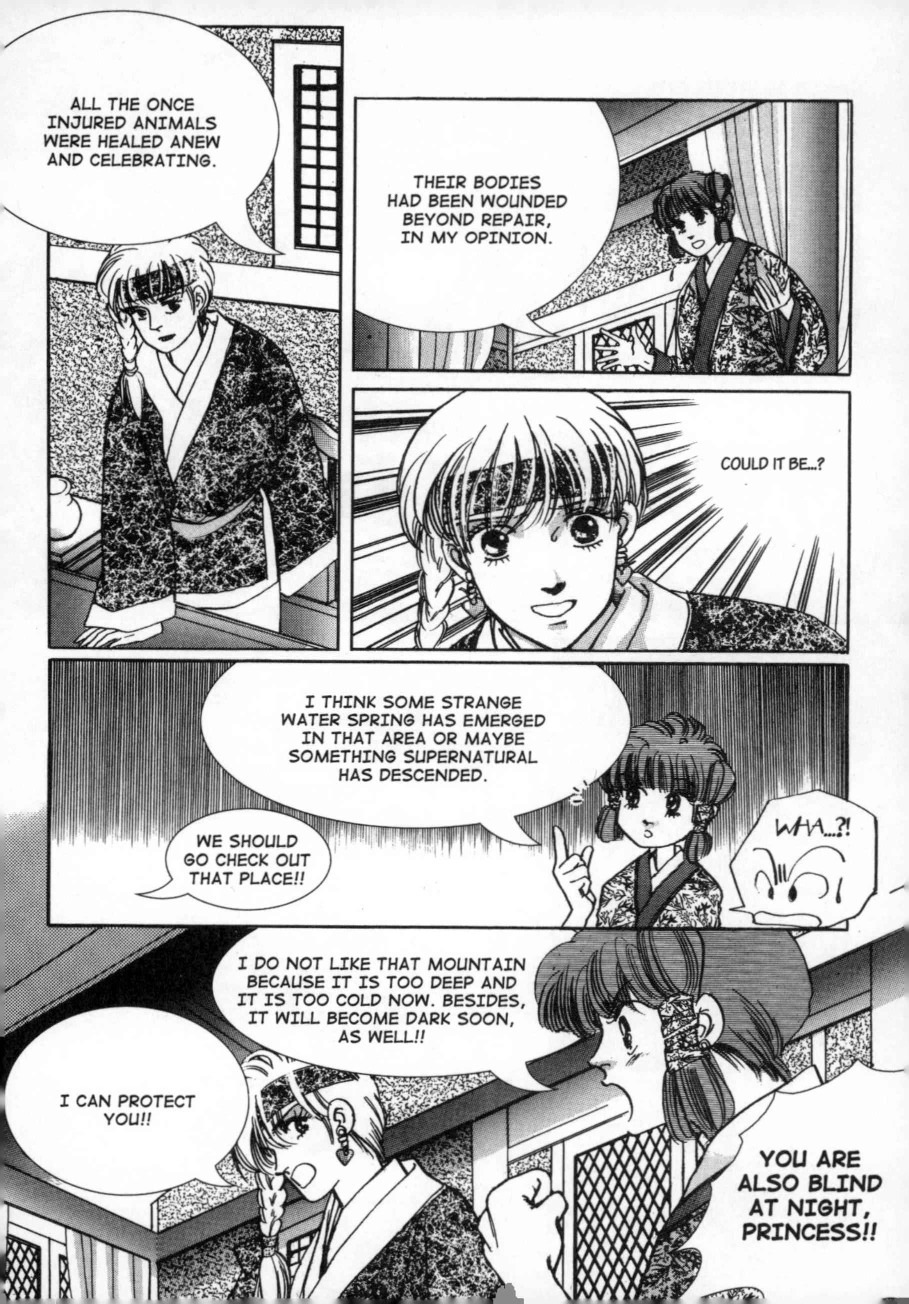
ALL THE ONCE INJURED ANIMALS WERE HEALED ANEW AND CELEBRATING.
THEIR BODIES HAD BEEN WOUNDED BEYOND REPAIR, IN MY OPINION.
COULD IT BE...?
I THINK SOME STRANGE WATER SPRING HAS EMERGED IN THAT AREA OR MAYBE SOMETHING SUPERNATURAL HAS DESCENDED.
WE SHOULD GO CHECK OUT THAT PLACE!!
WHA...?!
I DO NOT LIKE THAT MOUNTAIN BECAUSE IT IS TOO DEEP AND IT IS TOO COLD NOW. BESIDES, IT WILL BECOME DARK SOON, AS WELL!!
I CAN PROTECT YOU!!
YOU ARE ALSO BLIND AT NIGHT, PRINCESS!!

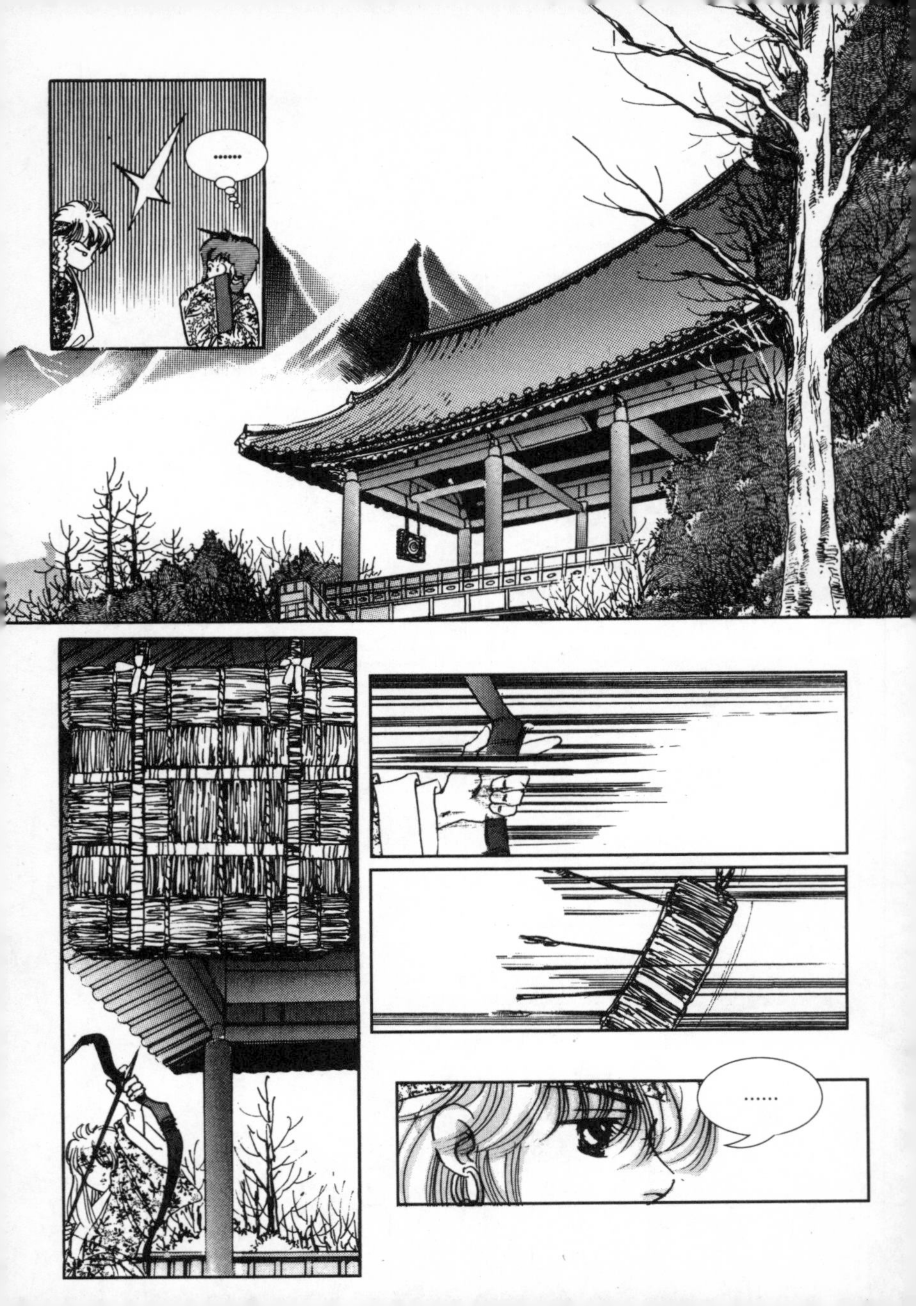

......
......

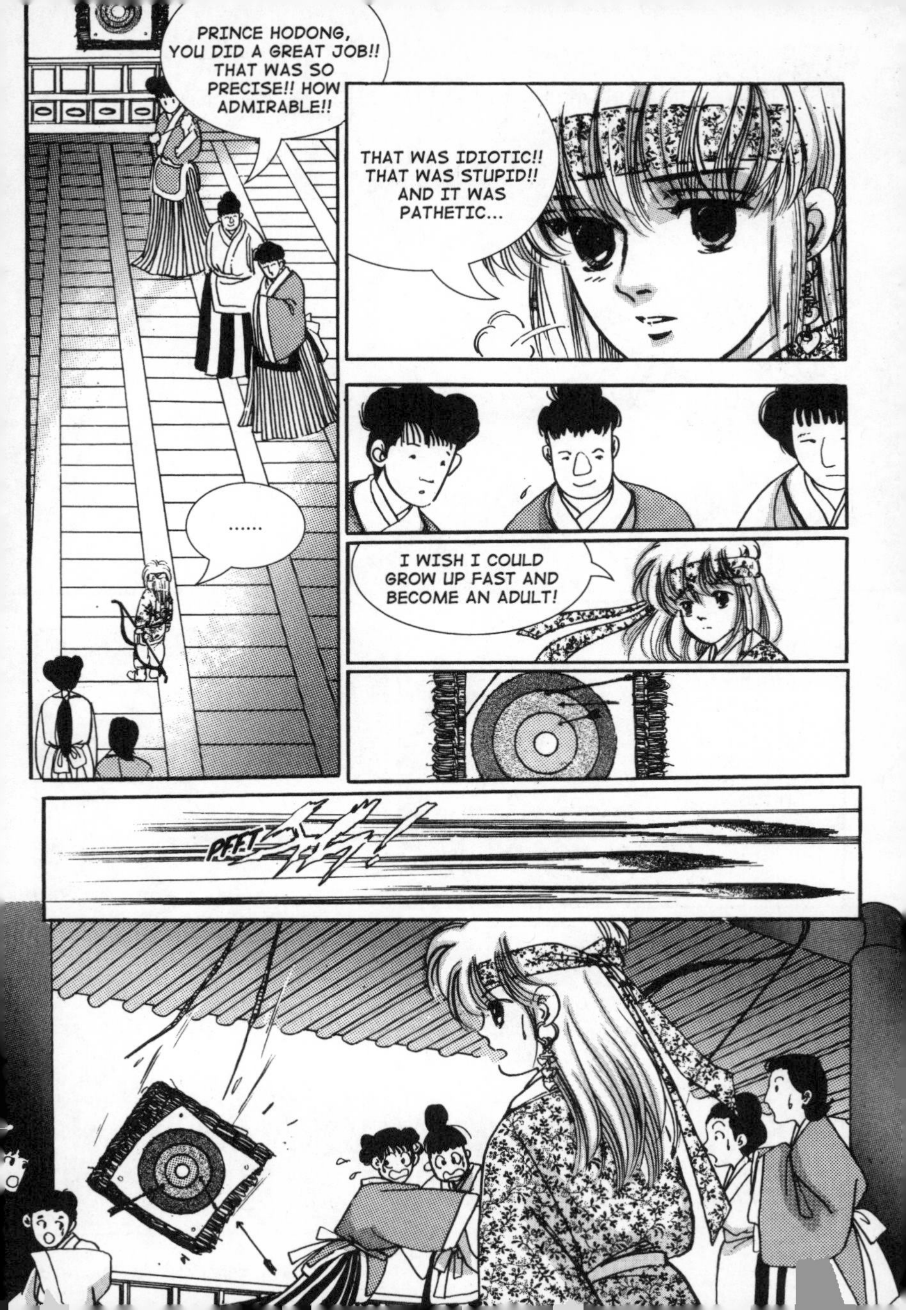
PRINCE HODONG, YOU DID A GREAT JOB!! THAT WAS SO PRECISE!! HOW ADMIRABLE!!
......
THAT WAS IDIOTIC!! THAT WAS STUPID!! AND IT WAS PATHETIC...
I WISH I COULD GROW UP FAST AND BECOME AN ADULT!
PFFT

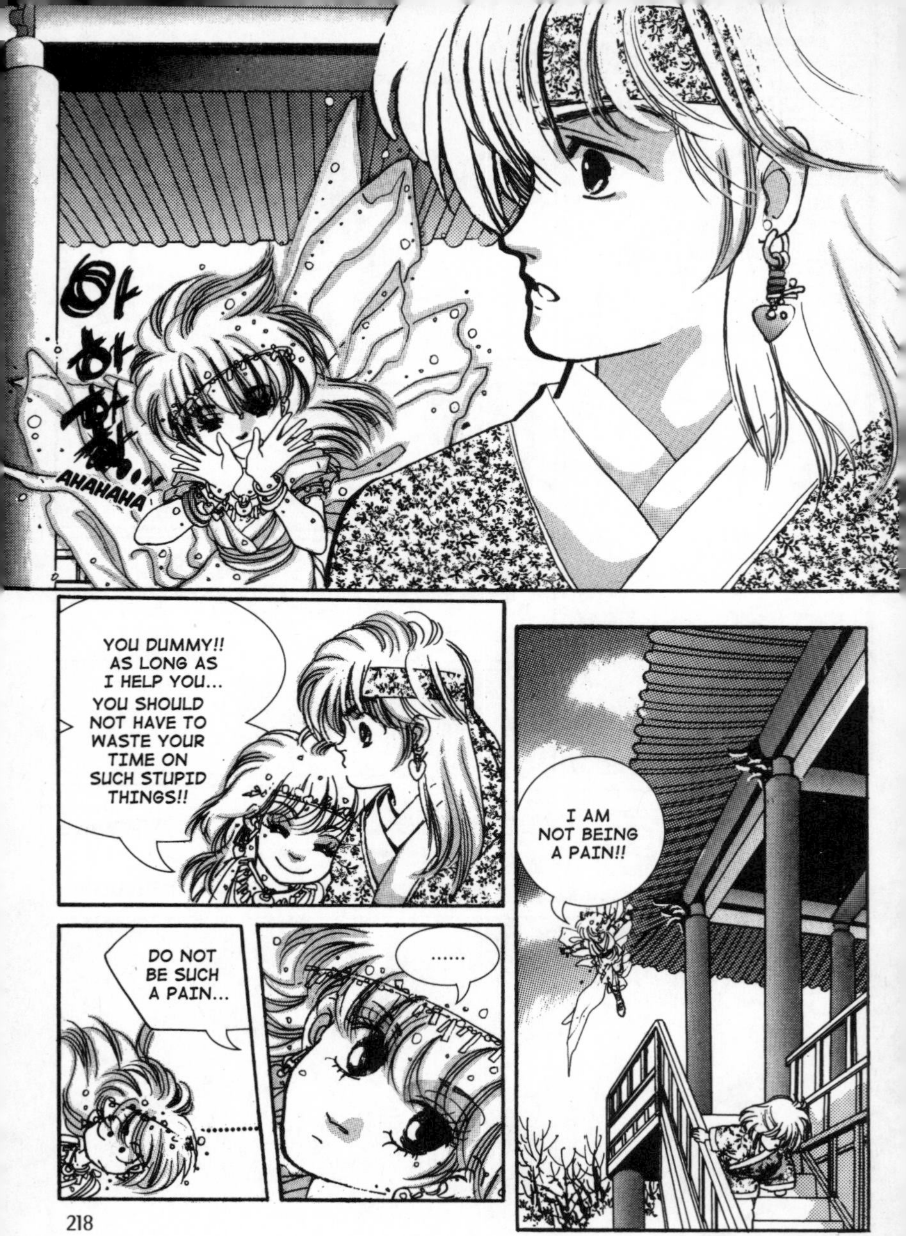
AHAHAHA
YOU DUMMY!! AS LONG AS I HELP YOU... YOU SHOULD NOT HAVE TO WASTE YOUR TIME ON SUCH STUPID THINGS!!
DO NOT BE SUCH A PAIN...
......
I AM NOT BEING A PAIN!!

THE END.
To be continued in Volume 3.

바람의 나라
KINGDOM OF THE WINDS Vol. 3

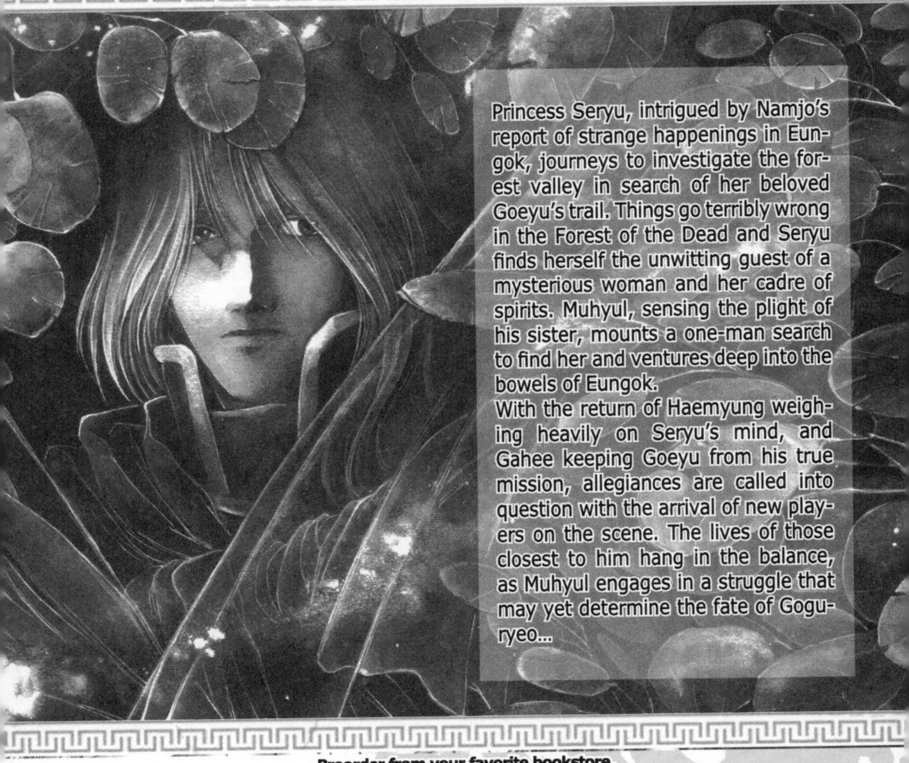

Princess Seryu, intrigued by Namjo's report of strange happenings in Eungok, journeys to investigate the forest valley in search of her beloved Goeyu's trail. Things go terribly wrong in the Forest of the Dead and Seryu finds herself the unwitting guest of a mysterious woman and her cadre of spirits. Muhyul, sensing the plight of his sister, mounts a one-man search to find her and ventures deep into the bowels of Eungok.

With the return of Haemyung weighing heavily on Seryu's mind, and Gahee keeping Goeyu from his true mission, allegiances are called into question with the arrival of new players on the scene. The lives of those closest to him hang in the balance, as Muhyul engages in a struggle that may yet determine the fate of Goguryeo...

Preorder from your favorite bookstore.
Read it ahead at www.NETCOMICS.com!

Kingdom of the Winds

PERIOD MAP OF GOGURYEO

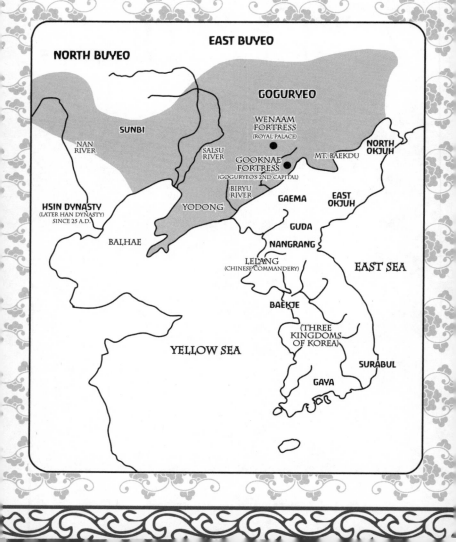

EAST BUYEO

NORTH BUYEO

GOGURYEO

SUNBI

WENAAM
FORTRESS
(ROYAL PALACE)

NAN
RIVER

SALSU
RIVER

GOOKNAE
FORTRESS

MT. BAEKDU

NORTH
OKJUH

(GOGURYEO'S 2ND CAPITAL)

BIRYU
RIVER

GAEMA

EAST
OKJUH

HSIN DYNASTY
(LATER HAN DYNASTY)
SINCE 25 A.D.

YODONG

GUDA

BALHAE

NANGRANG

EAST SEA

LELANG
(CHINESE COMMANDERY)

BAEKJE

(THREE
KINGDOMS
OF KOREA)

YELLOW SEA

SURABUL

GAYA

CHRONOLOGY

EUROPE		KOREA
	37 B.C.	Goguryeo founded by Jumong
The Battle of Actium	**31 B.C.**	(King Dongmyung).
Augustus rules as	**27 B.C.**	
Rome's first emperor.		
	24 B.C.	Lady Yuhwa (Jumong's mother) dies in East Buyeo.
	19 B.C.	King Dongmyung's 19 years of reign ends. King Yuri's reign begins.
	1 A.D.	Crown Prince Dojeol dies.
	3 A.D.	Goguryeo moves its capital to Gooknae Fortress. Builds Wenaam Fortress.
	4 A.D.	Prince Haemyung becomes crown prince. Prince Muhyul is born.
	5 A.D.	
The Battle of	**9 A.D.**	Crown Prince Haemyung commits suicide
the Teutoburg Forest.		at the command of his father, King Yuri.
	12 A.D.	Wang Mang of the Han Dynasty kills Goguryeo's General Yunbi.
	13 A.D.	Prince Muhyul annihilates Buyeo's army and drives out the Buyeo people.
Tiberius Caesar Augustus	**14 A.D.**	Prince Muhyul is crowned and is in charge
rules as Rome's second		of the national army and matters.
emperor.		
	18 A.D.	Prince Yeojin drowns.
Julius Caesar	**19 A.D.**	Prince Hodong is born.
Germanicus,		King Yuri dies in the Dugok Palace.
best loved of		King Yuri's 37th year of reign. Crown
Roman princes,		Prince Muhyul ascends the throne at 15,
dies of poisoning.		becomes King Daemushin.
	21 A.D.	Goguryeo attacks Buyeo.
	22 A.D.	King Daeso dies at the hands of Goeyu.
	26 A.D.	King Daemushin conquers Gaema and annexes it into the Goguryeo empire.
	32 A.D.	Prince Hodong encounters Choeri, king of Nangrang while travelling in Okjuh.

GOGURYEO:
History at a Glance Divine creatures

Vital to the history and mythology of Goguryeo are the four divine creatures. Bound to the cardinal directions and essential elements of our world, each creature has a different responsibility and purpose in the celestial realm, some being messengers of death, and others being champions of the people. Every creature is indicative of a constellation in the sky, and these constellations were used in the star charts of peoples across Asia for hundreds of years.

All four divine creatures were most often found manifested in death, as they were often found as wall paintings in Goguryeo's ancient tombs, each one adorning its corresponding direction.

<CONSTELLATIONS OF THE EAST>

TERRITORY	CONTTSTELLATION	CENTER STAR	TERRITORY	CONSTELLATION	CENTER STAR
EAST (Chungryong: Blue Dragon)	Gak (Horn of Chungryong)	Virgo Spica (α)	SOUTH (Baekho: White Tiger)	Gyu (Tail of Baekho)	Andromeda (η)
	Hang (Neck of Chungryong)	Virgo (κ)		Kyuh (Body of Baekho)	Aries Sheratan (β)
	Juh (Chest of Chungryong)	Libra Zubenelgenubi (α)		Wie (Body of Baekho)	Aries (35)
	Bang (Abdomen of Chungryong)	Scorpio (η)		Myo (Body of Baekho)	Taurus Electra (17)
	Shim (Heart of Chungryong)	Scorpio Al Niyat (σ)		Pil (Body of Baekho)	Taurus Ain (ε)
	Me (Tail of Chungryong)	Scorpio (μ)		Jah (Head of Baekho)	Orion Meissa (λ)
	Gi (Anus of Chungryong)	Sagittarius Al Nasi (γ)		Sahm (Front legs of Baekho)	Orion Alnitak (ζ)
WEST (Hyunmu: Black Tortoise)	Du (Head of Tortoise and Snake)	Sagittarius (φ)	NORTH (Jujak: Vermillion Bird)	Jung (Crown of Jujak)	Gemini (μ)
	Woo (Body of Snake)	Capricorn Dabih (β)		Gue (Eye of Jujak)	Cancer (θ)
	Nuh (Tortoise)	Aquarius Albali (ε)		Ryu (Beak of Jujak)	Hydra (δ)
	Huh (Tortoise)	Aquarius Sadaluud (β)		Sung (Neck and Heart of Jujak)	Hydra Alphard (α)
	We (Snake)	Aquarius Sadalmelik (α)		Jang (Craw of Jujak)	Hydra (ν1)
	Shil (Earth Dragon)	Pegasus Markab (α)		Ik (Wing of Jujak)	Crater Alkes (α)
	Byuk (Blood Dragon)	Pegasus Algenib (γ)		Jin (Tail of Jujak)	Corvus Gienah (γ)

Blue Dragon

The Blue Dragon is an auspicious omen and is associated with the East and the season of spring. Its dominion included control over weather and the elements, and is symbolic of the will of living things. The element of Chungryong is wood. In ancient times, it was drawn or painted on the left side of caskets and graves as a symbol of protection.

Vermilion Bird

The Vermilion Bird reigns over the element of fire. Its season is summer and it is thought of as the bird of the South. Vermilion Bird embodies the principals of knowledge and scientific skills. It is often represented by a bird of fire, or a phoenix, and has an aversion to the night. On caskets, it was drawn or painted at the foot or at the head.

White Tiger

The White Tiger is a symbol of strength, both in a physical sense and in terms of military prowess, inasmuch as it corresponds with the element of metal. It guards the West and is tied to the season of autumn. Occasionally described as an evil creature, it is painted on the right side of caskets and graves.

Black Tortoise

The Black Tortoise, or Hyunmu, is traditionally viewed as a messenger of death. "Mu" means armor and it is said that its shell is impenetrable to any weapon. From its head, it sprays fog and poison. The direction of the North is Hyunmu's, as is the season of winter. Its element is water.

Giraffe

The Giraffe has the body of a deer, head of a wolf, hooves of a horse, tail of a cow, and a horn. Its skin is five colors: red, blue, yellow, white, and black. It's also a creature of the air with a wide wingspan. The bottom end of its horn is wrapped with its own skin, to reduce the chance of injury during a fight. Possessing a meek disposition, the Giraffe doesn't even like to disturb healthy grass by walking on it or other plants by eating them. Like the Phoenix, an appearance of the Giraffe is believed to be a sign that a wise king will soon take birth and rule his kingdom in peace.

Phoenix

The Phoenix is a bird symbolizing the Sun, prosperity, and eternity. From the front, it resembles a wild goose and a giraffe looking from behind. It has the chin of a swallow, beak of a chicken, neck of a snake, tail of a fish, forehead of a stork, cheeks of a Mandarin duck, ears of an owl, body

<GIRAFFE>

of a tortoise with the feather pattern of a dragon. Phoenix feathers have five colors: red, blue, yellow, white and black. It sings five different beautiful tones when it cries out. It is known as an auspicious bird that only appears during the peaceful reigns of wise kings. It dwells only on the paulownia tree and, being very benign, refuses to peck at plants even when hungry. The Phoenix can fly a distance of over 200 miles in one flight. Often used in ancient Chinese mythology, the Phoenix symbolizes the emperor.

<BULGASARI MEANS "TO DIE BY FIRE.">

Bulgasari

The Bulgasari is a mythical creature in Korean folklore. It is said to have the body of a bear, eyes of a rhinoceros, claws of a tiger, tail of a bull, teeth like a hacksaw, and the body hair of a porcupine. Only females have stripes on their bodies. It appears when the land is in turmoil and devours all metal in order to stop warfare. No one was able to kill this creature, not with arrows or spears, but a sage divined its vulnerability to fire and it was finally slain.